A Crying in the Wind

A NEW
Map of
VAN DIEMENS LAND,
FROM THE BEST AUTHORITIES,
And from the most recent
Surveys.

1825

British Statute Miles.

Longitude East from Greenwich.

London, Published 1825, by J. Souter, St Pauls Ch. Yard.

A Crying in the Wind

A TASMANIAN STORY

Elizabeth Fleetwood

© 2017 Elizabeth Fleetwood

ISBN: 978-1-925590-20-3

Published by Vivid Publishing
P.O. Box 948, Fremantle
Western Australia 6959
www.vividpublishing.com.au

Cataloguing-in-Publication data is available from the National Library of Australia

This book is available in printed format via the environmentally friendly POD (print-on-demand) system, which dispenses with the traditional process of printing a large number of copies, which then must be warehoused and subsequently distributed by fuel-hungry means around the earth, according to demand. Instead, the new POD technology will, on receiving an order for a single copy (or more), send an electronic request to the geographically closest POD printing facility, where the book(s) ordered will be printed and then posted to the purchaser. The author thanks you for your generosity in taking part in this system; by being willing to pay for the necessary postage, you are protecting our environment and helping to preserve it for future generations.

To order your copy, go to: www.vividpublishing.com.au/acryinginthewind

It is also available to download in paperless format as an e-book at:
www.vividpublishing.com.au/acryinginthewind

10% of profits from this book go to support Deaf Children of Central Asia, a Tasmanian supported charity operating in Tajikistan and providing help to deaf children, through training and supporting adult sign language tutors. This provides a common language for parents and their children, and helps the latter prepare for formal education.
For more info on this work, please see: facebook.com/Deaf-Children-of-Central-Asia

Book cover design: Cathy McAuliffe at www.cmdesign.com.au
Front cover photograph: Rob Blakers at www.robblakers.com.au
Back cover photograph: John West at www.tierstealounge.com.au
Family Tree design: Carolyn J Foster cfosterbusiness@gmail.com
Frontispiece map by courtesy of the National Library of Australia
Maps of Tasmania in the text used by courtesy of TASMAP, Dept. of Primary Industries, Parks, Water and Environment, Hobart, Tasmania.

The wound is the place where the Light enters you.
Rumi

You will not fear the terror of night…
Psalm 91

Very little is needed to make a happy life;
it is all within yourself,
in your way of thinking.
Marcus Aurelius

It's really a wonder that I haven't dropped all my ideals,
because they seem so absurd and impossible to carry out.
Yet I keep them, because in spite of everything,
I still believe that people are really good at heart.
Anne Frank

The things you do for yourself are gone when you are gone,
but the things you do for others remain as your legacy.
Kalu Ndukwe Kalu

AUTHOR'S NOTE

This book is a true story. Although the majority of the characters are fictitious, they have been placed among events and people that did exist. Their settings and the historical facts presented are all closely based on the scholarly work of many researchers and authors. By narrating the personal stories three typical families, it is my intention to give a broad but accurate picture of Tasmania's European 200-year history, leading from settlement in 1803 to the present day and some of the complex issues that are with us now. If the reader gains a good understanding of what makes up the rich background of the ordinary everyday people he could meet on any street here, then my mission has succeeded.

But that is only a part of the big picture. There is another very important story to tell alongside that of the immigrants, and one that the invading English blundered into and totally failed to see. The ancient culture of the Tasmanian Aborigines, living on Tarena* for at least 40,000 years, had created a sophisticated adaption to local conditions, providing great stability and richness of experience. Because this is an important but not yet well-known part of Tasmania's story, I have chosen to write about real Aboriginal people in the indigenous history sections. Naturally, this has required some speculation on my part, as the records on the subject are very limited. My guideline in this has been our shared humanity. Only in the contemporary characters of Victor and James Mayne have I created fictitious indigenous persons; however I trust that the accuracy of their setting will be recognized.

The Aboriginal Community is therefore respectfully advised that the names of deceased Aborigines are mentioned in this book.

Too much has been lost for the story to be complete. The rapid destruction of that ancient way of life has left us with an irreplaceable loss, an absence of living myth and a deep understanding of the land itself. Many sense the emptiness, a strange absence, that often makes it difficult to be at peace here. It challenges us to look after this island properly, as we have so often failed to do. It questions the meaning of our identity and belonging. Ultimately, it asks us to face and acknowledge what has been done here. If we fail to do this, we will continue in a forlorn struggle, and our souls will continue to cry in the wind.

I must, of course, take responsibility for any personal thoughts and motivations attributed to all the characters, fictitious or otherwise. Gaps in the documentary records at times required some educated guesswork – occasions when I sat and pondered long in the silence of the evening, inviting the characters to come and tell me what it was all about. And they did, shy at first but then with an eagerness that has left me awed and humbled. Thus, very little in this book has actually been invented by me. I see myself rather as a facilitator, enabled to open a window into the grand panorama of life, with all its good, evil, and the possibility of redemption that is found only in love.

* To save confusion, I have used geographical place names that are in common usage now, that is, generally the current English terms. While we are aware of many of the Aboriginal appellations, these have all been recorded by white people and there is still much confusion over spelling. Also, there were several Aboriginal languages in use on the Island, resulting in several different names for the same place. However, the story requires an Indigenous name for the Island itself, and among the various possibilities, I have chosen the word "Tarena" to represent this.

CONTENTS

PART THREE

PART FOUR:

The Tasmanians: **James Mayne, Ellie Fairfield, Denise Turner, Alan Dijkstra – and Ty**

THE PEOPLE IN THIS BOOK

Persons directly significant in the story are shown in **bold**.

IN PART I:

THE ABORIGINES

Tom Kickerterpoller

ca1808-1832

From the East Coast Paredarerme Tribe. Loved Tekartee (ca1808-1831).
Lived with Pagerley from Bruny Island Nuenonne Tribe. No issue.
Died 12 May 1832 at Emu Bay.

THE FAIRFIELD SETTLERS

Susannah

1799-1887

She married William **Fairfield** (1796-1861).

Scottish farmers arrived in Hobart 1823, and were given an initial land grant of 600 acres
on the Macquarie River in the northern Midlands. They called it 'Fairbourne'.

Andrew	Nancy	Edward	Rebecca	George	Stillbirth	Margaret	David
b 1818	b1820	b 1821	b 1823	b 1826	b 1827	b 1828	b 1830
						Married Henry in 1847.	

Isabella

b 1848

THE CONVICT TURNERS

George Turner

b 1803 Yorkshire, England

Had several siblings.

Arrived in Hobart in September 1825 as a convict. He was assigned to 'Fairbourne'
and then out to the VDL Company in the far North West.

THE DUTCH DIJKTRA FAMILY

Katrijn Dijkstra in Amsterdam 1828.

IN PART II:

THE ABORIGINES

Thomas Beeton (White, ex-convict)

He married Emerenna (known as Bet Smith, a full-blooded Tasmanian Aborigine
from the North East Pyemmairre Tribe).

Lucy Beeton	James	Henry	Jane
b 1829	b 1831	b 1833	b 1836

No Marriage. No issue.
Died 7 July 1886
on Badger Island.

THE FAIRFIELD SETTLERS

Isabella Fairfield

b 1848

She married Phillip Charles Briermont **Cowley** (of Corinthia pastoral estate) in 1867.

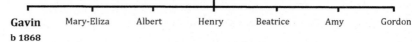

Gavin	Mary-Eliza	Albert	Henry	Beatrice	Amy	Gordon
b 1868						

THE CONVICT TURNERS

George Turner

b 1803

He married Rosie Meagher in 1842. Rosie was from a poor ex-convict Irish family.
He died 1851 at Emu Bay (Burnie).

Howard	Stillborn	Stillborn	Henry
1843-1908			1849

He married Anne.

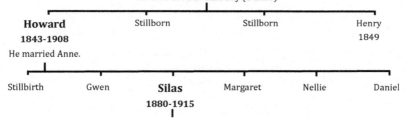

Stillbirth	Gwen	**Silas**	Margaret	Nellie	Daniel
		1880-1915			

In 1914 he married a cousin
Lavinia Turner.
Silas died in France in 1915.

Daniel

b 1915

THE DUTCH DIJKSTRA FAMILY

Berndt Dijkstra

b 1924 Java

Descendant of Katrijn.
He returned to the Netherlands after WWII.
In 1952 he married Anna and they emigrated to Tasmania.

IN PART III:

THE ABORIGINES
Victor (Vic) Mayne
1920-1969

Born on Cape Barren Island from a Straitsman Islander Family.
He married Bessie (also from an Islander family) in 1948.
Family moves from the Islands to Launceston in 1953.

Rachel	William	**James**	Erica
b 1949	b 1951	**b 1952**	b 1954

THE FAIRFIELD SETTLERS
Anthea Fairfield
b 1932

She married Terence Reid in 1951.

In 1952 they had a child **Eleanor ("Ellie") Suzanne Reid.**

THE CONVICT TURNERS
Daniel Turner
b 1915

He married in 1941.

Reginald
b 1944

Had several siblings. He married Aileen in 1968.

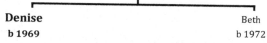

Denise	Beth
b 1969	b 1972

THE DUTCH DIJKSTRA FAMILY
Berndt and Anna Dijkstra

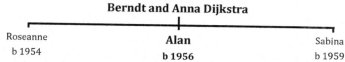

Roseanne	**Alan**	Sabina
b 1954	**b 1956**	b 1959

IN PART IV:

This part draws together and completes the stories of:
James Mayne,Ellie Fairfield,
Denise Turner, Alan Dijkstra and Ty.

PROLOGUE

For aeons, Tasmania has been the lonely southern outpost of the Great Southland, encircled by the cold surging waters of the Southern Ocean. Ice ages came and went. At times the land was covered with glaciers and in other, warmer, periods the waters rose to make it an island. Volcanic eruptions created minerals in the dramatic mountain ranges, through which wild rivers carved deep gorges, particularly along the western and southern coasts. There, huge cliffs rear up against the great sea storms; between them great waves roar onto long, empty beaches. One of the world's few remaining temperate rainforests covers much of this area, interspersed with buttongrass plains. Behind the mountains, high in the interior, lies a cold, exposed plateau filled with lakes, guarded to the north and east by a tremendous rampart of rock now known as the Great Western Tiers. At the foot of these lies deep rich soil, once covered in the north by a huge forest. To the east is a gentler land, well-watered, that once teemed with wildlife. The coast beyond it, facing out into the Tasman Sea, has softer granite hills, warm beaches and gentle breezes, the waters rich with shellfish. Whales came to breed in the estuaries, dolphins too; a vast array of birds from eagles, ducks, geese and black swans through to tiny honeyeaters filled the air and forests with their gliding and fluttering presences. It was a cornucopia of vibrant life, the air charged like champagne. The sea glittered from turquoise to darkest purple, and the land lay peacefully through the ages, a small Eden on the rim of the world.

The people who lived there knew their land intimately. They sheltered their families in well-chosen campsites, made love against the warm soft sandstone, and followed the season up into the highlands in the spring when the lakesides teemed with eggs and young birds. Here they met other tribal groups to swap stories, settle scores, trade ochre and utensils, and build friendships. They consulted their knowing ones, their old men, on the meaning of dreams and sought wisdom about life. Along with the music, song and dance, they also broke hearts and conducted affairs. There were seven distinct tribes, with separate dialects – some were so different that the people of the west coast could not understand those from the northeast. Already fine hunters, their occasional feuds made them into formidable fighters, deadly accurate with their spears and able to slip invisibly through the landscape. Their fire farming methods created park-like valleys of rich verdure where hunting could be conducted efficiently. Life was largely satisfying; fiercely they loved their island, believing it and its creatures including themselves to have been created by the star gods, and one of the names they called it was Tarena.

But it was fated not to stay quietly forgotten on the outer margins of the world. Far away, in Rome during the 12th century, the popes decided that Christianity does not have to mean withdrawal from the world, but rather encouraged a very material engagement with it. Power-hungry kings and potentates with coffers to fill began explorations for trade and to loot such wealth as could be found. Stories of great riches in mythical places had long abounded, and with the building of the seaworthy caravel, the Portuguese were among the first to venture forth into unknown seas, rounding the Cape of Good Hope in 1488. Inside 30 years they had established trading posts on the rim of the Indian Ocean, along the African, Arabian, and Indian coasts and right out to the Spice Islands of eastern Indonesia. Though they always travelled under the sign of the cross and in Christ's name, they imposed their rule with violence instead of trade, massacring the people and looting and burning the cities of unbelievers mercilessly. Soon after, Christopher Columbus acting on behalf of the Spaniards, took the same approach to the Americas, where entire nations were pillaged and dispersed within a handful of years. When the Dutch and the English followed suit in both the east and the west, their greed for gold and trade generally overcame any Christian concerns for the well-being of their newly-enslaved peoples. A reign of terror had begun, and its dark shadow reached out into the most remote corners.

In the rush to claim first any new lands and access their gold and silver, secret expeditions were sent out. Maps of unknown shores were made and guarded jealously. Sometime between 1519 and 1523 such a one, outlining in astonishing detail the eastern coast of Australia, called Java Le Grande, was made. It is believed that it was charted by three Portuguese caravels under Captain Cristovao de Mendonca, who appears to have also rounded Cape Howe and sailed through Bass Strait and along the southern Australian coast as far as, possibly, Port Fairy, before the great storms roaring out of the Bight forced him to retreat, back up the east coast again and returning through Torres Strait. It was, by the standards of the day, an epic journey, though perhaps no greater than Ferdinand Magellan's, also around 1520, from Spain west across the Atlantic, passing below South America and crossing the unimaginable vastness of the Pacific. By the time Mendonca returned to the Portuguese stronghold of Goa in India, he had only one ship left. Two were wrecked along the way, and given the prevailing winds, it is entirely possible that one of them was driven onto the Tasmanian West Coast. The people of that area had a legend of 'a big canoe with a house on top' that came with men who looked different and had no wives. Perhaps the expanding finger of Europe's unstoppable takeover had already brushed upon Tarena's Dreaming, 121 years before the official discoverer, Abel Tasman, arrived in 1642?

There are some possible indications that the other lost ship, staying on Mendonca's intended course a bit longer, started to break up just as they rounded Cape Howe. Maybe it limped for safety to nearby Bittangabee Bay, or perhaps some survivors were swept in there, clinging to debris or a ship's boat. The feisty Captain Mendonca himself did eventually make it back to Goa, with the precious portolan maps he had so painstakingly made of the entire Eastern Australian Coast, including a section of New Zealand's North Island. Why the Portuguese never publicly claimed their discovery remains a matter for speculation, though commercial secrecy as well as the Pope's arbitrary division of the world into Spanish and Portuguese sections respectively, would have played their part. Australia's East Coast fell squarely into the Spanish sector, so their rivals would have moved very cautiously and perhaps they were intending to approach the

Pope for a revision. Whatever their plans, the more ignominious likelihood is that Mendonca's maps were stolen from him before he could bring them back to Portugal. Certain is that the information ended up in France, where the superb Dauphin Map of 1536 was created, clearly showing that extraordinary journey in remarkable detail, some of it more accurate than Captain Cook's mapping of 250 years later.

Abel Tasman's 1642 impact upon the Tarena was a mere passing by, leaving no more than some campfire tales about the brief visit by men with very big boats and white faces. Not until six generations later was there reason to change those stories, when French explorers and later English settlers started turning up. It is almost beyond our imagination today to visualise what the Tarenians thought as they looked upon the ugly and clumsy newcomers, but none of them could foresee that their world was about to be invaded and their ancient culture all but destroyed inside thirty years.

Tom Kickerterpoller's father would have seen, from his family's campsite opposite Maria Island, the strangers' ships hunting whales, filling the white beaches with gore and blood and stink and noise. Did he convey his astonishment, perhaps concern, to his little son by his knee? Not that he would live to see young Tom grow up among those same invaders. Nor could he begin to imagine the subsequent generations of struggle, racial alienation and bare survival that would lead, 150 years later, to James Mayne, small business owner with a ute and a dog named Bonnie, embodying some deep lessons about redemptive love.

The strangers kept coming, more and more of them. In 1824 the Fairfields arrived, straight from Scotland, from a modest farming family with not enough land for its younger sons. Stories of the free land grants in faraway Tasmania, then known as Van Diemens Land, tempted William to risk the long journey with his wife Susannah and young children. Initially entirely unaware of the brutal blood price paid for the acres of sweet green land that in time became their pastoral estate, the unease of the lost Tarena seeped into their bones, especially when one of their family died under the clubs of Tom's warrior tribe. How this upright Presbyterian family reconciled itself with the fact of their unwanted presence in an alien culture entirely beyond their understanding, would guide much of Ellie Fairfield's thinking, 180 years later.

Convicts came, also: 73,500 men and women already burdened with their own shadow of displacement. One of these was George Turner. On the torn and bleeding island, instead of the rehabilitation that was held out as a possibility for all prisoners, a demon seemed to fasten upon him. He saw too much of what was done by apparently upstanding men, the unhindered killing and raping, and when he thought he'd finally fought free of it all, the demon came and got him again. That dark shadow followed most of the Turner generations, and though some fought it bravely, precious little peace was ever granted them. Denise, restless hair-dressing apprentice at the Launceston Technical College, took the hard knocks life doled out to her with the same mixture of hopeless defiance.

Much later the Island received another large group of displaced strangers. These were fleeing the devastation of WWII; the peaceful and remote Tasmania with its green valleys offered a refuge. Alan Dijkstra was born there of his recently-arrived Dutch parents, but in his genes also lay the knowledge of war, several times over. He remained a stranger to himself and the land he lived in. His ill-fated affair with Denise did nothing to help him. But one day the keys were handed to him, a challenge to see life differently and find the moral strength to meet it.

Today, Tasmania is widely known as a wilderness paradise, sold to tourists for its clean air and pristine environment, particularly the golden beaches and red rocks of the eastern coast and what remains of the great rainforest in the west. Exclusive resorts are placed for the best views. There are countless attractions, vine yards, restaurants offering fine seafood, cruises to spot seabirds and dolphins. Visitors come by the score and are genuinely enthused by what they see.

There are others, those who live ordinary lives on the Island, who see something else. Behind the glittering lodges lie dark hills, holding a long story about demons that trample over Eden. One of these has clothed the hillsides with a mutated tree. Another has filled the valleys with a strange presence. The sparkling vitality, too, has gone from the very air.

"My, how hopelessly miserable one can feel in Australia: to the very depths. It's a dark country underneath – like an abyss. Then, when the sky turns frail and blue again and the trees against the far off sky stand out, the glamour, the un-get-at-able glamour! A great fascination, but also a dismal grey terror underneath..."

Written by D H Lawrence to Katharine S Prichard, at the end of his visit to Australia in 1922.

Many can hear the crying in the wind; those who confront it will experience fear and challenge, but they are the very ones who can also rise above it and soar with the angels.

PART ONE

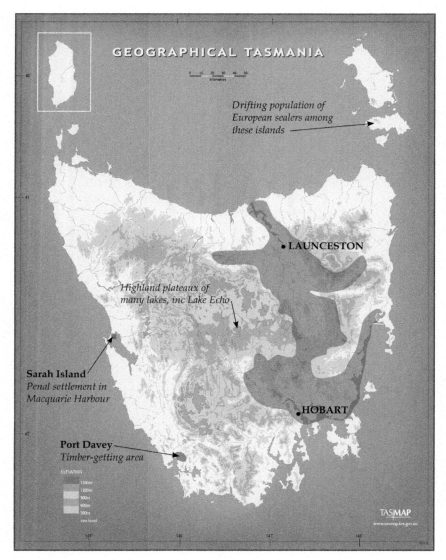

GEOGRAPHICAL TASMANIA

*Drifting population of
European sealers among
these islands*

• LAUNCESTON

*Highland plateaux of
many lakes, inc Lake Echo*

Sarah Island
*Penal settlement in
Macquarie Harbour*

•HOBART

Port Davey
Timber-getting area

ELEVATION

Map 1 – *Tasmania by 1826*

The indigenous Aborigines were settled in virtually all parts of the Island, and certainly familiar
with every part of it. They were divided into seven tribes, each with their defined home areas, but
there was regular and seasonal movement across many parts, with clearly defined tracks, specific
camping sites, and well-established places for ritual and celebratory gatherings.

*Area of European settlement, primarily through the Midlands between
Hobart and Launceston, also on parts of the East Coast.*

Remaining areas, particularly in the West, had mountain ranges covered in vast forests, wild rivers
and open buttongrass plains, and were mainly unknown to the Europeans.

THE ABORIGINES 1812-1832

TOM KICKERTERPOLLER

...and never a saint took pity on my soul in agony
S T Coleridge

1. TOM'S CHILDHOOD LOST

We'll call him Tom, decided Sarah Birch, eyeing the petrified little boy. Wrapped in the remnant rags of what might have been a man's shirt once, he was being held very firmly by the agent. Two sealers from Mr Birch's boat had found him on the East Coast, and thought the gentleman might like to have him. They had him sent up to the house after their ship had returned back to Hobart. He's a fine boy, he'll grow up strong and good to work.

Yes, Mr Birch would certainly like to have this boy. Sarah was also pleased, it being quite the fashion now to have a black child, and anything that served to underline her status as part of the leading set of Hobart, was very welcome. Had she not married one of the most successful local merchants? Had not her father, George Guest, arrived here as a free man, bringing valuable sheep to the colony in 1805? Unjustly convicted and sent to Norfolk Island in 1790, he had long demonstrated that he was a cut above his fellow prisoners there while he worked off his sentence. The island commandant, Major Foveaux, had personally commended Guest as a most industrious person, and when the Sydney government decided to forcibly re-settle everyone from Norfolk elsewhere, he was allocated a land grant in then barely-established Hobart. Here he settled with his

1

wife and six children, and was soon making the most of the commercial and social opportunities.

The latter were quickly realized when his daughter Sarah married Thomas William Birch four years later. Previously trading in India with merchant interests, Birch had arrived in Hobart three years after the Guest family, and he quickly established a brisk business in whaling and sealing, employing men in small boats to scour the shores of Van Diemens Land for the sea creatures that yielded the valuable oil. It was in this process of their duties near Maria Island that the two sealers said they had found the boy now shivering before her.

He's around five, she judged, old enough to sleep in the stable with the coachman. You'll need to keep him locked up for a while, Mam, so he doesn't run away, advised the agent. The harness room will do, at any rate till Mr. Birch comes home, and she directed the man to take the boy there. How would she dress him, so he could be properly seen as belonging to her household? Clothes, or even plain cloth, were not readily obtainable in the settlement. Hobart, barely past the condition of a camp, was only eight years old. It had around four dozen houses made of brick that could be called decent habitations. The rest were paling huts thatched with grass, or – if lucky – covered in timber shingles. But finally there was talk of lifting the harbour restrictions, and plans for warehouses to be built and filled with goods from England. Meanwhile perhaps Annie could be sent to the Whale Fishery Inn, where a sailor had died the day before – the publican, if he still had them, would likely be willing to sell the man's clothes. They could be cut down to fit the boy.

Sarah Birch went to the kitchen, in quest of Annie the cook – a servant as insolent as they all were, but the best that could be got. Convicts, especially females, were not at this time being brought to this colony directly, as there was no official place to house them. They had to be found in Sydney, where there was great competition for them. But Annie was a real servant, the free daughter of a convict. Sarah was forced to pay her well for the privilege of having a proper cook, but William could afford it, thank goodness. She thought briefly of her good fortune in having become Mrs. Birch. There were very few marriageable women in Hobart at the time, and his choice therefore had not been wide, but that was not a line of thought Sarah wished to pursue. She considered instead, with great satisfaction, her husband's new plans to build a fine residence: the only one in town with three stories and of solid brick. Governor Macquarie, on his visit to Hobart the previous year, had laid out a proper street plan, and their new home was to be on the best street, named after the governor himself. She briefly looked in upon her own sleeping child, 10-month old Jessica, tucked warmly into a small cot. All was peaceful with this little one, quite the opposite to the roiling energies of her first born, George junior. He would be keeping Annie busy in the kitchen, and, as Sarah hastened there, she wondered if she would get used to the rolling white eyes of the black boy.

***

Kickerterpoller – now to be known as Tom – was in a numb daze, sitting in that dark little harness room, overwhelmed by the violent change in his young life. Everything was incomprehensible to him, from the moment the strange men rushed their camp at night, the sudden loud bangs, and everyone running, the thumps and the screams. His mother disappeared immediately, grabbed by one of the men, and his father lay on the ground not moving. Kickerterpoller didn't know what to do, and as he stood there shocked and crying, one of the men caught him by the arm and pulled him away. Roughly handled, and tied to a tree by the beach, he saw one of those strangely-shaped canoes. The men were roughing up his mother, sister and the other girl, despite their screams. There was coarse laughter and sounds the little boy had never heard before, but he knew it was bad. His special friend, little Tekartee, was there too and being hurt. There were more thumps, and presently none of the women said anything more.

The men placed the three women and the little girl into the canoe, and rowed out of the small bay. Kickerterpoller watched it go, straining against the ropes that held him, but it was useless – he could not free himself. He cried out loud, some of the others must hear him, surely? But nobody replied. From where he was tied, he could not see that the three men were all lying dead in the spreading stains of their blood. The fourth man, old Tapete, was still alive, but too badly wounded to crawl to his grandson and comfort him. He heard the terrified child's sobbing and tried calling to him, but there was something wrong with his throat and he couldn't even croak. A few hours later, he too was dead.

In the morning, the big canoe returned with four men. The boy woke from a dazed sleep as one of the men came up to him, and cowered in fright before the man's horrible pale face. He was dragged to the boat, and roughly cuffed across the head when he tried resisting. After checking out the camp, all jumped in and made it move smoothly with sticks that they dipped into the water.

"Shut up, you!" growled one, and though the boy could not understand the words, the meaning was clear and he ceased his whimpering. They moved swiftly, rounding the headland, where one of the huge ships of the strangers sat. There were more men with fearsome faces on it.

"Here's something for Mr. Birch…get it delivered to him when you get to Hobart."

Kickerterpoller was hauled up, and tied by the leg to a heavy round thing on the ground. Faint with fright, he watched as the ship stretched out a huge wing above him which flapped at first and then tightened. He felt the movement as it got underway, but was too low down to see the shoreline, his homeland, sliding away. The wave motion and the awful stink around him made him feel sick. He was hungry and desperately thirsty, too. The men were moving all around him, shouting and pulling at ropes, and there was a lot of noise, flapping, creaking and water sloshing.

Presently things settled to a steadiness, and different sounds and smells began to fill the space. An older man squatted down beside him, holding a round thing with something in it. Kickerterpoller, terrified as unintelligible sounds rumbled, presently realized that he was not being hurt. The man made eating gestures, picking from the bowl, indicating that the boy should do the same. Presently he put it down and went away, returning with another round thing that had water in it. He offered it to the boy, and laughed when he tried scooping it up with his hand. No, no, like this – the man drank from the cup to demonstrate, and handed it back to the boy.

The left him pretty much alone for the rest of the journey, merely providing food, water, and a smelly bucket at regular intervals. The same man came with a sack in the evening, indicating that the boy could cover himself with it. Even though it was bitterly cold, the sack stank so badly that Kickerterpoller couldn't bear it, and he rolled away from it as far as his short rope allowed. The next day they untied him, and roared with laughter as he darted from side to side, seeking to escape. Finally one of them scooped him up high so he could see over the gunwale. After his first fright of seeing the sea all around him, he understood. There was nowhere to run.

The men were rough but not really unkind; he got used to their hideous faces after a while. The rhythm of the boat began to make sense to him. Arriving in Hobart was too bewildering to take in. Later he would understand about houses and ships and oxen and carts and dogs (oh marvelous creatures!), streets, and the many white-faced people. For now he was carried through the noise and terror of it all, until he was suddenly in the cave with the strange woman who eyed him over and sent him to this dark hole.

Escape was impossible. There was only one tiny window high up, with bars across it. As his eyes got used to the gloom, he made out the shapes of the harnesses, and sacks and boxes all stacked about. It all had a strong, rather nice animal smell, and it was rather exciting, too. Was it related to the animals he could hear snorting close by? They sounded very big; he could not imagine what they might be. So much frightening stuff had happened to him lately that he was unable to process more. Utterly exhausted, he began to whimper for his mother and his family. There was a yawning hole inside him, a torn woundedness, and no one to soothe it away.

***

Hobart, the 'town' that Tom had just arrived in, was officially founded by David Collins, first governor of the colony of Van Diemens Land, in 1804. He had transferred his settlement to the Derwent River after an unsuccessful attempt to colonise what was later known as the Mornington

Peninsula in southern Victoria. Collins knew that a small camp had already been established on the eastern side of the River by young Lt Bowen from Sydney, with some seventy men, a mixture of free settlers, soldiers, and some convicts.

"A poorly chosen site, without good water, as yet only some rude huts built and miserably few acres under cultivation," he wrote to his superior, Governor King in Sydney, "not surprising, given that the convicts here are the most intractable and sullen lot I've ever come across."

Jaded by the harsh, dry landscape he had just done battle with over the previous seven months, Collins eyed the grand tree-covered mountain opposite, noted the lush greenery in its foothills that promised reliable fresh water, and promptly declared that he would settle on that side. Accordingly, on the 24th of February he moved his ship across the water, ceremoniously planted a flag and named the new site after Lord Hobart, the Secretary of the Colonial Office in London. A kindly and well-meaning man, already experienced in colonial matters after eight years as judge-advocate in the newly established Sydney, Collins had taken a compassionate interest in the Aborigines around that area. He was not ignorant of the problematic complexity caused by attempts to include them in British ways, and had concluded that the best thing would be for there to be the least possible amount of contact between the two races. His new position as governor of Van Diemens Land required him to dispense justice for all, including 'the natives' who were in theory to be considered the subjects of the British monarch. But however noble his intentions, he was hampered by the strictures of his time that declared him a representative of the greatest civilization on earth, whose right to enter upon other kingdoms and dominate them could not be questioned. Thus even he was blind to the ancient culture on whose shores he had just settled.

Tarena had been inhabited for at least 40'000 years. Its people had traditions and legends which made their society work and explained the world to them. Intensely practical, they hunted efficiently with spears and waddies. They climbed the tall trees with home-made ropes and simple notches, in search of the delicious possum. Adept at diving among the rocks and kelp for oysters and other seafood, including the succulent crayfish, their diet was healthy, and they had wonderfully white and even teeth that lasted them for most of their life. They knew every animal that moved, every bird that flew, and every insect that scrabbled in the under-growth. They built fish traps, harvested the bounty of the land, lived and loved and fought, and were mostly free of disease.

Kickerterpoller's family made their home on the gentle eastern coast. His father Terpollee had come up through the various levels of initiated wisdom with honour and had many beautiful scar patterns to prove it. He hunted well for his family. His wife was Mirnermannerme from the Little Swanport group; Terpollee had to wait some long years for her to become a woman, and lovely she turned out to be.

At his own camp fire, he tenderly held her hand and admired her youthful shape. His finger traced her closing eyelid, his face nuzzled her neck, and he felt her willing form arching beneath him. Soon, there was a boy and then a girl; Kickerterpoller was the third. As was the custom, the group included several others, mostly the older relatives, and they closely co-operated with a similar family group that included little Tekartee, Kickerterpoller's special friend. The children played together, getting into mischief and learning their lessons in the important life skills. Terpollee and Maremmer, the leader of the other family, organized hunts, held council with old Tapete on important matters, and led their group along the interior pathways at the right seasons. Terpollee himself was looked upon as a coming leader, and took his position seriously. He set aside time to learn from old Tapete, debating issues with him, and discussing the rights and wrongs of recent decisions and events. Sometimes, bent over a shared job like re-working their reed canoe, they had time to dabble in the "what if..." questions that intrigue humanity in all parts of the world.

Their life was largely a satisfying one. There was food in abundance, particularly the shellfish and lobsters that the women dived so skillfully for. They wove practical baskets from grasses, and made drinking vessels from the leaves of the large kelp that filled the bays with acres of floating masses, on which the seabirds also found much sustenance. Skins from kangaroos were used as coat-like covers in the colder months, especially by the older people, and they built bark-covered shelters in front of which they lit their fires. Much time was spent in scraping and sharpening their spears, but there was time for ceremony and fun, also: both men and women took delight in decorating themselves with charcoal and ochre patterns rubbed onto their skin. They helped each other shave their hair, often leaving one or two artistic rings of fuzz around the skull, complemented by their shell and grass fibre necklaces. Some of the men kept their locks and wore them heavily laden with ochre, and nearly all trimmed their facial hair quite short. Only the very old men sported longer beards. When one of them died, the funeral ceremony was a complex one: the body was cremated and a site selected, often near a spring or small stream, where the remaining bones were carefully laid into a shallow hole. Over this they built a mound containing the ashes, covering it with turfs of fine young grass, held down by a neat pattern of sticks that, in turn, were held in place with flat stones. The whole was then covered with a tent of bark, some sheets of which were decorated with patterns, and tied at the top with strands of grassy string and sporting artistic loops. The departed spirit thus having been set free with the correct ritual, the site was left alone for nature to complete the process.

Terpollee had a fine woman, good children, and they lived in the soft gentle climate of the warm eastern coast. As long as no tribal war erupted, his only real danger should have been the possibility of an accident, but his world was changing as another race of people appeared who had no understanding of the right customs. For almost the length of a man's lifetime the white-faced foreigners had been unpredictably turning up in their huge canoes. Sometimes they stayed only a few days, other times several moons, coming ashore in smaller boats with many men and no women. Why they were coming, and where they were from, remained a mystery. They seemed to be initially quite friendly, actively seeking encounters. At such a great many useless things were handed out, but then the strangers got inexplicably angry when the Tarena peoples requested some of the other items they had. And they carried no spears, but had a fearsome weapon that made a big noise and could kill an animal – or a man – at a great distance. The word quickly spread among the tribes that these men were uncouth and not to be trusted, and anyway, why were they here in the first place? Though they were fascinating, it was always a relief to see them go away again.

But then another lot came, and this time it was different. Uninvited, they settled on the river below the great mountain, building huts from bark and poles. They hacked at the trees, making them fall the way only a big storm normally could. This lot had women and children with them, and began to breed more of themselves. Soon, those men were coming into the forest, and the use of their strange weapons brought devastation to the hunting grounds. The loud bangs made the kangaroos fall over dead, and they took far too many.

The Tarena people mostly stayed out of sight, watching with growing dismay. But life had to go on, and in the autumn of that year, 1804, the big hunt on the eastern shore was on as usual. Several sub groups got together to drive the kangaroo into the handy fold of the hill by the Risdon Creek, where they would be trapped and enough speared for a great feast. This was to be held beside the chain of lagoons that lay in the Risdon Valley, beautifully sheltered by the hills and home to myriads of ducks and swans. It was one of their favorite gathering places, where the richness of the summer just passed was to be acknowledged with feasting and dancing. Over two hundred men, women and children fanned out, and at the signal given, began running and hollering and chasing the creatures out of the undergrowth, round the cliff and up the valley. They paid no attention to the startled white faced men of the first camp, barely six months there, who came straggling out of their huts, until the loud bangs started and some of the Tarena people began falling over. Then an extra loud bang – later they would learn these were called cannon shots – killed and hurt many, and the hunt disintegrated in confusion and terror.

It took a long time for the shock of this event to settle. The destructive power of the new weapon was terrifying. The impact of so many sudden deaths was a serious disaster for the tribal group – husbands, fathers and sons had been the main victims, being out front and so taking the main brunt, along with some of the women. A small boy, Kalliderer, was also missing, snatched in the confusion by Dr. Mountgarrett, and later named James Hobart May. David Collins, the governor, barely settled on the other side of the big river, was horrified when later told of the 'attack' and the soldiers' response to it. He also sharply ordered Mountgarrett to return the boy to his family, though this was never done. Indeed, even had the attempt been made, it would probably have failed. The shattered tribe kept well away from the invaders, as well as the killing field, fearing the spirits of the dead there, condemned to roam the land without the proper funeral ritual. Never again would the southeastern people gather for their annual autumn hunt on that eastern shore of the River Derwent. Kalliderer was the first of many Tarena children to be taken into a white man's house; by 1820 there were several dozen in the Hobart area alone; Tom Kickerterpoller was one of them.

At the next spring tribal gathering by Lake Echo, safely out of reach, seemingly, up on the highland plateau, the talk was all about the new situation. Not only were the whites showing no sign of leaving, having been there now for more than a full round of seasons, but also the sheer impact of their magic sticks and many strange ways was endlessly discussed and wondered over. It was remembered that the previous foreigners – those that had gone away again – were always very keen to get hold of the Tarenas' spears; were they trying to dis-arm as many men as possible? Some of those foreigners had shown no respect, desecrating the dead's funerary constructions on Maria Island, disturbing campsites and taking baskets and tools. Clearly, they were not to be trusted! Even more disorienting were other stories that were trickling in, especially from the north eastern tribes. Another group of similar strangers had started a settlement up there on the Tamar River, also building their huts and hunting in the area. And that more of them were coming with many big canoes onto the islands in Bass Strait where they were killing the seals, and taking women.

"Our women," confirmed Lapetenner, from the Cape Portland peoples. "They come and steal them, and use them ill, and take them away, and they kill our men if they try to stop it."

Stealing women was nothing new; many of the tribes fought each other quite regularly over such incidents. But having the white faced men do it was quite another thing.

There was also talk of a strange new animal, which, confusingly, seemed to come in various sizes, shapes, and colours, but it was very good at hunting and could outrun any kangaroo. The young men were very interested in that. That 1805 spring gathering was a-buzz with talk. Not too many as yet noticed the odd cough, here and there, mainly among the young warriors who had been courageous enough to investigate the strangers' doings more closely.

Over the next 18 years, most of the Tarena people experienced a great many rapid changes to their lifestyles and assumptions about everything. More and more strangers arrived, until their numbers far exceeded the Tarena's own. The invaders hunted anywhere, observing none of the tribal customs that allocated areas to each tribe, and thus interfered with the vital food supply. With them came diseases such as had not been known on Tarena before, killing a great many in hideous and unstoppable ways, the wise men having no cures or explanations. The strangers also brought many more unknown animals, particularly the wooly creature that ate the greenery intended for the native marsupials. These sheep were presently brought up even into the highlands by brutish men, and when the Tarenas defended their pastures by spearing some of the animals, the revenge wrought on them was terrible beyond words. Once, a tribe of 40 were driven by the strangers with guns into a marshy lagoon, where all of them were ruthlessly shot, excepting a very old man and his wife who were suffered to leave.

The stealing of women continued and increased. After David Collins' death in 1810, the strangers also starting taking the children in larger numbers. Any native man who offered resistance was shot, and sometimes, it seemed, they shot them simply for fun. Or maybe it was target practice?

The strangers put up fences and chased away, or killed, anyone who tried to pass through. It was no longer safe just to walk through the forest in the old, time-honoured way. Inside the fences – and later also outside of them, roaming the countryside in wild flocks – were enormous horned creatures that also ate the grass. Probably the only welcome change to the Tarena lifestyle were the new dogs, whom they quickly learned to appreciate for their hunting skills. These they attempted to steal whenever they could, and the puppies became a valuable item to barter.

In time, the Tarena people learned to communicate with the

strangers. Their language was incomprehensible, and their ways equally so, but some things were gradually understood.

"Not all the newcomers act in the same way; some of them, especially in the settlements, are friendly or at least not aggressive. They offer what they call 'gifts' of clothes and food and blankets, and seemed to think that we all need some kind of help… Some willingly share out flour and sugar and tea, others do it with fear in their faces.

Beware of those in houses that stand alone, away from the settlements – they are usually too frightened to do anything other than shoot… Best keep out of their way, but as the strangers' ways are often inscrutable, this is not always easily done. A valley that had been untouched by them only a moon or two before, can suddenly be occupied by one or several and their animals…"

To add to the confusion, the white men had among themselves groups that were kept separately and made to do what was called work.

"Take extra care with these men – single runaways or the groups that look after their animals, especially up on the plateau. They are violent and will kill and rape, if they can get you…"

The tribes were increasingly pressured to find enough game, even in remote regions, or a viable area where they could still live in peace. It was not a situation that could last much longer.

Meanwhile, other Tarena groups had more regular contact with the strangers, got used to the white men and began to move among them regularly. They were called the Town Mob, and a degree of familiarity developed. The stranger's tribal chief, called the governor, was always pleased to see them, and it was known that he had issued orders that no one was to harm them. Freely given food, and often offered clothing as well, the Town Mob would put these on, and caper around in them to please the white men. But the garments were uncomfortable and upset the body's senses, so they never wore them for long, discarding them in careless heaps as they left town. But they always took any blankets handed out; these were actually useful.

The Tarena watched the ceaseless labour in amazement. Did these people ever take time out to dance and sing and tell stories? The nearest they seemed to get to it was in the shanties where the grog was. Enough of that, and the white man became foolish and unsteady and then he would sometimes sing. On one astonishing occasion, in the middle of a time when the strangers appeared to be very short of their food, a ship arrived that had mostly only rum in barrels on board. For the next two weeks, nearly every man in the settlement was rendered incoherent. The Tarena tried the stuff also, and some became addicted, losing all pride and health, and stayed in the town, no longer hunting with their group like proper men. But that was only some of them; others drifted into the settlements only at intervals to look and wonder. After all, there was real life to be got on with, the pleasure of the hunt, the family life, the ceremonies and rituals that had to be observed, and the sharing of their new information with the other tribes.

Gradually, however, a gap grew between those who visited town and those who did not. The former were accused of fraternizing with the invaders. So they went less often to the tribal gatherings. Life somehow seemed to continue without the regular ceremonial rituals. Sometimes, back in Hobart, they would camp near the house of that funny little man whom everyone called the parson; he seemed to be a man of some importance despite his feeble frame, and he had planted small trees that eventually produced some delicious fruit called apples. The Tarena also learnt some of the new language, enough to get by on. This parson was very friendly, letting them make camp beside his house – which stood in a particularly favoured corner – and a group of mainly young native females took to virtually living there. One of them, whom he called Catherine, disappeared in 1821, along with the parson's housekeeper, on one of the big ships going to England. Rumour had it that she was pregnant at the time.

***

Tom Birch, as he was now called, had all the resilience and adaptability of a young person. In due course, his early memories faded, and he adjusted to his new life. He was endlessly fascinated by the two horses in the household, whom the master called Dragon and Dare. There were not many such animals in Hobart at the time; some officers and wealthy settlers had a few; the parson Knopwood had a small white pony. Keeping horses was very expensive, much of their food still having to be imported. In any case the priority at the time was on clearing and cultivating land; lugging heavy trees and ploughs was more readily done by oxen. Edward Lord, temporarily holding the post of governor after Collins died, had the finest steed of all. When Mr Birch rode out on one of his, Tom loved to watch the harnessing and the cool swing of the man's leg over the horse's back. Tom dreamed of doing the same.

Dogs were his other joy. Every man in Hobart kept one to hunt and guard, if he possibly could, jealously protecting them, for they were much sought by thieves and sold for good money. This was Tom's job, along with cleaning in the yard, oiling harness, feeding chickens and collecting the eggs, mucking out the pigs, and any other errand Mrs. Birch should think of. For this he was fed alongside the man servant, who was described as a convict. Like him, Tom was never allowed inside the house. Once, the son of the family, George, had come into the yard and started playing with him. They'd had some fun throwing stones along the drain until Mrs Birch came flying out and grabbed her son back. It was understood that the Birches did not consider Tom a suitable companion for their boy.

So Tom spent a lot of time with John Crips. That convicts were beneath the notice of fine folk was not surprising, but the one who treated John with the most contempt was Annie the cook. This caused him a great deal of consternation, frequently expressed in vitriolic language to young Tom. He had grown to like the black boy, after his first outrage at being billeted with 'a stinkin' native'. Crips was from Newbury in England, where he had laboured loading drays for a carter, until one day by some unlucky chance a crate of goods broke open and revealed several very fine garments that were just too easy to hide and later sell to one who didn't ask inconvenient questions. Unfortunately for Crips, the owner had money and could pay a policeman to follow the trail, and presently he found himself in prison. Sentenced to seven years transportation, he arrived in Sydney in 1791.

Sent on to Norfolk Island, he kept out of trouble, completed his sentence in 1797, and then became a general servant to Samuel and Ann

Hussey, ex-convicts themselves but hardworking and much liked by all. They cultivated 30 acres and gave the little man a steady home. After the forced closure of the Island, the three of them arrived in Hobart together in 1807. Sam Hussey, old and unable to face starting all over again, hanged himself soon after. This knocked John off his steady path; soon he was in bad company and re-offending with theft and sale of un-licensed liquor. Thus he came back into servitude, allocated to the Birch household.

He was around forty years of age, but could not be exact on that, recalling no parents who might have given him a precise date. Even his name was uncertain. His earliest memories were of surviving the hard way in the mean and dirty alleys of Newbury; his small body remained stunted from malnutrition. But there was enough goodness in him to find compassion for another outcast. In time he was warmed by Tom's affection, in his gruff way beginning to look out for him. He explained a great deal of Life to the young boy, who quickly picked up John's broad English. It was an unconventional education, for Crips could neither read nor write, and had never seen life from any other place than the bottom of the pile. But he knew a great deal about surviving, managing his assignment to the Birch's in masterly fashion. Some nights he quietly absented himself, and then there would be some extra food to share, or perhaps a 'found' jacket to ward off the cold. Greatly distressed that he could not find any shoes to fit Tom, he returned with a piece of kangaroo skin from which he laboriously stitched some moccasins for both of them. His duties involved all the heavy outside work, procuring and sawing firewood, fetching water from the creek, caring for the horses. Seeing Tom's fascination for the latter, he had on occasion sat him up on Dare, who could be trusted to stand still.

He also encouraged Tom to meet the other natives – the Town Mob when they were about, and the other black children. In 1820 Governor Sorell ordered a census taken of all such being kept in white men's houses. In Hobart alone there were over twenty who were admitted to, with many more out in the country. Those in town formed a small gang of their own, whenever they could get away, and they were swift and for the most part lawless. They formed a curious connection with the

Town Mob, hanging around with them at times, and despising them at others. Some black children were too well guarded, growing up entirely in the white man's way, and taught to read, write and cipher by settlers who were genuinely well-meaning. They believed civilizing the 'dusky children of the forest' was their Christian duty. But more generally, black children soon were seen merely as useful labour.

Tom's master T W Birch was exceptionally energetic and entrepreneurial. In addition to the whaling and sealing, he was soon trading grain and timber in Sydney on his own ships. Then he built a warehouse, began importing much-needed goods and making handsome profits. Some of the land grants he cultivated with the labour of the convicts allocated to him, others he simply kept for later speculation. In Hobart, his fine three-story house built in 1816 was the finest in town, often the setting for official banquets and let to Governor Macquarie on his 2nd visit in 1821 as the only suitable house in town, better even than the existing Government House. Birch also provided building services, such as the wall around the gaol, and his ships under Captain Kelly were among the first to exploit the Huon Pine timber on the wild western coast. And he supplied the commissariat stores with meat, a lucrative contract indeed. His marriage had yielded four sons and two daughters, and he was soon among the most influential and wealthy men in Hobart.

His wife Sarah was not an unkind woman, merely a conventional one, and over time she began to notice young Tom as a person. Gradually, more contact with her own children was allowed, though it always remained clear that he was not family. He was obviously intelligent and soon fluent in English, so she made some attempts to teach him to read. In the house on Macquarie St there was plenty of space and he was allowed a corner of his own, where he could study his primer. Sarah expected that he attend church on Sundays, sitting in the servant pews along with John and Annie, and wearing a neat coat bearing the Birch insignia. She described him as good and honest, even gentle and obliging. Later, when he was in trouble, she interceded for him.

Young Tom's best moments were when his master took him out into the country. Birch's land grants were in varying areas, in Cambridge, Richmond, Hollow Tree, Jericho and Lovely Banks – all parts of Tarena that Tom' s family had regularly travelled over as part of their normal life. His memory of these journeys was gone, but his connection with the land lay in his blood and soul. Here he felt free. He rejoiced every time Birch, riding out to inspect his far-flung properties, took a cart with supplies and allowed young Tom to come along.

The visits to Lovely Banks excited Tom the most. Among the convicts and others who worked there was a black girl, a little older than Tom. Where had she come from? What tribe did she belong to? Had she been taken by force from her family, or was she one of the many orphans whose parents had been shot or driven off? Neither she nor Tom ever knew that, or her real name. On the farm, they called her Sal. She worked on small chores like Tom, and later the men made use of her. Like most of these children, she died young of abuse and disease, simply vanishing from the landscape. What broken spirits did they leave behind, this small army of dislocated young people? How many of the men gave her another thought?

Tom and Sal, on the rare occasions that they saw each other, felt like family and provided some solace to each other. They had carefree moments when they scampered among the trees, irrepressible as children are, rejoicing in the birdsong and the sunlight on the water. Later, when Tom was a well-grown fourteen-year old and had been loaned by Birch to surveyor Evans' party as a carrier, he remembered Sal. By the Prosser River on the east coast, Tom deserted and made his way to Lovely Banks. He worked there alongside the convicts and at night Sal took him to her sleeping corner. Here he learnt about sex, and for the girl it was the only time she lay with someone who held her warm and close. The farm men dropped her as soon as they had had their way with her. She knew nothing else. By the time Tom came to her, she was already broken, her system battling invading organisms and her spirit too sad and lonely to survive much longer. It was too late to save her.

In December 1821, Mr. Birch died very suddenly at 47, probably of an apoplexy, leaving behind him a chaotic situation. His widow Sarah, now left with six children, had enjoyed the advantages of being a wealthy merchant's wife, but she was not an entrepreneur herself. The many business interests, some of the acreage, and the fine home in Macquarie

St had to be sold; the complexities of the will took thirty-three years to finally sort out. She hastily took refuge in a second marriage, to Edmund Hodgson who held the neighbouring grant to Lovely Banks. With his help both land pieces were managed, and she was comfortable enough, especially after the will was declared. Hodgson then ran a very successful tannery on Birch's land grant, which extended up along the creek in South Hobart, and later they built the now-famous 'Islington', as well as Glen House nearby.

In the fluster of all these events, Sarah had little time for Tom, but she was pleased that he had turned up at Lovely Banks. Both the Birch's had been surprised to hear of his deserting the surveyor's party, though Sarah had been aware how, in the months before, Tom had shown great distress when his early companion, the convict John Crips, suddenly disappeared. The latter's fate was never really established, but it was believed that he had been murdered in some drunken brawl. Tom had genuinely loved the crusty little man.

Doing the hard physical work made Tom grow into a fine figure, showing all promise of being tall and already very strong. He was good-looking, vitally healthy and moved with an animal grace. Then one day he disappeared into the bush.

Tom stopped, sitting in a quiet nook where the creek twisted back on itself, and carefully absorbed the environment about him. All was quiet. No birds chattered warnings. No animal showed extra alerts. No strange scents wafted on the breeze. The silence deepened. He felt as though he should be slipping into something he was somehow familiar with, yet an invisible but tangible barrier prevented him. Although he was alone, unquiet spirits were about. He was not comfortable. Something was missing and it bothered him, but he was unable to decide what it was.

He was not going back to the farm. That much he did know. Sal was dead, her broken frame unceremoniously interred out the back by one of the convicts. Tom had seen the look on the men's faces. There was no acceptance for her, or him, there. But he was growing into a man, and needed to prove himself. Where, then, if not with the white people?

Tom's own people, along with the other East Coast tribes, were fragmenting. Increasingly unable to move, hunt and meet freely, they were reduced to isolated groups moving cautiously through the landscape, ever wary of attack. From 1817 on, huge numbers of settlers began pouring in, and valleys that had been peaceful camping and hunting grounds, were now empty of game and filled instead with invaders' huts and animals – and guns.

Tom knew all this, for he regularly spoke to members of the Town Mob. He had also heard that a tribal warrior called Musquito was organising resistance at last. Powerful and forceful, this Aboriginal man was armed with extensive knowledge of white man's ways and, importantly, their weapons. And driving him was an implacable hatred of the invaders with their hollow promises and condescending attitudes. He encouraged Tarena men to fight back and defend their homeland. Every man was needed.

"That is where I'm going," Tom decided. "I'm strong. I can be a man among them, and they will be proud of me."

He had proved his manhood with Sal, and now he was going to avenge her. Besides, there were women among the tribes.

The matter decided, Tom was unsure how to prepare. Most of the tribes, even the Town Mob, generally went about in their natural and proper naked state. To belong to them, Tom would have to do the same, but he had spent the last nine years wearing clothing, and to go about naked did not come easily. His feet, fortunately, were adequately hardened. Since he grew out of John Crips' moccasins, he had generally preferred bare feet, grudgingly putting on shoes only for church attendance. This was not so out of the ordinary; many assigned servants didn't have any either. But neither did he have any of the tribal cicatrices to denote his status and journey to manhood. In the end he hid his shirt in a hollow tree where it could stay dry, and be found again if needed. He set off, wearing trousers only and carrying a possum rug and a musket, both of which he had taken from Lovely Banks.

Then he went to join his own people.

2. KICKERTERPOLLER THE WARRIOR

The next two years were exciting. Tom had been welcomed with open arms. The women appreciated his youthful body and were generous with their own. The men quickly saw to it that he had at least the essential initiations, and he proudly wore the new scars. He learned that his real name was Kickerterpoller, and who his family was, and even met some relatives. Nobody could tell him about the fate of his mother. She had vanished with the whalers, killed, drowned or died of disease, there was no telling.

But he did hear of Tekartee, his little childhood friend. She was given to a sealer, John Harvey, and lived with him on the islands in the Bass' Strait. Later, he sold her to another sealer, John Myetye, a Maori black. She was still with him.

Tekartee! Only three when she was taken, still only about fourteen now. What had she met with in her short life? Tom could guess, for he had seen Sal's fate, and his heart hardened. She might still be alive, but he was going to avenge her, too.

Tom began to learn the art of bush warfare. He watched the experienced Musquito closely, flattered that the great man occasionally consulted him about the local manner of white man's arrangements. Ironically, they had to converse in English; neither man knew the other's language. Musquito, an Aborigine from the Sydney area, had – as a result of a murder that was never proved against him – been sent to Norfolk Island, and on to Van Diemens Land in 1813. Sent to work on Edward Lord's estate, he was quickly recognized as a skilled tracker, and the colonial government called him up to help find many troublesome bushrangers. He was promised that he would be repatriated to Sydney, which he had expressed a great desire for, if he helped catch Michael Howe. This he did, but the promise was never kept, although Governor

Sorell did send the request to Macquarie. It is not known why the Sydney governor did not follow up on it. Perhaps he simply didn't see it as important enough. Had he realised the rage that yet another dismissal would fuel in Musquito's heart, and what savage consequences were about to be unleashed upon the settlers, he would certainly have made haste to attend to it. It was Musquito who united the Tarena tribal people into a skilled guerrilla force.

Filled with new hope, they allocated Musquito one of their few remaining young girls, Gooseberry. Eventually he murdered her in a jealous rage. But he clearly had great charisma, and further enhanced his status by killing the convict Kemp in 1818 and the following year, one Huxley was, it seems, another of his victims.

"Why should you put up with white man? Is he not taking your land, your women, your children? Fight back!"

He taught them many clever tricks. Wear some clothes, knock on the door of an isolated settler's hut, and ask him nicely in English for some food. He'll relax, thinking you're 'tame', and meanwhile surround the hut from the back and be ready to set fire to it. Grab his provisions. He's always got flour, tea, and sugar; above all take away his weapons. If you can get him to fire his gun, you've got time then to rush him; he'll have to reload it before he can fire again. Burn his crops – that will really hurt him – and spear his sheep and cattle. Take his hunting dogs, you'll find those useful yourself, and why should he have them to take yet more of your food supply? Do all of this often enough, and the white man will give up and go away…

And so Tom learnt to attack and harass the invader. He was good at it, often taking a leading part, silently guiding his group to the back of targeted homesteads, or pointing out the best season to most effec-tively damage crops. He understood which barns had vital grain and seed stored. As their attacks became more successful, other tribal mobs began to join them, and they soon saw the advantage of large numbers. Besides, that meant more women, and Kickerterpoller made the most of it. He grew almost as tall as Musquito, but always took care to remain respectful of the great man. Gooseberry – by far the most attractive girl there – was sadly and definitely out of bounds. But perhaps she also saw the attractiveness of the keen young man? Maybe it was an unguarded moment in that direction that brought about her violent end.

Late in 1823, when Kickerterpoller had been with Musquito's band for nearly two years, things began to change. The group had camped at Grindstone Bay, on the eastern coast, for several days in a peaceable manner, then suddenly attacked and killed two convicts without, apparently, any immediate provocation. Kickerterpoller, who had been further down the bay at the time, could not work it out. Had Musquito lost control and let his rage boil over? Had the other warriors simply followed suit? The white men had been wary, but not unfriendly, and had shared some of their food.

A third white man, however, got away and back to Pittwater, raising the alarm. George Gatehouse, a settler of that area, quickly mustered some men to ride north to the scene of the murder. On the way, near the Prosser River, they located a different Aboriginal group encamped in a valley, and attacked them in the night, killing men, women and children indiscriminately. Thirty natives slaughtered in retribution for two convicts, – the perpetrators congratulated themselves on their success, but continued all the same north along the coast to Grindstone Bay, in pursuit of the other Aborigines.

When Musquito heard of this latest outrage, his fury got really dark. Now there was no stopping him. Over a period of seven months, in an area from the East Coast to the higher Central Plateau, he killed at least eleven people, mostly assigned convicts. At times, his band joined up with the Big River tribe, and groups of up to three hundred were reported to be making the hills unsafe. They also attacked and severely wounded a Mrs. Osborne, who later testified that Musquito had been the leader and that Kickerterpoller was with him. Both black men were by now well-recognised among the settlers, but even in the grieving over her husband's violent death by spearing, that lady indicated that she did not see Kickerterpoller, whom she called Black Tom, administer any of the actual violence.

This was uncommonly observant of her. Most settlers spent no time ascribing human qualities to the black savages. As the attacks increased, blind panic was spreading among the whites; in their eyes, all blacks were undiscriminating, violent and out to murder. But Kickerterpoller was in a great dilemma. Killing was part of a great warrior's fighting job. Musquito was his hero. But the truth was that he had encountered an unexpected resistance within himself to throwing a spear with genuine deadly intent. Defending the land, yes, and destroying the invaders' stuff for vengeance, that too, but his gentle nature recoiled at the idea of actually destroying another human being. Being such a softie in this group was a real handicap, so he went to much effort to prove his usefulness in other ways, desperately hoping to avoid an actual confrontation. So far, he had been successful, roaring around with much bluster and wild love-making.

Regular raiding parties were organized to counter the attacks. One, led by Lt Gunn and assisted by a 'tame' Aborigine called Tegg, finally caught Musquito and brought him, quite badly injured by Tegg, to the Hobart Hospital until he recovered enough to be transferred to the town gaol. He and another captured Aborigine known as Black Jack were sentenced to hang for the murder of a convict and a settler known as McCarthy. It was a farcical trial which caused honest and thoughtful men much concern. What thoughts it provoked among a large group of captured natives, brought into Hobart just at that time, was not inquired into.

Governor Arthur was delighted to have so many Aborigines under his control.

"We'll build them a village of their own, on the eastern shore, across the river from Hobart Town, and provide them with food and clothing. They'll see that we mean well, and have good things to offer."

That group remained for nearly two years, making occasional hunting excursions into the countryside. But in September 1826 two more Aboriginal men were hanged 'for depredations upon white man'; with this news every last native decamped from Hobart, satisfied that nothing worthwhile could be received from the hands of the traitorous invaders.

Kickerterpoller was now, by default, the leader of the ever-smaller group of defending warriors. It was a chance to prove himself as a real man, no longer overshadowed. He led several highly effective strikes, perfecting the art of the lightening raid, and melting back into the bush with his group before effective pursuit could be organized. He was one of several such leaders across the island, but he had learnt well and his attacks were particularly infamous and feared.

It was during the raid on Jones's place near Oatlands that he came up against his own scruples. The band, surrounding the cottage which stood close by the river bank, watched Kickerterpoller applying his usual tactic of taunting the settler and his wife with strong language, calling them cowards and bastards, hoping they would fire their pistol. But he had done it too often, and the Jones' knew of their danger if they actually used the weapon. Finding himself thus made ineffective, Kickerterpoller flew into a rage, driven by conflicting emotions. He had to be seen as the strong leader, yet was unable to bring himself to actually inflict direct bodily harm. Especially on a woman. Somehow, Sarah Birch's image stood between him and Mrs Jones, the hapless woman in the doorway of her hut. So easily could he dodge her wavering pistol and grab her! He was entirely quick and strong enough! The whole mob was waiting for his signal. In total frustration, he leapt up and down, roaring out what he hoped were fearsome-sounding threats.

"I'll put you in the river, ma-am, I'll burn your hut, ma-am..."

Perhaps it was a kindness of fate that caused the riverbank behind him, softened by recent flooding, to suddenly give way. With a spectacular splash he fell in backwards, and by the time he had floundered out to the contemptuous laughter of his group, a signal from their lookout up the hill warned of approaching armed men, and they had to flee.

Kickerterpoller had come close to being undone. The memory of that laughter smarted, though perhaps the ridiculous situation had – just – saved him. But now he had to be decisive, and when they heard about settler Browning holding a native woman against her will, his opportunity came. Driven, perhaps, also by the memory of Sal and Tekartee, he didn't wait for any conflicting feelings to get in the way, but swung the axe in a blind rage so hard that it virtually decapitated the man, killing him on the instant. Shortly afterwards a stock keeper at Thompson's hut was also speared to death. The Colonial Times in Hobart reported both incidents with great outrage. No mention was made of Browning forcing a native woman to be a sexual slave, nor that three of the stock keepers and an accomplice had captured and pack-raped another native shortly before the attack. What reading skills Kickerterpoller once had were sadly in disuse, but no doubt he knew of the way these things were spoken of among the white men.

His leadership beyond doubt re-instated, Kickerterpoller continued to lead many raids, but the killing sat badly with him. The spirits of the two men he had dispatched seemed to be hovering in odd places, fearsome and revolting. He got ever better at dodging the deed itself, instead making his raids especially ferocious. It was a desperate war that his people were fighting, and he could not avoid it. The murder of Herbert Fairfield, brother of a settler on the Macquarie River, affected him particularly. The Fairfields were known to the Tarenas as one of the benign sort. Although they were occupying land along a particularly fine stretch of the river, much favoured for campsites, they had offered no aggression, and it was even said that they would not have any of those convicts to do their labour. Young Herbert, though, had employed some as shepherds, in the foothills of the Great Tiers, a long way out of sight of the Fairbourne homestead. Most likely Herbert, a young and amiable idealist, had no idea of those shepherds' part in the depredations upon the Tarena tribes, but that did not save him when he accidentally blundered into the camp that Kickerterpoller's warriors had just set up.

So he watched, torn by his own conflict, as his group, and those other tribal remnants that had joined them, became ever more brutalized, taking pleasure in the killing, hacking into Herbert Fairfield without mercy. But what was he to do? Most whites were equally awful. In late 1826 the news that other hanging of two black men reached them. One had been an old man, sick and feeble, who could no more have killed anyone than sailed through the air with the black swans.

Kickerterpoller and his band were finally caught near Richmond by Constable Laing and his men. Since some men swore that he had been complicit in Musquitos' murder of a white settler, banishing Kickerterpoller to the convict colony on Sarah Island, in Macquarie Harbour on the remote West Coast was proposed, but at this point Sarah Birch, now Mrs Hodgson, spoke up on his behalf.

"Not only is he baptized a Christian, but he was brought up in a Christian household, and was always good and honest…"

It is something of a mystery why he was released without further punishment. Sarah Hodgson was member of the small social elite in Hobart, and therefore had some influence, but that seems insufficient reason for the eventual 'discharge by proclamation', which was normally only done when there was insufficient evidence for a conviction. At any rate, his adoptive mother, being willing to have him return 'home' to Lovely Banks, prevailed. No doubt she meant well, but she could not contain the wild young man. Her husband resented having a black around the place, and soon Tom was out raiding again. The only real sense of belonging he had found was among his own kind.

Not that there were many of them left by now, but in the last three years of the decade, they mounted a last desperate war against the invaders. Given their low numbers – there were probably no more than 200 – 300 active natives left by then in the settled areas – they were re-markably successful. In 1830 the hysteria reached such levels that Arthur had no choice but to declare martial law, under which, effectively, no white man could be prosecuted for shooting a black one.

But Kickerterpoller found that somehow the steam had gone from him. The role of warrior did not suit his naturally sensitive mind. Had he lived before the invasion, he would have become one of the wise men of the tribe, perhaps a thinker or a prophet, his status confirmed through those abilities. Early exposure to white man's religious thinking had given him the concept of hell – the place where murderers go. He was appalled by his own actions, weary of the burden he was carrying increasingly unwillingly. His acuity lessened; at the end of 1827 he was captured again, and this time he was held in Richmond Gaol for eight months.

***

The district constable at the time in Richmond was Gilbert Robertson, a man with an unusual background in the predominantly British setting of early Hobart. The son of a Scotsman with property in British Guiana, his mother was slave brought from Africa. Sent to Scotland in 1812, young Gilbert's appearance had just enough of 'the touch of the tar brush' to meet discrimination frequently, in subtle insults and avoidances. Not even his father's wealth and position could protect him entirely. Thus he gravitated to Methodism, a strong proving ground for working class men seeking living wages and a natural egalitarian justice for all. Gilbert found acceptance there, and developed strong opinions against the establishment of wealth and privilege. All his life he remained resentful, a man quickly ready to pick a quarrel, frequently embroiled in litigation and legal cases, always suspicious of others' motives. For some years, he ran a newspaper *The Colonist*, in which he spent much time criticizing the establishment. No doubt he often had right and justice on his side, but the prevailing racial attitudes ensured that he was never taken seriously. Eventually, the Colony got sick of him and he was appointed agricultural supervisor on Norfolk Island.

He had married in 1820 and persuaded his wife to the idea of emigrating. They arrived in Hobart with their first baby in 1822, Gilbert – after a disastrous land-deal-gone-wrong episode that brought him to bankruptcy – eventually found work as superintendent of the government farm at New Town. His humane and lenient views made him popular with the convicts, but the authorities wanted a stricter discipline, and – probably to get rid of him – granted him land near Richmond and made him district constable, where he encountered the young black warrior, now reduced to being a prisoner.

What conversations did Gilbert and Kickerterpoller have in the Richmond prison? Strangers in their own cultures, both knew rejection and neither had found a comfortable niche. Whatever Gilbert's other shortcomings, he did genuinely concern himself with this desperate young man. As the black and the café-au-lait heads were bent together, Gilbert shared his faith in God's acceptance of all, irrespective of colour.

Tom – for now he was known by his old name again – disputed this.

"This god is white man's idea – he never did me any good, and neither did most white men."

Tom was prepared to concede that there were some good white people. Both Sarah and convict John Crips had been nominal Christians, kindly enough and accepting that one should at least attempt to live according to the ten commandments – which in John's case was definitely a struggle as he often decided to conveniently forget the one about not stealing – but never had Tom been in the close company of a believing Christian. Gilbert's personal God-experience was incomprehensible. Yet Tom could see that this man had some inner sustenance, something that helped him hold his head up. And this man came to see him, daily when he was able, and talked with him as though he, Tom, mattered.

One night Tom had a nightmare in which he was tied to a tree and forced to watch as men tore Sal apart, limb from limb, laughing insanely as they tossed the pieces that had been a living human being into the fire. In vain he fought against his ropes. The scene was in the dark of night and the flames leapt higher with each piece of flesh. Then he saw that the men were actually devils, leering and dancing about, and to his horror they pulled the burnt pieces from the fire and began to devour them. Then they turned on him…he woke howling in fear.

"Oh, shut up, for Chris' sake, you fuckin' nigger!" snarled one of the five convicts that were stuffed into the small cell along with Tom. The local road gang was locked up there every night, and they spared him none of their contempt. The concept of convicts as an underclass among white men took a while to understand, although he had heard much about it from John Crips, but that those same men, despised by their own race, should find it necessary to look down upon himself and dark-skinned men generally, he could not come to grips with. Was he not – like them – an outcast? Why did they hate him so?

Sweating with fright, he moaned under the curses that rained on him. In the morning, he was exhausted and empty, sitting listlessly in the small yard where he was allowed to take some fresh air. His depression deepened. All he had tried to do seemed to have been of no avail. He had no one to belong to, his tribe had been scattered with many killed, and it was entirely clear that the white invaders held the winning hand. Here he was, in *their* prison! He, the warrior, who had fought to save his people! He, now treated as less than dirt, and exposed nightly to the insults of convicts. Tom shuddered. Some of what those men did at night was unspeakable – at least they kept away from him on that subject – but he couldn't help being aware of it. Each group of men was the same – the gangs changed all the time – and each lot had the same attitude towards him. Sometimes he thought he caught a brief look of sympathy from the odd one, but it was quickly suppressed. It didn't do, in this crowd, to show anything other than the mob attitude.

As the weeks went on, Tom began to despair. The nightmares became more frequent, each more horrible than the last. Sometimes it was Sal, and other times his dear little Tekartee, Tekartee! Tekartee! stolen and used by the sealers! until he felt his very soul shrinking. He began to behave irrationally, howling and pounding the prison bars until they put him into chains, where he lay either listless or raving.

Gilbert found Tom in this desperate state on his return from an expedition.

"My dear man, you must come and live at my house. I'm sure Governor Arthur would allow you to work with me."

Better food, some kindliness, and relative freedom quickly revived the young black man. With Gilbert's constant expounding of Christ's law and God's love, one day Tom was ready to bow his head and thank God that he had been spared and was being given another chance at a better life. A deep peace came into him, a wonderful, calming blessing into every part of his body.

***

That year, 1828, more roving parties were formed, led by men like John Batman, Jorgen Jorgenson, and Edgar Luttrell. Officially, the objective of the parties was to round up the natives and hand them over to the authorities, 'for their own safekeeping'. Governor Arthur insisted that conciliation was to be employed as far as possible, and violence kept for a last resort. What actually happened in the bush was well away from the public eye, but it was noted that very few live natives were brought in by this method. Gilbert, hoping to make his mark as one who helped solve the problem of the natives, included Tom in his own party so he could convince any Aborigines they met up with to come peacefully. And one of the few successes they did have was the capture, in November, of Eumarrah, the feared leader of the Stony Creek Tribe who had been the terror of the white settlers in the Northern Midlands for the last two years, involved in numerous killings, burnings, and lootings. Eumarrah, his woman, and several other members of the tribe were all brought to the Richmond Gaol, and then released into the care of Gilbert Robertson on condition that they all help with the roving parties. Between expeditions, they lived at Gilbert's, and played with his children. By then, no more native children were being born in the south eastern parts of Tarena.

"I'm not going along with that!" Eumarrah was bitter. "They've beaten us and now they want us to betray the rest of our people…"

"But don't you see, the Governor has promised that we may live in peace if we go to this place on Bruny, and leave the settlers alone. He said the white men would not be allowed into our area." Tom was sick of fighting.

"I don't believe it – it's all empty words like everything else they've said. Anyway, why should we stay in only one part of Tarena? This is *our* place! I *want* to kill the bastards! Look at what they've done to us!"

"I know. Haven't I fought them also? But there's too many of them, they just keep coming, and we're not getting anywhere. Maybe this is our only chance to survive. Anyway, I want to get out of here. I want a woman!"

"You keep your hands off mine, you craven bastard!" Eumarrah's wife was the only younger woman in the group, and he knew Tom's reputation as a great seducer. "Besides, there are lots of white men on Bruny already, and they've been messing with our women there. You really want to tamely go and say 'yes, Governor, and thank you for offering me a bit of land and I'll be a good boy and learn to work it'. Bugger that – it's already *our* land, don't you see!? He can't bloody well *give* it to us! What's the matter with you? Lost your guts altogether?"

Tom drew himself up at this insult, but quickly let it go again. Gilbert's words about being gentle and kind were still fresh in his mind. The warrior spoke the truth, indeed, but what was the use?

"No, Eumarrah, I'm being a realist. I just want to be left in peace to go hunting and have a woman and live a normal life. There's a fair few of the

Nuonene tribe on Bruny, they're all hanging out there and the Governor promised he would provide food and all we need. It would be better than this, even though Gilbert's been pretty decent to us."

Eumarrah spat. "You're just chicken! He's made you into a softie! I know you sit with him and read in his big black book. What's that going to teach you? White man's disgusting ways when we've got our own good traditions? How long is it since you danced properly and called up the old stories?"

Tom flinched. He couldn't deny it. It was true that he missed the excitement of the real corroboree. He also knew that white men thought it a ridiculous notion, having grown men dancing wildly for hours round a camp fire. A real longing to be with his own kind filled Tom. He ignored Eumarrah's last remark and insisted that he wanted to go to Bruny.

"Even if the Gov is lying, at least we'll be together. And then we *could* dance!"

The other man made a disgusted sound.

"And meanwhile, I suppose, you're going to continue to help them catch the rest of us, eh? How does that fit with your scheme? Can't you at least leave those that are clever enough to survive alone?"

More flinching on Tom's part. The condition of their relative freedom here was that they continue to help bring in more natives, and Tom was deeply conflicted over this. Half of him felt that it was betrayal indeed, and the other half desperately wanted to believe that he was doing his people a favour, that the governor was really his friend and was telling the truth, and that he, Tom, could help by bringing them all to a peaceful place. In the face of Eumarrah's scorn he made an effort at a compromise.

"No, I'll not betray more of our people. I can lead the stupid whites in circles and pretend to be reading tracks. They won't know any different. It won't be my fault then, if we don't catch anyone. We'll just keep them going till they get tired of it."

And so it was agreed. All three of the roving expeditions attempted thereafter were completely unsuccessful. Just occasionally, Tom caught Gilbert looking at him speculatively, but if the latter had any thoughts, he kept them to himself. He also had his doubts about the justice of their actions. He later observed: "...they [the blacks] consider every injury they can inflict upon the white men as an act of duty and patriotism… having ideas of their natural rights which would astonish most European statesmen".

Meanwhile, Governor Arthur sincerely sought a peaceful solution to the settler/native conflict – always providing, of course, that nobody questioned the fundamental land grab the English had committed. He planned to build a village for the natives on Bruny Island, provide a school and chapel, and teach them the skills of tending the land, growing vegetables, and domestic arts. Some of the local Nuenone tribe came voluntarily, lured by the hand outs, but they were not accustomed to European ways. They soon caught the fatal chest infection, probably exacerbated by living in the confined quarters of the huts, and the survivors left, creating a precarious existence as best they could outside the compound. Much to their men's resentment, the women spent time at the white men's sealing camps. Venereal diseases from there quickly rendered them infertile. Someone was desperately needed to provide leadership and create some order. When George Augustus Robinson came to Arthur's attention, he seemed the perfect answer.

3. TOM'S LOVE LOST

"April 1830: Can I imagine for a moment that the white man, my fellow man, has murdered their [the Tarena people's] countrymen, their kindred and their friends, has violated their daughters, and has forcibly taken away their children under pretext of taking care of them? Yes, it is only too true. Regardless of all laws, human or divine, they have imbued their hands with the blood of these poor unoffending people."

Thus wrote George Augustus Robinson, a self-educated builder from London and fiery evangelist, who arrived in Hobart in 1824. It was a view that grated with the already-tender consciences of the white settlers, and won him no friends among them, but it was the very outlook that Governor Arthur seized on. Here, at last, was a man who could conciliate the natives without violence, and Arthur wasted no time in sending Robinson to Bruny Island, to rescue what he could of the settlement.

Robinson's original intention was genuinely well-meaning, believing all men to be equal before God. In this, he was similar to Gilbert Robertson; both had the same evangelical piety bred by the Methodist Church. But they were destined to become acrimonious rivals over the Aboriginal question, both aspiring to be recognized for having the answers and practical solutions on the matter. In 1829, Robinson requested the group at Gilbert's be sent to Bruny, thinking that the best progress would come with real numbers and the fullest possible involvement of the wider remaining Aboriginal community. He also planned a journey up the remote and wild west coast to establish initial contact with the tribes in that area, who were largely unaffected by white men. A 'civilised' native like Tom, who had an understanding of the governor's intentions, would be invaluable on the journey, providing an effective communication. Tom was only too happy to follow the call, but Gilbert Robertson resented having one of his star performers taken away from him, and hung back until forced by a direct order to relinquish them. In December Tom, Eumarrah, and the rest of their group, joined up with some of the Nuenone from Bruny, in readiness for Robinson's trek. Among the latter group was Truganini, young, petite and attractive, both in the eyes of white men and of woman-starved Tom.

Alas, Truganini had a husband… Woorraddy, no mean warrior himself. The two men were destined to fight each other several times, and once Tom attempted to draw the other natives into a vendetta against Woorraddy so he, Tom, might have Truganini to himself. The excitement grew even more when the lovely lady, who was delightfully generous with her charms, ensnared Robinson himself, and Woorraddy had to be restrained from murdering him, also. The nightly intrigues over who was sleeping with whom enlivened their long journey greatly.

Fortunately for Tom, a friend of Truganini's called Pagerly was also in the group. She was somewhat more mature than her young companion, and had in fact been married to Truganini's father Mangana, before he died "from the effects of a loathsome disease". But she was wise in the ways of sex, and Tom quickly staked his claim. The two remained together for the next two and half years, forming a steady friendship that was not seriously affected by any of the other fluid sexual encounters that various tribal meetings called forth. Friendship with a special person – marriage as the white man called it – was for life, but that did not interfere with the tribes' greatest entertainment and pleasure. The generous sharing of sex, the impulsive acting upon the pleasure of meeting, the fulfillment of a natural drive, was the simple and uncomplicated way of Aboriginal life. The smallest child knew that it was growing up to be a sexual being when its proper time came. It saw the sexual couplings of the adults, and there was no mystery about it. A large part of the children's amusements was to track lovers and plot disruptions to their trysts. There were strict rules around who was available and who was not. Kinship patterns had to be observed. Totemic connections could not be violated. Real trouble came when a couple ignored those tribal laws, or when one tribe stole another's women without making the appropriate approaches, and then persecution and even death were swiftly administered. These were ancient rules that had been followed for millennia, and they worked. The tribes had survived, and were in good physical and mental health.

Rape was largely not a feature among individual tribes, although it probably happened during inter-tribal raids. The women were as active in, and initiative of, sexual involvements as the men. Nor was the matter of a child's paternity ever questioned, for the child's spirit entered the womb from the landscape, and the children grew up safely within the tribe and were valued for who they were. They learnt their traditions and the tribal groups spoke their stories and danced them in the excitement of the intricate weavings of sound and movement. The younger warriors being what young men are, occasionally there would be outbreaks of sexual jealousies leading to great fights, even killings, and these entered part of the folk lore and were re-told with great relish. The stories of the creation spirits and their doings were also repeated regularly, each in its proper season and location, and formed the other great entertainment round the camp fires.

Tom re-entered the world of Aboriginal life with joy. As the group of twenty, comprising Robinson, six convicts acting as porters, and the thirteen natives, walked along the wild coast into areas where no white man had yet stepped, they did so in their traditional style, hunting along the way. To Tom, who had never been in this part of Tarena, some of the local myths themselves were new, and he listened with concentration as they were told by the fireside. At Louisa's Bay, now known as Cox's Bight, Woorraddy pointed to the great split rock.

"That's where Moinee, falling out of the sky and grabbing hold of a star on his way down, crashed to earth, scattering flaming sparks in all directions. These glowing pieces turned into the fire-tail finches flitting about in the ferny parts of the bush. They have to seek the green coolness to quench the fire that gave them birth…"

Woorraddy was a natural story teller, and loved to be in the limelight, nightly detailing the great stories of his people and their quests for love. After hearing many of these performances, Tom felt it was his turn to contribute something. After all, did he, Tom, not have a great knowledge of white man's ways? Could he not speak their language fluently? And did not he, Tom, know *their* story of the world's creation? Had he not encountered *their* God, who was greater than Moinee and even Parnuen and Vena? And, anyway, who was Woorraddy that he put himself up as the great authority on all things? The thing that really stuck in Tom's craw was the simple fact that the other man was Truganini's husband.... Truganini had smiled and winked in Tom's direction in a few discreet moments and had even invited him into her delicious body, which only fired him up for more. Damn Woorraddy! Why doesn't Raggeowrappa take him in the night! To have to listen to this annoying man's nightly self-posturing was becoming intolerable....

Tom was also deeply conflicted, torn between the ease and joy that his own culture afforded him when he was among his kind, and yet already deeply impacted by the white man. During their first journey along the west and north coasts of Tarena, they made contact with many natives, some of whom had never seen a man other than their own kind. Tom had closely observed Robinson, as he conveyed to the tribes that white men actually meant well, that there would be a safe place for all of them, that all they needed to do was to trust him. Was this really true? And anyway, why worry about the tribes on this remote west coast? They were a long way from the parts that white man wanted, and surely could just be left alone to get on with their normal life. Tom could not entirely fathom what Robinson was getting at, but by now he had so much at stake as the one in the group who understood white man's ways best, that he could not openly challenge him, and therefore nodded wisely and supportively whenever appealed to by the little man.

Occasionally Tom set himself aside to wrestle with the problem. It was hard. White man had so much that was impressive – horses and carriages, houses and dinner plates and saucepans and bottles and glasses, books and a way of writing things down, fancy clothes and guns and big ships which were capable even of taking the giant whales....surely such clever people must have the answers to everything? In truth, beside them his own people looked a poor lot, running about naked, dancing round open fires, and having no clever instruments. Part of Tom, ashamed of belonging to such an unsophisticated kind, longed to have, and be, what the new men were. Desperately wanting to be equal to Robinson, he worked to make himself as indispensable as possible. And he listened carefully when the latter expostulated about his God. A lot of it made little sense to Tom; indeed, his own people's explanations were far more understandable and fitted the natural order of things far better than this unseen deity with mysterious, unfathomable ways. But there was that undeniable sense of deep peace that had so gloriously filled him when he had bowed his head in prayer to this strange new god. Maybe he really was more powerful? Tom couldn't get words in his head to formulate the problem, but his soul knew that something was not quite right with all this... what *was* it?

Of Robinson's genuine efforts to protect the natives, when they arrived in Launceston after their 10-month journey, there could however be no doubt. In that year, 1830, decisive events had taken place while Tom and his group were isolated on the west coast. Governor Arthur, constantly appealed to by terrified settlers, had in desperation decided to settle the native problem once and for all, by calling for the formation of the Black Line. Every settler and man who could be spared, along with most of the soldiers, officers, and Arthur himself, were to form a human chain and sweep down the entire east coast and midlands areas, driving the natives before them into the Forestier Peninsula, where they were to be gathered up and taken to a safe place. It was a complex and enormously expensive undertaking involving 2600 men, and as is always the case when action has been called, the men's blood was running high. At last official permission had been given to go and get those pesky blacks! This will finally free us of the problem! And we're not going to miss a single one of them! Even if we have to shoot them!

Tom's group, unaware of any of this, arrived into the town just as the Black Line had mobilized and was getting underway. Robinson and his band of blacks caused a sensation, with every man who saw them ready to kill. The hatred was palpable, the insults flying and the threat very real.

"Nothing was to be heard in town but that they were going to kill natives..." Robinson recorded in his diary.

He had intended to have the natives camp just north of the town while he found the Governor for further instructions; but the danger was too great. Finally a humane person offered the shelter of his house, and on the way there, only his (white) presence prevented an immediate tragedy. Tom, once recovered from the fright of being such a public target, had much admiration for Robinson's courage. So why was there still something that *just wasn't right?* It was not until Tom got the chance to talk to Mannalargenna that some clarity began to form in his head, but before then, his world was turned upside down with the arrival of Tekartee.

Robinson had caught up with the governor at Ross and was provided with letters securing him all assistance as well as the use of a boat. Well aware that sealers on the Islands had many black women with them, he determined that these must be wrested from them. To this effect he sent the boat, piloted by James Parish, on several expeditions. By early December, Robinson had also used the boat to ship himself and his group of natives over to Swan Island "for their own safety", and while they were there, Parish returned from another trip with six women on board. All had been abducted by sealers and, forced to live in captivity with them, were made to hunt kangaroo and seals. They had stories of brutal treatment, often were used sexually by several men, and knew of other women who had been shot, beaten, and in one extreme case, hung upside down and left to perish. One of the six was Tekartee.

Tom ran his tongue up her body, from her belly button to her throat. He breathed her in, his strong arms under her as he lifted her up into him. She was slight of form, a fragile thing, and somehow just like the picture he had dreamed of her, all these years. Tekartee, Tekartee… This was more than just being man. This was a melting of his heart, a blending of his body into hers, an inside warmth the like of which he had never felt before. And she was just as full of desire for him. It was magic, ravishing, gut-tearing, agonizing and magnificent, all rolled into one. He wanted to soar like an eagle, protect her forever, be her hero, listen to her smallest breath. He was almost afraid to enter her, but when he did the passion overwhelmed him and he tore some of the shrubs from the ground around her in his effort not to knock her about.

But she was smiling, thank goodness, her face dewy with her own sweat, and her eyes full of love. They were lying among the low coastal scrub, well away from the camp. The first sighting of each other, slow recognition growing out of disbelief, that immediate connection even though they had not seen each other for eighteen years! Tom at twenty-three was a powerful handsome man, already very battle-scarred and soul-weary. She, a year younger, had survived by her wits and the only gestures of kindness she had ever experienced since her abduction had been occasional, stolen moments of solidarity with other women in the same situation.

Both of them had been forced to grow up too fast. They had faced a complete loss of identity and belonging. Their very souls were in permanent crisis. And now this magical upwelling, this coming home to each other, this unbelievable gift! Nothing would do but they *had* to go off together.

Pagerly, Tom's companion since they left Bruny Island a year ago, had understood immediately. She liked Tom well enough; they had grown a good friendship and respected each other. She knew his and Tekartee's early stories, and her heart was joyous for him when he encountered his little childhood friend and their early love blossomed. She actively enabled their meetings, and amusedly listened to Robinson's outrage:

"That good-for-nothing, after any woman he can get!"

Apparently Robinson had a notion that Tom was betraying *her*, Pagerly, though exactly what this was supposed to be about she could not entirely fathom. Robinson was well-meaning, but totally incapable of recognizing that before him lay an ancient understanding of the human being, practiced successfully over thousands of years, an effective philosophy that accepted human emotions and allowed them to be expressed within a carefully constructed framework. All Robinson could see was a man misbehaving sexually:

"You should be faithful to Pagerly! She's your woman, isn't she? You've got no business eyeing other ones! I thought you were a better Christian than that, Tom, you should be an example to the others. I'm disappointed in you…"

For her part, Pagerly patiently listened to Robinson's rantings and devised ways of deflecting his attention from the lovers.

And oh! did the latter two have a blossoming of love, a passion so entwined, that for quite a while they were insensible to all else.

"You have a child?" Tom asked, tracing the lines of her belly.

"Yes, little John, he's seven now… Mytye has him. He wouldn't let me bring him. But he's ok there. Mytye is quite kindly – and he's more like us, being a darkie. He'll take care of Johnnie, alright."

She told Tom about Hervey, the sealer who had taken her from her family that same terrible night; how he'd used her from when she was quite small, which wasn't so bad once you got used to it, but it had been awful when he had offered her – for money or rum – to other sealers, sometimes several together, and they had been rough and uncaring. Tekartee had come thus to womanhood. It could well have gone really badly with her, but for the chance drowning of Hervey. The man who came to tell her was Mytye, also known as John Miree, a native of Otaheite, and he offered her a home. She felt better with one who was almost as dark as herself, and when she was fourteen her son was born. But her physical reproductive structure was already badly damaged, and when she recovered after the appallingly difficult birth, she was no longer fertile.

"I came here because I wanted to see my own people, I'd heard that some from our group were here on this island…but I didn't know *you* were among them…I didn't know you were still alive…"

And her tears spilled, the tears for so much lost, for the years of aching loneliness, and for the sheer blissful agony of their love. Tom cried also, in fact he howled, shuddering into her, and they shared their pain till both lay exhausted in the sand.

In the face of such a release of emotion, Robinson's blind and outraged moral fulminations were a complete waste of time.

***

Robinson was anxious to get back to Hobart – he had already missed Christmas with his family, and been away from them for almost a full year. There was also the urgent and essential question of where the Aborigines were to be more properly settled. The little Swan Island that they were currently occupying was simply too small, and not that far from the shore. Robinson considered the only really safe place needed to be further away, in Bass Strait itself, for the contempt and fury of many white settlers was unbounded. It was not beyond them to attack his camp in the night – even with himself, Robinson, present! – and destroy them all. In this, Robinson was probably correct, and genuinely concerned for the safety of 'his' natives.

But there was more to his motivations – one, that having them all confined on an island put him in much better control over them; and two, Robinson's path to becoming A Person Of Importance in the colony was closely intertwined with his being seen as the one who had solved the native problem, the one with the answers, and the one who could speak with authority on the subject. In fact, *the only one*. Robinson was aware that other people were putting forward different suggestions, and that the Governor had established a Committee for Aborigines. He was most anxious to be interviewed by them, and have his position as The Conciliator confirmed. And, importantly, he needed to make sure that the Governor put in place his, Robinson's, just reward, which he in due course triumphantly recorded in his diary as being: "2,500 acres of land free of restrictions, a bonus of £100, and a salary of £250pa from the time of my appointment".

The government boat being needed elsewhere, Robinson set out in early January 1831 to walk down the East Coast to Hobart. In the group accompanying him were Truganini and Worraddy with their two sons, Tom, Pagerly, and Tekartee. Tom would not even consider leaving without the latter, but Robinson made no objection. He needed to arrive in Hobart with an impressive collection of natives, to underline his success with them. Leaving the rest of the natives on Swan Island under the care of an army officer, they walked steadily south. On the 11th January they overnighted at Francis Cotton's farm at Kelvedon south of Swansea, and Robinson's protectiveness of his position of authority is clearly demonstrated by his totally failing to record in his diary that Cotton had sat himself down with the group of natives and had pains-takingly interviewed them about their beliefs. Cotton, being a practicing Quaker, saw the divine in every man, and his record of their stories is the most sympathetic and delightful account that has been preserved to us.

Once in Hobart, Robinson bustled importantly about and successfully suggested Gun Carriage Island, south of Flinders, as a suitable site for a permanent native camp. Arrangements were made to have his group, along with seven other natives, shipped up there along with provisions, a carpenter and a secretary of sorts. However, the ship designated to him for this, the government cutter *Charlotte*, had a captain who was going to make the most of the journey, and thus gave preference to his better-paying cargo for Port Arthur. There were also some convicts to be delivered there. What with the additional cargo for the natives, there was no room for the latter except on the open deck itself. Robinson was outraged by the callous handling of the latter, and correctly predicted the disastrous results – that the exposure to such cold, as well as close contact with convicts straight from the gaol, would make them sick.

The unfortunate natives huddled on the windswept deck, sheltering as best they could among the casks of meat and other cargo. Among the seven newcomers, two were quite sick already. The ship sailed abruptly without Robinson – probably a device by the captain, who could not see why there should be such fuss made over some natives, and wanted to avoid putting up with the fussy, self-important little man.

Thus left behind, Robinson set out to walk overland to Prosser's Bay opposite Maria Island, where he hoped to catch up with the *Charlotte* and the Aborigines. Going the same way were a number of locals, who freely conversed about having shot natives, apparently simply because they were there. One pointed to a ridge, saying he'd seen "the man walking along with a waddie in his hand; he did not see me and I shot him dead". Robinson hurried on.

At Maria Island, he did catch up with the *Charlotte*, after her trip to Port Arthur. Two days passed while other cargo was unloaded and water taken on board; apparently the captain continued to make trouble by which Robinson, who was staying with the commandant at Darlington, felt greatly insulted. He also became most indignant when the soldiers demanded sexual favours from the native women they knew to be on the boat. Most of all, Robinson was cross due to being severely bitten by flies and mosquitoes…

...and meanwhile on the *Charlotte,* Tom 's heart was breaking as he desperately wrapped himself around Tekartee, who was dying. Shivering despite her raging fever, she clung to him under the few smelly sacks that had been thrown to them. Jail fever had come on board in Hobart, and the icy sea wind had done the rest. She started coughing. Presently the sputum was streaked with blood. She was short of breath and her chest hurt. Her lungs felt like they would burst. Her skin went clammy. In the space of two days, all the flesh fell off her. White man had brought with him a bacterium previously unknown in Tarena, and the people had no immunity. It killed them, mostly inside two weeks or so, and in the years 1831 and 1832 there was a particularly virulent strain about. Tromee-hennea, who had joined the boat from the hospital, was still ill, and the other little girl from there, Mary, would herself be dead in a few days.

And now Tekartee....Tom was beside himself. He and Pagerly tended the sick girl as best they could. Her eyes sank and death stared out of them. Tom would have done anything, died himself if it would help her, but there was nothing he could do as her lungs disintegrated and she gave up the fight. It's a wonder that Tom did not catch the illness then, bent over her as he was for hours on end, trying to keep her warm and give what comfort he could, tenderly wiping her face and trying to encourage her to take a little food. But she could not, and in the night of the 10th of March, the dark shadow moved closer.

Tekartee lay still. Tom had finally fallen asleep, his arms still about her. Her world was reduced to the simple fact of his holding her. Nothing else mattered. Mytye would be good to his son, she knew. She settled her head against the shoulder beside her, grateful for Tom's presence. Presently her breathing stopped its labouring, becoming light and infre-quent. She laid her hand, spread wide, on his chest, and slipped away to her ancestors up among the stars.

There was a plain interment the next day at the back of the Darlington military station on Maria Island, with no words spoken over the grave. Robinson mentions in his diary that "the death of this woman is a severe loss to the mission", and goes on to describe how pleasing her features were, *resembling those of a European.* To do him justice, he did comment at length that this death had been brought about by the poor treatment afforded the natives on board the ship. The rest of that day's journal entry concerns the incompetence of the captain. Tom rates no further comment until some weeks later. Did Robinson – one of the few to concern himself with the Aborigines at close quarters – really miss the entire love story, or did he simply not consider it as having any importance?

4. THE DARKNESS UNLEASHED

"What's not right about it is that he says you must accept his ways and believe his stories, and yet when you do, you still aren't acceptable."

Mannalargenna's deep voice expressed the insight sadly as he sat, his hand on Tom's shoulder, after listening to the younger man's distress. His own wife, Tanleboneyer, was sister to Tekartee, and his own four daughters were all living with sealers.

The old chief had had plenty of time to assess white man and his ways. Out of the Ben Lomond tribe, he had spent all his life in the north east, observing the arrival of the white sealers from 1800 on. He adjusted to the new situation by visiting his daughters when they lived on the islands, bartering kangaroo skins with the whites, and being on close, familiar terms with the sealers Briggs, Kelly and others. The only warrior leader to succeed in retaining his accustomed lifestyle while also gaining a good understanding of what was happening to his country, he was considered the greatest among the Togee, the wise men of Tarena. By 1830 he was in no doubt that his people were doomed.

Thus, he had met with Robinson in November of that year, just at the time of the Black Line, and for the sake of his people, fell in with the latter's suggestion that they go under his protection to Swan Island, where they would be safe from the line of soldiers and armed men. He was there while Tom witnessed Tekartee's dying on the boat near Port Arthur, and it was to him that Tom poured out his grief after the group had returned to the island in March 1831.

"Besides," added Mannalargenna, "these men are a strange lot, and they do not know much. They do not live by laws that make any kind of sense. They have no respect. They have many fine things, but they are not content, and they tell lies, even to themselves. They do not know how to be."

He looked gently upon the younger man, seeing his confusion and his hopeless attempts to find an identity in an alien culture. He himself had come to maturity before the invasion, and was therefore grounded in his understanding of life, but Tom had no such advantages.

"Do not try to ape them. But, what you can do – indeed, what we must all do – is play along with them, for they have outnumbered us and there is no end to their coming. So many of us have died already. Robinson is not the leader he pretends to be, and I don't really trust him, but we are safer with him than with anyone else. Besides, he has the ear of their chief, and if we can get an agreement through him, there's a chance for us."

And so both men actively assisted Robinson. First they re-settled the entire group over to Gun Carriage Island, and oversaw the tidy ordering of huts and daily rations. Then they set out, along with several other natives including Pagerly, Tanleboneyer, and Truganini, to an arranged meeting with Governor Arthur at Campbell Town. Robinson was most anxious for this, as having the great chief Mannalargenna with him, and apparently supportive of his efforts, was a major triumph. He also realized that the latter would be impressed to have finally met his, Robinson's, own big chief, Governor Arthur, and that Mannalargenna wished to discuss the Aborigines' grievances with him.

Arthur greeted the famous warrior with due ceremony. This impressive man was clearly no fool, so he conducted the discussion with care and attention. That the people of Tarena should seek safety for the time being on an island, was understood by all. But, Arthur indicated, when the settlers' upset had calmed down, it would surely be possible to set aside an area on Tarena itself, that could be declared the natives own, and where they could pursue in peace their own lifestyle. Possibly the north eastern most part of the Island would be suitable? Then, in due course, Mannalargenna and his people could be settled there, back on Tarena. In the meantime, would the great warrior spread the word to those tribes still remaining at large, and persuade them to cease their guerrilla warring in return for safe passage? Certainly, they would be supplied with food, shelter and all things necessary, at the government's expense. And so it was agreed.

After that meeting, Robinson and his group of natives including Manalargenna set out in pursuit of the Big River Tribe. Considered the most aggressive warriors of all, they were the cause of much anxiety in the northern Midlands. Robinson's position would be fully confirmed if he succeeded in conciliating them. What he didn't know was that Mannalargenna remained unconvinced of Arthur's sincerity and was determined to subtly sabotage the expedition. Perhaps he hoped to buy time, to see how the situation would further develop. While he accepted the value of being offered a temporary escape, especially for the women and children, the thought of clearing all the Tarena men off the highlands, did not sit well with him. Once they were gone, there would be an unfillable vacuum.

They were joined, unexpectedly, by Eumarrah. Having been ingloriously caught three years previously by Gilbert Robertson, and then moved to Bruny Island with Tom's group, he initially had come along on Robinson's first west coast expedition. But he soon disappeared into the bush, preferring to make war on white men rather than trek along tamely on a mission organized by one such. The local gossip line told of his being in the Launceston area. Mannalargenna, catching up with him in the bush, persuaded him that joining Robinson, but with their own agenda, might be equally effective. The two of them, along with Tom, managed to spend several months in pleasurable strolling along, hunting, camping, and story-telling every night, while Robinson, helplessly in their power, fulminated furiously.

Tom watched. He envied the old chief's detached wisdom, but also admired Eumarrah's unquenched warrior fire. The latter considered it his patriotic duty to kill as many whites as possible, and submitted to the relatively uneventful trek with difficulty. He made up for it by telling lengthy stories of war and brave deeds. Tom enjoyed these, but when that Woorraddy – jealous husband of the desirable Truganini – also joined in with more creation stories, Tom could no longer contain himself. He *had* to demonstrate his own superior knowledge! So he said that he didn't believe any of those stories anymore, but only white man's explanation. But this backfired badly, with Truganini rounding on him sharply, saying: "Where have you come from? *White* woman?!"

With Mannalargenna's delaying tactics, all the while pretending to Robinson that they were leading him on the trail of the Big River Tribe, the journey stretched out over many weeks. As they moved down the eastern side of the Midlands, the remains of murdered natives, skulls with bullet holes, and burnt bones, were found. Another hazard was white man's cattle gone wild. Also feral were increasing numbers of wild dogs, but these, or their pups, could be tamed and trained to hunt. As the group crossed over the main Hobart to Launceston road, Mannalargenna observed with surprise and interest the method of broken stones to lay a solid permanent foundation. Concealed nearby, he watched the traffic, particularly the horse-drawn mail coach, clattering by, unimpeded by any mud. It was marvelous indeed, but what was it for?

Robinson moved with caution, knowing that stock keepers would shoot on sight any group of black men, and that his own life, as well as theirs, was constantly at risk. As they moved further west into the higher grounds northwest of Bothwell, through Native Hut Plains and in the direction of Lake Echo, the group showed him where terrible outrages had been committed. This was where some of the earliest settlers had sent their assigned convict shepherds with flocks of sheep, and where, from the earliest days, rape and murder of natives had been the order of the day. These men, so far beyond the reach of the law, were still a dangerous lot, and Robinson knew it only too well.

The women also showed Robinson many sites, often hollow trees, where they had hidden the guns and powder that they had made a point of taking from stock keepers' huts. There is not a single recorded instance of an Aborigine in Tasmania ever using a gun upon a white man, with the possible exception of Walyer, an amazon-like Aboriginal and the only female known to have actively led a group in making war upon the invaders. Although several of the warriors were familiar with the mechanism of the weaponry, they preferred to rely on their skills in throwing spears. But moving the guns out of harm's way was a long-standing tactic, and there were many caches of them on the plateau.

Tom was delighted to be introduced to the cider gum. An old Tarena custom was to notch this particular tree on the north side, and above a point where the roots formed a convenient bowl, to gather the sap. This turned into a delightful, mildly alcoholic drink much sought after, and whenever they got near such trees, there would be a great rush to get to them first. Tom had possibly been in this area as a small child, when his family gathered with others for the spring festivities, but this was his first time as an adult here.

He also enjoyed the cat-and-mouse game played by the two chiefs. Robinson had no idea how closely they were informing, by means of noise and fires, their quarry, the feared Big River Tribe, of their progress. But when they doubled back numerous times on their own tracks, and were clearly in no hurry, he became suspicious. For Tom, these few months of relative freedom were the last time he would hunt, trek, dance, and mate. Pagerly was still his companion. They had lived together through the death of Tekartee, and that of so many others, and valued their companionship and the warmth of a familiar body at night.

Tom was somewhat nervous of actually catching up with the fierce Big River Tribe. There had been wars between his, and most other, tribes and this one. Their leader, the legendary Montpelliata, was unforgiving and there was the little matter of his brother having been killed by Mannalargenna… But the times were different, and somehow the matter was put aside. Tom realized that Eumarrah and Mannalargenna were disappearing regularly at night, and in fact were in discussions with the very same Montpelliata. That his group had been moving alongside them for weeks, simply blending into the landscape until they were willing to be seen, was a fact that Robinson sensed but was unable to pinpoint. He well knew that they were playing with him, but his need to be seen as being in charge permitted no such admission.

When on 30th December 1831 they finally confronted Montpelliata and his tribe, of which there was only the astonishingly low number of fourteen men, twelve women and one child – had the settlers' hysterical fears really been over such a small group of people? – Robinson always presented this as his triumph and their surrender. In fact it was a voluntary meeting negotiated between the three chiefs. They all knew themselves outnumbered and out-armed; their only hope of survival lay with the little white man. On 7th January 1832, Robinson brought 'his' tribes to Hobart, declaring this to be the last lot of really troublesome ones. He paraded the 40-odd natives through the streets to the astonishment of the inhabitants, and all were received at Government House.

It was Tom's moment of glory. Here he was, included among the great Tarena chiefs and also speaking fluently with the great leader of the white men, Governor Arthur himself. Showing himself to be in command, he understood how the kitchens and the other facilities of the fine building functioned. Later he actively organized a spear-throwing demonstration. At 50 yards, he also could land a spear accurately into the target, but that counted far less than the fact that here, he was on familiar territory. He went to wash himself, had his hair trimmed, his beard shaved, and got fresh clothes – proper white man's gear. Standing next to Arthur, he facilitated communication. Was seen by all as educated and civilized. A man who had adapted. A man in his prime, in the know, and on top of things.

"Here, Eumarrah! Over here!"

Tom hastened to show that the proper way to relieve oneself here was to use the privies. Eumarrah was revolted.

"By Moina, this is disgusting! They really use such stinking holes?"

To accumulate waste in one place was unhealthy, when the proper way was to move out of any given spot after a certain amount of time, and let nature clean it up.

"Every house has one of these? No wonder these men stink. Their women are even worse… And what are you doing, wearing their fancy rags? You got something to hide? Naw, you're just sucking up to them! Have you got no pride, man?"

Eumarrah was a hardliner.

But Tom, on a roll, for once felt confident enough to override his friend:

"No, Eumarrah, if you want to get anywhere in this place, you've got to be like them!" and he pulled himself up to his full height. His feet hurt badly in the abominable shoes, but he wasn't going to admit that. He strutted off importantly, to organise everyone round the tables that had been set up for the feasting, and to prate knowledgeably on the dishes as they were presented. When Robinson and Arthur re-emerged from the office, Tom was clapped on the shoulder by the Governor and thanked for his services to the great mission.

Mannalargenna watched the two men, Tom finally fizzing with stature and Eumarah the angry warrior reluctantly present, in the extraordinary setting of the Government House grounds. He would have been mildly amused by their interplay, but his smile faded as he perceived the dark shadow stalking them both.

***

Four months later, Robinson was making his way through the vast dark forests of the north west coast, on another tribe-gathering mission. He had received reports of trouble between local Aborigines and stock keepers belonging to the Van Diemens Land Company. The latter held vast acreages of this coast and its hinterland, all the way out to Cape Grim on the most westerly point of the Island. Aware of the likely killing going on in such a remote and unregulated place, he was in something of a hurry. Two years earlier, some 30 to 40 natives had been massacred there, at Cape Grim, and it was he who would eventually bring together such evidence of that crime as could be found, though no official investigation was ever conducted.

Along with Robinson on this new mission were Tom, Pagerly, Mannalargenna and Tanleboneyer, Worraddy and Truganini, seven other natives, and three convict porters. Eumarrah should also have been with them. All of them, including the Big River Tribe members, had sailed from Hobart in January – after the great festivities at Government House – back to Gun Carriage Island. Arriving there after a rough trip, they found that the Aboriginal camp had meanwhile been shifted to Flinders Island. But the place chosen was a miserable spot on the exposed western side, set about by stagnant lagoons with little fresh water or real shelter. Many of the natives there were already not well, and when, after a brief stay, Robinson re-gathered this group for the new mission, it had only taken the two days' boat journey to Launceston for Eumarrah to fall really ill.

Again Tom was holding close a dying friend. The sick warrior lay on some sacking in the shed at the back of the Launceston hospital, covered in sweat and reduced to delirious moaning. That strong man, who had been so full of fight and burning with anger! He who had remained unimpressed by the Governor himself ! Tom was shaken to the core that such a mighty warrior could be felled so quickly. Truly, the white man had brought a great weapon with him, an evil creeping malediction that you couldn't see coming or duck away from like you could from an honest spear.

And now, some weeks later, they were all utterly miserable, having trudged for days through the wet dense forest in cold and relentlessly pouring rain. Tom began to cough painfully. The damp, almost wet, blanket around his shoulders only made his shivering worse. Oh, for a proper possum skin! He had not felt really well since their visit to the camp on Flinders Island. He was also deeply upended by Eumarrah's death. Now here *he* was, also, for the first time in his life sick in body and he couldn't stop the illness from invading him to his innermost fibers.

The party finally reached the VDL Company's huts in the Hampshire Hills. The next day, Tom was unable to go any further. Even Pagerly's warmth had not been able to help him; he was shaking with fever and too weak to stand. As five of the thirteen Tasmanian natives were not well, including Tom and Pagerly, Robinson arranged for four of them to be conveyed by packhorses to Emu Bay, leaving the most indisposed one behind at the huts. He himself continued his journey with the rest of the group, making a loop through the back hills in search of more natives. When he arrived in Emu Bay two days later, he found Tom and the other sick natives huddled outside the back of the store, no indoor space being available and none of the few white persons there having been willing to shelter them in their huts. Tom was by now dangerously ill.

Robinson, anxious to get on with his mission, was glad to hear that the sloop *Fanny* was expected shortly, and made arrangements with the storekeeper that the invalids were to be placed on board and conveyed by the ship to Circular Head, where he himself was headed. He admonished the store keeper, George Rouse, to make better provision for the sick ones, assuring him he would be paid for his exertions. Then he and his group continued on.

"So they got me too..." Tom croaked, cradled in Pagerly's arms.

"They're taking all of us, one by one, we can't fight them....when they're not shooting us, they get us with this...this..."

'Curse' was the word he was seeking. That dreaded dark demon that had gradually come over them, even more to be feared than any gun, which a fighting man at least could understand. It had taken so many already. Tekartee, also. And, just two moons ago, his friend Eumarrah.

"It's no use..."

Tom was mumbling. The women crowded round him, his Pagerly, Karnebutcher, and Woolaytopineyer, who had been Eumarah's woman. All three were also unwell, but they gave him what body warmth they could under the flimsy shelter of a few packing cases and boughs leant against the back wall of the store. The store keeper, somewhat more attentive now, and knowing that the miserable blacks would soon be gone on the *Fanny*, cooked them some potatoes and helped them make a fire to keep warm by.

But it was too late for Tom.

On the night of the 12th of May he began to rave. Somehow, despite his inflamed lungs, he found the strength to howl, howl out the agony, the sheer waste of it all, the loss of his proud manhood, his beloved Tekartee, his people, his country. The women joined in with their own keening, and every white person in the tiny miserable settlement was touched for a moment by an ancient dread. The terrible wailing echoed over the bay. The very water shivered. The animals in the forest turned their heads to listen and the tigers added their own strange howling, as they poured out the knowledge of their own impending doom. Then a dark shadow came down over the land and flowed through every valley. And it has remained there, to be found on the underside of every leaf even on the sunniest smiling day.

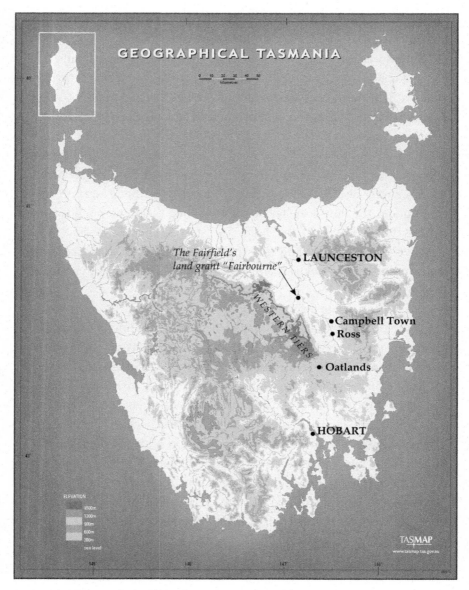

Map 2 – *Tasmania by 1830's*

A "main" road of sorts, running through the Midlands towns, connected Hobart with Launceston. Before 1828, private postal services went once a week on foot, taking 5 days. By 1833, a one-horse chaise carrying the mail and one passenger only covered the distance in 19 hours. In 1830, Hobart's European population was 5,700 and that of the whole Island was approx. 20,500. The Aboriginal population has been estimated as being anywhere between 3000 – 15,000 at the time.

THE FAIRFIELD SETTLERS 1823 – 1831

SUSANNAH

There's a long, long trail a-winding into the lands of my dreams, where the nightingales are singing and a white moon beams; there's a long long night of waiting until my dreams come true, till the day when I'll be going down that long long trail with you.

Stoddard King

5. I NEVER WANTED TO BE HERE...

Susannah Fairfield stared in astonishment.

"No milk? What do you mean, no milk! I have a baby to feed! I can't just go out there into the wilds without a cow...and what about the other children?"

"My dear, I understand your concern. But there are no fences out there just yet. There isn't much of anything, except that fertile land grant – that's *ours* now! – and that's worth every effort, isn't it?"

William looked at his beloved wife pleadingly. He knew he was asking a lot of her. Although, despite being so fair and delicate looking, she had proved herself to be very resilient. Four children had not taken away her youthful figure. She had managed the long sea journey from Scotland to Hobart really well, keeping up a small daily school for their oldest, Andrew, and the children of some other emigrant families on the ship, and she even saved the birth of little Rebecca till after they landed in Hobart in 1823.

In the town, almost no accommodation had been available. Eventually, he and Andrew Gatenby, who had arrived with his family on the same ship, were able to rent a reasonable house in Macquarie St. between them. It was a little further up from the fine house that the merchant William Birch had built in 1816, although that family no longer appeared to own it. Once their two wives were settled in, William and Andrew rode out to inspect possible land tracts in the Midlands and, having made their respective applications, had to wait for the governor's approval. After eleven long months, their grants were confirmed, and now the Fairfields were making ready to move there. The sheer cost of living in Hobart made it necessary that they should do so as soon as possible.

William gently stroked his wife's soft, rosy cheek.

"It's not going to be easy for you, my dear, I do know it. I will do the best I can to build us a reasonable house quickly. It's wonderful land – Gatenby is over the moon with his piece. It's only a short distance north from ours, so you'll have friends close by when they follow us soon. My dear, this is our big chance. In time, we can be independent and successful farmers, far more than we could ever hope for in Scotland. You can see that, surely, Susannah?"

All I can see is that there really isn't much of anything out here, thought Susannah, as she watched, a week later, the landscape slowly jolting past the bullock cart on which she and the children sat. It all seemed so strange, the ragged-looking silvery trees with their bark peeling off in long strips. At first she thought there was some disease in them, but it was perfectly normal, she was told. Some had blackened trunks as though they had been recently burnt, and between them was mostly a scrubby sort of grass. How any of it could become the rich pasture lands that had been talked about back in Scotland, she could not imagine.

The Scottish glen she had grown up in was fertile and had been cultivated for centuries, with family farms cosily surrounded by proper green trees and neat stone walls. But the men had been so sure – letters had repeatedly spoken of the fortunes to be made in Van Diemens Land. Great tracts of land were available, free of charge. Putting sheep on cost very little and had the money coming in quickly, even before additional improvements were required. It all sounded very promising, so they had arrived with a letter of commendation from the Colonial Office in London. The Gatenbys, whom they had met on board ship, were similarly placed. The two families found much in common, and were kindly received on their arrival in June 1823 by Governor Sorell in Hobart. In his view, they were exactly the right kind of settlers with experience, capital, and a willingness to work hard on improving their grants.

It sure will need some improving, Susannah continued her musing. Not that she doubted William's ability to do so. He had always had plenty of energy. That handsome young man on his fine horse, second son of a long-established and respectable farming family, had been hard to resist with his laughing blue eyes and mischievous grin. His family, staunch Presbyterians like her own, all agreed that it was a suitable match and they celebrated its union on a bright spring day in 1816. It was a time of depressed farming conditions, with the prospects for younger sons not looking very hopeful. The news that the young colony of Van Diemens Land had plenty of good land free for the taking up, proved irresistible.

"All we have to do is go there," enthused William. "They want people like us. Think of it, Susie, we could have rolling acres of our own, with a great flock of sheep. I'll build you such a fine house then!"

It was too good a promise to ignore. But the process was not simple, requiring much planning and organizing. Many times Susannah's heart flailed at the thought of leaving her own dear parents and siblings behind. How much she would miss the sight of cultivated gentle farmland, she was only just realizing as she looked at this oddly empty land that had never, so she thought, seen a yeoman's care. All this travelling for *this?* The sea journey had taken nearly seven months, and had been simply horrendous. Once the first seasickness was over, she found herself pregnant and thus remained nauseated most of the time. Mercifully the three children stayed healthy, and she was grateful for the daily diversion that her little school provided.

Her first impression of the Island was an alien wonderment. The mountain was undoubtedly magnificent, but the darkness of the forest all around the little town of Hobart was only broken here and there with a few small farms and cultivated fields. And it was such a strange forest, with huge trees of wild shapes – how could the locals call it "the bush"? Nor was it filled with proper birdsong, but rather with shrill and unmusical notes, or else with a fearsome silence. But when the wattles began their golden bloom in late July and filled the air with a heady fragrance, she took the children for walks among the edge of the trees and gradually her eyes took in the flittering of small birds. She heard their excited tiny chirping as a whole flock descended on a shrub and darted among the branches, and began to see that there was beauty here too. But oh! how she missed the deep peace of the blackbird's evening song.

They had been in Hobart for nearly a year before their grant was finally approved, and then, it being winter, there was a further anxious delay till the better weather. She was sorry to leave the small town, where slowly a sense of familiarity had begun to form, and she had got on well with Hannah Gatenby. Sharing the house had worked well for both wives, making the childcare and household duties easier and providing an effective defense against the depredations of convict servants. This was perhaps the hardest aspect of the whole venture for Susannah. Convict labour was the only kind available. Paid servants hardly existed at all and the few that did were in huge demand. But convicts, though requiring no wages, were largely unskilled, and often unwilling as well. They did nothing more than what was spelled out to them. Every drawer or box in the house had to be locked even for the shortest absence, and many were the clever excuses that a convict found in order to draw her from the room, so another might dart in and take whatever they could lay their hands on.

Susannah was of strong farming stock and expected to do much of the work herself. In Scotland, farm labourers cared for the domesticated animals, cut firewood, and did the heavy jobs. Inside the house, a general servant to help with everything from child care to cooking was part of the family, and in return for kindly treatment and a small wage cared as much as the mistress for the wellbeing of all. Thus Susannah – who had a sunny and kindly nature – could not come to grips with the convicts and their apparent lack of all moral constraint. That her trusting friendliness should elicit no similar response left her baffled. In time, she saw that some convicts were good people also, but it was unfortunate that her first experience with them was not a happy one. She was grateful to have the support of Hannah, who had a more direct manner and fewer scruples about ordering people to get on with it.

In this respect, Susannah was glad to leave Hobart. Convicts assigned to individuals all somehow managed to be on the streets in large numbers, especially at night, and picking of pockets or even blatant snatching of hats, coats or any other unguarded possession was common. Soldiers, traders, even some officers, regularly rubbed shoulders in the pubs. Drunkenness was widespread. Susannah also saw the black men, the natives of the island. Some hung around all the time, and seemed sad, derelict people in rags who refused to do any paid labour. But occasionally their numbers swelled when the Town Mob arrived. This mixed group of men, women and children caused her great embarrassment as they were for most part entirely naked. Susannah viewed them in uncertain astonishment and some fear, having heard of increasing depredations by these savages on the outlying settlers' houses.

"They used to be entirely harmless," Isabella Lewis, the merchant's wife, told her. "But now lately they have a leader, called Musquito, who is stirring them up and making them angry. I cannot think why – we have treated them perfectly well. The governor ensures that they have plenty of food and blankets from the stores whenever they want. We have had them on our properties at Pittwater, where they were allowed to camp, but now they have taken to setting light to our hay stacks or standing crops. They have attacked and killed some farm servants. There are not enough soldiers to protect us out there, so I persuaded Richard to build us this town house."

"But what will we do when we move out to our land?" cried Susannah. Her husband re-assured her that they would bring guns, and have two extra convicts to keep guard.

"They can be kept in check by pointing the guns at them, for they fear our weapons, thinking them to have some black magic."

It was cold comfort, and she resolved that the children would never be allowed out of her sight.

Susannah sighed and watched her husband, riding ahead of the plodding wagon. He had their son Andrew, now nearly six, sitting proudly with him on the horse. The other two, Nancy and Edward, were amusing themselves in a large basket behind her, and little Rebecca slept on her lap. They were all well-behaved for anything less in their loving but strict household would not do, but they would reasonably enough get tired and cross soon. Five days of bone-jarring travelling, camping out overnight under their wagon, was no longer an adventure. At Oatlands they had stayed at the Inn, and now they were hoping to make it to the Ross Hotel before night fell, even though the comforts of the hostelries were dubious. There had been fleas in the bedding at Oatlands. At least the weather had held, so far, with sunny days and high white clouds sailing by on the brisk and fresh spring breeze. She had to admit that the climate seemed bracing and healthy, and even the wettest winter days in Hobart were not as cold as her snow-filled Scottish valley had been.

Home! Tears welled as she thought of the cosy farmstead and her parents' durable kindliness. The steady patterns of life and the seasons, the assurance that she had her place and that it was a good one, had made her the happy girl she was. But the challenge of trying to make a similar home for her own children in this wilderness, this alien place with savages lurking in the darkness, with no certainty of anything and even the seasons upside down – spring in September! – for a moment nearly defeated her. All this because of her love for William, now her only support and comforter. Was he able to see this mad adventure through?

For a moment Susannah fought a wave of bitter anger. How dare he expose them to this uncertainty and danger? In enforced company with these, these …. Susannah's descriptive abilities failed. The convicts deeply confused her, for she was not one to dismiss anyone and had always been taught to see the good in everyone. Did not God command that? But their coarse detachment and utter unreliability was beyond her, and now, without Hannah's firmness to guide her, she felt unable to manage them as a house mistress properly should. Thank goodness the Gatenbys would be moving nearby soon. There had been some complication with the final granting of their land, which meant them remaining behind in Hobart, but it was hoped that the matter would be resolved within weeks.

Having been granted 640 acres, and qualifying as a substantial and respectable settler, William Fairfields was allotted six convicts to work his land. Two were walking alongside the wagon now, helping with the bullocks and managing the baggage. The other four had been sent out to the grant a few days earlier, to convey their stores and set up camp, under the oversight of a hired man, Connelly, loaned to them at a high wage by the merchant Lord but recommended as competent and honest. You can't trust the convicts on their own, was the advice in town. With them also went their small flock of precious sheep. Andrew had selected five rams and twenty ewes from the best herd available in their Scottish glen, only to watch more than half die on the long journey across the sea. But at least they had a few to start with. They could have sold each one for ten times its proper price, such was the value of any good stock. Success hung on building a big flock quickly, for the cost of keeping the animals was negligible and the demand for wool in England huge.

Susannah had not wanted to take a convict woman as a house servant, thinking she would rather do the work herself than be in such close proximity to someone she felt she could not trust. Besides, they had slovenly habits and were less than clean. But William would not hear of it.

"Of course you must have some help with the children and the washing and all! I'll find you someone decent."

But try as he might, in this he failed. The few who did have a 'good' convict were not willing to part with them, not at any price. Finally, he heard through the Reverend MacArthur that the Presbyterian Church's ladies' team was caring for an orphan girl who would soon be going into service. The Reverend thought that she would be well off in a stable family and out in the country – meaning away from the temptations of town – and Susannah would be a good motherly influence. Sick when found in the street, the child had recovered now and, though small and barely twelve, was wiry and would surely be of great use around the house.

Susannah vividly recalled the wrenching of her heart when she first saw the thin bones, dull dark hair, barely enough of it to tie back, transparent skin, eyes lowered apart from a quick glance. Was there anything useful in this stray child? But she could not turn her away. Another responsibility.

"What's your name?"

"Telah..." barely whispered.

"Telah? Did you say 'Telah'? But that's not a proper Christian name! How did you come by that?"

Susannah stopped herself. The child had most likely not been given any name at all, having lived on the street and not apparently having recollection of any parents. How had she survived at all? Gentler, she said:

"Shall we call you Theresa? It's a pretty name."

"Yes, ma'am..."

But Susannah was wrong about Tess, as they soon started calling her, not being useful. The child had little knowledge of what might be expected inside a household, but she was a quick learner and proved very willing. Given a small corner of the kitchen to sleep in, she fitted in with both families and never forgot a single thing she was told. In the three weeks before they left Hobart, the regular good food, warm clothing and kindly treatment changed her noticeably. Not that she said a word in her halting speech about herself, but Susannah did not pry, letting time do the healing. Instructing Tess in basic household matters, and how to keep personally clean, she also found her a pretty hair ribbon and taught her to plait what eventually turned into waves of lustrous black curls.

Tess was now sitting beside the basket containing Nancy and Edward, playing cat's cradle with them. Susannah had shown her how to do it, noting that behind the scarring of chilblains the child had fine sensitive hands. But she knew nothing of threads and yarns. How one could grow up not knitting or spinning or darning, the older woman could not imagine, and her heart ached for the loveless waif. Tess relaxed readily with the children, but remained wary of most grown-ups. The game with the ball of string was not very successful, due to the jolting of the cart, but caused much hilarity until the ball escaped to the ground, and was triumphantly carried away by Fuller the dog. William had bought him at a great price and with some difficulty, for dogs were hugely prized as hunting animals and to keep guard. Tess and Fuller formed an immediate bond, and the only time Susannah had seen the girl smile was in play with the dog.

Reaching the Ross Hotel was a welcome relief.

"Only one more full day, a night at Campbell Town, and then we're almost there," pronounced William.

"How do you like the name *Fairbourne* for our new home?"

More likely *Fairburn*, thought Susannah but forbore to say it. She had not the heart to dampen his enthusiasm, as he spoke of his visions for the place.

"It won't be long before the flock builds up, and we shall get a return on the wool. Meanwhile, there will be much to do with the clearing and the fencing, and sowing good grass – I've placed an order for seed with Bethune's – and first thing we'll build us a cottage and some outhouses for the men. You'll see, in no time we'll have it all really nice," his boyish grin gleamed through the more usually serious face, "and I'll make it a grand place for you!"

They made it to Campbell Town the next evening. That night, the weather changed, bringing heavy rain., and Susannah was grateful for the inn's shelter. It would be quite a while before she could experience such luxury again.

The next day they continued, still in the rain, on the very last part of their journey, fording the fine Macquarie River at Morningside. Just before, William had pointed up a track to the right, indicating that was the place where the Murray family, also from Scotland, had settled only months earlier.

"Until the Gatenby's arrive, these will be our nearest neighbours. We will call on them soon."

Another two hours later, they arrived at Fairbourne.

All Susannah's forebodings came together that wet day when the wagon finally jolted to a halt at the camp that Conelly and the four men had prepared. A big fire in the centre of a clearing. A part bark, part canvas hut for herself, William and the children. A tent for the overseer. Nothing, apparently, for the men. Stacks of their goods, all strewn around, some of it broken. Conelly himself there to greet them, looking apologetic, and in the background the chorusing of the men, who had found the barrel of rum and could not be prevented from liberally partaking of it. William immediately set off with him to inspect the precious sheep, corralled to one side in some rough fencing. All their bedding was damp, and there was no food prepared. If it had not been for the needs of the children, Susannah would have laid down on the ground and cried through sheer disappointment and exhaustion.

But little Tess, who had nothing much to compare all this to, was not dismayed. She dragged off their bundles, arranging them with glee in the little hut, seeing it all as a great adventure. Presently the two men returned, complete with a shot kangaroo, and the meat was fried in great chunks over the fire. A billy was set to make hot tea, and the last of the sago pudding warmed in a pan for the children. The two assigned men who had travelled with them could barely be prevailed upon to attend the four bullocks before they joined the others. Susannah provided for the little ones as best she could, in the dubious shelter of the little hut, and wrapped them with everything she could spare, fearing for their health on the damp, cold ground. She lay down next to Tess, knowing William would stay out, watching the sheep while the men were not fit to do so. So she lay, grimly enduring the night without adequate covers for herself, trying not to think of what might be scrabbling in the vegetation beneath her, or what the growling noises in the bush might mean. Somewhere in the night, as the rain got heavier, she listened to a fight among the men for a space beneath the wagon. A sense of utter devastation filled her. Not even the awfulness of the sea voyage on a crowded ship full of vomit could compare to this.

***

Just over two years later, in November 1826, Susannah sat on the slight rise to the left of their house, enjoying the warm spring sun, and taking stock. William had been right after all. They really were on the way to becoming the fine landowners he had promised. Not that it had been easy, and much hard work had been necessary, but God's provision had been with them, also. Their few sheep had multiplied wonderfully, and the previous year William had been able to buy a further twenty pure merinos, including a precious ram, from a shipment brought to the Colony from Macarthur's fine Camden flock. And just two months ago, by a wonderful piece of luck, he and Andrew had put together to buy a further two hundred sheep from a settler who was forced to sell as a result of a family dispute.

William spent much of his time supervising the management of the land. The assigned men, after their first drunken bout, had settled into an unwilling workforce of sorts that gradually improved. Their master was essentially a fair man. He expected good work, but he also insisted that they have Sundays free, and provided generous rations of tobacco and a weekly dish of rum. No man ever went hungry at Fairbourne. Once the two most recalcitrant men in the gang had been sent to the magistrate and thence to a chain gang on the highway, the group worked steadily enough. But William was unreconciled with the convict system in general. To solve the problem, he had sent a notice to his home county in Scotland, offering to pay the passage of any skilled labourers who were willing to come out and work for him, promising each a cottage, provisions, and a salary on condition that they worked with him for at least two years. To his – and Susannah's – delight, fourteen families were now making preparations to sail on the next suitable ship. William had borrowed the necessary money from his father, but he knew he could repay it well within the terms agreed to.

Before Susannah lay – at least in the immediate vicinity of their home – an attractive vision of grassed land interspersed with some fine trees beneath which grazed their precious sheep. The land sloped gently away to the sparkling curve of the Macquarie River, beside which lay some fields sown to turnips, oats and wheat. These had been fenced to keep the kangaroos out, although they still needed watching. By now she had seen that the soil was fertile indeed. All it took was time and consistent effort, and neither, she reflected happily on that pleasant sunny morning, was lacking on Fairbourne.

Their house, also, had improved. Before the first winter came, William had felled enough timber to cut boards and build them a sturdy cottage with four rooms and a shingled roof. She had a small dairy, for they had eventually managed to purchase a cow from the government flock kept near Ross. Getting the animal to stand quietly for milking was a nightmare until Tess attempted it. Now Susannah could make milk and butter, and they had eggs from the chickens, although the latter were lost with depressing regularity to hawks and the spotted wildcat. Susannah still hated these alien creatures that threatened their lambs and any unguarded stock. She thought them ugly and her anger rose every time she heard the snarling and screaming of the devils in the night. The rasping of the possums, appallingly like heavy breathing, made her shudder, and when she discovered that the wretches were eating everything from her precious garden, and were capable of climbing any fence William could devise, she felt helplessly defeated by them. But she truly learned to hate them when they ate the buds off her one treasured rose bush, sent to her all the way from Scotland. It was her luxury, her personal mark on this alien landscape. That its unfriendly creatures should deprive her of the much anticipated blossoms was a bitter, personal loss.

For their first twelve months they had lived from the stores supplied by the commissariat in Hobart, enough for each of them and their assigned men. William had taken the wagon to the town three times to collect their allocation, a three-week absence that she only survived with the help of the Gatenby's, who sent one of their sons over to act as overseer.

The latter family had in due course arrived, bringing with them not only Andrew's strong and sturdy boys, but William's own younger brother Herbert, who had arrived in Hobart a few months after the Fairfields had left the town. This attractive young man, even better-looking than his brother William, and with an irrepressible larrikin streak, quickly made havoc in the bosoms of the few young ladies in the district. For all his light-hearted fun, he proved his worth, willingly helping out at Fairbourne while meeting the requirements of improving at least two acres of his own grant, which he had chosen on an adjoining piece to the west of William's. He built himself a neat little cottage and kept an eye on the four convicts who watched his small but growing herd of sheep and a few beef cattle. Susannah loved him most for his laughter. He brought a light-hearted ray of sunshine to her, with his Scottish burr and way of seeing everything in a golden light. His nephews and nieces adored him, calling "Herbie, Herbie" as soon as his tow-head appeared among the trees, and they had many bush adventures under his supervision.

Before Kirklands Church nearby was completed in 1836, the families of the area gathered in each others' homes for informal Presbyterian services. At Hugh Murray's place, Herbert's eye fell upon their oldest daughter Lillias, who was only fourteen at the time but a pretty little lass for all that. Watched over by her strict mother Jean, the young girl still managed to send a long look in Herbie's direction. She had violet eyes that were devastatingly fringed by long black lashes, and he was hopelessly lost.

From then on, he spent rather a lot of time at Murray's place, only a short ride away. Many were the excuses he found for errands in that direction, but nobody was fooled. In the end, tall kindly Hugh took him aside and told him that Lillias was simply too young, and that Herbert had better cool his ardour for a few years. In a stolen moment, the two young lovers – she as conniving as he – breathlessly promised to wait for each other. This being agreed to, a genuine friendship grew up between her father and the young man.

Hugh Murray, from Edinburgh, took the word of God more literally than many. This induced a much more kindly attitude towards the natives, whom most of the other settlers nervously barely tolerated. But on Murray's place, named St. Leonards, the black bands were always welcome. Murray taught them to enjoy cooked potatoes, and would often sit with them. He learned that this area was a 'highway' that the various tribes used regularly. It was prime hunting ground, tended by the natives with regular burning, so the scrub remained cleared and the new grass tempted the kangaroo out to graze. Murray, having wondered why the countryside had in places the look of a well-tended park land, began to see the connection – this was a loved and cared-for land. Whenever a tribe made camp there, Murray came out to greet them courteously and supplied them with tucker.

When the blacks began to fight back under Musquito's urging, the bands remembered Murray's attitude. No one ever attacked anything belonging to St. Leonards. The majority of the settlers remained in a state of fear, never working without a firearm nearby, staying as close as possible to their homesteads and families. Upset at their continual stock and crop losses, and verging on hysterical if any band was nearby, most held back from actual violence. Some handed out food, especially the craved flour, sugar and tea, in the hopes of conciliating them. Others, no doubt, were more genuine, even downright uncomfortable, with the whole situation, but no matter what the individual's attitude, they all wished the problem gone.

Thus most settlers rejoiced when news came that Musquito had been hanged in Hobart, along with another black trouble maker. They hoped it would mean one problem less, for another that harassed them greatly were the white bushranger attacks. But Hugh Murray was greatly distressed when he heard about it.

The matter will not simply go away," he told Herbert. "There are other warriors who can take Musquito's place. They all can throw their spears with deadly accuracy – they are, after all, fine hunters. No, nothing will be achieved by hanging them. On the contrary, I think it will probably make them more bitter and resentful. And who can blame them? We have after all taken everything from them."

Murray's view was unusual. Most settlers did not question their ownership of the land. They were the ones who, with industry and zeal, were turning this untamed wilderness into a cultivated land of bounty, and therefore it properly belonged to them. The natives, being savages, had never cultivated anything, or had any of the symbols of culture such as churches or proper homes. A few rude huts did not count. And they went about naked…

Susannah, already buffeted by her experiences with convicts, the alien bush and the elusive but destructive animals it contained, was just as apprehensive about the natives. So far, she had not yet looked a single one of them in the eye. They were an unknown force out there, and the less she had to do with them, the gladder she was. It was simply, for all her kindliness, more than she could take on board. The survival of her family was her primary concern. William's occasional reports of a band being camped nearby made her angry and impatient, insisting that none of the children go beyond earshot of the house. By now young George had been born, a lusty little bundle at this moment being watched by Tess. Murray's view, related to her by Herbert, left her thinking that he was probably putting his family more at risk by consorting with the blacks.

Susannah sighed, her stolen moment on the little hill coming to an end. The baby will need feeding soon, and lunch prepared for the men and Herbert. Where *is* the boy? He should have been here quite some time ago! As she gathered her skirts about her – here was another complexity, how to obtain in this remote place enough cloth to keep everyone decently dressed – she heard in the far distance a hullabaloo. Those blacks again with their wild dances! Then she froze. No, no, not in daylight. And not with this kind of a sound.... With a cry, Susannah ran down the hill. William! William! Where are the children? Oh, my God, be with us!

6. ...BUT I MADE THE MOST OF IT

Herbert was on his way. That morning, he was gaily whistling a tune as he turned his horse down the path towards his brother's house. It had been a good decision to come to this island. Here, all the land about him was *his*. Not for him the labouring for someone else, as would have been the case in Scotland for a fourth son, or at best the renting of someone else's farm.

"And I'm loving it, this opportunity, putting my mark on it, clearing, sowing good English grasses, pasturing some beef cattle, building fences... and the pride of owning my own sheep. I'll soon be able to offer Lillas a decent home, too... right there on that hillock. Plenty of sandstone about. We'll have a really big veranda where she and the children can play, whatever the weather. And I'll lay out a fine garden for her, properly fenced, and send away for some English flowers to gladden her heart. Some violets in particular, to match her lovely eyes..."

But first the farm had to be made to pay.

Herbert got on well with his assigned men, having gained their respect through his own fair dealings with them, and helped along with generous rum rations. He largely left them unrestricted as long as they watched his precious stock. This was often in outlying parts some distance away, up towards the rising hills culminating in the grand Tiers. Here he had built them a sturdy bark hut, stocked regularly with stores and arms; they took turns being up there when not actively needed on the farm. What the men got up to there, he did not inquire. It was none of his concern. Although, since starting to talk with Murray, he had felt some unease. Some very nasty stories had begun to circulate. Perhaps he should check on his men a bit more closely.

Later than intended, he urged his horse to a canter. Susannah's good grub was worth hurrying for.

Near the river, he noticed a movement through the trees. Surely those were some of William's sheep? Were they meant to be there? Herbert didn't think so – he remembered that they were down on the southern side. If they had got away, then it was important that he stop their progress. Quickly he rode down towards the water, and yes, there were at least fifty of them, but he was too late. Already they were spreading out over the unfenced plain. Nobody seemed to be with them – the only hope of containing them now was to keep them close to the river. Round the next bend a steep bank came right down to the water, and he would be able to hold them penned against it until help arrived – as it surely would, and soon, for these sheep were the apple of William's eye.

Racing his horse up and down, hurrahing and waving his hat, Herbert didn't notice the group of natives encamped by the river until he was virtually on top of them. The sheep sheared away as the black figures in their turn took up the yahooing, and in the melee his own horse took fright and bolted. He landed with a heavy thud, and was instantly surrounded by a menacing, spear-waving group.

Once again, Kickerterpoller watched a murder and was frozen, unable to move. His group had recently met up with warriors from other tribes, including two with a long-standing grievance over the murder of a brother. Realising that larger numbers were more frightening to the settlers, the two groups had however agreed to set aside, at least for now, their disagreements. Resting by their campsite, and planning their next attack, the herd of sheep erupting round the bend and followed by a yelling, menacing man on a galloping horse, took them by surprise. The suddenness of it triggered the already-high tensions, and in no time several spears were plunged into the dazed man on the ground. One of the chiefs then spat on him, before they hastened to disappear silently back into the hills. Seeing the white man's silly sheep still fleeing confusedly all directions, gave them great delight.

***

Five years later, in 1831, Hugh Murray announced that they were leaving.
  "But why?"

Susannah was dismayed.

They had been doing so well, as indeed they all had, this little conclave of hard-working Scottish settlers with their ever-growing land grants and well-paying flocks of sheep. Murray by then had acquired 2560 acres, over one hundred of which was in cultivation, owned 1800 sheep, had built a fine house, and was particularly noted for his two miles of fine four-railed fencing. Surely this was home now, so hard worked for but now also much easier, with a modicum of real comfort, and both the natives and the bush rangers mostly under control?

Susannah herself was by now the mistress of a fine home and the mother of seven children, ranging from Andrew, now a boy of thirteen, to little David, barely toddling. Knowing that they could have done so much worse, her eye gradually attuned to see some beauty in the place, and her homesickness lessened over the years. William expanded into the satisfactions granted to a successful and increasingly wealthy land owner. Particularly practical had been his idea of sending for tradesmen from his homeland.

The fourteen families had duly arrived, finally solving their desperate shortage of real, skilled labour. He much preferred to pay regular wages to a man who was voluntarily there, rather than have the free but generally unwilling work of convicts. All the settlers in the district had benefitted from it, other landowners following the example. Thus the area became quite a community. The mothers shared the teaching of all the children, as best they could. All believed in education, and Sundays were always spent in learning, singing, sketching, debating, as well as the shared church services, each suitable home taking their turn.

It's turning tail to leave, thought Susannah, after all these hard years of tears and battles to get established! And just now, when you're so well set at last? Don't you care about that, Jean Murray? At the same time, you're lucky, too – I wouldn't mind being in Hobart...shops, warehouses, schools, proper churches, a bit more company...and I don't want to lose you, either, you're a special friend to me. Oh, please don't go!

But the Murrays did, selling St. Leonards to the Viveash's, and moved to Hobart. There, Hugh ran a business as a wine and spirit merchant, doing well out of it, and became an important citizen, a co-founder in the

Hobart Savings Bank, and most active within the Presbyterian Church. With him went the violet-eyed Lillias, who never looked quite the same after Herbert was murdered. In the five years since, she had grown into a young woman as lovely as the early promise, but no young man had yet been able to make her smile.

Oh Herbie, Herbie! He had been a terrible loss to them. In the shattered months after, they sorely missed his friendly laughter and the children looked in vain for the blond mop to turn up and take them out to play. In less than two years he had become a much loved part of the family. To William and Susannah the guilt was the worst bit. Herbert had come with such high hopes, and they had failed to keep him safe. Susannah could not forgive the blacks.

She had rejoiced when Governor Arthur was forced to declare martial law, and the roving parties were formed to comb the bush for them. Jorgen Jorgenson, in charge of such a group, wrote to police magistrate Anstey at the time: "…if the parties have hitherto not been very successful in capturing *and destroying* the Aborigines, yet we have presented an imposing check to their attacks on settlements and farms." The natives, growing desperate, hit back harder than ever, and that year alone, 1828, there were 126 attacks on whites, resulting in 33 deaths. Two years later, the Black Line was formed to sweep the nuisances finally off the island. Many men from the Macquarie River district rode with that line, but not Hugh Murray. Instead, he quietly sheltered some black women and children on his farm, thus keeping them safe when the line of soldiers came through. If he had not been so completely respected in the district, other settlers would have come close to lynching him. As it was, some would no longer speak with him. Perhaps that was the reason he decided to leave, or maybe his spirit was weary of the unsolvable war. At times he thought he could hear in the wind the lonely keening of the dispossessed people.

There had been other losses as well. Not long after Herbert's death, their fifth child was born to live only a few days. With the birth of little Margaret barely a year later, Susannah's radiant health seemed to leave her, and she became something of an invalid. The baby was raised on cow's milk and oat gruel, but grew well all the same. Not so their last one,

David, who was as frail as his mother. Hannah Gatenby, on observing this, sent her husband to have a private word with William. If he valued his wife, he had best not risk there being any more children, at least for the time being... William kept his distance, deciding that, for the comfort and convenience of both, the marital bed had better not be his for a while. Both prayed over David.

There had been devastating stock losses at times, also, including the sheep scattered at Herbert's murder, some of which were never recovered. Another herd simply disappeared, most likely taken by bushrangers. But overall, the remaining sheep thrived and time made up for the lost ones. And, ironically, they gained from Herbert's death, for the family in Scotland decided that his land grant and the stock on it had best be given to William.

And then there was the day on which the bush rangers attacked.

It was Tess who saved them, that still hot afternoon when hell broke loose. Tess, whose body had been so starved in her childhood that it was still, after several years of good nourishment, pitifully small and slight, was just struggling to put on the first shy curves of womanhood. She had slipped wordlessly into this family and was simply part of them. Susannah relied totally on her, wishing in odd moments that the girl might open up a little, but respecting her choice not to. No one had ever heard her string more than four or five words together. The older woman had wondered if the girl was even capable of proper speech. Yes, but something's knocked it out of her, she decided. She says more to the animals than to us – recalling the soft crooning that she one day accidentally overheard Tess bestowing on the dog.

The girl certainly had a special touch with animals. The cow stood patiently and gave her more milk than anyone else could persuade her to yield. The dogs obeyed her instantly, the chickens fluttered eagerly around her, and any orphan lamb she cared for simply thrived. For the rest, she worked alongside Susannah, cooking and washing and cleaning.

"We should regularize her position with us properly," William commented. "Either give her wages, or adopt her."

Although she was perfectly friendly, perhaps even happy, the girl's silence had a forbidding quality and nothing had been done about it. She was so much a part of them that it didn't seem to matter.

That afternoon Tess was in the vegetable garden behind the house, gathering what was needed for the evening meal. Stooping low, her eye was caught by the wink of some heavenly blue beetles, and she paused in her pulling of carrots to watch them. It was her attunement to the animal world that alerted her. Not many bird sounds were to be expected in the hot stillness of mid-afternoon, but there was an odd chirring in the air, an uneasy movement that suddenly struck her forcibly. She lifted her head, covered in the glorious black curls that were forever tumbling from their ribbon – the only bit of her that had recovered, luxuriantly, from her early deprivations – and one of the bushrangers, on his belly in the undergrowth not far away, noted its gleam.

She straightened up and forced herself to walk calmly back to the house – bejeezus, she's got a fine figure too! – fighting every instinct to run. But inside, she raced to pull up the guns that were always kept handy along with the powder and shot, wordlessly conveying the danger outside. William was far out with the shepherds and the dogs, but fortunately the children had all been driven in by the heat and the two farm men at that moment were having a break by the kitchen door. The attackers – there were seven of them – were no doubt waiting for those two to go back out to their fencing before springing, but Tess' fast action had spoilt their plan. They could have withdrawn silently, but were much in need of supplies, and this tidy farm was bound to have plenty. Surely they were a match for two men, a woman, a girl, and a bevy of children? Better strike now while the master and the other men were still well away!

But they were met with a volley of shots as they exploded out of the trees. William had prepared his family well, and supplied plenty of fire arms. Inside, Tess organized the oldest two to keep re-loading the used guns, while she and the adults shot from the windows at all movement outside. The attackers fell back, holing up behind trees and sheds, and waited their chance to dispatch the men so they could overwhelm the two women. But no such chance presented itself, and as the tense afternoon wore on, they had to make do with taking from the barn some harnessing, snatching what chickens could be caught, pillaging the vegetables, and driving off the two young goats. They could have fired the barn, and even the house, but that would not have served their purpose. William had wisely designed the cool store rooms to be part of the main house itself, and it was in those that the bushrangers' real target was to be found – provisions and rum.

The silence around the house deepened. But Tess kept them alert, shaking her head at the slightest sign of relaxation, and managing to make them hot tea to help. She reassured the three small ones, huddled under the kitchen table, and, flitting from one to the other, somehow held them all together until William and his men rode up. Susannah collapsed into his arms in hysterics, overcome by the tension, but they all rejoiced at their light escape, making much of Tess' help.

Tess herself, however, did not escape the bushrangers. The one who had especially noticed her did not forget the lithe form and gleaming hair. With the instinct of the deprived, he had noted her servant status – this one was not part of the actual family – and therefore was fair game. The gang had moved north, succeeding better at another homestead. After they had enjoyed their ill-gotten gains, he separated from them, turning south back to Fairbourne, where he hid close by, watching for his chance.

He got it when the girl, having taken the cow to be tethered in a new patch nearer the river, wandered a little along the bank, singing to herself. Her broken body was found, torn and bloodied, with earth and twigs embedded in those enticing curls that never got a chance to be put up with a pretty comb. Susannah would really have doubted God's justice had she known that the man, by leaving the gang for this act, succeeded in not being there when the bushrangers were finally captured two days later near Launceston.

Yet again, the Fairfields had failed to keep one of their own safe. It was another, bitter loss, felt all the more by Susannah, who was deeply bereft, missing the silent child far more for her presence than for the work she had done. One of the workmen's wives started coming in to help her, and thus life continued, but for a long time she had to fight the feeling that this land harboured something that was malevolent and just lying in wait to send yet another horror upon her.

***

But, three years later as the Murrays were packing up, she had to admit that they were doing all right. Gradually, her frailty had lessened. William took her and the children on a shopping trip to Hobart, were they attended a reception at Government House and were especially commended for their spirited self-defence against the bush rangers. The town had developed greatly in the eight years since she had arrived. Merchant houses with fabric, clothing, fine furnishings, and general goods, made shopping great fun, and their home more comfortable, even luxurious. William was making a name for himself for particularly well-bred sheep, and his stock was sought for a high price. He had bought another neighbouring grant from a retiring settler, intending it for young Andrew, and which meanwhile carried an ever-growing herd producing fine wool for the avid English market.

He was also proud of his fine house. Its plain, classical Georgian lines began to take shape as he sketched some plans for it, on the kitchen table in the snug cottage he had initially built.

"What do you think, my Dear? A veranda along the entire front, either side of the front door? "

"That would be a great place for the children to play…and I could send for some roses to grow up the posts! That would be so lovely! Now we've got enough dogs to keep those wretched possums off them…"

"Hmmm, plenty of sandstone about – we could start cutting blocks in the slacker times. Take a while, of course. "

As his income grew, and the first few years of heavy labour passed, he directed his energies towards completing it. Susannah's precious blooms in due course thrived in a glory of white, gold, and pink. William built the house entirely himself with the help of his men, designing it carefully to meet the family's needs for comfort as well as security. One of the better houses of the district, much admired, it was a long way from the humble, rented farm that would have been their likely prospect had they stayed in Scotland.

Things had settled down, also, in the wider Macquarie District, for the conciliator Robinson was now efficiently gathering up the remaining natives and shipping them away to a small island in the north. There were still some bushrangers about, but with increased numbers of soldiers and ever more settlers arriving, they were confining themselves largely to the outer fringes of settlement. It was now possible to go about in relative safety.

The Fairfields had paid a high price in blood and tears for their growing wealth and comfortable life, but now they could put that behind them. The other settlers of the area felt the same. Country balls, hunting meets, breeding fine horses, drawing lessons for their daughters, became the pleasant round for most. By an unwritten agreement, nobody ever spoke of the past. Many were still uncomfortable with the displacement of the natives, and everyone knew terrible stories of cruelty and murder. Even those who had not taken part in any of the violence felt guilt by association – for was it not the coming of white man that had brought about the end of the poor unfortunate savages? The dark shadow in the land made them keep their eyes and hearts turned firmly towards England, which they continued to call Home, and which was the source of all that was culturally desirable and properly civilized.

Particularly, Susannah thought, when the first proper songbirds were brought out from England. Captain Langthrop's ship had docked in Hobart, and the singing and warbling that emerged from the cages on the deck soon brought an excited crowd. Some were openly crying on hearing the familiar sounds of home, and even tough men stood in silence as the blackbird's evening ode first rose into the Tasmanian dusk. These, and many others – thrushes, robins, wrens, tits, warblers, larks and others – found their way into the gardens and woodlands, were released, and gradually spread across the Island. It was a matter of great pride when a family could report that a pair had settled near their home. Surely they would soon come to Fairbourne, also!

So she attended to the growing of her family, taking pride in her fine upright sons and the grace of her daughters. Her last-born, David, so frail as a child, had survived and grown into a sensitive type unlike his heftier brothers, preferring the home garden and the writing desk to the run-and-tumble of the outdoors. His dreamy eyes saw other worlds than his siblings did, and when he wandered in the bush his ears were more attuned to the feather-light chittering of the native birds than any possible blackbird calls. He saw beauty in the dancing silver of the leaves stirred by the wind, breathed deep the heady fragrance of the wattle flowers in spring, and perhaps he sensed the strange emptiness in the land. In the wind, sometimes, there was a lonely calling, and now and then he thought he could see dark figures just slipping out of sight. He quickly learned that such fancy ideas were not tolerated among his peers. Even his own family laughed gently at him, so he remained a shy loner.

Susannah occasionally looked at him protectively and thoughtfully, hoping that he would soon get over his odd notions, for they made her uncomfortable. Somewhere in her soul, Susannah resented the refusal of this land to yield her the deep peace that had cradled her in the misty-blue glens of Scotland. She had desperately missed the warming comfort of her home village clustered around its ancient church, and its seasons of celebration and thanksgiving. Determined to make a home in this new land, they had built a fine chapel here, along with their gracious farms and community, and faithfully observed all the old rituals. But those did not belong here, and the spirit of the land was not seduced. Susannah knew that she was still, despite all, a stranger here.

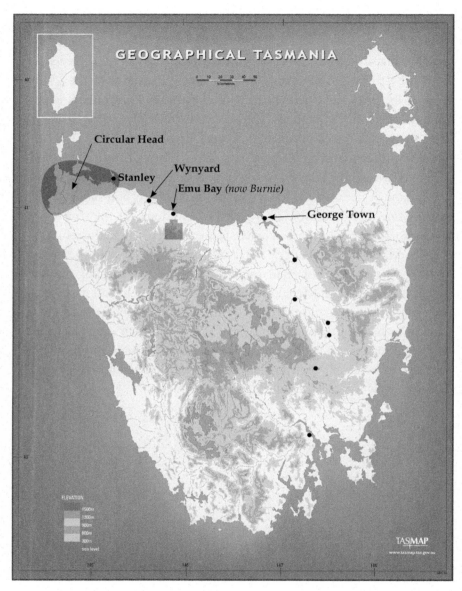

Map 3 – *Tasmania by 1832*

 Landgrants made to the Van Diemens Land Company

At this time, most of the North and West Coasts were covered in vast and almost impenetrable forests, excepting some coastal areas in the far North West. The North West Coast was bifurcated by numerous dangerous and often torrential rivers, adding to the sense of isolation.

THE CONVICTS 1825 – 1833

GEORGE TURNER

"Humanity probably invented exile first and prison later.
Expulsion from the tribe was, of course, exile. We were quick to
realise how difficult it is for a man to exist, divorced from his own
place, his familiar territory. Everything is wrong and awkward..."
Alexander Solzhenitsyn

7. FROM ONE HELL TO ANOTHER

It's just my rotten bloody luck, isn't it, thought George Turner bitterly as the soldier marched him back to the cells. That fat lousy bastard... He meant the magistrate at the Launceston courthouse, who had suddenly turned indisposed and retired before completing the jobs in hand. Which meant that George's co-convicts, Jones and Kershaw – all three of them here because their previous assignment to Herbert Fairfield had ended suddenly with the man's murder – had already been allocated to the road gang, whereas George was left to stew in the filthy gaol until the magistrate felt better.

I wouldn't have minded being in the road gang. Might be 'ard work, but it's close to the town. Sure would be better'n being stuck out there in those bloody hills, guardin' a rich man's sheep. Might even find a woman, or go to the pub...better'n forever seein' only sheep and them other two, lucky bastards...

Best of all would have been an assignment into the public works, but only skilled men were taken there. They had the extra privilege of being allowed to sell their labour in the afternoons for money to the settlers, and in 1826 there was a great shortage of carpenters, blacksmiths, mechanics and the like.

But I never 'ad a chance to learn a trade, George continued musing, not back there in Pontefract. No time then for any proper schooling, and definitely no chance of any apprenticeship.

He jerked inside at a brief memory of his careworn mother, his rough and desperate father, the squalling little ones and never enough to eat.

The magistrate was still prostrated with a bad attack of the gout when, two days later, a request arrived with the constable for another convict to join a ship currently at George Town, on the mouth of the river Tamar. The *Lady Nelson* had come up from Hobart with goods for the Northern settlement, and was due to sail on immediately to the far northwestern coast, carrying fourteen convicts assigned to the Van Diemens Land Company. Only thirteen men had been found in the hurry before sailing, so having one sitting idle in the Launceston gaol was handy, and the constable was sent to fetch him.

George was given little time to think about his new situation. The hasty departure, the forced march of 25 miles, and the unceremonious bundling onto the ship, left him cross but resigned. What were they packing him off into now? And he hated ships with their unstable motion, a nasty reminder of the long journey from England on the *Medina*. Confined to a tight corner of the overcrowded deck with the other men, he was filled with nausea as the ship got underway, clearing the dangerous Hebe reef and turning west out into Bass's Straits.

George was twenty-three, of medium height, well built and strong. He had very pale flaxen hair, almost white, and the unusual condition of having one brown and one blue eye. The contrast was not particularly stark, but it was enough to confuse people and they rarely looked straight at him. George found himself doing a lot of the looking, instead, and he sometimes saw things others missed. He was the first to see the natives as they crept up on their isolated hut, up in the foothills of the Western Tiers, where he and the two other convicts had until recently been shepherding. They'd held them off successfully that time, by staying united in the hut and shooting from the doorway, but you had to sleep sometime and you never knew when the savages might burst in upon you. The other two, Kershaw and Jones, had been there somewhat longer than George, and told him of an occasion when they had shot and killed a native:

"...a real savage he was, too, covered in scars."

"The bastards are getting real clever, sending flaming spears into the thatch to force you out. You can't wait for them – the only way to survive here is to shoot them before they get near you."

George was stunned by such stories, but hid his thoughts, for the other two clearly gloried in anything that got the black bastards their just deserts, and couldn't wait for the next chance to kill some more. All of them were sullen and resentful at being forced into this remote and dangerous place, with only occasional turns down at the homestead where the master's brother's wife was kindly and provided them with generous and good grub. Mr Herbert Fairfield, it was known, had an informal agreement with a neighbour's fair daughter, and was planning to build a house for her, so there were sandstone blocks to carve and foundations to dig when the husbandry had been done. But leaving only two convicts up in the hills had proved insufficient and risky, so Fairfield's brother William had loaned George to make up an additional presence. It was to Fairbourne that George had been assigned on his arrival in Van Diemens Land, in September 1825.

George, feeling alienated and exposed, got into the habit of keeping a sharp and constant lookout into the strange and threatening landscape that surrounded him.

He had been born near Selby in Yorkshire, England, the oldest of seven, and only his first five years saw any sort of settled life. His father, Jake, the brown-eyed one with a wild Gaelic streak in him, worked as an occasional farm labourer and the family supplemented his irregular income by growing vegetables, keeping chickens, and a cow on the common land. It wasn't a bad life, up there on the edges of the big moor. For little George there was a reassuring comfort in the song of the lark, the warm sunlight, and the fat eggs he collected for his mother. Some of the hymns they sang in church spoke of the beauty of nature. Later, he would see no such kindliness in the landscape of Van Diemens Land.

The little family's life, while humble, should have been pleasant enough, until the effect of the enclosures act of 1801 caught up with them. Ejected from their rented cottage and denied use of the common land, they gathered their very few belongings and migrated south to Pontefract, where they hoped to find work, perhaps in the liquorice fields. But the industrial revolution and mechanization meant that unskilled agricultural labourers were wanted in ever smaller numbers. In 1786, the infernal threshing machine had been invented; by 1808 its use was widespread.

The Turner family was one of many unable to find a place for themselves. They did not qualify for parish relief, the poor law insisting that you had to belong to the area and also be physically unable to work to be considered as 'the deserving poor'. For several years they got by in the barest existence on odd jobs and in the poorest of rented cottages, but the babes kept coming. Things improved briefly when Jake found work in one of the weaving factories, but that ended when they brought him home with his right arm torn off by the machine. Years of malnutrition had depleted his body beyond recovery; they buried him at the paupers' end of the cemetery; his wife left with an unpayable debt to the doctor.

George, by then thirteen, had spent the last eight years scrounging the streets for anything useful for the family's sustenance, and seeking any paying errand that someone might give a small boy. He blended into the rabble of such children, noticed only by a few for his odd eyes, and grew adept at snatching any opportunity for survival. As his mother's desperation grew, he got closer to overlooking the difference between right and wrong, and sometimes succeeded in stealing some vegetables, and once – gloriously – a bone with the marrow still in it.

Anne Turner, the flaxen-haired and blue-eyed one, could no longer keep up any niceties beyond survival. She was born into a poor but respectable tenant farmer family, and her parents had taken her to church regularly. She could read a little, as the priest had taught the children of the parish on Sundays, using the bible as a primer. She had continued to attend there, after marrying, as often as could, taking little George with her. Her husband Jake was not interested.

"That's a wild one" her father had muttered, "nothing good will come of it," and his opinion was confirmed when his first grandchild turned out to have such odd eyes.

"It's like he's two people in one," thought the grandmother uneasily. "The fairies have split his soul."

But Anne was young, strong and capable, and tried to make up for her husband's waywardness. She had made them a good little home, with her parents nearby to help, until the land was enclosed by the local squire and suddenly, all was taken away from them with no redress. George, just old enough then to take it in, over time built a deep resentment against men who could do such things, and the system that allowed it.

He adored his mother. She was his only comfort, the one who did all she could to shelter him and who held him when taunts over his eyes got too bad. He imagined her as an angel. At times, Anne had made some attempts to teach her children basic reading, using the one book she possessed, her bible, but eventually that had to go, too. George had only attended real school during the brief months before his father's death. Now all he had were lessons at the Sunday school, conducted by Howard Walker, a tall, educated, plainly-dressed man with a sensitive face and kindly eyes. He was the only other person in George's life who took the trouble to notice him, sitting beside him and carefully guiding his childish hand around the mysteries of the alphabet.

In the closing years of the 18th century, a movement had grown up that believed the working classes could be bettered and kept from crime by providing them with education; this was done on Sundays as the boys were usually required to work during the week. Known as the Ragged Schools, philanthropically-minded men like Howard Walker would do the practical teaching. He was interested in his pupils, genuinely delighted when he saw a spark of understanding or a gleam of bright intelligence among them, and deeply grieved at their poverty, both physical and spiritual. He spent extra time with George, for the clearness of the moor's wide skies had not yet been entirely erased from the boy's eyes, though it would be soon.

It was Howard Walker who spoke for the boy the first time George was caught stealing; the magistrate respected that and let the boy off with a warning. The second time he went to gaol for a few months; it was that spell on his record that later convinced the visiting judge at the quarterly sessions in the old Pontefract court house that he was dealing with an unredeemable criminal, a taint on proper society, and best sent as far away as possible.

"To Van Diemens Land, in fact, for fourteen years, where you will have plenty of time to learn about doing some honest work."

Walker himself had been unwell and knew nothing of this; when he recovered he was very distressed about George's abrupt departure. He attempted to find the mother, but Anne had also disappeared. It was known that she had wept in the courthouse on hearing her oldest son's fate; after that she vanished into the dirty back alleys and no further record of her or the children could be found.

George did have plenty of time to learn to hate the authorities; from the rough soldiers who collected him, and others like him along the way, prodding them on the long walk south through Nottingham, Leicester, Oxford, Reading and into Portsmouth; to the jailers who locked them into the filthy hulks with hundreds of other convicts, and the overseers who had them chained and made them labour on the dock structures. Many men died from accidents, infections, and disease. By the time George was allocated to a ship that would bring him to Australia, he had already been a prisoner for nearly two years. The journey took five months, packed nightmarishly below decks among so many stinking bodies; the men ranging from the equally resentful just trying to survive to the downright evil. George coped by being wary, going with the crowd and trying not to stand out, which was extra hard on account of his unusual eyes, and trying to out-guess every guard's intention before it could befall him. His resentment of the rich and his fear of authority, reinforced by the other convicts, made him lose his faith in humanity. The world was a threatening place and everyone was a potential enemy. There were no Howard Walkers here.

The *Medina* docked in Hobart in September 1825. George was then 22 and still had twelve years of hard labour ahead of him. He had no idea what had happened to his mother and siblings, and no hope of finding out. He could not write properly; nor had he money to pay for a scribe or the postage. The relative inactivity on board ship and the regular, if plain, food had put some flesh back on him; his youth did the rest and he was assessed as capable of hard work. Perhaps it was that early memory of the Yorkshire moor's wide horizons that made him state 'agricultural labourer' when asked; on the basis of that, he was allocated to William Fairfield of Fairbourne near Campbell Town. William promptly passed him over to his recently-arrived brother Herbert, who was having difficulty keeping his sheep together in the remoter hills at the back of his grant. Thus George suddenly found himself in the most alien place he could imagine.

Nothing in his life could have prepared him for the strange bare trees, the thud of the kangaroos bounding amongst them, the harsh caw of the ravens, the dry undergrowth with a multitude of insects including the horrifyingly large huntsman spider. The other two, having had longer to get used to it all, laughed and assured him:

"It won't hurt you..."

But they also didn't find the nightly snarling and growling of the devils and the heavy breathing of the possums particularly funny.

"Heathen place, this..."

There was the elusive native cat, another possible threat to the lambs. They knew one had taken all Susannah Fairfield's chickens several times until an adequate enough enclosure had been built. Initially, it being summer, the weather wasn't too bad, though the sun could be unexpectedly fierce and sometimes it got really hot. The vast dense silence, filled only with the ceaseless zirring of the cicadas, made George nervy. There were big black tiger snakes, known to be deadly poisonous, and smaller ones too. Once, he had stopped among the trees for a brief rest, only to jump back in fear as he found a copperhead hanging from a branch, its flicking tongue inches from his face. There were strange yippings and unexplained snufflings, striped shadows glimpsed, and every dark space among the trees might be a native savage with a deadly spear aimed at him.

The winter rolled in with thick, wet mists, hiding anything that might be out there. Properly watching the stupid sheep became almost impossible. He admitted that Herbert Fairfield was generous with both food and rum rations; when the weather turned colder he had ridden up with extra blankets and coats, and made sure that they always had enough powder and shot for the muskets.

"You're lucky, not many masters are like that," George heard from convicts on the run.

"Men get beaten, made to work in terrible places without adequate grub or slops. Often no shoes, either."

Some of them banded together with stolen guns and made a regular living from plundering settler's homes; often they would come past the hut on their way to hide in higher hills. George was glad to be accepted as one into this network of men; together they could drink their fears away, ridicule the rich men whose livestock they were condemned to watch, and curse the injustices of the system that had brought them into this awful exile.

Though he found it abhorrent, George would join in the coarse laughter when talk was of native women, caught and kept tied up, to be used by the men. Once, lured by this, Kershaw had taken the risk and disappeared for several days over to a hut further up where such a 'gin' was available. George was sure that their hut was singled out after that by the natives; spears had come flying out of nowhere and once, after the sheep went into a massive stampede and all three men were required to manage them, the hut was plundered of all their stores.

He was glad when his turn came to do the labouring down on the farm. There was also the pretty, silent Tess but George, impossibly shy with women, of whom he knew almost nothing, dared do no more than briefly glance at her. He minded his work with somewhat better care whilst on his valley spell, and was there working on a fence when his own master, Herbert, was killed by a group of natives down by the river.

Once the worst shock was over, William Fairfield decided to sell off his dead brother's cattle, and bring his sheep down to join his own on the Fairbourne pastures, until the will was sorted out. Accordingly, he sent Herbert's three convicts to the magistrate in Launceston for allocation to some other assignment.

Thus George found himself, yet again, abruptly being taken to another unknown place. On the ship he reflected bitterly, between bouts of nausea, that life had dished him out the dirtiest of deals. Every time things had gotten a bit better, it was snatched away again. It was no use expecting anything good to happen, for even if it did, it wouldn't stay that way. He even hated people like the Fairfields, knowing that their solidarity and security was not for the likes of him. It was in the blackest of moods that he watched the coastline going by, not in the least surprised to see the utter desolation of the darkest, dankest, most forbidding forest man had ever encountered. This was where he was being taken to? Yes, that would be right...

Here he was, along with thirteen others like him, all to be at the beck and call of some superintendent, made to labour like dumb animals in some godforsaken place, and all of it because he tried to keep his family from starving. There was no hope of escape from here, no going back, and no way of knowing what had happened to his mother and siblings.

8. IT'S NOT GETTING ANY BETTER

The night on the *Lady Nelson's* deck was bitterly cold, the icy sea wind sweeping all before it. The next day they reached the Circular Head area, anchoring below The Nut, a huge dark rock rising straight out of the sea, providing a dramatic end to the long promontory coming off the coastline. Not yet understood by any aboard was the climate there, so different from the more familiar parts. Massive rain, sometimes for weeks on end, cold and penetrating, could kill sheep and even men; drive rheumatism into the joints, cause wounds to fester, and – in winter at least – could bring people to a deep depression, even despair. But for now it was November, with summer about to start, and there was a wild beauty in the sea creaming green, white and azure onto the endless pale golden beaches. Those who could see the lovely even in strange places would find the sweeping vista glorious, as did Henry Hellyer, one of the VDL Company's surveyors.

This Company, formed two years previously in London by a syndicate of wealthy investors, was intended to be a large-scale sheep-raising venture. They appointed one Edward Curr as agent and manager, who had previously already lived on the Island for two years, written a book about it, and had returned to England to oversee its publication. Requesting a grant of some 500'000 acres in some as yet not-taken-up part of the Island, the governor had decided that the far North West would be most suitable. Thus Curr employed several surveyors, Henry Hellyer among them, as well as one Alexander Goldie, an agriculturalist, who spent the last two years beating their way through the unknown mountains, massive forests, along coast lines, across swamps, and fording dangerous rivers – all in a desperate attempt to find that piece of land, all 500'000 acres of it, that might prove suitable for the raising of fine-woolled sheep.

So far, the only piece with potential lay in the very northwestern tip, from Circular Head to Cape Grim, where they found some 60'000 acres of mostly open pasture. Curr hastened back to Hobart to convince the governor that the land grant needed to be in several pieces, not one continuous one as originally stated. The area so far identified as useable at Circular Head would be the main headquarters; the Company's surveyors would continue to map the land with a view to selecting further pieces later.

The company's own ship, *Tranmere*, had arrived inconveniently early before all the land grant matters were settled, and had started to unload at The Nut. A total of 23 convicts had been assigned to the new settlement, George's group of fourteen being the second lot to arrive. Soon they were all at work, building huts for shelter, caring for the precious sheep and other livestock. As soon as the most basic amenities were established, Hellyer and the other surveyors got ready for more exploratory trips to find that suitable land.

George Turner was one of two convicts chosen to accompany Henry Hellyer and his two companions, Richard Frederick and Isaac Cutts. The other convict was Abe Wells, who had already taken part in another such exploration. With the party were three packhorses to carry provisions as far as the terrain would permit. They left Circular Head on the 1st of February 1827 and five days later had reached a high point on the southernmost peak of the Dip Range. Before them lay the vast panorama of the Arthur River basin, an endless unbroken sweep of heavily timbered ridges, intersected by deep ravines. Far to the southeast rose two distinct mountains that Hellyer was able to name as Mt. Roland and Black Bluff, much to George's astonishment. Hellyer also pointed out Mt. Cameron to the west and the Dial Range to the east, but his chief interest lay on a distant peak like a volcano rising steeply out of the dark forest, to the southeast.

"That's where we are going," he said.

George had already found the trek this far very difficult, even though he was assured by Wells that this was 'comparatively easy going'. Hacking their way through dense tea-tree, the stems so close that a man could not slip between them, and the coastal marshland underfoot making every step a mud-sucking effort, had exhausted him.

"This is *easy*?" George asked.

"Wait till you get to some real forest," Wells had warned him then.

Along the Dip Range the going had been easier, the ground mostly clear if stony and often very steep, but now that forest lay before him, a forbidding, vast, and darkly brooding mass, impenetrable surely to any civilized man.

"Well, it's quite clear that the horses cannot come any further," commented Hellyer the next morning, after they had climbed down from the peak to a heathy flat area on the eastern slope.

"You two can stay here with them, and the dogs. We will be back in about fourteen days."

He and his companions filled their kangaroo skin bags with a fortnight's provisions and a blanket each, and set off, every man carrying a gun. George and Wells were left behind to guard the three horses. They had a tent, flour, oatmeal, tea and some sugar, one gun and two dogs to catch them some additional sustenance.

As the three men disappeared into the dense undergrowth of the myrtle forest, a huge fear descended upon George. What lay out there? What was waiting to prey on them, hidden in the edge of the trees just over there? They spent their first night alone in secret terror, tensing at every sound as the forest came alive. Some of the noises he was already familiar with, the kangaroo's thudding, as it bounded along, the possum's harrking, and the snarling of the devils fighting. But there were other rustles, some terrifyingly close, and at one point the horses neighed in fright as a strange yipping bark sounded through the dark. Surely those were footsteps and whispers? What strangers were creeping up on them? Swarms of mosquitoes descended upon them, adding to their misery. They wanted to keep their fire going, yet felt it might draw attention to their presence. Sleeping in the tent gave some relief from the flying insects, but disallowed them the opportunity of keeping an eye on their surroundings. Not that they could see anything much anyway – the black darkness was impenetrably dense. The men huddled miserably in their blankets, unable to sleep. Towards morning, they came alert as a roaring noise brought a strong wind and a wall of drenching, cold rain. Their desolation was complete.

George came to hate the wind more than anything. It was so big and powerful, and came out of nowhere, not like a proper English gale that slowly built up and gave you the time to batten down the hatches. He had heard that sailors feared this wind, known as the Roaring Forties, and he could see why. It was like a monster, ready to slash at you any moment and destabilize your footing or send a tree crashing down on you. It was another thing that added to the horror of their situation – the third night brought a real storm, and amid the roaring the groaning and breaking of trees and branches made up a veritable cacophony. It also effectively masked any approaching sounds, and heightened their sense of vulnerability.

Gradually, they settled to a routine as they got somewhat used to it. Nights were still an uncomfortable experience, with their nerves constantly on edge, but the days were tolerable when it wasn't raining, which it did quite often. The two men hid their fear under nervous laughter and crude jokes, but as the time lengthened and they were thrown upon each other to deal with various situations, they stopped pretending.

"That horse looks sick – what d'ye reckon?"

"Hmmm...don't know what's the matter with it."

Presently it died. The dogs gave off hunting as there was so much fresh meat right at the camp. The men dragged the carcass further away, disturbing the big black flies that descended by the million.

"God, that's disgusting," said Abe, indicating the black moving mass, around which the bloated dogs were still poking. "And now that other horse is sick, too – what is it? Something in the bloody grass? Wouldn't surprise me – look at the coarse stuff, it's a wonder they're eating any of it. Or maybe some leaves around here are poisonous?"

Neither man was willing to try the horsemeat. They made do with oatmeal gruel and bread, blackened on the outside from baking in the ashes, and made unsuccessful attempts to hunt.

"I don't like this, Abe," said George. "I reckon we should not just be left here. We haven't seen any yet, but who knows when the natives might find us here? Christ, I've seen them, throwing their bloody spears out from behind the trees – you don't even know they're there until it hits you."

He looked over at the dark forest edge. The surface soil there was rank with decaying matter, littered with dead logs and branches, impeding any progress by dense thickets of interwoven growth. Above, the myrtle trees formed a dark canopy, shutting out all sunlight, and above them again towered the immense eucalypts, their enormous trunks measuring up to three to meters across, and reaching up into the sky, dead straight, some over one hundred meters tall, before their scraggly crowns started to spread out. The men were awed and subdued by this forbidding place. No man in England had ever seen a tree that big, let alone thousands of them.

"That Hellyer must be mad to try to go through stuff like this," said Abe. "Even if they do manage it, the natives will get them for sure. I don't reckon we'll see any of them again. We might as well pack up and go back; no point sitting it out here any longer."

"No," reckoned George. "They took food for a fortnight, so we've got to give 'em that much time. It's only ten days since they left."

Neither man was properly literate, but both could count the pennies in the shilling. Neither had ever handled more than a few of the latter; a full pound was unimaginable riches to them. They were marking the days by incising a tree nearby.

"I'd be glad to get out, for sure, but they'll be pretty hungry when they do get back – if they ever do."

George was in two minds over the surveyor Henry Hellyer. His negative expectations were immediately fulfilled, on arrival, by the Company overseer's sharp and dictatorial manner. That man, Alexander Goldie, brooked no nonsense, which might have been alright but he had little regard for fairness. At Christmas he had issued a celebratory rum ration to the men – but provided more for the indentured servants that had been hired by the VDL in England, and less for the locally assigned convicts. The latter naturally objected, ending up by forcibly taking all the rum. The inevitable drunken fight was only uneasily settled when the drink itself ran out. Goldie had one of them, Harley, whom he considered the ringleader, chained to a tree until Edward Curr, the manager, returned from Hobart on 21st January, who then had all the convicts flogged and the indentured men's pay stopped. This further confirmed George's view that all men were in a state of enmity against him, his flayed back painful proof of it. Particularly as he himself had had no part in the actual taking of the rum, though he had drunk plenty of it once others had secured it.

But Hellyer the surveyor was another matter. Perhaps the man's accidental likeness to Howard Walker, George's kindly early mentor and teacher in England, was a factor. Like Walker, Hellyer was tall and thinly built, though very strong, and his face was sensitive and gentle-looking. After a few days in the surveyor's party, George decided that this man had a different attitude, even towards convicts. He was considerate, and naturally assumed that all would eat together by his camp fire. He made sure both Wells and George had enough blankets, handed them a daily rum ration to lift their spirits in the evenings, and thanked them for their effort during the day. Even their opinion on a number of practical things was welcome. Nor did he expect more of the men than he was willing to do himself, and was impressively handy with managing the work of bush-bashing and setting up campsites.

On reflection, George decided that "being left out here alone" with Abe Wells would not have seemed to Hellyer as expecting anything too much; the man would have done similar things many times himself.

"I don't understand it, Abe," George tried hesitantly one evening. "Hellyer doesn't seem to think the natives are dangerous?"

"I don't think he's had any problems with them, so far," his companion remarked. "I was with him on another trip, and we saw huts and campfires, but we never saw a native, never had any trouble. The men that went with Goldie and Fossey down the coast out by Cape Grim said the same."

"Then why was it so different in the Midlands? You couldn't turn your back there without risking a spear in it."

"I've heard stories…about the stock keepers there – and in other parts – and the savages. Like they shoot 'em on sight and take their women…"

George knew those stories, too.

"So you reckon the natives are taking revenge?" he asked.

"Sure thing."

"And what about out here?"

"There's not been any stock keepers out here yet," Abe pointed out, "not really any white men much, either, apart from the surveyors goin' through the bush. I reckon the natives here got no reason to hate us. Won't last, though. Goldie's going to send some men out with the sheep to the Cape, and I heard Gunshannon saying about what he'd do to any native that tried to mess with him."

"That Russell has the same ideas," said George.

"Yep, be careful of him – a nasty piece of work. Most of the men that came with the ship from England, they seem to be alright, pretty friendly sort of bunch, particularly James Morton. Not that any are liking it here; reckon no one told them what to expect. They're not gettin' enough pay, either, they say. You can understand it; there's not much here except bloody hard work, Goldie to boss 'em around, and no comfort. Reckon we'll see a few disappearing, despite their two-year indentures. One went with a sealer that called in, not long ago. Anyways, that Nat Russell is different. Keep away from him."

"Curr ain't much better, what do you reckon?"

"That bastard…" Both men still had sore backs from the flogging that Curr had ordered, and which he had stood by and watched.

George could not quite bring himself to say out loud that he thought Hellyer was a decent sort, unlike Curr. It would sound soft, a weakness in their mutual defense against the bosses, but he was warmed by the thought and it made him determined to stay put, despite his fear, until the surveyor and his companions returned.

Both men were unable to help the second horse, either, and presently it died. This time, they immediately dragged it away as far as possible, over to the forest edge. The dogs, already overfed, showed little interest when the dark, snarling devils came out in the night to feed on it; the noise and crunching of bones was most unpleasant but inside two nights the carcass was mostly gone. Despite the convenience of that, to George there was something nightmarish about those creatures emerging in the darkness to fight over dead meat.

The days ticked by slowly, with no sign of the surveyor's group when the fortnight was up. Three days later, with both men by now on the point of giving up, the third horse went down, clearly also suffering from whatever had poisoned the other two. Wells was having no more of it.

"We'll leave the tent and put most of the food in it, so they'll find that and shelter if they do make it back. It's only five days walking back to the Nut; we can carry enough food for that without the horse."

"You can't just leave the beast to die! Those damned devils might attack it even before it's dead."

"We could shoot it before we go – put it out of its misery."

"Wish I knew what is getting it…must be something that's growing here." George was hesitant. "We could wait a bit longer – all we'll get back there is more work. Here at least we're just sitting."

That was undeniable. Abe agreed to another day or two, but: "…no more than that. Even if they've extended their food with hunting, this is too hard a place. They'll never make it through."

"I'm not so sure," said George. "He's a clever man."

George's faith was rewarded on the nineteenth day. A shot rang out nearby. After the first fright, they replied with one of their own, and an hour later the three men, barely able to walk, with their clothes torn to shreds and covered in festering wounds, staggered into the clearing.

Restored with porridge, hot tea and warm clothing, they planned to walk out the next morning. Hellyer was most anxious to get back with his news of the good land he had finally found, east and south of that peak they had climbed. All three men were dismayed at the loss of the two horses, and the sickly state of the third one, for any livestock was valuable and scarce. Richard Frederick looked closely at the barely surviving beast, and decided that, rather than poisoning, the likely cause might be malnutrition. He insisted they try and save it, even if it meant a delay in their departure. Feeding it warm gruel made of oatmeal, and wrapping it in blankets, the animal was standing and rapidly regaining its strength inside two days.

"But they were eating all the time!" the two convicts assured him.

"Maybe the grass here isn't sufficient. It doesn't look particularly succulent, does it?"

It was a prophetic observation, and a great pity that Hellyer, full of excitement at his great discovery that would finally solve the Company's problems, did not take note of it at the time. But he was a surveyor, not an agriculturist, and treated the incident as a passing curiosity. Back at Circular Head, he expounded to Curr about: "…the grassy hills and knolls that resembled a neglected old park, a 1000 to 1500 acres to a patch without a tree except some clumps of blackwood…" and Curr was delighted to hear it.

The latter had his own urgent reasons for finding suitable land for his employers, the VDL Company. Still young, having just turned thirty, he was not only ambitious but keen to demonstrate the rightness of the claims he had made in his book. After all, they had employed him on that basis. What they did not know – and what, in fairness, nobody including Curr knew at the time – was that here the climate was so much wetter and colder, even bringing icy conditions with snow, as well as having a brooding isolation calculated to strike despair into most white men's hearts.

Curr wrote immediately to his directors, urging them to apply immediately for Hellyer's new found land. They set off to assess the coast nearby for a port to service the new area, investigating the mouth of the Inglis River, later the site for the town of Wynyard, and then the Emu River. Hellyer recommended the latter, as being closer to his find, even though the Inglis provided much better anchorage.

Before the matter of the land grants was settled, Hellyer began, with a group of assigned convicts including George, to build a road from the coast up into his Hampshire Hills, thus effectively founding Emu Bay, later renamed Burnie. They constructed a jetty serviced with a crane, to save expending energy on building major landing facilities, plus a small store and some basic huts. Every day, he and his men emerged from them to do battle with the massive forest, felling enough to create a strip six yards wide, clearing and burning the tough and wiry undergrowth, attempting as much as possible to avoid the huge labour of dropping the towering eucalypts. Every yard they so painfully cleared immediately turned into a morass of mud, in which the bullocks sank deeply and every step was an effort. The men cursed and swore, injuries were frequent, leeches attached themselves to every bit of bare skin and caused festering sores. Their clothing went to pieces and was not replaced often enough.

Amidst the communal misery, George again observed Hellyer's personal qualities. Kept burning by his vision, the surveyor urged his men on. He ensured their comfort as far as possible within the primitive conditions, and provided himself with nothing better. But despite all the effort, for years Hellyer's "road" remained infamously difficult and virtually impassable in winter. What they didn't realise at the time was the sheer, astounding fertility that lay within that brown, cursed-over mud.

Meanwhile in Hobart, Governor Arthur decided to send out his own surveyor, John Helder Wedge, to assess the situation up in the North West, as he did not trust the VDL Company's claims and was alarmed at their request for several separate blocks of land. In his 1828 report, Wedge stated what the VDL Company, in their focus on the breeding of sheep, were unable to see: under the massive forest, at least in parts, lay great tracts of good quality and rich soil, that would yield substantial returns if cleared. Wedge conceded the great effort that would be required to achieve this, but presciently suggested the fine timber could be exported to advantage, and each acre thus cleared and paid for could then be cultivated, in turn providing an income to prepare the next piece of ground. In this, Wedge was the first to foresee the remarkable farmlands of Tasmania, where in time millions of tons of potatoes and other vegetables would be grown, dairy cattle kept, orchards planted, and a thriving farming community established, all in the shadow of a vanished forest.

In his otherwise highly observant report, J H Wedge made no mention of the Aborigines. That they could be anything other than an inconvenience to be disposed of, was not considered. It may be, however, that the respectable surveyor Wedge had personal reasons for not mentioning them. He himself, on that trip, captured and took prisoner a black boy. He also kept, at his estate of Leighlands, three other native youths, as did his near neighbour, John Batman.

After much wrangling the separate grants were finally drawn up and officially sealed. The total irony was that the VDL Company ended up, with the sole exception of the Cape Grim piece, with land totally unsuited to its intended purpose, the raising of sheep, but had effectively at the same time deprived itself of nearly all the potentially good quality soil where it might have built an agricultural fortune. And, as chance would have it in a further bit of bad luck, their Hampshire Hills boundary was only a few miles east of another fortune: the fabulously rich mountain of tin, found at Waratah in 1872.

"This land is no good at all...the grass is too coarse, no good for sheep, and it's damn cold up here, too..."

Curr had finally managed to visit Hellyer's find in up the Hampshire Hills, and recognized immediately that a big mistake was being made. But by then he had made too many recommendations and expended too much money to establish the Company.

Even more ironically, the shareholders in London were at the point of cutting their losses and withdrawing completely, and had Arthur not agreed to the grants, they would have been saved much further loss and heartbreak, for the original investors never made any significant income.

George Turner and his fellow convicts knew a great deal about this process, in the way of the mute servant who, while never consulted in any matter of importance, has plenty of time to observe and assess the men above him. George's silent admiration for Hellyer did not extend to anyone else, and he was as ready to heap abuse on the bosses as his fellow sufferers. Personally refusing to badmouth Hellyer, he did not stand up for him either out of fear of being different from the others, and occasionally he felt some ashamed guilt about his cowardice.

But presently Hellyer disappeared on other exploring expeditions, and George, moved along with other convicts into service directly under Goldie, found his attention caught up in his old fear: the natives.

9. ENCOUNTERING THE DARKNESS

At the very time when Arthur was handing Curr the right to use the land, the latter's stock keepers were demonstrating to the local natives that white men were bad news, bringing the most terrible and merciless destruction. Natives were shot on sight, or tricked with friendly gestures until they were within range. Later, George Augustus Robinson heard of poison, supplied to the men to kill the Tasmanian tigers, being placed into the flour in the huts, as the men knew that the blacks would particularly take flour as prize plunder. Robinson estimated that hundreds of natives were killed in this way. Their women were taken and raped. Natives, accustomed for millennia to hunt on this fertile corner, suddenly found it full of strange animals and very dangerous men.

"The natives killed about 120 sheep – drove 'em over the cliffs!"

The prompt reprisal – led by none other than the Richard Frederick who had saved the third horse – resulted in 12 natives killed. A few weeks later, stock keepers came upon another group of blacks, whom they shot without warning, throwing their bodies over the 200-meter cliff. Some of them were still alive, or possibly even jumped to their death.

Curr, who knew of the massacre, gave a modified version to his directors, suggesting that the natives were the attackers and the total killed was 'perhaps three'.

It is noteworthy that Curr, in his position as the only magistrate and justice of the peace on the entire Northwest Coast, never attempted to investigate the matter, as he should have done. He also personally captured a black youth, Nicermic, officially to demonstrate that the Company was well-meaning towards the natives, but why the supposedly 'kindly treatment' required that the boy was kept prisoner on a boat for four months, was not explained.

That isolated stock keepers were nervous when placed in a strange and alien situation, and fearful of the dark savages that were capable of slipping silently through the landscape with deadly spears, was understandable. These men were completely out of their depth, often coming from non-rural backgrounds, as well as angry and resentful. But their willingness to brutalise and to kill, and to do so with pleasure, went a step beyond anything that could be described as ensuring survival. Had the activity remained among them only, perhaps excuses could have been found. But such was not the case, as George was about to find out.

As Hellyer's road was completed, he found himself back at the camp at Emu Bay, assisting with the building of stock yards and other facilities. On the morning of 21st August 1829, west of the camp in an area now known as Cooee and Ocean Vista – where suburban houses now line the main highway and occupants sip drinks while enjoying the serene view over the Bass Strait – George arrived with two other men under Alexander Goldie's direction to construct a shed.

With his ingrained habit of keeping a very sharp lookout: "There's some natives further along the beach! They've seen us – they're running off."

The white men could have simply let them go, and – possibly with a guard posted – continued with their building job.

But to George's surprise, Goldie and Richard Sweetling immediately galloped after them, succeeding in cutting off two women and a child. And, right beside George, Nat Russell got down on one knee, took a line of sight with his gun, and shot one of them. The other woman was grabbed by Goldie, who, on snatching her up, wheeled his horse back and called out:

"Don't kill her!"

Sweetling, however, leapt off his horse beside the other, injured, woman and killed her with a blow of his axe, severing the jugular vein. He then snatched the terrified child, but was prevented by Goldie from killing it also. The shot, the blood, the screams, the thunder of hooves, it all happened so quickly that George was unable to take it in.

Later, after the body had been dumped in the scrub and Goldie had tied the woman and the child to a nearby tree, he tried to focus on the job of building the shed, but was too overwhelmed to concentrate. How the others, Russell and Sweetling, could simply continue working without the slightest apparent disturbance, astounded him. For the rest of the day, he was uncomfortably conscious of the presence of the captives, to whom nobody had offered anything. But he could not bring himself to go near them, to offer at least some water, and at lunch he too joined in the laughter and the lewd jokes.

It was soon clear to him that Goldie was not concerned with saving the women out of the goodness of his heart. This had been a deliberate kidnapping. In his report to Curr, Goldie was to write:

...the woman is in irons I make her wash potatoes for the horses and intend taking her to the hills and making her work...the woman will not speak and is often very sulky. She broke her irons once and was nearly getting away I think she is about 20 or 22 years old. I have no doubt she will work. [the man] Barras can make her do anything...

That evening as the group returned to Emu Bay, dragging the naked woman and child with them, George got close to her on one occasion and briefly caught her stare. Too afraid to give her a human look, he veiled his soul and turned away.

The woman was kept, with Goldie's sanction, near the Burleigh camp in the remote hills, as a slave for the use of the men. Goldie kept the little girl for himself. A year or so later, on his departure from the area, he sent her to Mrs. Cameron, where the child soon died. One can only speculate on the reasons why a single man would want to keep a small female child chained up in his hut.

Curr, who was well aware that slavery had been outlawed, and realised that news of this incident could possibly eventually reach Hobart, attempted to make Goldie the scapegoat in his official report. Goldie retaliated by sending Governor Arthur detailed information about numerous killings of natives that, he indicated, Curr was aware of and had sanctioned, including the Cape Grim massacre earlier that year. Two years later, the matter was investigated by Robinson on Arthur's orders, but nothing came of it. The conclusion was that nobody could be accused of murder, because at the time a state of martial law had been in force, under which it was legal to shoot Aborigines.

Relations between Goldie and his employer, Curr, soured from that point on, and by the following year, Goldie resigned from the VDL Company. Retreating to Hobart, he found respectable and successful employment as general manager of Edward Lord's estates. Based at Orielton near Richmond, he got married and in 1846 bought for himself and his family of eight the Laburnum Park property nearby. He became a justice of the peace and died in April 1889, aged 89, a most respectable and honourable founding settler of Tasmania. The main street of Wynyard is named after him.

***

The darkness in George's soul deepened. Deeply troubled by what he saw around him, yet unable to speak out against it or to go away, he dragged himself through his day's obligatory labour, drinking as heavily as he could. His time as convict still stretched endlessly before him, till 1837, before he could hope for freedom. At 27, he still had not had a woman nor any hope of one – white females were extremely rare in the area, turning up only occasionally as wives of other men. He thought about absconding, but did not believe that things would go well for him elsewhere anyway, and he was afraid of the authorities who were bound to track him down sooner or later, so he stayed. He began to cultivate a bit of a skill for carpentering, hoping to avoid being sent on any outlying shepherding jobs.

In May 1832 he was in Emu Bay when a group of four natives were brought in on horseback. Sick and needing care, they had been sent by the man Robinson, who was now walking through the bush to collect up any remaining natives and take them away. The four blacks made a little camp at the back of the company store. George watched the poor shivering creatures from a distance, feeling he should help by giving them some food and perhaps his spare blanket, yet held back by his fear – of them, of his own mixed and inexpressable feelings, of his need to remain accepted among his own.

"What the…?"

The frightful keening that filled the night when one of them, Tom, died, made George's very soul shudder. The next day he was asked to dig a grave; two weeks later, another hole for another dead native. Both bodies were interred without ceremony in the small cemetery, where Spring Street now runs through Burnie. Robinson records in his diary some three weeks later that he had ordered a service, and railings to mark the site, but there is no evidence that this was ever done.

Their bones most likely found little rest there. Many years later, long after the little graveyard had been forgotten, a street widening scheme dug up an old coffin containing only a thigh bone. It is reasonable to assume that those who made money by selling Aboriginal bones to the Royal Society and other collectors had not been long in coming by to make their ghoulish income.

The surviving two, both females, were presently collected by the ship *Fanny* and taken to Circular Head to join Robinson. By coincidence, George Turner was also ordered onto the same trip along with three other assigned men; their labour was needed at headquarters. On the ship, the two black women stared defiantly at the men. George kept his eyes averted, after a brief curious glance at the semi-naked bodies on hearing the other men making lewd comments. More embarrassed than anything, he wished they were decently dressed, for their own sake, too.

It was the last time that George was to be near to any natives. They re-joined their group and disappeared from his sight. As Robinson completed his job, the blacks vanished from the landscape, either through death or banishment to Flinders Island. People stopped fearing them, and they also stopped talking about them, a guilty secret best left alone. The dark shadow remained locked inside George's head.

***

The VDL Company's headquarters had grown into a village known as Stanley.

"That's a mighty fine-lookin' place Mr Hellyer's designed for the manager, the lucky bastard…"

George and his old friend Abe Wells sweated as they dug the necessary foundations. In the evenings they got acquainted with James Morton and George Bromley. The latter two, originally indentured servants but now free men, had chosen to remain, doing waged work. Bromley acted mostly as personal assistant to Edward Curr. George and Abe were more comfortable with them than with the rougher men congregating around Hartley. At day's end they often talked about the state of things, about work, the situation they found themselves in, and no doubt also about their bosses.

And, in September 1832, they talked a great deal about the suicide of the surveyor, Henry Hellyer. The body had been buried almost immediately, and Curr, as the local magistrate, had conducted an inquiry the same day. A few days later, the four friends found themselves together one evening.

"It was really horrible, finding him with his head blown off like that. There was blood everywhere…"

Morton had been the first in the surveyor's room. When Hellyer had failed to turn up for breakfast, the cook asked Morton to rouse him. Getting no reply, Morton peered in the window and what he saw was enough to run for Dr. Hutchinson, who ordered him to force the door.

"I can't understand how Curr knew Hellyer was dead when I went to tell him," Morton added

"I don't believe that Hellyer took his own life," said George. "He… he just wouldn't do that." He remembered working for the surveyor and his many kindnesses, his cheer when things were difficult, his enormous energy. "Besides, him was a believin' Christian, one of the few that attended the services. It's against the bible, to kill yourself."

"Hmmm… it does seem strange," agreed Morton. "Especially as he had finished his job here, and was to go to Hobart soon to his new appointment as government surveyor. They were saying in the kitchen about how much he was looking forward to being on His Majesty's Service."

Wells laughed. "You'd be pleased too to be leavin' after seven years in this bloody place…and working for this fuckin' company. Especially when your boss is a bastard like Curr."

Bromley looked up. "I reckon he and Curr had a big falling-out that night."

"Why do you say that?" Morton asked.

"Because I saw Curr going into Hellyer's cottage that night, after Golding collected his boots."

"That wasn't mentioned in the inquiry. Besides, someone would have heard that…though it is strange that no one heard the shot, either."

George recalled that night as a particularly riotous one. That evening, the *Fanny* had called in with the mail and as usual, some rum had made it on shore despite the official sanction against it. The convicts and labourers had made the most of it.

The four men were silent for a while, each cautiously edging around their uneasy thoughts. Beyond the hut in front of which they were sitting, another wallaby fell to the hunter's gun.

"No, you wouldn't have noticed the shot. Especially not that night, with lots of gun-happy men about," Morton commented. "What do you reckon Curr and Hellyer were on about? Why do you say it was a disagreement?" he asked Bromley.

"Maybe Hellyer was planning to leave in a hurry, on the *Fanny* the next day. Just maybe he was also planning to take a lot of evidence against Curr to the governor…you know, with all this fuss now about the natives. That man Robinson had been talking a lot to Hellyer, and we all know that Gov Arthur had told him to investigate about how the Company had been shooting the blacks. Now that he no longer had a job to lose here, he could have had that in mind."

"Swayne said something about how Hellyer was reading a book that night on the treatment of natives," Morton agreed. Swayne was the Company clerk.

The men continued to sit. An unspoken thought was growing between them. Not something anyone was ready to express just yet. They all had reason to dislike Curr, who was arrogant and unpleasantly forceful, and all knew that Hellyer, also, had been the recipient of his boss's contempt. George in particular knew that Hellyer, with his moral uprightness and sensitivity to any injustice, would have been deeply concerned about the treatment of the natives. Curr had certainly condoned the killing, and possibly taken part himself. If he was to keep his well-paid job and position of power, he had much to cover up. Hellyer's evidence, if presenting it was what the latter had in mind, could indeed be very damaging to the manager.

(It is ironic that Curr's son, also Edward, after becoming a substantial settler in Victoria himself, became a real champion of the natives and spoke out openly against their killing and displacement. Edward Jnr had been left in England when the Curr family returned to Van Diemens Land in 1826, to gain an education, and was 19 before he finally rejoined his parents in Stanley. By then the natives had mostly gone from the area, but no doubt the young man would have heard some stories. How much he knew about his father's involvement in their demise, is a matter for speculation, but he grew to develop a warm sympathy for the original peoples of Australia, took a great interest in their lives and wrote down and published his extensive observations.)

The days went by and much more talk with them. It was noted that the inquiry had concentrated on some slanderous gossip about Hellyer being 'of unnatural leanings' that was rife, particularly among the convicts. It seemed odd that so much weight was given to it at the inquiry. None of the thinking men believed such a thing for a moment of Hellyer, and readily accepted Dr. Hutchinson's evidence that the surveyor had a groin wound that required regular dressing. Presently it was realised that no coroner had been called to investigate the evidence. Curr was indeed the official magistrate for the region, but given his close involvement, the proper proceeding would be to call in another opinion. The body, also, had been hurriedly buried the very next day. The government itself had doubts about Curr's actions, it seemed, for within two months he had been stripped of magisterial duties and Alfred Horne was appointed instead.

But the speculation, rumour and exaggeration continued. Was it really suicide?

"Could it be that Hellyer had taken to heart his mistake in recommending the Hampshire and Surrey Hills as good land? That really had been a disaster – thousands of valuable sheep had died there in the winter." Morton put forward this thought, and George felt that it was possible. Some of the stock keepers he talked with had personally seen that carnage.

"But if the Company was upset with Hellyer about this, why had they continued to employ him for another five years?" Bromey interjected. "And anyway, would anybody in their right mind worry that much about *this* Company?"

George wondered – Hellyer might have done just that.

George had, lately, begun to feel a little hope. By now, 1833, a large part of his sentence was behind him. Only two more years before he qualified for a ticket-of-leave! Then he could finally leave this place, and look for paid work anywhere, under the terms of the final two years' probation before full freedom was granted. He had got used to the island, the seasonal rhythms, the climate and the animals, even the hated wind. Not that there was much to like about the place, but familiarity meant his nerves were less taut.

"In Launceston I might find someone from Pontefract, that might know something about my family..."

Still young at just thirty, he very cautiously allowed himself the thought that a woman, perhaps even a wife, might actually still be within the bounds of possibility. Only two more years. He could hardly wait.

Back in Stanley after a spell working on outlying stations, Abe Wells filled him in on how Curr, not long after George's departure, had angrily demanded that all talk about the surveyor's death and the inquiry was to stop at once. As the man would readily flog any offender, this had been largely effective. But some whispering continued. How it was odd that the suicide note found in the surveyor's room had disappeared, and the only copy of it was in Curr's own handwriting. How there was uncertainty about whether the key was in the door of the fatal room. How none of the officers of the Company were prepared to talk about anything...

Only when chance found Morton, Bromley, Wells and George alone together one evening, they cautiously risked speaking more of the matter.

"I still don't think Hellyer took his own life," George said, greatly daring, and motivated by his improved outlook on life to actually stand up for the one man in Van Diemens Land that he had found worthy of admiration.

"Well, if he didn't then someone must've killed him," Wells stated the obvious. "And would ye be thinkin' of anyone in particular, wise guy?"

They all looked at him, daring him to say what they had all been thinking. He squirmed, but he had started it and he needed to know.

"Like they said at the inquiry, that the door was locked from the inside with the bolt…but…but nobody said nothin' about the window. You said you looked in it that morning, James, round the blind, *but was the window locked?*"

Morton, thus addressed, looked away. He too had had thoughts about this. Not on the day, it had all been too distressing then, but later, when things stopped adding up and he'd had time to think about it. He hesitated a moment longer, for it was risky to say anything and he neither wanted Curr's wrath nor to lose his job just yet. But he was also an honest man.

"I don't know if it was properly locked. I didn't think to look. But yes, it would have been possible for someone to shoot Hellyer, make sure the door was bolted on the inside, and then climb out of the window and pull it shut behind him."

"But what about the suicide note?" Wells put in.

Bromley answered him: "There were a lot of scratched out lines on it. They said it was a real mess, and it was put down to Mr. Hellyer being of an unsound frame of mind at the time."

"But if he wrote a suicide note, then he must've taken his life?"

"Not if someone else, who knew him well, wrote the note…"

"And then went back to the room to put it there…"

And maybe that someone had something to fear from Hellyer's going to Hobart, so he made sure that it didn't happen. Perhaps that someone had cleverly planted some rumours, so Hellyer would have something to be upset about, or maybe that someone simply lost their temper when they couldn't buy his silence, and then did a very good cover-up job. Just maybe, if that someone was in a position to do that, like perhaps the man holding the inquiry and therefore able to direct it, then maybe….

George leaned forward. "So you think C…"

The other three looked at him, but their retreat from him, from his rashness, reached him before he said the fatal name. There was simply too much to lose. It was also too destabilising to admit that the structure they lived within, this little outpost of civilisation perched so precariously on the outer fringe of a wild and savage place, was in fact rotten and with that, it challenged their very being.

They all knew it was possible. Curr was an arrogant man who ruthlessly imposed his will on others, as his own son later described him. All had seen him lose his temper and act impulsively, and then use some very devious ways to repair the damage. He could easily lie and pass the blame to others for anything, if it saved his skin. And he'd been willing to kill before, when he organised, and rode with, that hunt to 'teach the natives a permanent lesson', and had urged his men to bring back the heads of any blacks they shot.

The four men looked at each other, and knew that the price of community was to stay silent. Thus they parted, and the silence held and deepened. Whatever thoughts George had were added to the darkness already inside his head.

THE DUTCH DIJKSTRA FAMILY, 1820

Was it a vision, or a waking dream?
John Keats

10. KATRIJN'S DREAM

Katrijn sat by the window, for a brief, stolen moment resting her hands, empty of any darning or other work, in her lap. Through the glass she looked out on the street, busy with tradesmen, carts, women coming from the market with laden baskets, and beyond them, the masts of barges crowding the adjacent canal. Inner silence descended on her, the kind she knew only rarely in her busy life, and only in the shimmer of the mid-afternoon. Though she was fully awake, her normal world became faintly unreal, a lucid vision filling her senses instead. A filmy curtain was pulled aside to reveal another place – a place where people she somehow knew were bustling about doing ordinary things, and yet they were strangers at the same time. Behind them lay a verdant valley, ringed in the distance by blue mountains. It was unspeakably beautiful…

She was shocked back to reality by the cheery hello of her neighbour.

"Those are fine flowers coming up, Katrijn. You must be proud of them. And I do love the bowl they are in!"

Hendrika had entered by the open door, as she often did when passing by. Attracted by the flowers, she had not noticed the strange look on her friend's face.

"Yes, indeed, it is pretty. But not as fine as those in the order for Mr. van Wallenstein, on the Heerengracht. For his daughter's wedding, you know. He had the bowls brought over, and wants the bulbs all to flower together on the big day. But I don't know if I am going to succeed with it, and I'm so nervous having all that fine china in my house."

Katrijn's husband Willem Dijkstra was a weaver, and worked every day except Sunday for as long as daylight lasted. Despite that, their income was small and the family large, and Katrijn, who had green thumbs proved by her productive vegetable garden on a communal plot outside the city wall, had turned to making some extra guilders. Her pretty bowls of bulbs flowering in the very early spring, before nature outdoors had shrugged off its grey and dismal winter mantle, were famous and much sought after. It was not easy to get the bulbs all to flower together, requiring much moving about from a warm spot to a cooler one, finding the right level of light, and a fine sense of which bulb was doing what. Particularly famous were her mixed ones, where tulips, freesias and hyacinths bloomed fragrantly above their beds of moss. Katrijn added to their attractiveness by using most unusual, imported bowls.

The Dutch merchants of the early 17th century had sent many navigators in search of the spices, silk, sandalwood, and other exotic luxuries that were to be found in the Far East. In Amsterdam, by the 1820's, many including Katrijn's brother Kaspar Tehrendt were benefitting from such trade links. He had some minor investments in the Dutch East India Company, and thus was able to alert Katrijn when a shipment of the pretty blue and white bowls from China had arrived. For her, it seemed a lot of money to invest in what was an uncertain venture, and she could not have started with it without Kaspar's generous financial help.

It paid off in time, her fragrant bowls soon famous in the town as a desirable spring gift, and now one of the fine folk from the Heerengracht had placed this special order with her. He wanted twelve of them for daughter's wedding table. The bowls from his household's china had been brought to her house three months ago, so she would have time to bring them to their finest at the right moment. Even Mr von Wallenstein's fancy gardeners on his country estate could not do what she could! It was an order to die for, likely to bring much future custom, and he would pay her well for her artistry.

But right now, Katrijn was more inclined to curse the bulbs and their bowls. Heavily pregnant with her eighth child, moving them around all the time was hard work. Their small house had only two windows properly facing south, at which she could effectively nurse the bulbs in the feeble winter light. Both were in upstairs rooms, crowded already with beds, and the children were cross and fraught at having such precious items to try not to bump into, in the already insufficient space. The two oldest, Miriam and Theodor, were temporarily sleeping downstairs in the kitchen on makeshift bundles. The best room in the house, on the ground floor and with a sunny window, was occupied by two spinsters, one a sister of her mother's and one from Willem's family. The frail old ladies could not be expected to tiptoe round such an inconvenience.

And would she manage to have them all ready and flowering when they were meant to? Failure would be terrible. There was also the worry of the fine china – what if one of the precious pieces got broken? She could never pay for it, she knew, and she was half wishing she had never been given the job in the first place.

However, the bowl that her neighbour Hendrika was commenting on was not one of von Wallenstein's, but one she had chosen herself the previous autumn in the big warehouse. Every year, she had one in her front window, and this one was not for sale, but for her family's delight and the pleasure of the passers-by. As the first flowers began to bloom, the word spread, and people came by to see them. She always readily sold any other bowls she had prepared, blessing her brother for his encouragement.

The extra money made life much easier; they had several better furnishings and could afford better cloth for the clothes she made. All the children were able to go to school, and were decently dressed. Now, they were hoping to put down the necessary guilders for an apprenticeship for Theodor.

"You'll be fine with it," encouraged her friend Hendrika.

They helped each other out, these two doughty, uncomplaining women, often sitting together whilst sewing and watching the littlest ones. Katrijn was the classic blue-eyed blonde with her thick hair wound in a heavy plait around her head. Both women, now in their late twenties, were mildly round and fleshed-out after bearing large families. They were inordinately proud that they were managing to be above the poverty level, able to rent small but nice houses in a respectable street. Katrijn had, in the opinion of her family, married 'down' with Willem who had no material goods to offer his bride, but in Dutch fashion they gave him time to prove himself, and he turned out a decent and sober enough fellow who worked hard.

It was to Hendrika that Katrijn had confessed her longing to be out of the city of Amsterdam. She wanted to go to Groeningen, where her family had come from thirty years ago, and where she still had relatives.

"Aunt Minna writes that they have so much space there; you can have a garden by your house. Not like here, where we have to go outside the city walls for even a small plot." Katrijn dreamt of a little house surrounded by a garden, full of wonderful flowers, roses even, and dahlias...

"But it's colder up there in the North," cautioned Hendrika. "And there's no work. Isn't that why the Tehrendts came here in the first place?"

She was referring to Katrijn's family, who had left the northern town during a period of stagnation, to seek better work conditions in the lively hub of Amsterdam. The big city with a good harbour and excellent banking houses very interested in providing credit for commerce, remained lively even as the country's golden age faded away. Katrijn was born there. Never having seen anything other than tall and crowded houses, she had a longing for wide and uncluttered spaces, for the sound of the real, unfettered sea, and above all for that garden.

"Yes," she agreed with a sigh. "There's no chance of going there, I know."

And she had much to be grateful for. All of them were healthy, and the older four were by now able to help around the house. There was enough to eat; they could put a penny or two in the alms box, and occasionally buy a precious book or some sheets of music. Of an educated class, family evenings gathered over songs or readings were their delight. Katrijn came from a staunch Protestant background. The love of God, daily prayers, a humble and thankful attitude, and compassion for others were unquestioned basics of their life.

Once a year, the mother made her children go through their small possessions, and each one had to find something to give to a child in greater need. On one such occasion her littlest daughter Minna had nothing to spare. Her only toy consisted of a treasured doll with a cracked china face. Mother wouldn't surely make her part with that one? It was a terrible dilemma. Minna sat for a long time in a dark corner, hugging the doll, and praying for an answer. But God did not speak, and eventually the little girl descended the stairs in tears, and tremblingly held out the doll to her mother. Katrijn understood, touched that Minna was willing to sacrifice so much for some unknown child who might have no doll at all. What to do? Her daughter's decision, arrived at after so much agonizing, would have to be honoured, but to take her only toy away altogether was very hard. What would Jesus do, wondered Katrijn, and she remembered that a coat could also be shared.

"What about we give your doll's dress as a present? Some poor child might not have anything to dress her dolly in…"

Later that day, the mother and littlest daughter sat together, just the two of them in rare and precious companionship. Katrijn found a small scrap of spare cloth, and showed Minna how to take the first few stitches to make a new dress for her doll. From then on, they shared special moments on a regular basis; many years later when Minna as an old woman looked back, she counted those times as the most precious in her early life.

God had spoken after all.

Katrijn made coffee for her neighbour, and agreed that the wedding bowl project was worth the effort and inconvenience.

"The money will pay the guild fees for Theodor's apprenticeship, and the tools he will need to get started. He wants to be a jeweler, you know."

Older daughter Miriam was becoming a fine cook and would no doubt marry soon; the van der Woude boy had been visiting quite often lately and her daughter's blushes had not escaped Katrijn. Well, that would be fine; he was a proper young man from a God-fearing family. But it was a bit soon as Miriam was barely fifteen – they would have to wait a little while. And so it would go, all her children starting their own separate lives. The mother hoped that God would let them remain well, and their children would live and be without any real want. More, she did not ask, for more was not necessary.

But, dear God, it would be so nice to have a garden round my house, thought Katrijn. She remembered the strange moment earlier in the day when, as if from behind a veil, an unknown place had been revealed to her – with valleys and mountains that she, a person of the endlessly flat Netherlands, had never seen yet felt strangely at home in. She did not know that, 186 years earlier, one of her own countrymen, one Abel Tasman, had briefly sighted that place of the blue mountains and green valleys. He had called it Van Diemens Land.

PART
TWO

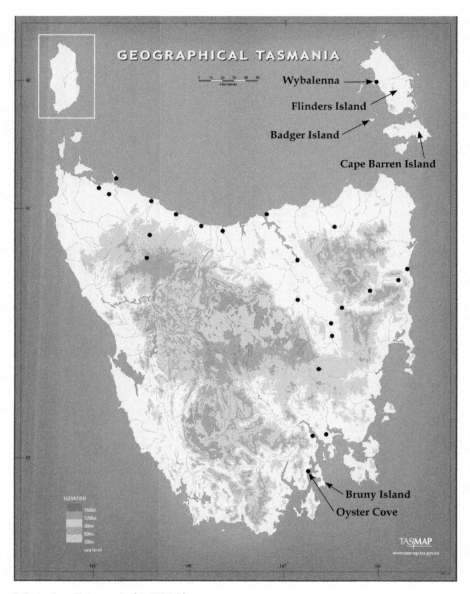

Map 4 – *Tasmania by 1880's*

The group of islands around Flinders were extremely isolated by the highly dangerous sea surrounding them. Shifting sandbanks, strong currents and violent storms were frequent. Infamous for wrecks, to date over 200 are known, including one of the earliest, the *Sydney Cove* on Preservation Island in 1797. Attempts to salvage her cargo (mostly rum) brought the existence of plentiful seals on the islands to general notice, and started the sealing trade that nearly exterminated them inside 20 years.

THE ABORIGINES 1829 – 1886

LUCY BEETON

"[The Aborigine] Walter George Arthur represented something altogether different and ultimately more challenging. He was able to successfully synthesize Aboriginal identity with Christianity and European education. His career pointed the way to the possibilities of the future rather than the past; the politics of rights rather than those of guilt. He appealed to the principles of British and colonial society – he wanted justice, not pity."
From: 'Fate of a Free People', by Henry Reynolds, in a reference to Walter Arthur, a full-blood Aboriginal who had as a boy been sent to the Orphan School in Hobart

11. I KNOW YOU WILL BETRAY ME

ON BADGER ISLAND, BASS STRAIT, APRIL 1885

"We shall not meet again on this earth, Reverend Brownrigg."

The old lady extended her hand.

"But Miss Beeton! Don't say such a thing! We still have much to do...."

The usual conventionalities died away as her direct remark caused him to look at her searchingly, for the first time actually seeing her in the fullness of her humanity. They had worked side by side for fourteen years, in what had seemed a common cause, but now she had cut through all that. There was no yielding in her eyes, framed by the old black face. Shocked and shamed, he reached for both her hands and held them.

"Miss Beeton....Lucy...."

***

Just over one year later, in May 1886, Lucy was sitting by the window of her neat cottage on Badger Island. Age and her huge bulk now often obliged her to rest idly like this, but she didn't mind, for before her lay a grand vista of ever-changing interest. The sea – at the moment calm and gentle – looked like a quilt of dark velvet pieces interspersed with shiny satin ones, the sun winking off the wavelets. White lines creamed along the shores of Chappell Island to her left, and directly in front of her lay the panorama of the Strzelecki Mountains on Flinders Island, some three miles across the water from Lucy's gaze. How often had she seen the same scene in storms, wild and threatening, and had waited, sick with fear, for news of missing boats and men.

Bass Strait, 200 km wide, is the narrow channel between mainland Australia and Tasmania, in which the immense powers of the Indian Ocean in the west and those of the eastern Tasman Sea collide. It is also a notoriously dangerous waterway. Originally dry land, it was swamped by the rising seas around 12,000 years ago, and its lack of oceanic depth can create immense waves in no time at all. Tides rush savagely between the many islands, half-submerged rocks, reefs, shifting sandbars – all requiring the utmost skill to even go near. The locals, living daily in these conditions, had become legendary as some of the world's most skilled and daring boatmen.

But there were still accidents, men drowned and smashed on rocks and never found. Even the most experienced of men can suddenly find themselves in unexpected difficulties. Beginning in the 1840's, much-needed lighthouses were built on Swan, Goose, and Deal Islands. They are remarkable, well-engineered structures, made under huge difficulties by convict labour; it was hoped they would reduce the huge number of wrecks. The worst had been the *Cataraqui* in 1846, smashing into the rocks of King Island on the western end of the Strait. Of 423 persons, mostly immigrant females and children from England, only nine survived.

The sheer inaccessibility of these wild islands made them for some time the sole domain of the white sealers, landed by merchant ships from Sydney and Hobart from 1798 on. The many thousands of seals, taken in unrestricted manner for their oil and skins, were decimated inside twenty years, so the trading ships stopped coming. A few of the men stayed anyway, some because they had nowhere else to go, and others because they liked the wild remote life, well away from the authorities. But not all of them were desperate men or runaway convicts.

Among them were some educated men from good families, who had either fallen foul of the law in their younger years or found a personal freedom away from the restrictions of polite society. Such men were Thomas Tucker, Richard Maynard, and Thomas Beeton. Most had changed their names, seeking anonymity, and – after some wild years among gangs and convicts – began to settle in the Islands, building small cottages, cultivating gardens, keeping pigs, chickens, and goats. Later, they added sheep and a few cattle, but their primary income was in trading seal and kangaroo skins, mutton bird eggs, oil, feathers and some garden produce.

Naturally they also wanted wives, but none of the few white girls available would have been willing to come to such primitive conditions. Besides, the men had a reputation for being the scum of the earth, and – while there were without doubt some really rough and low characters among them – this view was continually and indiscriminately reinforced by frustrated authorities who could not control this outlying group of people.

So the sealers turned to the only women who were to be found – the natives of Van Diemens Land and New Holland. One man even brought a woman from India. There were stories of forcible abductions and the summary killing of native men who objected, and some cases of women bartered for produce or dogs. But there were also many situations – perhaps the majority – where women agreed to go with these men, as part of trading deals and exchanges, probably initially intended for a period of time only. These women were skilled at managing the dogs to hunt and kill kangaroos, and in pegging and drying the skins for trade. Some suffered greatly, being subjected to sexual slavery and harsh treatment, but others found homes and shelter with the men, and gradually some stable families were formed. These became known as the Straitsmen, and their offspring labelled 'half castes'.

***

'Lucy', the good Reverend Brownrigg had called her when momentarily shocked into realizing that she was not just a charitable project for his church's missionary society. She did not blame him for this, knowing well from bitter experience that white men – even this good man, who genuinely exerted himself on behalf of her people – were caught up by the idea that dark-skinned natives simply didn't entirely count. Even less so the half-castes like herself, doubly cursed – it was believed – by all that was weak and low from both white and black. How would he have looked at her if they really had met once more? She already knew, as his boat sailed out of sight that April in 1885, that it would not happen. A hacking cough frequently racked his too-thin frame, his fine sensitive face often tight with pain. He would not be able to stay in this demanding environment for much longer. As for herself, she too would soon be gone. The old people had appeared to her several times lately.

Had it not been completely unthinkable, she would have embraced him as they said goodbye and prayed the Lord's mercy on him. The agony of a long lingering death, her own father's fate, was familiar enough to her. Spare him, dear God, she had thought, and let him die easily.

"My father," Lucy now thought, her chair creaking as she adjusted herself more comfortably by the window. "You were a good man too… you were not anointed by God, as the good Reverend is supposed to be, but you had more love in your heart for us than he. You stood up for justice, too."

Sitting together with Truganini and the other Aborigines, at Wybalenna on Flinders Island in the 1840's, they had exchanged their stories. Lucy's own was one of the luckier ones:

I was born on Guncarriage Island in 1829, and my mother was Emerenna, more generally called Bet Smith. She came from the Cape Portland Tribe, in the North East of Tarena. When she was still very young, the sealer John Harrington abducted her. He was later drowned, and another sealer, Thomas Tucker, got hold of Mother. She had two boys to him, and told me that she deliberately killed them both. How some of our people at first feared those half-breed children! Some had our beautiful dark skin but a mop of red hair or such strange blue eyes! But those children were also all we had to love. I think Tucker was real rough with Mother. He sold her around 1825 to my father. That's just what some of these sealers did with us – we didn't count as anything better than some property. Sometimes they did real worse things to us, too…

But Mother was actually lucky in this. My Father was a kind and decent man. He treated her really well. We were living on Guncarriage Island at the time, my parents and me and my brother James, and two more were born after we had moved to Launceston. In 1831, when Robinson brought out to these islands all our remaining tribes that he had collected from around Tarena, he issued an order that all the sealer's native women were to be delivered up to him. But my mother did not want to leave Father. He successfully wrote to the Governor in Hobart, asking that he might have his native woman Emerenna returned to him from Robinson, showing that she had a decent home with him.

When Robinson turned up, he also demanded that all sealers living on Guncarriage leave their homes so he, Robinson, could have the entire island to settle our tribes on. All the families, including ours, were forced off, and while most made do as best they could on nearby islands, Father decided to go all the way to Launceston.

He had good reasons for doing so. His real name wasn't actually Beeton, but Thomas Herbert and he had come from a family of goldsmiths in London. An educated man, trained in commerce, in a moment of youthful madness he had committed the theft of a ring that he had expected to replace 'in a sure deal' that went wrong. Caught and convicted in June 1817, he was shipped out on the Lady

Castlereagh in December to Van Diemens Land, where he worked off his sentence, mostly in Launceston where he was initially assigned to the constabulary, and then as clerk in a merchant's warehouse. Having completed his time without further blemish to his character, he received his ticket of leave in 1825. There is also a story that he had taken part in a mutiny on the ship, along with his mate James Everett, but Father never mentioned that bit to me so I don't really know the truth of it. Work opportunities then had brought him out to these Islands, possibly because that same Everett was also out here, already sealing, and had suggested he join him. And of course it was out here where he met my mother.

So Father knew Launceston quite well. Although he had been there as a convict, he had got on well with his master. His main reason for going back there, however, was that he had received word from a ship's captain that this same merchant was searching for him, on account of an inheritance. This merchant had trading and banking links with London, and had been charged with finding the ex-convict. When we arrived, Father learned that he was to receive a modest sum of money every year. There was also a parcel with some gifts, and for many years these would continue to come, including each time a fine dress in the latest London fashion, for his wife. The good merchant, on hearing that Beeton had a family, had sent this news to England.

Was Father tempted to return to England at this point? I have often wondered. He now had the means, but he never did. Nor did he ever speak about it. Who knows how he stood with his English family, the Herberts, and whether they had disowned him? His annual remittance was from an aunt. He probably realised well enough how his relations in England might have turned away from him if he had appeared with a coloured wife, and half-caste children, and he was not prepared to abandon them here in order to seek his own re-entry into English society.

Whatever his innermost thoughts, he decided to stick with what he had created, his family here. With the help of the remittance, and a job he now secured as clerk in a warehouse, Father was able to rent a pleasant house on the fringe of the town. I remember it well. He kept a small library, and taught me my letters. We sat together of an evening, while I learned to shape the alphabet on a piece of slate, and Mother would be nearby, listening intently. She spoke little English, you see – and Father of course had none of her language. They seemed to understand each other perfectly well, all the same. By 1837 I had three siblings, James, Henry and little Jane. Father wanted them to attend school, too, the one I was already at, and we should have been able to live a normal life that way.

Given his education and pleasant manner, he might have overcome the slur of his convict past, but white society was not going to forgive him for having a native 'wife'. That men should be cohabiting with Aboriginal women was an accepted situation, but for her to be in the same status as a real wife was not to be tolerated. No member of Launceston society would have us in their home. Even at church we were shunned. It was soon clear that we would not be able to attend school in peace, either. Even though I loved learning and was a good student, the other children taunted and mocked me for my dark skin and the teacher really did nothing much to prevent it. The hatred of the native was too strong. Some individuals here and there were friendly, but not as a group. Perversely, they would have taken Father in, even with open arms, had he abandoned Emerenna and us children. Yet white man claims that in his god's sight all men are equal! I could only admire Father for his principles that did not allow him to do this. The temptation to return to his own society must have been there – he could have made good, or started over elsewhere such as in Sydney, forgotten the past and become respectable.

Father got to have no time for the church and its hypocritical ministers. He had more courage than they, too. One day I was playing out in the street with James when some white children began to jeer and throw sticks. Father, happening to return home at that moment, told them off and safely shepherded us back to our house. He took me, and all our family, seriously and stood by us despite being rejected by his own kind, and I loved him so for it.

Mother, also, suffered. In the town, she was completely cut off from all social contact, from her own tribe as well as the people of the town. Nor did those fancy dresses that kept arriving from England, which Father had at great expense altered for her, help any. In fact, they seemed to draw more outrage than anything else, as if the latest fashion seen on a 'darkie' were the final insult. Of course, Mother could not sew or darn, and was struggling to learn how to cook English food on a wood stove. Father would patiently show her how to make a stew. Bravely she tried, but it was hard going. I often saw her crying over another failed attempt. But worst for Mother was being confined in a small house with no natural open spaces around her. We did have a garden, in which she spent a lot of her time with the little ones, but it was fenced and gave her no real sense of being out in the open.

Eventually, Father decided to move back to Guncarriage Island, to escape the discrimination and where the proximity of the sea and coast would provide the freedom his wife so bitterly missed. But it was too late for her. Already on the journey back out, Mother started coughing. She had caught – perhaps from the crowded unhealthy conditions in town, or maybe it was the social rejection she encountered there – the dreaded lung complaint. Within very few weeks she had died, like so many of her own people, unstoppably wasting away, and leaving Father with the four of us. She was buried on the Island. I was then thirteen years of age, and to me fell the all daily care of the two boys and the youngest, Jane, barely five.

Father tried hard not to let bitterness overtake him. In one thing he was determined: his children should not suffer any more for their half-caste status than he could help. Being back on the Islands, among other families of the same kind, was an improvement, for here we were all the same.

Robinson, after turning us out of our homes six years earlier, had meanwhile moved our gathered tribes to Flinders Island, eventually settling them at Wybalenna. Our original cottage, though badly battered both by Robinson's use of it as well as the wild storms of these parts, was still there, and after some restoration useable.

Other families like ours were coming back to Guncarriage, too, and others were living on islands close by. It was great for us – we loved the new freedom and here we finally had proper playmates.

Father also set himself to teaching all of us, for there was no school, and he was glad he could spare some time for this, due to his remittance income. All of us were to have the advantage of a proper education, not only in the three R's but also in business. He developed his own trading in skins, produce and sheep, and taught me the keeping of the books. He took me with him on boat trips to Launceston, to visit the merchants and get supplies. Like most Islanders, he built his own boat, and James and Henry soon learnt the handling of tools and timber.

He became a respected member among the several Straitsmen families, valued for his kindly and generous nature. He willingly shared his business ability, taking other men's produce and getting them a decent price.

A much closer market for our produce, particularly for potatoes, was at Robinson's village, Wybalenna. I remember my first trip there as though it was yesterday. I'd heard of it, of course, but the reality of meeting so many who were not only like Mother, but who were close kin to her also, was overwhelming. There I found aunts and uncles and other relatives. I heard their stories, and those of others, and most of them were so sad. Dispossession, rape and murder. Rejection and betrayal. The plains and valleys filled with wailing spirits unable to go home. Though there was joy in finding relatives, there were more tears than anything else. And worst of all was that the dying was still going on, even here in Wybalenna that was supposed to be a refuge for my people.

"A temporary situation to keep you safe," Robinson had told the great Chief Manalargenna, "only until we can sort out an area for you to manage your own lives in peace on Tarena, and then you can return."

But it was never carried out, that promise. Not for the few remaining of my people, and certainly not for the half-castes like myself.

Lucy sighed and shifted in her chair. Outside, the view was changing as another of the frequent fronts blotted away the glittering waves and the air cooled. Rain would be falling shortly. Only a brief shower, Lucy thought, deeply familiar as she was with this sea. Many times had she sat in a boat herself, travelling to Launceston or among the Islands, sometimes in serious peril. For all its danger, she loved it, its wild beauty daily another reason for praising God.

Would Brownrigg, that man of God, have accepted her father, if he had met him? Lucy wondered, knowing that among white men one who had been a convict was often spurned, no matter how well and decently he rebuilt his life. But her father had a gentle nature, an educated manner of speech and was most insistent on keeping cleanly personal habits. Brownrigg would probably have overcome his prejudices with Thomas Beeton. But that man's half-caste daughter, born of a dark-skinned native woman? No matter how well-read, how clever, kindly, honest and proper Lucy was, this man of the church would not see her as his true equal, even though she genuinely believed in the same God as he.

When the representatives of the Anglican Church started coming to the Islands, first Bishop Nixon, then the Rev Fereday with Archdeacon Reibey, and now Brownrigg, it had seemed so hopeful. At last someone official, with a respected presence at Government House, was taking an interest in their well-being. These men had taken their requests and petitions to the Governor. They openly argued for the need for school teachers and churches for the half-castes, helped them with land lease issues, and in some cases established useful trading links for her community's produce in Launceston.

Lucy was at first overjoyed, collaborating enthusiastically. But over time she realized that she, and her beloved families, many of whom were true believing Christians and lived sober lives, were never actually asked about their own concerns. Bishop Nixon had taken tea with her, in her own cottage several times, and described her "as the greatest lady it was ever my privilege to meet". But what use was that, when the bishop was convinced that he, and only he, knew what was best for them?

Lucy sighed again. All her life she had fought for acceptance for her kin and her community, who were making decent lives in such difficult circumstances. Now, as she herself prepared to die, she had to accept that it would never happen. Could she have done something differently? Sitting back in her armchair in her pretty cottage with the million-dollar view, Lucy went back to her reminiscences.

We were luckier than most, what with Father's small but steady income. He rebuilt and extended the old cottage on the island. All the fencing had to be replaced, before any cultivation could be done, and then we got some sheep. Our home was nicely placed, sheltered in a hollow behind the dunes. Being near the beach was important – much of our life centered on the sea and our boat, for trade and staying in touch with the other families. On Woody Island were the Maynards and Everetts, on Tin Kettle the Smiths, and a bit further away, on Long Island, was the Mansell family. Others on Clarke and Cape Barren Islands, also turned up at times.

There were lots of emergencies – men caught in storms, ship wrecks, sudden illness and accidents. We helped each other as best we could. No doctor here – getting to one in Launceston, even if we could have afforded it, could take several days depending on the weather, and a rough ride with it. Anyone really sick wouldn't survive that. It was best to treat them where they were. Father got several books about how to do it; one even had a section on child-birth. I studied all of it, and later helped many a baby into the world. Sometimes you could only watch someone die, when the injuries were too bad, like the man who got washed ashore from a wreck, so smashed about on the rocks that his flesh was torn off and he hadn't a whole bone in him. All we could do was wrap him in a blanket and pray for him. Real awful too was watching the last agonies of snakebite. Sucking out the poison only worked if you got there quick enough. There are lots of snakes on the Islands, those big black tiger ones, real dangerous they are.

There were fleas too, millions of them, brought in by the dogs. As our people got taken away from Tarena, the dogs stayed behind in the bush and bred. There were so many in the end, the governor in Hobart put a tax on any owned ones, and many who couldn't afford to pay up either shot or dumped them on the Islands instead. The dogs didn't survive long, but their fleas did well enough and for years it was a constant battle to keep them out of the house.

Father specially got some housekeeping books for Jane and me, knowing how Mother had never learnt any of these things. I could already do some basic stitching before we left the town, and we carefully studied the construction of each of the wonderful dresses that came every year in the parcel from England. How I longed to keep them, for they were always beautiful, but they were no use out here on the Islands. So Jane and I unpicked them, and turned the fabric into sensible skirts and jackets. We learned a lot that way, and soon could sew all the usual things needed in the household. Father would take the lace and other trimmings to Launceston on his next trip to sell, and with some of the money he always got us something special. As we got older, he allowed us to keep some of the fancy lace and beadingss, so we each could have one good dress. It was just as well that I learnt to sew, for when I was fifteen my body started to swell and I got real big and had to make special clothes to fit me for the rest of my life.

In the same parcel there would sometimes be a ladies' magazine, showing fancy clothes and ladies sitting in carriages or even on horseback, wearing hats with feathers and pictures of houses and gardens like we had never seen before. Father explained about the big town of London and how people lived there, and it all sounded so wonderful. But he always finished by saying how glad he was to be away from there, and to be here with us instead.

"Our life here is simple, and we haven't got any fancy things, but it is true and honest and we can stand upright before any man," he would say.

So we worked hard and kept ourselves and our cottage clean, and learnt always to speak the truth.

We had lots of fun too. When the chores were done, Jane and I went with James and Henry to play, most usually along the beach, and often the children of those families who lived nearby, the Riddles and the Kelly boy, would join us too. In the evenings, we'd repeat our lessons and Father would listen carefully, correcting any mistakes and explaining things to us. He held a small school once a week for as many of the children that could get to us, which was on different days depending on the weather – the boats couldn't always come over if the sea was too heavy. We had some books – only a few for they were expensive and not many could be bought anyway – so they were mostly practical ones about seamanship and husbandry, but Father said never mind, it's still good English and you need to learn, so we would take turns to read out loud. Just occasionally a real story book would come our way, which was very exciting. I remember 'Robinson Crusoe' in particular, about a man who got stuck on an island. We could have told him a lot about how to survive!

One day, word came to us that someone from his Herbert family in England had come as far as Launceston to look for him.

"He's sent Captain Greatbatch out to the Islands to look for you," we heard.

Father watched carefully for that captain to show up, but when he did, we were caught unawares, being out in a boat. Father signaled to the man to go away, that he didn't want to have communication, and some said later that he threw a sail over us, so he wouldn't have to be ashamed of his coloured half-native children before the captain who would report back to the relative waiting in town. But that's just malicious and jealous gossip. If Father was hiding us from anyone, it was to protect us from the racist label that we would inevitably be given. I don't know what the captain said when he got back to Launceston, but the relative apparently went back to England and from then on, the annual parcels stopped coming. I suppose for all Father's efforts, the word had got out anyway. This would have been a bit before Bishop Nixon first showed up, in 1854.

Some years earlier Thomas Beeton had applied for a lease of Badger Island. The community was beginning to settle down, developing some trading patterns, and the value of grazing leases, as well as the mutton-bird rookeries, were recognized as their most likely avenues of survival, now that the seals had been largely decimated. However, the application was turned down on the grounds that Badger might be needed for a lighthouse. (It was, in fact, built in 1846 by convicts on neighbouring Goose Island.) A factor was probably that the government was not anxious to legitimize a community that had long evaded regulation. This changed somewhat after surveyor-general Robert Powel made two visits, to decide the future uses of the Islands. He took an unusually positive view of the community there:

"… I find them kind and gentle, upon the whole I consider them a primitive and amiable people, and believe that the greatest harmony prevails among them. The men are excellent boatmen and possess a capital description of a whaleboat…every encouragement should be given to a class of men most invaluable as pilots."

His second visit, in 1854, was with Bishop Nixon. The Islanders had applied to Governor Denison for a teacher-catechist to educate their children, the cost to be met from a fund that had been set aside for assistance "to the poor natives of Tasmania". It was refused on the grounds that they "could not be fairly termed Aborigines", despite there being at the time at least seven full-blood native women among them. However, Denison suggested that the Anglican Church might take an interest in the Islanders' welfare, and so the Bishop came out on Powel's second trip.

He agreed with the surveyor.

"The Islanders have an air of quiet domestic union, and an innocence of drunkenness and theft…"

He was made aware of the problems facing the Straitsmen, the main one being the increasing occupation of the islands by white men who were bringing sheep and cattle out to graze. This damaged the mutton-bird rookeries, and interfered with the annual birding. With two sympathetic reports arriving at Government House, finally some efforts were made, resulting in a few modest leases to half-caste families, including a part of Badger Island for Thomas Beeton.

On this visit, Bishop Nixon stayed with Thomas Tucker and his Indian wife Maria on Guncarriage Island. He visited every home within reach, including the Beeton's, where he noted that Lucy, now twenty-five, had become the teacher for the Island children. Nixon had an ample demonstration of the Straitsmen's vital community, as more and more boats arrived, all coming for the announced divine service – the first ever to be performed in the Straits by an official clergyman. Twenty eight adults crowded into Tucker's house, whose bedroom had to be opened to accommodate them (it was very severe weather at the time), and in the bishop's own words:

"…a more quiet, orderly, and attentive gathering I never witnessed…… there was a deep earnestness, too, with which my half-caste congregation joined in the several parts of the service, that I should be glad to witness in more educated and polished gatherings of Christian worshippers."

He observed further that they had taken the prayer-book as their guide, and were not too proud to kneel, and that they could sing the hymns with an accuracy and fervour that 'would have done credit to a well-trained village choir'.

What Nixon's innermost thoughts were about this astonishing find – a truly Christian and believing community in a place widely reviled as disreputable and savage – he did not convey to his diary. From later chance remarks we do know that he found it difficult to reconcile it with his ideas about the half-caste character. In time, Lucy made the painful insight that perhaps this was the bigger problem than her dark skin – the fact that she, and most of the half-caste families here, were living better Christian lives than many of the whites did.

He just couldn't come at it, and I guess he – and all the others after him – handled it by imagining us as children, easily led and too innocent to discriminate. What did he think – that someone had chanced to throw us a bible and we believed it because we knew no better? Did he not wonder how our belief, so strong back then – it really held us together in those early days – had come about, and how it was that we had studied the word of God and lived by it?

It had come to us, that real true believing in the love of God, through one of our own people, Walter George Arthur, one of the Ben Lomond Tribe who was at Wybalenna while I was visiting there regularly. Walter was a really special person.

He was the son of Rolepa, the Ben Lomond Chief, and had been stolen from his tribe as a small child. Up to about twelve or so, he was on the streets of Launceston with other riffraff, surviving on petty theft. Someone reported him to Robinson, who sent him to the boys' orphan school in Hobart. He probably took a bad knocking there, but at least he had several other young ones from our people with him, including Peter and David, sons of Woorrady. Walter did cope, though, not only by being tough, but he turned out to be really clever. He learnt to read and write real quick, and do his numbers, just like Father had taught me. It was there that he found a real, living belief, and when he was brought back to Wybalenna in 1835 he was all fired up. At 16, he already had a good authority and some white people respected him, especially the missionaries. He taught some of our people to cipher and read, and led them in religious services. Most of the older ones could not understand him, and had many arguments with him about God. They felt it would be a betrayal to accept a white man's god, given how much harm and damage had been done to them, but Walter consistently conducted himself with so much dignity and justice that they had to respect that, even if they couldn't fathom it.

Walter also edited and produced a small newspaper for Wybalenna, in which he further exhorted his beliefs. The paper was literate and intelligent, proving without doubt that black people were as capable of intelligent reasoning as any white man.

It was here at Wybalenna where Walter finally met his father again, old Rolepa, and many other kin.

It was to us half-castes, especially the younger ones like myself, who were at Wybalenna regularly with produce to sell, that Walter's belief made sense. We did not know anything much of our mothers' old stories, and mostly we spoke our fathers' English anyway. Not that many of them were serious about religion, and my own Father, of course, had by then retreated in bitter disappointment from anything to do with the church. But he was fair and let me talk to my brothers and sister about it, and the other children too, and bit by bit it took hold among the families. It was not just a consolation, but a structure that filled our lives with a real meaning. We started sharing bible readings and hymn singing. That was why we were so excited when Bishop Nixon came and held the first proper service for us. Father refused to commit to the end of his days, but he acknowledged that if living sober and decent lives was the result of such belief, then he was alright with that.

"You seem to be doing a better job at living it than some of those clergymen can manage," he would say.

I am glad he died before it all came apart and so many lawless and vile men came amongst us with their alcohol and deceiving ways. They brought a corruption that we could not stand against for long. It really started with the wreck of the <u>George Marshall</u> in 1862...

12. THESE WERE MY PEOPLE

Lucy shivered as ghosts began to crowd into her memories:

At Wybalenna I found so many of my kin, apart from Walter's understanding of real Christianity. Walter himself had gone, along with several other of our people and his wife Mary Anne, with Robinson to Port Phillip in 1838, but it was a disastrous trip and those who survived came back to Wybalenna in 1842. That's when I first started going there, and I met him – and so many others.

Here was an aunt of mine, known as Mother Brown, from the same Cape Portland tribe as my mother.

Here was Mary Ann, now married to Walter Arthur, and Fanny, too, both daughters of Tarenootairer, also from that tribe.

Here in 1842 were the 76 remaining relatives of hundreds of other tribespeople who hadn't even made it this far, who had been shot or died of the mysterious lung disease. 73 had died at Wybalenna before I started visiting, and 22 more during the next five years. Among them also were the memories of Tom Kickerterpoller and of Tekartee, and I learned that the latter's boy, Harry, was growing up right here on the Islands with his father Myteye, another sealer, that dark man from New Zealand. In time, I got to know Harry well. He lived at Killiecrankie Bay on Flinders, and did a lot of boat work around the place with the fine little craft he'd built, the Dora.

And here also they remembered Pagerly, who had held Kicker-terpoller in his distress at loosing Tekartee, and later had cradled his shivering, dying body to her at the back of the store shed in Emu Bay. Brave Pagerly, who was on the last mission to round up our peoples when she made a bid, along with another woman, for freedom down on the West Coast. Both were caught, and Robinson ordered them sent to Wybalenna, but she disappeared somewhere along the way. Did she, too, die of a broken heart like Tom?

Over the settlement also hung the shadow of the famous chief Manalargenna, who had died here a few years earlier, in 1835, already knowing his fate as he stood on the ship's deck for his final journey away from his ancestral lands. He had The Sight, you see. Crying and howling he was, the great man, forced by circumstances to put his people's fate into the uncertain hands of the man Robinson who ultimately betrayed them. All he could do was hope that some might survive, and I, Lucy, am one of them... And, equally restless beside Manalargenna, roamed the lost spirit of his wife, Tanleboneyer. Both had walked with Tom, and she was the sister to his Tekartee... I also learnt that Nimerana, who lived with our neighbour John Thomas on Cape Barren Island, was a daughter of Mannalargenna.

For me, a whole new family and many close connections opened up, and for the rest of my life, I worked for those that remained here, my people, fighting for recognition, for access to hunting, grazing and rookeries, education, and sometimes simply for the right to be who we were.

And then there was Truganini herself...

Lucy the old woman, soon to die herself, stirred in her seat by the cottage window. Her memory of Truganini was sharp, indelible. How she had grieved for that once strong, active woman, who had followed Robinson on all his journeys, believing him to be their saviour, a white who had their real interests at heart. Truganini's desolation, when banishment and rejection was all they actually got, was terrible to see.

During the four years that Lucy was visiting at Wybalenna, she often sat beside that older woman, seeing her despair at all hope finally lost. All her people there were steadily fading away. Lucy tried to make them some extra jackets, for they were often in damp clothing. But she was already so busy with the teaching, house-keeping, helping her father in the business and cultivating the garden, that it was not easy. Nor could she show the older ladies how to sew for themselves – it was too alien, too nit-picking for those whose life had revolved around hunting and climbing trees and diving the waters – always nude and natural. For them, it was simply too late.

Things meanwhile were changing for the Beeton family. Their fifty-acre grant on Badger Island meant that Thomas and his sons were spending much time there, building a cottage, erecting fencing, creating a suitable jetty, and all the other preparations required for a permanent move. Lucy often had to manage on her own with the younger Jane, who was growing up and making eyes at George, one of the Everett boys. This was not too difficult, because both Lucy's brothers were also interested in the daughters of that particular family, and there were many trips between Guncarriage and Woody Islands. Presently there were three marriages, two solemnized in George Town by the Rev. Fereday, and Henry Beeton's ceremony in Launceston. All parties insisted it be done properly, in church, even though this involved uncertain boat trips at the weather's mercy, and the Reverend's fees had to be saved up carefully, too. But they all did it.

Lucy and her father settled permanently on Badger around 1860, into the same cottage that she was now sitting in. It was comfortable, neat and always scrupulously clean, the kettle singing on the hob ready for the unfailingly friendly welcome any visitor experienced there. Her brother James and his wife Rachel had nine children, and came over frequently. Brother Henry and his Sarah – another Everett girl – moved onto Badger, also. Often in the summer, many families congregated on Badger for weeks on end, so the children could be taught by Lucy. It was also enjoyable and working tasks could be shared, particularly so in March when the mutton birding took place. Nearby Chappell Island had the best rookery in the area.

After her father's death in 1867, Lucy became the matriarch and spokeswoman for the community, and visiting government or church officials headed straight for her cosy cottage. Old Thomas Beeton had died slowly and painfully, and was much missed by his daughter, who nursed him to the end.

My Father had been my special companion. More than anyone else here, we two had shared the experience of living in town, of being literate and accustomed to the dealings of business. We were very close, and I guess it's not surprising. Father had lost our Mother a long time ago now, and no Island boy would have looked at me – I was a bit too bookish for them, and anyway, I was always very big indeed. I don't know why, really – it wasn't that I didn't work, and work hard, same as everyone else, or even that I ate more, because I didn't – but it caused me a lot of grief. Of course I wanted to be married. I had quite a fancy for Harry Miti, half brother to Bessy, who lived on Cape Barren with the Rews. But it was no use hoping. In time, I learned not to mind. I was always busy, writing petitions, teaching, and doing business for all. And I was proud of our community with our fine strong men who were the best boatmen around. They had saved many, many lives from the wrecks.

There was hardly a year without at least one, often several. The worst place was the eastern side of Cape Barren, but they could happen anywhere – there'd been five around Chappell and Badger alone in the time I've lived here. Our men would be out there with boats and ropes hauling the crew and passengers to safety, often risking their own lives. There were people who said that some ships had been deliberately lured onto the rocks, so they could be plundered, but that's just not true. Nor did any Straitsmen ever take anything from a wreck until every last possible soul, including any animals, were saved. If it took the insurance salvage crews a while to get there later, well that was another matter. I guess everyone thought in such a situation that any goods sitting out there were fair game.

A change came to us with the wreck of the <u>George Marshall</u> in 1862. She was a big ship, out from London and on her way to Sydney, carrying a cargo valued at £70,000. She got holed on a rock and was lucky that the captain managed, despite the heavy weather, to run her onto the sandy beach north of Wybalenna. All sixty passengers and crew got safely off, and one of our men took the captain to Launceston, where several boats were hired to go and collect what could be salvaged of the cargo. They managed to get most of it, though the ship itself eventually was a complete loss and sank into the sands. It was a pretty good outcome, given that most wrecks around here tended to get too smashed up for such extensive salvage to be possible.

But for us it was a real bad thing. They should have hired our people to do the job, but there were not enough of us, nor were our boats big enough, so they brought in anyone they could get, and there were some really rough and low characters among them. These men thought they'd make some extra business along the way, so they brought out alcohol and tobacco to sell. They'd give some away, to start a taste for it, and of course it wasn't long before some of our men wanted more of it. And then these intruders started messing with some of our girls, promising them all kinds of fancy goods, but none of those men was serious or decent. They brought out some pretty trinkets, and it kind of turned the girls' heads, and of course our boys didn't like it and then there'd be fights.

I suppose it was our isolation before this time that had kept us from such contamination. Also, by the 1860's some steam ships were being seen here and there, the three light houses had been built to make the passage safer, and it started to be quite a thoroughfare. More strangers, always white men, came to the Islands and it broke up our peace and unity. Those of us who had learnt to live properly, we mostly stayed that way, but our children saw a wider world and it wasn't always a good one.

But I'm getting ahead of myself. There was another big event that affected us greatly, back in 1847, when the governor was ordered to move all those of our tribal people who were at Wybalenna. Not that there were so many left – only 47 of them, including Truganini and Walter and his wife Mary Anne. It all started three years earlier, when Walter wrote a petition to the Queen in England. Oh yes, his English and writing hand were entirely good enough for that, and though he got it checked by Dr Milligan, they were his words, spoken on behalf of all of them. It was to do with that awful Jeanneret, who was the overseer there after Robinson left in 1837 and never really came back again except for a short visit. Jeanneret was unfair and unkind, and didn't treat our people well at all. Requests to the Governor in Hobart went nowhere, so Walter decided to write directly to the Queen. Not only did he ask to have Jeanneret removed, but he reminded her that his people had agreed with Robinson to freely come to Wybalenna for a while, but that the Governor had not made good his side of the promise, which was that they would be allowed to return to Tarena and have a part of it for themselves, where they could live in peace.

This petition went to England and was read to the Queen, but we never got a direct reply. It is true that after some long time, Jeanneret was replaced, but the really big result was that the Queen decided that the Aborigines of Wybalenna must be immediately moved back onto Tarena. At first, there was rejoicing – at last! – back home! – especially for Truganini, for it was known that they were to be taken to a place very near Bruny Island – but in the long run it turned out to be a more miserable and unsuitable place even than Wybalenna. It was an old convict station near Oyster Cove. Even though it wasn't so good eventually, I was glad for them because they immediately planned to go on hunting trips to their old grounds. Of course, it wasn't home ground for everybody, but white man had never understood that we came from different tribes that belonged in different parts – he just lumped us all together and expected us to get on. Well, we did, in time. Most, of course, never again got to see their home places, but I was glad for Truganini that she, at least, got that chance.

So then, after 1847, we half-castes were left behind on the Islands. Not that there was ever any suggestion that we should be included – the governor only wanted those of us who were, as he called it, of 'pure blood'. We wouldn't have wanted to go, anyway – we loved our free life here. But it left a big hole in our lives, no longer having our last few elders to speak with, and we sure were out on our own after that. We didn't count anywhere then – not as proper native peoples, nor as whites. It's no wonder we turned away from white men generally, and learnt to be very tough and self-sufficient.

So we got on with life. We raised enough money ourselves to

employ a teacher from Melbourne. In time, the governor in Hobart did relent and sent one out – mainly because of Rev. Brownrigg's efforts. Our families grew, and married, and turned into fine strong people. In time, we settled in many parts around here; my nephew Harry built himself a place in the northern corner of Flinders. And some of the white men and women who came to these parts were good people – we married into their families, too. We all knew each other, and we kept to our ways and were proud of them.

***

Governor Denison, having been ordered to re-accept the remaining Aborigines into his domain, decided to make a good showing of it. For the first two years, there was much publicity. Famous people went to visit the by-now 'exotic' blacks at Oyster Cove, and they were even invited to Government House for Christmas dinner. Allowed considerable freedom, and initially given very adequate provisions, some hope blossomed among them. Even their health improved.

But it all soon wore off. Whites did not like being reminded of their earlier transgressions against these people, and were only too happy to reinforce the thought that 'they will soon die out anyway'. Interest flagged, and with it the amounts of money made available for upkeep of the blacks. The old convict station proved damp and poorly built, and it wasn't long before the dying started again.

Of the ten younger ones among them, six were sent to the Orphan School at the time of the move, including Fanny. But these few, who perhaps could have prevented the final dying out of the pure-blooded natives, began to die there, also. Fanny managed to survive, and, after a short period as a domestic, married a white man, Smith. They settled on a farm not far from Oyster Cove, where she became a respected and long-lived part of the community and had many children, whose descendants are very much a part of Tasmania's community today.

Walter Arthur and his Mary Ann soon established themselves in business, first running a boarding house in Hobart, and then a dairy farm near Oyster Cove. Their adoption of the best of white man's ways

– a clean, neat cottage, literacy, good Christian lives, hard work, was noted by visitors. That did not prevent the government refusing Walter's application for a convict labourer.

"The thought of a black man issuing orders to a white one, even if only a convict, is intolerable."

They had no children. With insufficient labour, Walter was unable to make a full living on his little farm, so he and another full blood from Oyster Cove, William Lanne, began to work on the whaling ships. On a return trip in 1861, their boat was swamped and Walter drowned. His wife presently re-joined the few remaining natives at Oyster Cove, where she died 10 years later. William Lanne continued to work the whalers until he expired in great agony, possibly of liver failure, in a hotel in Hobart in 1869.

One by one, the Aboriginesfaded away at Oyster Cove. News of this gradually filtered through to Lucy on the Islands. On learning that Truganini was virtually the only one left, she had begged the Reverend Brownrigg, at their first meeting in 1872, that the old woman be allowed to join her on Badger Island, for her final years among her own kin. Lucy would gladly give her a home and all the care she needed, and she wrote a letter of invitation to Truganini for the Reverend to take. The latter also wrote to the Governor, pleading that the invitation be passed on and such a move facilitated, if the old lady wanted to come.

In his own record he added, mysteriously, that he feared:

"…that the kindly wish of Miss Beeton is not likely to be gratified."

What did Brownrigg know that Lucy didn't? Was the government determined that the aged and now-feeble remnant of pure blooded natives from Wybalenna be kept away from those half-caste Straitsmen, who were so infuriatingly alive? That nothing should be permitted to interfere with any official proclamations that the entire race of primitive indigenous Tasmanians had 'sadly passed away'?

Lucy did know something of this, in her heart. Even in 1872, when she first met the Rev. Brownrigg, was she beginning to realize how it was to be, and now, in the last year of her life in 1886, she knew it for sure. But she had hoped that the Christian love, which white man was supposed to act by and which Brownrigg represented, would finally overcome the prejudice. Disappointed in that also, it was this final and unutterable realization that had made her turn away from the Reverend on the beach at Cape Barren Island, just one year earlier.

Truganini never did come to the home that was offered her, and it is highly unlikely that she was ever notified of the invitation. Her death there would have been gentler than the one she experienced in Hobart, screaming that the dark spirit was coming to get her. She had begged that her body be kept safe from the ghouls who had dismembered William Lanne's, and the government actually did manage that. Nevertheless she was dug up later and her skeleton displayed for many years in the Hobart Museum. Her remains were handed back to the Aboriginal community in 1976, exactly 100 years later. Her ashes were then scattered on the waters around Bruny Island, where she was born.

As for George Augustus Robinson, after placing the natives at Wybalenna, he had no intention of being incarcerated with them. In 1839 he achieved his ambition by being appointed Chief Protector of Aborigines in the Port Phillip area, and thenceforth spent his time there, where his effectiveness as 'protector' was virtually non-existent. His most valuable contribution consists of extensive journals made on his many trips over a vast area, which include observations on local native tribes and early European settler life. He made only one brief visit back to 'his' Tasmanian Aborigines, in 1851, after they had been moved to Oyster Cove. It is said that Truganini, in despair at his betrayal, on that occasion refused to acknowledge him.

In 1849 Robinson's position in Victoria was abolished, leaving him free and comfortably off with a pension. He appears to have had few cordial connections with his now adult children, and – his wife having died the year before – he sailed back to England in 1852, married again and had another family of five. He spent some years living in France and Italy, eventually settling in Bath, England, to social acceptance and a very comfortable living. There he died, in 1866. One may well wonder if Truganini's 'dark spirit' came to get him, also.

Lucy Beeton shivered with her sad memories. White man came to beautiful Tarena, and took it away from the black people who had lived there for many thousands of years. They spoke of a god who had made everything and all men equal, and who commanded that all should love and accept one another. It was a gospel of freedom, and when many of the half-caste Straitsmen, including Lucy, took it to heart and became genuine believing Christians, living sober and decent lives, it should have made them equal, too.

Lucy Beeton died on the 7th of July, 1886, and was buried on Badger Island. By the time of her death she was a well-known local character, meriting a full-page obituary in the Launceston paper. Acknowledged as a fine lady and a great example to her people, the article even finished with her own words: *"Why do you, blessed with civilization and Christianity, neglect to afford us poor half-castes the simplest duties laid upon you by the requirements of Christian charity?"*

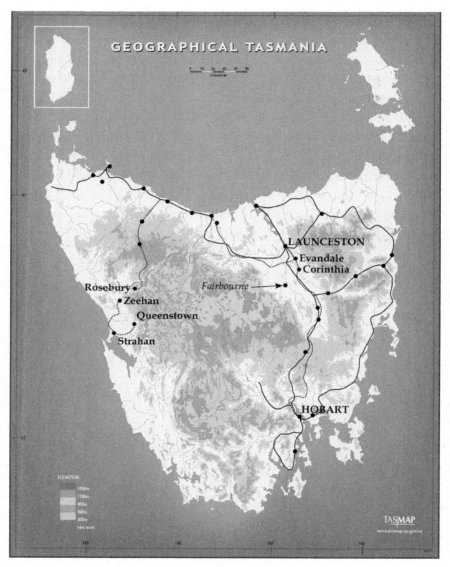

GEOGRAPHICAL TASMANIA

0 10 20 30 40 50
Kilometres

LAUNCESTON
Evandale
Corinthia

Fairbourne

Rosebury
Zeehan
Queenstown
Strahan

HOBART

ELEVATION

1500m
1200m
900m
600m
300m
sea level

TAS|MAP
www.tasmap.tas.gov.au

Map 5 – *Tasmania 1880's*

 Tasmanian Main Line Railway and Western Railway   *Main formed roads*

By the 1880's, all the major towns we know today had been formed, with roads, mail and coach services connecting most. In 1876 the Hobart–Launceston railway opened, reducing the traveltime of at least 15 hours (by coach) to seven.

The West Coast, despite having significant mining centres at Queenstown, Zeehan and Waratah, remained largely isolated with only a railway from Burnie, and from Queenstown to the coast. Access was mostly by ship, the journey rough and unpredictable and often taking weeks.

THE FAIRFIELDS 1868 – 1887

ISABELLA

Yet each man kills the thing he loves,
By each let this be heard,
Some do it with a bitter look,
Some with a flattering word.
The coward does it with a kiss,
The brave man with a sword!
Oscar Wilde

13. AFTER THE FIRST BALL

In January 1868 a grand ball was held at Government House in Hobart, the culmination of many festivities in Tasmania for Prince Alfred, son of Queen Victoria, making the first ever royal visit to the Island. Invitations from Governor Gore Browne had been sent to most leading citizens, including the owners of the larger Midlands grazing properties. Dancing in the gay throng was the pretty Isabella Cowley, born a Fairfield, and now expecting her first child.

The pregnancy was not yet in the slightest affecting Isabella's youthful waistline. She looked enchanting in her pale cream gown, elaborately trimmed with lace and ribbons. Her husband Philip watched her with possessive pleasure as she twirled to the waltz with the Governor himself. Philip had been pleased to make a marriage with this granddaughter of William and Susannah Fairfield who had built up one of the finest merino sheep studs in the Midlands. They were a bit strict in their

Presbyterian faith, and Philip hoped that Isabella was of a lighter heart, but she was eminently suitable, from respectable stock and would be a faithful wife and a good mother to his sons. And she was very pretty...

Also closely watching Isabella, with more anxiety than pleasure, was Susannah Fairfield herself. Nearly seventy but still in good health, she had decided to make the long and arduous journey by coach to Hobart, partly because balls at Government House were rather special, but mainly to keep an eye on her granddaughter. Something was not right there, with that girl who should be glowing with happiness in the early months of her marriage. Susannah wondered if Philip was aware of his approaching fatherhood, and thought possibly not. Nothing had been said by anyone. To her, Isabella's condition was obvious, a natural and expected matter, so why was she unable to push away the sense of unease?

Being a new wife and now suddenly facing motherhood as well was naturally a big adjustment for an eighteen-year-old girl. Philip seemed a nice young man despite the difference in family culture, and would surely be considerate in their marital relations. Susannah herself had had a largely happy experience in her own marriage, she and William always being comfortable and devoted to each other, despite all the practical difficulties their life had presented them with. There were times when she had cordially hated him for bringing her to this alien and barbarous place, but even at such moments she never lost sight of his essential goodness and her love for him always returned. She said a quick prayer that Isabella might experience the same happiness, and retired to the ladies' room to adjust her ribbons.

Nineteen years later, in June 1887, another Fairfield descendant danced at a ball in the same Government House. It was in fact young Gavin Cowley's second time at such an occasion, though he was not aware of the first one, hidden as he was then, deep in his mother's belly. Now nearly nineteen himself, just as his mother had been then, he too had a dark shadow in his eyes. Not that this was obvious at the moment, excited as he was by the grand occasion, stepping out along with the other bright sons and daughters, most making their debut in Hobart. His features were regular rather than handsome. Nor had he inherited his father's tall stature, being medium in height and somewhat squarer. But strong. He was already noted for his ability to manage horses, indeed any animal, and was at his happiest among them and out in the countryside. But for now he was youthfully excited, enticed by the pretty girls and the music, the grand setting and the general fun.

This Fairfield child was also being anxiously watched, just as Isabella had been. His Uncle David was keeping the sorrowing vigil, though this time the cause of the sadness was known to the watcher. David Fairfield, youngest son of William and Susannah, the dreamer who heard the crying in the wind, had watched young Gavin grow up and had come to love the vulnerable boy, protecting him as best he could. He had made the effort to attend this ball, simply to be near him. He did not care for such occasions and would have happily remained at quiet Fairbourne beside the Macquarie River, eschewing the long journey, first by cart to Campbell Town, and then by the new train to Hobart, laden with the luggage necessary for presenting oneself in a reasonable turnout at the Governor's residence. There were plenty of Fairfields, Cowleys and other relatives of Gavin's attending the ball also, but David was propelled to all this effort by a sense of impending doom. Besides, a visit to Hobart meant access to the bookshops, and that would be a great treat for David.

***

The years between these two balls were only nineteen in number, but they saw great changes in the Island of Tasmania, still struggling to find its place in the world. Many wonderful advances had come.

After ten years of failed attempts, in May 1869 the new submarine cable under Bass Strait finally worked effectively. Now it was possible to know the news from Melbourne and Sydney, inside a few hours. In 1872, the telegraph had been completed all the way to England, and the newspapers could print the latest news from Home the very next day.

There had been long and bitter battles, too, over the establishment of the railway line that finally linked the two major cities through the Midlands. The economic recession that had held back the advancement of the Island since the late 1830's did not start to really lift until its own gold and other mineral resources were finally found, culminating in the great mountain of tin, in 1872, at Mt Bischoff in the vast forests of the West Coast. With that came a new sense of optimism, and it was fully displayed in 1887 for the amazing Jubilee illuminations, made with the gas lighting that had recently changed the streetscapes of the two cities. These formed a major component of the celebrations, being much admired and commented on. At the earlier 1868 ball gas had barely arrived, making the brilliantly lit chandeliers a huge sensation at Government House and the Town Hall, while most homes still were making do with candles and oil lamps. Now Tasmanian rejoiced that they were finally joining the rest of Australia in sophistication and advancement.

Great changes were taking place in the Midlands too, though the ones that concern us here were mostly hidden under the outwardly placid surface of the landowners' properties.

***

Back home after the first ball in 1868, Susannah Fairfield was taking stock. She did this regularly, having taken over the management of Fairbourne's paperwork after her husband's death, five years earlier. This work came easily to her, as William had been in the habit of speaking with her about all matters concerning their property including the financial ones. Their oldest son, Andrew, was busy making a good success of his own property further north along the Macquarie River. Their second boy, Edward, had only just turned seventeen when the excitement of the great plains opening up to the west of Port Phillip – later known as Melbourne – caught him. He had crossed over there along with a group of other young adventurers, and after some years of working on one of the huge developing properties there, the Campbell's, he had successfully applied for a piece of his own, well-chosen and well-stocked with sheep from his father's own flock, and was doing as well if not better than his brother Andrew.

Susannah sighed. She was glad of her son's success but wished that he had not gone so far away. A letter from him had come, announcing his intention of marrying a local girl. He was already forty-six and it was high time that he did, but the trip across the Bass Strait and the long jolting journey out west was not enticing, even though she would much have liked to meet the girl and see any grandchildren. Susannah now much identified with her own parents, who had to let her go when she and William, as a young couple, had left Scotland for Van Diemens Land in 1823. Forty-five years ago…she had never seen them again, and now they were both dead. So much change in those years, too – even the name of the island they had come to was now altered to Tasmania. It was a good name, better than the old VDL, that place of exile. Exile it had been for her, too, despite their subsequent success. At odd moments, a loneliness and a rage would assail, nearly choke, her. She had done her part, and very well at that, loyally supporting her husband's vision, had found many satisfactions and had fine children along the way. But her heart still longed for a Scottish glen, and the sound of the lark in that free and familiar air. So she kept busy to keep those thoughts at bay, and God knew, there was always plenty to do.

Edward's removal to Port Phillip also caused their fourth child, Rebecca, to go there. Or, more accurately, Edward's mentioning of his pretty sister had been heard by a serious young man, one James Littleton, engaged in merchandising in Melbourne, with whom Edward had struck up a friendship. James was looking for a nice wife and was sufficiently intrigued with stories of Rebecca to find reasons why a trip to Launceston – for business purposes, naturally – could bring about an excuse to visit the parents of his good friend Edward. He was blessed in both endeavours, as Rebecca liked him greatly and he was also able to secure a good supply of wanted wares from Reed's merchant house. The goods were shipped over sometime before his bride arrived in Melbourne, and while Susannah was sad to see her daughter go, she was glad for her as James was a stout Presbyterian – from Scotland too, a good business man, and a kindly soul. Rebecca would be happy enough.

Their oldest daughter, Nancy, was also content. Busy with ever more children, she had married into the family of the Mackerseys nearby, within easy visiting distance.

And George, their fifth, had naturally slipped into his father's place when William died. It was for him that she kept the long ledgers that accounted for the farm's doings. Listening to George's plans and ideas, she had no concerns there – he was a chip off the old block, showing his father's good common sense, and had learned well all that was needed to carry on the family's highly successful estate.

That left their last two, Margaret and David.

Margaret had married Henry, the second son of a Midlands grazier, in 1847. The couple moved to Launceston, and there Margaret gave birth to Isabella and died two days later, the doctor unable to stop the life from haemorrhaging out of her. The young widower took the child to his mother-in-law, Susannah Fairfield, who – shaken by the early death of her daughter Margaret – took in the helpless bundle and let its needs fill the sudden gap in her heart. She came to love her dearly, and raised Isabella at Fairbourne until the girl married Philip Cowley, heir to one of the largest properties around, near Evandale.

And David, dear different David, the quiet one who never wanted a farm of his own or even a wife. He had remained living on Fairbourne, doing his fair share of work alongside his father, brothers and the labourers. But it was clear that he really lived to wander alone in the countryside, his mind filled with incomprehensible dreams. He often rode over to Evandale where the Reverend Robert Russell had started a lending library. Barely twenty when baby Isabella arrived so unexpectedly, he quickly became a big brother to her, and began to take her with him as soon as she was able to ride the distance herself; they would return happy, having had a wonderful adventure every time, and bringing back quantities of books. These too, they shared, and while not one title could ever have been said to be unsuitable for the tender ears of a young miss in a strictly Presbyterian household, somehow David made the reading of even the most sober tome into an exciting flight of fancy. Susannah had often watched the two fair heads bent close together over the pages.

"Perhaps," thought Susannah, "that's when the mischief started…"

Somewhere along the line in an unguarded moment, a new element had joined those two young ones and bound them tightly together.

Susannah was glad that William was not there to see it, though she much missed his steady advice. Five years earlier, when Isabella was just thirteen, he had died suddenly of a heart attack. One moment he was checking on some sheep nearby, and the next he had fallen over by the gate. They found him soon after, and carried him to the house, but there was nothing anyone could do. His stout soul had fled, and Susannah, who would miss him deeply for the rest of her own life, was glad for him that his death had been quick and dignified. She could not imagine her strong, capable William any other way. Her children were a comfort to her then, and even Edward and Rebecca had managed to cross the Bass Strait from Victoria to visit her, but they could not replace him, his kindly commonsense and unshakeable goodness, nor his body beside her in bed. They had had a full, rich life together, a truly happy marriage.

But that's not what Isabella is experiencing now, Susannah mused. Still, it's early, she reminded herself; any girl might find the first few months of marriage a bit awkward. And it takes time for familiarity and trust to build up. Susannah remembered that it had taken nearly twenty years before her body actively started welcoming William's embraces. When it did, a new, rich dimension had entered their life, the warmth of which was an astonishing reward for the long years of disciplined and self-sacrificing love.

But no amount of sensible reasoning could shift something in Susannah's head, something she'd seen, perhaps without even knowing it. Isabella and Philip should be pleased to be together. He'd certainly courted her ardently enough, riding over frequently from the Corinthia estate.

"It should be a very good match, even though that family is Anglican and therefore somewhat lax. Isabella will fit in well enough with their fine mansion and the hunting meets and balls – enough to turn any girl's head – but she's not happy..."

It was a surprise that young Philip should have chosen Isabella to court, but he was determined once he had caught sight of her coming out of the Reverend Russell's library.

That Reverend, thought Susannah. There always was something a little odd about him. Why has he not married? It seems unnatural for such a presentable and obviously good man. He's a deeply esteemed minister, tireless on behalf of the poor in his parish, concerned for justice and dignity for all. She could not find any fault with him, and –

other than a faint curiosity about an old whispered-about scandal: he'd proposed marrying his *sister*? – had hardly thought about him, until his library became instrumental in providing David with the means of turning his niece's head and then completing his mischief by introducing her to Philip Cowley as well.

Susannah had a healthy respect for education, and had always fostered it in her family. Reading worthy material that broadened the mind was very desirable, even for girls, and she had welcomed David's early trips. At some point, he had begun to borrow sheet music, also, the tunes of which he could now and then be heard singing or whistling in the fields. Both Susannah and William's strict views considered music suitable only for hymns, and their house had no piano. Dancing was absolutely not permitted, and they stuck with this though the daughters of families like the Cowleys were taught the quadrille, minuet and other dainty steps, as well as to sing pretty songs and tinkle tunes on the keys. At Fairbourne, Sunday afternoons were spent in reading out loud, drawing the flowers and birds of the countryside, going for gentle walks or in serious con-versation. Their books were always informative ones, about places and travels, philosophies or the classics, poetry and history, natural and applied sciences, dictionaries and essential manuals on home medicine and remedies both for the house and the farm. But no outright fiction, especially novels of any kind, was permitted. They will only put fancy and unrealistic notions into their heads, declared William, and they all humbly followed his dictates because he truly loved them and wanted nothing but the best for them.

And so had David. Keeping his love of music strictly to himself, not once had he brought back an unsuitable book, but somehow he had still managed to imbue his reading of them with just that romantic nonsense that his father had feared. The boy was gifted and perhaps he should be writing poetry in his spare time, his mother thought, after he had entertained them one evening with a spirited rendition on the history of Scotland. By the time she became aware that his troubadour's spell had fallen upon Isabella, it was too late.

***

In Hobart, Philip and Isabella returned after the ball in the early hours to Webb's Hotel, in 1868 the best in town, where several Cowley family members had taken rooms for the occasion. That day was to see the departure of Prince Alfred, on the yacht Galatea, and most were intending to crowd the wharves and nearby lookout points to wave him away. Before that, some sleep was necessary.

"You were certainly the belle of the ball, my dear Isabella," Philip complimented her, "and your dancing was perfectly fine."

He had been a little shocked to discover, practically on their wedding day, that she could not dance, and had employed a tuition master to teach her, in the company of his sisters. Isabella was relieved to hear his approval. Corinthia's way of life was so very different! She was hard put to acquire the easy style of Phillip's sisters, and much of it was greatly exciting to her impressionable young mind – the fine clothes that were especially made for her in Launceston, the many servants, the music and the wide range of books suddenly available to her – the Cowleys had a magnificent library – including those romantic novels.

***

The first widely-read work of true fiction – that is, writing unfettered by any constraining facts – was Daniel Defoe's *Robinson Crusoe* published in 1719. It had an extra-ordinary impact on eighteenth-century society, bringing a liberating freedom to the imaginations of everyday people. Tales of wild adventures, descriptions of exotic and strange places, of people, usually wealthy nobility, behaving in unconventional ways or indulging in wild affairs of the heart – all represented a thrilling new escape from the daily round of poverty and drudgery. Defoe's outstanding success was quickly followed by many more such books, like Samuel Richardson's *Pamela* and Henry Fielding's *Tom Jones*. The masses loved them, and while most could not afford to buy the actual volumes, serialised editions in papers and magazines and copies from circulating libraries were in huge demand.

To thoughtful people, however, the novel represented a seduction into realms of unreality. Indulging in such romantic flights of impossible fancy was not only a complete waste of time, but could start dangerous notions and expectations among the impressionable young. Serious parents routinely banned any such books, believing their children should be raised to deal in what was real, and worthy, and tested by time and the demands of everyday life. The Cowleys on the other hand had shelves laden with such books, and being of a much more liberal mind than the Fairfields' tradition, saw no harm in encouraging their daughters to read them. Their impact on Isabella was enormous.

Hiding herself away as often as she could in some quiet corner, she thrilled over *The Trials of Margaret Lyndsay*, groaning with the heroine as she withstands an attempt at seduction, or the magnificent potential of 'in the dark and stormy night' from the novel *Paul Clifford*. The sad romance of *Jane Eyre*, the heroic stories of Walter Scott, Mrs Porter and Mrs Bray, and many others, held her captivated. It was a whole new world, so wildly exciting to her that she quickly earned herself a reputation of 'being a bit of mouse' over the many times she would turn down a proposed drive to visit friends or even to town, preferring to read yet another book.

Perhaps it would all have been quite harmless, had Isabella been a happy young wife. But she wasn't, for she had tasted romance even before she knew what it was, and now that she was separated from it, just as Jane was from her Mr Rochester, the pathos of it filled her heart and turned her head and led her down paths she had no business to be on.

Her husband Philip, in whose breast the only romance that fluttered occasionally was the thrill of a successful stag hunt, an advantageous deal well made, or the highly satisfactory ledgers of the estate accounts, soon decided that his wife would be very worthy but not very exciting. Somehow, her simple and dignified innocence had taken his fancy, being a refreshing change from the cloying frothiness of his many sisters and their friends. And indeed, Isabella would prove to be sensible and capable to a high degree; in time the management of the fine house was handled extremely well by her. But for now, she was a bit disappointing, seeming to lack any real ardour in his direction. Perhaps he was expecting too much of a still-young girl from such a sober family? Though what he knew of her parents did not suggest that there had been any lack of warmth between them.

His sexual experience had been quite vivid to this point; the usual young man's excursions to the town brothel were later augmented by a couple of discreet dalliances with older married ladies. But faced with Isabella he felt a bit unsure, and restrained himself greatly, especially in the bedroom, not wanting to frighten her. Children however were to be expected, so he exercised his conjugal rights with the minimum necessary ritual. He accepted her occasional rides back to her family home, knowing that she was very fond of Susannah, whom she thought of more as her mother than anything else, and for whom he himself had considerable respect. Meanwhile, he remained charming and attentive, taking his wife out on drives and to see the sights of Launceston and now those in Hobart. They had been there for nearly three weeks.

On Regatta Day, Isabella's attention had been caught by two figures on the steps of the pavilion. A man and an old woman, both completely black-skinned. Never having seen anyone other than ordinary white people, she whispered to Philip about who they were? Before he could answer, Prince Albert, having just arrived, halted beside the same two and was being introduced to them. *The Mercury*, reporting the incident, described them as "the last representatives of the Aboriginal race of Tasmania, King Billy and Queen Truganini, with Mr Dandridge, their protector, present with them".

Isabella was fascinated. This was something to tell David about! He had told her of the dark-skinned people of the island, and how they had been displaced by families like her own, and that there had been battles and how Uncle Herbert had been killed by them. The matter had eventually been peacefully resolved by gathering them up and providing for them on Flinders Island, so the good farmers could properly till the soil and raise their sheep in peace. David had not said anything more, no doubt wishing to shield her from the more horrible stories and she had no idea that there were any Aborigines left around to be seen.

"But why 'the last', Philip? What happened to them all?"

"They were no match to civilised man, being heathens and not able to adapt to proper ways. So they wasted away – the last few were brought back from Flinders about twenty years ago and these two are the very last ones."

She watched them again a bit later, as they were chosen to hand the prizes to the race winner, which 'Queen' Truganini did with the greatest of grace. King Billy, properly known as William Lanney, then initiated another cheer for the Duke, which was soundly taken up. Both performed their parts, but Isabella was filled with sadness, seeing two puppets dancing to an alien tune. Who were they really? What did they think and feel, now that there were only the two of them? She must ask David.

Oh David! Again and again she caught herself wanting to share things with him – he who had been her natural companion and confidant and was always the first in her mind, every day. And now she couldn't do it anymore, indeed he himself had told her to go, and not come back again, when, when… Isabella shivered. Dutifully turning her attention back to Philip, she couldn't resist a small sense of fearful triumph as she passed her hand gracefully over her stomach. One thing of David's she did now have, and if the price for that was to be a good wife to the wrong man, then she would pay it gladly. Once they got home from Hobart, she would tell Philip that he would soon become a father.

Having waved the Prince away, they prepared for their return to Evandale in their carriage, a journey of two days with a stop overnight at Oatlands. They were followed by a cart filled with fancy goods. Philip, observing the complete novelty to her of such sprees, took her to the best merchant houses, and indulgently urged upon her fine fabrics, silks and taffetas, lawns and laces, fashionable bonnets and elaborate trims, dainty gloves, parasols, soft calf leather booties with many buttons, and much more. But there was one more shop she wished to visit, the only one she had planned ahead for, and that was the bookshop. There she would find a gift for David, and nobody would think twice about her riding over to bring it to him, along with the particularly fine lace she had found for Susannah.

14. DANCING ON HOT COALS

William would have known what to do about Isabella, Susannah thought sadly. He had died at the wrong moment, just as the girl was coming to womanhood, and – Susannah now realised – she should have sent her then to live with her father Henry's family. The latter had gone on to marry again, and despite now having a numerous family, he had stayed in touch with his first-born daughter. She had also visited them in Launceston, but all seemed satisfied that Isabella's home was at Fairbourne.

"I should have sent her away then, before she got to be womanly and fell in love with David. I should have separated them then, I should have seen it coming but I didn't. Too full of my own grief over losing William, and anyway, who would have thought of it? David is simply part of the family, my own son, just as Isabella had grown to be more of a daughter to me than a grand child. Any question of impropriety simply never arose…"

Nor, Susannah was sure, had there ever been any such thing between the two of them. Yes, they were close, too close, but both had been properly raised and anyway, other young men were starting to turn up and it seemed the most natural thing that Isabella's thoughts would soon be turned by some dashing young suitor. And by the handsome and well-connected Philip Charles Briermont Cowley, of all people! In her eagerness to get the matter safely settled, Susannah had ignored the small warning voice within. No man was ever going to replace David in Isabella's heart.

***

Rolling along in the coach on their way north, Isabella kept her delicious secret close to her bosom in the best romantic manner, and daydreamt about its delightful possibilities. There was no doubt in her mind that she was carrying a boy.

"How would you like a trip to Melbourne?" Phillip asked her. "We could visit your brother's place – see how he's getting on out there. Your sister Rebecca could put us up in town; you'd like that, wouldn't you?"

Melbourne was indeed a place of glittering excitement, in contrast to Tasmania. The Island Colony had undergone a painful change of status, from the second leading place in Australia to a too-quiet and too-frequently bypassed corner. The great days of the 1820's and 30's, when men like his father had created their pastoral estates with the free labour of assigned convicts, were well and truly over. The 1840's brought a bitter recession as credit failed, banks collapsed, and many businesses ceased to trade. Those with sheep, like Philip's father, had survived because demand for wool did not cease, although the price dropped severely for a while, and only those with large herds and already-established estates coped adequately.

But only just, because the foolish Colonial Office in London had at that precise time decided to replace the convict assignment system with the poorly-implemented probation one. It effectively deprived the big landholders of their labour force. Then the gold rush took nearly all the able-bodied men away across the water. Many of the remaining labourers were those incapable of doing it – the feeble and feckless, and those already weakened by the Irish famine even before arriving as convicts. Such men roamed the roads, and most – unable to get regular work as the landlords pitched one against the other, taking on only those willing to work for the least wage for a few hours or days – eventually retreated into the margins of the great forests, forming their own, reviled underclass. One of them was George Turner, one-time assignee to Isabella's grandfather.

The poor economic situation of the Island was then further aggravated by the ending of transportation. The great majority of the people wanted no more convicts arriving to further stain their reputations, it being bad enough to be known as the place where all the scum from the English prisons had been dumped. The probation system had made it all worse by receiving much bad publicity over the darkly hinted-at, unspeakably disgusting practices supposedly common among men locked up together in large numbers. Passions flared high, moral outrage was expressed by the churches, and many readily signed or supported petitions to London that the convict system should cease. The government in London resisted this, reluctant to lose their conveniently distant and carefully built up penal colony, into which they had invested a great deal of money. But public opinion prevailed, helped by the anti-slavery agitations in England, and the last convict ship sailed from there to Van Diemens Land in 1853.

Much rejoicing followed the decision; a focal part of the celebrations being the changing of the Island's name from VDL to Tasmania. It was to be a brave new place, where all men could stand proud. Those with the big landed estates did not see it that way.

"If England cannot send her felons here, she won't send money to support the system here, either," Philip had argued with a neighbor. "They'll withdraw all the military and most government staff, and will leave us with the responsibility of providing policing, hospitals, and the general management of the prisoners already here."

In this, he was entirely right. Together with the painful loss of the local trade that feeding and servicing the military had provided, and coming at an economically difficult time, Tasmania now found itself severely challenged to cope. Granted full autonomy in 1856, it elected the hopefully-named Responsible Government, which – composed largely of landowners anxious to maintain the status quo – had little unity or common direction, setting the tone for many years of general governmental incompetence. With little money available, and attempts to raise local taxes understandably unpopular, not much was done to provide for the poor and infirm, of which there were a great many, particularly ex-convicts. Regular outbreaks of typhoid were caused by virtually non-existent sewerage and inadequate supplies of clean water. Even investments with obvious economic advantages were wasted in the competition between rival party factions and favour-currying among those who should have had a long term vision.

Melbourne, by contrast, had surged ahead, fueled by the goldrush. The streets there were lit by gas, begun in 1855, bringing great advances to the safety of citizens and delighting the eye with its bright twinkling. Some larger stores were using such illuminations to great effect, creating wonderlands that drew great crowds.

"And we could ride on the new railway," added Phillip. The first railway in Australia, built in 1854, from Flinders St in the town to the pier at Sandridge, was quickly followed by several lines servicing Melbourne and the surrounding districts, and were being extended even as far as Geelong, Bendigo and Echuca.

"What we need is a proper railway right here, through the Midlands," Phillip continued. "If we could get our cattle and produce to the markets more quickly, we would see much more economic activity. But they won't vote any money for it, the fools, so we'll have to raise it ourselves, like Dry and others have done."

Philip Cowley, forced to sit idly in the jolting coach on his way home after the grand ball, found himself speculating on the possibilities. How many of his grazier friends would be willing to invest in a railway scheme? He could think of a number, though he doubted if his wife's brother George, now head of the Fairbourne property, would be one of them. Not that he couldn't afford it, far from it. But he would be too cautious to consider such a venture, too old fashioned and too, well, severe. Those Presbyterians, sighed Phillip. They're solid and worthy and hardworking, but they have no idea of a bit of fun. Whatever did they do for amusement? No horse-racing for them. (Phillip was proud of his fine stable that had bred several highly successful chasers.) Certainly no gambling, no card-playing, no unnecessary trips just for the pleasure of it, no music, not even dancing!

And no sexual yielding? He glanced at his wife beside him, expecting her face to be in its usual serious repose, and was surprised at the soft smile that rested there. What was she thinking about? Impulsively, he leaned over, cupping her chin to kiss the inviting mouth. Maybe he had been wrong to hold back. Perhaps she was just waiting to be swept off her feet in a passionate rush? He let his ardour mount, his hands seeking the creamy skin, urgently struggling with the buttons and hooks of her underclothing. He didn't stop, but had his way with her right there in the swaying coach, and he didn't think more about the fraction-of-a-second look of estrangement in her eyes, as they snapped open upon his approach.

"Just shy", he thought, and letting himself fully go, covering her with passionate kisses, he thrust in. She not only submitted but suddenly he found her responding, or at least not remaining as passive as she had been hitherto. The coachman meanwhile kept on observing the horizon and made sure that the horses maintained their steady trot, even urging them on a bit. He did permit himself the whistling of a little tune. It wasn't the first time his master had been distracted while travelling in the coach, but with his own wife? Well, now, that was something new.

Over the next few weeks, Philip was stunned and delighted to find Isabella eagerly awaiting him in the bedroom every night. It was not long after that she told him he would be a father soon. Pleased, he forbade her to go riding out, for the safety of herself and the child, and she accepted this quietly, but pleaded for just one last trip, to tell her mother the great news. He offered to call the coachman, but no, she wanted to go alone. She promised to maintain a sedate pace.

***

Susannah fingered the lovely lace – indeed it was of remarkably good quality, a beautiful length – and wondered how she would ever find a use for such extravagant frothiness. Perhaps some neat trimming for christening dresses?

"Thank you, my dear...."

She studied her granddaughter. There finally was the looked-for flush of young wifehood, a blooming as girl turns into woman, and she was relieved to see it. There was a baby coming, was there? Susannah wondered why it was only being announced now, but perhaps it was simply that Isabella had not been sure herself? The first time, and all that – it took some getting used to. Clearly, their recent sojourn in Hobart had done them both good and maybe the excitement of it had infected them in the bedroom as well.

"Is David here?" Isabella was holding another parcel. "I got him a book. There were so many in the shop in Hobart!"

The older woman stifled a brief flare of unease.

"I'm not sure where he is at the moment, dear. I'll send Jane to check his cottage."

"No, no, don't bother her, I'll go myself." Isabella eagerly gathered her skirts and practically ran from the room.

∗∗∗

David had moved into one of the old workmen's cottages after his father's death, leaving the main house to his older brother George. Tucked away on the far side of the courtyard, David had the freedom to sing or whistle his tunes, study a few books that his mother was better off not seeing – no need to disturb her – write or just sit and ponder in peace. Not that he was lazy. He still did his fair share of work, but was satisfied with that, having no interest in owning and running a farm. Content at Fairbourne, he found all he needed among the birds and trees along the waters of the Macquarie River and in the foothills of the towering Western Tiers. Those great brooding ranges, blue and ringing with life during the day, purple and unapproachable at dusk, and shining gold and orange as the sun rose opposite them up over the eastern hills, provided both a physical and climatic barrier to the farm. Above them extraordinary cloud formations could form, often vividly coloured and telling of the wild weather up there on the high plateau. The ramparts held it back and provided warm sheltered nooks along the foothills where the sheep and cattle would gather till the ice was off the grass further out on the plain.

These nooks were David's delight. Every animal was his friend, its habits known to him. The creatures had got used to his presence, as he moved quietly among them, lightly, never bringing a firearm but just to look and be, drinking in the living silence. He knew them intimately, from the charming blue flash of the fairy wren to the subtler greens, yellows and greys of the honeyeaters, finches, robins, wrens, thornbills, wattle birds and many others. He watched the rushing flocks of tiny whiteyes, setting a shrub a-tremble as they chittered their way along the branches finding sustenance. Every call was an announcing of his coming, and the bush welcomed him and allowed him to enter. His gentle presence was acceptable.

Here, too, the old ghosts would come by. As David was a kindred soul without judgement, they kept a gentle distance, allowing him to sense them only, for they carried great pain that they wished not to burden him with, and perhaps also to express their atonement for the killing of his uncle..... Much had happened back then that was sad and to be regretted, many mistakes made, but now it was time to be at peace. So they wrapped him around with their mature stillness, and he was grateful and sought it regularly.

Only sometimes, deep in the night, would he hear the crying in the wind, that howling of the dispossessed and lost souls, and once, when roaming a bit higher up the hills than usual, he had come to copse in which stood the ruin of a small hut. He had backed away, for here was the crying and the spilled blood and the terror, and he knew that awful things had been done there. He called on God, asking forgiveness for his race, and came away shamed by the stillness and acceptance he was being shown by those who had cause to hate him.

For a while he stayed away. He had heard some terrible stories. One of the worst was the one from the Western Marshes, just beyond Deloraine, where in 1827, on Bull's grant, a group of convicts on horseback, searching for straying cattle, had come upon some thirty Aborigines. What persuaded them to drive these unfortunates into the nearest lagoon, in which they shot a number, then forcing the remainder to walk to Ritchie's Sugarloaf only to dispatch the rest there? They did let one old man and his wife go, it was boasted... David knew that this had happened only a short distance from where the big merchant and landowner Henry Reed had a large land grant, and he wondered if the old man knew of the real price that had been paid for his now fine and lucrative farms. He might not – it had happened ten years before Reed got his land – but he was said to be on particularly friendly terms with all his workers and it seemed unlikely that he had not heard talk of it. Reed was an active Christian whose missionary efforts for the poor and un-converted were generous and legendary, but what of his conscience? Did it stir at night with unease? Did he hear the moaning of those who died so settlers like Reed might build their farms and profits on their bones?

David was a troubled man, all the more so as nobody would ever speak of any of this. It was an unwritten but unbreakable agreement, now that natives were out of the way and no longer a daily troubling presence. They might never have existed, and most children born to the white people had barely heard of them. Neither would his niece Isabella, had it not been for her uncle being killed by the Aborigines, which was family lore. But he had not told her anything except the briefest outline of the circumstances.

And here she was, rushing into his cottage in all her breathless young beauty, holding out a parcel.

"David! I brought you a book! David?"

He held himself back, gripping his armchair. She shouldn't be here, not after what had happened...they had agreed... He stood, and with grave formality motioned her to a chair while he took the present and held himself firmly back from her.

"Isabella. You're back then. You look well. Thank you," as he fumbled with the wrappings, "this looks very interesting."

"David..."

Shocked that he really meant it, that he truly was cold towards her and would not acknowledge her in that personal intimate way that had been theirs for so many years, she was at a loss. A yawning hole opened up in her, one she would fall into, screaming, for many nights to come as her heart rent in her and the man she really loved turned away from her.

"Did you have a good time in Hobart?"

The conventional inquiry was too much. A sob rose in her, stifled as she proudly lifted her head and gathered her skirts to go. *It's your child I'm carrying*, she wanted to scream at him, *yours, made with our love!* But it would never do and must never be said. She was married to Phillip Cowley, and to protect the child, it had to be known as Phillip's. Pulling herself up like one of the tragic heroines from her enthralling novels, she walked out and back to her horse for the ride home.

She did not see the man in the cottage, choking as he forced himself to stay, to let her go, his whole frame shivering with the effort. He too would spend many restless nights to come.

***

It hadn't been her fault! He had let it go too far! Thus Isabella tried to justify it in her anger and upset, but didn't get far with it, for she was too honest to hold the pretense for long. She had invited David's attentions, that time in the early days of her marriage when she had come home so distraught by the reality of a wife's obligations in the bedroom. Not that Philip had been unkind, and vaguely she had realised even then that he was trying to be as gentle as possible with the physical process, but for all that she found it uncomfortable and unpleasant. The first time had been painful and she remained sore for days after, and she found nothing attractive about the man heaving above her. David, she was sure, would have been very different, romantic and loving and her body would have yielded to his kisses like the married bliss that the novels alluded to.

She had accepted Philip because in the eyes of most, she and David were brother and sister. Romantic novels spoke of the tragic maiden who forsakes true love to save her beloved from social scandal. She would carry her real heart, devastated though it was, with courageous fortitude and do her best by her legal husband despite the tears inside. Thus she dreamed for some weeks, possibly still quite innocently though not harmlessly, for after she had wept out her woes to her mother, she had gone to David's cottage – just to say hello to her 'brother' – and had found herself in his arms, clinging and seeking for just that romance she was supposed to have forsaken.

David, who had watched his young companion turn into a lovely woman and could not help but be aware of her rounded breasts and clean female scent, was this time completely undone. Perhaps, subconsciously, the fact that she was now a married woman, that now he wouldn't be taking a pure virgin, broke that last barrier. His hands were on her in that new way, he began to kiss her and she kissed him back, and eagerly pressed into his arms. Their fervour grew and soon it was too late to stop. He invaded her body, and her loins melted and her womb stirred deliciously. The heat ran through her, as she became one with him, and she knew the real overall bliss of it. "David, David!" she cried, and the sweat ran down her limbs.

What was to be said afterwards in the shivering, embarrassed return to reality, the guilty knowledge of wrong having been done? Struggling with their clothes, longing but embarrassed to look each other in the eye, he had told her sternly that it mustn't happen again, that she was not to come back to his cottage, and that they would not see each other again except in public, and, shaking, she had agreed.

Now she knew the truth of the sexual response, and when she had the first inkling that she might be expecting – and it just had to be David's child; had she not felt her womb stir? – she knew she would have to play a game, so that Philip would have no reason to believe other than this to be his child. So she encouraged him wildly for a while after their return from Hobart, till she felt it safe to announce the pregnancy.

**

The trip to Melbourne had proved inspiring indeed, especially the new railway, and Phillip returned home determined that one would be serving the Tasmanian Midlands soon. If necessary, he would stand for government at the next opportunity.

In due course, he was elected, and pursued his goal doggedly. In 1876 the Hobart to Launceston Railway finally opened. It was beset with difficulties, having been built to the lowest quote offered and therefore of an inadequate standard with a narrow gauge, too-tight curves, poor alignment, and steep gradients. With insufficient funds for the necessary maintenance, its woes remained acute until the government had to take it over, in 1890, but meanwhile Phillip was very satisfied. He had succeeded in making sure that the new rail track ran directly past Corinthia, stopping beside his own cattle yards, and naturally also stopping there whenever any member of his family required it to. The commercial ad-vantages were soon obvious. On one astonishing occasion he found that, having railed several trucks of cattle to the Launceston saleyards and not satisfied with the prices being offered there, he was able to re-load them onto the Hobart train, sell them in the latter city at a better price and still make a profit despite the double rail charge. Every time he heard the cheery steam whistle as the train approached his estate, Philip was filled with the glow of being an Important and Clever Man.

Suited to his fine position, he was also among the first to have a private telephone installed, in the mid eighties, to connect him to his merchant's warehouse in Launceston. The estate staff were awed by this new machine; one old retainer, being demonstrated the voice coming through from city, leapt back, exclaiming: "That's the devil in there!"

It was an exciting time for the small colony of Tasmania, when its own mineral discoveries finally began to lift it out of its economic stagnation. Many of the main investors in the new mining ventures were situated in Launceston; with the opening of the smelters and associated trades came a great flow of money to the town. Attractive public buildings, parks and general amenities were built, agricultural and other exhibitions hosted, and for a heady spell of some thirty years the small northern town outstripped Hobart as the liveliest place in Tasmania. It was also the first place – indeed, the first in the Southern Hemisphere – to have electric street lighting, replacing the gas lamps in 1895. The port, too, was lively, handling among many others' the wool clip of the Cowley family, bearing it away to the insatiable mills of England. The fast Walker Line clippers did a round trip once a year, returning with immigrants and goods for the Launceston shops. The pride of the town, great crowds welcomed them home each time they were sighted approaching down the River Tamar. Among the cheering families Phillip sometimes stood with his sons, a proud part of the prosperity reflected in the great white sails.

The first of his boys, Gavin William Cowley, had been born with ease at Corinthia, causing his mother more heart-agony than physical effort. Isabella soon recovered, sitting in the sunroom crooning to her child and managing the care of him almost entirely by herself, ignoring comments about unladylike involvement with nursing and nappies when there was plenty of staff to do such work. She became known for her hands-on approach in a wider sense, too, even being seen on her knees in the mud beside a sick animal – and often able to heal it, too. She was liked by the servants and mostly willingly obeyed.

Gavin grew healthily; in time, he acquired brothers and sisters, and it looked like a most successful family. The dourness that Philip feared to find in his wife, proved unfounded. After an uncertain start – understandable, he had since decided, in any young bride of strict upbringing – the personal side of their marriage proved gratifyingly satisfying. She remained eager in the bedroom, between the subsequent pregnancies, and he found himself a contented man, surveying with steady pleasure his extensive estate, comfortable fortune, exalted social position, and large family. Life was good. For nineteen years, Philip continued in this comfortable state, unaware of the potential traitor growing within it.

**

Isabella had strictly observed David's request not to come near him, partly from wounded pride and partly for fear of discovery. But when Gavin was four, she had taken the coach to Fairbourne to visit Susannah, bringing her son along with his little sister Mary-Eliza and the newest baby, Albert. In the flurry of cooing over the littlest ones, Gavin had escaped into the courtyard and was wandering, entranced, among the chickens and rich animal smells till he encountered a man who hunkered down in front of him, and asked who he might be. He seemed a nice man with a kindly if somewhat sad face so Gavin announced himself readily enough. His four-year-old innocent clarity allowed him to observe the startled look this produced in the man, and feeling sorry for him, the child asked gravely if he had seen the chickens sitting on the fence?

They did indeed look rather comic, five plump white hens perched closely together like a series of round feathered balls, cocking their small heads in short quick darts and gutturally clucking about the things they perceived as noteworthy. The distraction proved welcome to the man, that he might put his emotions back under control, and when little Gavin turned back to him, he was smiling and agreeing that the chickens were great fun. So the two began to wander around the yard, looking in the stables, leaning on the fence where some old ewes were spending their last few days all unknowing of the butcher's chopping block awaiting them, the child closely observing their unfathomable yellow eyes. Man and boy together, no words were needed to make them understand that they were good mates.

David, having entered the yard directly from the fields and therefore unaware of Isabella's presence, now studied his sturdy small son. Half fascinated, he was also appalled. Here was his sin, his transgression, his guilt, and for many a night thereafter he pleaded with God for forgiveness. Only God could be told, for clearly the child was accepted as Phillip's son, and he – he who had desecrated that man's wife in his weakness – he had no claim on the boy whatsoever. His heart would never be allowed any say, and the best thing he could do was to keep away as much as possible. Despite the immediate bond he had felt with the boy, it was too risky to be seen in his company, in case he betrayed himself or a sharp eye picked up the likeness. Even less could he face Isabella, and for love of her he could not take any chances that could jeopardise her stability and respect as Phillip's wife. So he ushered the child safely back to the door and popped him inside, going immediately round the outside of the house to the kitchen to tell the cook that he would not be eating lunch today as some fence line was broken and needed immediate attention. Cutting himself a hunk of bread and cheese, he fled.

And so the star-crossed lovers went along for some years, each eating their heart out for the other, finding a perverse fulfilment in their frustrated love. When a meeting was absolutely unavoidable, such as at a family wedding, they would keep as far apart as the room would allow. But at a christening, David couldn't help himself, watching her, sitting a few pews in front of him, with such longing that his soul was naked upon his face. At that moment, as if drawn by the intensity of her child's emotion, Susannah turned around and saw his agony. In perceiving it, the puzzle of her youngest child fell into place, and then she, also, knew.

The shock was great. But it was not a complete surprise. She had known that David and Isabella were much too close, but that they had in fact consummated their love, illicitly, shook her. She tallied up the months again to the birth of the child, but – though he had come three weeks earlier than the officially expected birth date – it was nevertheless nearly a full year after the wedding. So, if they had not dallied before that marriage, it had to be after. It seemed so unlikely, surely, but there had been that time when the girl had come home in great distress. Yes, of course. That one fitted perfectly. Susannah became the third person to know, and though none of them ever spoke a word out loud about it, it became a secret that weighed on their consciences.

Nothing is without its price.

Isabella had come to the marriage with a part of her already locked away from it, her love for David engaging her heart entirely. Every day, he was the first thing on her mind, and all day long she spoke to him in her thoughts. Occasional family frictions between her and Philip she resolved by imagining how differently it might be if David were her husband. Her joys and woes she shared with him, seeing herself as one of the tragic and selfless heroines that she found in the novels she was so avidly reading. Her mind was constantly filled with such fantasies, giving her a remote and elfin look.

Yet it was also heroic, this betrayal of her marriage vows, for she was inwardly strong and very capable, confirmed in what was right, and never once could she be accused of the least outward omission to her duties as a wife. She was always gracious and kind, presenting a smiling face to all that required it, and the many visitors to Corinthia noted how good and happy a wife she was to Phillip. She knew that the early pretended passion, to cover her unfaithfulness, had laid a groundwork that she would have to maintain, so when the time came, she was as passionate a wife as any man could hope for. That her mind meanwhile pictured another one into whose embraces she melted so deliciously, never crossed her real husband's mind. Loving David became a habit to her. Her guilt made her a better wife than she might perhaps otherwise have been, but it took her attention away from seeing the real Phillip, who – despite being rather unromantic, occasionally quite irascible, and somewhat full of himself – was basically a kindly man, sincerely proud and appreciative of his wife, and concerned to provide well for her.

***

David had none of Philip's prosaic self-assurance, and his soul was deeply troubled. In desperation, he almost unburdened himself to the Presbyterian minister at nearby Kirkland Church, but was held back by the risk to Isabella, the church being local, the Reverend only human, and one of his own sisters married into that same family as well. But there was the Catholic confessional in Launceston, where he was unknown and no name was required for the speaking out of his guilt. The pronounced absolution left David unconvinced; nevertheless he did feel lighter at heart for having expressed his sin. His official reason for visiting Launceston had been to collect some stores and farming supplies needed at Fairbourne, and now he directed his loaded wagon along the road back home. Presently he found himself offering a lift to a man walking the same way.

"You're looking for work?" he asked, when the stranger was settled beside him on the driver's seat. The man assented, and David, taking in his strong physique and rather liking the look of him, continued: "What can you do?"

"Anything on the farm...shearing, building, fencing, mending, animals...anything except butchering. I won't do that."

Something in the way he said it made David look more closely. His age was hard to determine, the face being more mature than the youthful body suggested. They were unusually dark features that this man had, something foreign about him, gipsy, maybe, or Gaelic Irish? No, David decided, it's something else, and as the man unflinchingly returned his gaze, it dawned on him that here was a half caste, one with a lot of native blood in him. The man saw his recognition, and settled back. "I'm Marner Larkin."

They went some way in silence, the country spreading greenly out from the unmade road, along which the horses' shod feet clumped steadily and the wagon's axle creaked. David knew well enough that they didn't need another hand on the farm, but surprised himself at the anxiousness with which he was searching for a reason to bring this man home. Maybe they could bring forward the building of that distant fence line that had been spoken of so long, on the foothills of the Western Tiers, and attend to the strengthening of the shepherd's hut there at the same time? Take on this man, if he was willing, only for the time needed to complete that job? David thought he could square that readily enough with his brother George – these outlying jobs were often a nuisance and a drain on the man power. And so it came about that he and Marner found themselves alone out in the bush, spending their days cutting fence posts and putting them up, repairing the old hut, getting their food, and talking. And it was to this oddly familiar stranger that David began to speak about all his inner things, his loss of a love, about a son who shouldn't be there, of his not fitting in with the fairly simple ambitions of his own worthy family and even less with those of the worldly society around him, his sense of despair, and that awful crying in the wind that apparently nobody else could hear.

"I hear it," said Marner. "It's the cry of the wounded and dispossessed, it's the groan of nature destroyed for greed, the wailing of the animals driven out and the broken song of the birds shot for no real reason, the sadness of those who don't count, and those whose dignity was trampled on. It's the tears of the broken hearts and it's the cry of those who didn't love when they could have."

On the morning that the job was finished, Marner was gone, disappeared into thin air and never collecting his accrued wages. David was not entirely surprised, for the suspicion had been growing upon him that this man was not of this earth, but a spirit sent to take his burden, to open his eyes to a broader knowledge, and to show his soul that there was a place for it after all. From then on, David was more content within, able to return to a satisfying appreciation of nature's kingdom around him, and less disturbed by the doings of humanity. Next time he saw his son, he was more relaxed in his role as an uncle to be occasionally visited.

Such visits however became increasingly frequent, as young Gavin discovered how much he enjoyed his uncle's company. Both Isabella and Susannah watched with mixed feelings, for Gavin found little common ground with his father Phillip, being made of a very different clay. But as the company of an older man was most desirable to temper and guide a youth, everyone including Phillip himself could find no reason to object. Initially, he had been frustrated by his oldest son's disinterest in the matters of the estate – except in the well-being of the animals – but he had three younger sons who were all keen to take his place, and he was far too comfortable to get too excited about it.

"Give the boy time," Isabella confirmed soothingly, "he'll probably grow out of it."

There were moments like these to overcome in almost every area; Gavin, despite being an excellent young rider, point blank refused to go with the hunt, labelling it cruel and unnecessary. This was such a major break with Corinthia tradition that father and son nearly came to a serious falling-out. Isabella hosted the hunt ball later in the week, and made extra efforts to look wonderful and be the most gracious of wives among the gentry there. She also made much of her other children, Mary-Eliza at fourteen already promising to be a young beauty, Albert at twelve filling out confidently, Henry at ten daintily handing around bowls of sweetmeats to guests. Beatrice, Gordon and Amy were all considered too young to attend, though their nurse let them peep over the banisters at the throng below. To anyone asking Isabella where Gavin was, she said that he was away on business, and quietly hoped that he and David might perhaps be talking about some farming matters along with their much more likely discussions on the meaning of life or the size of the universe.

When the musicians next struck up a tune, she took her husband's arm and waltzed with him, the perfect and adoring wife.

15. AFTER THE SECOND BALL

And so came the time of another great ball at Government House, in honour of the Queen's Jubilee, in 1887. Most of the Midlands gentry prepared to go. The trip was easy now, for one could go on the train, in a few short hours. Some, like the Cowleys, even made their booking by telephone, as their favourite hotel, Webb's – by now known as Hadley's Hotel – had also installed the new invention. Gavin was not quite nineteen and youthful enough to find the prospect of such a trip exciting – lovely young ladies to dance with, well-stocked bookshops to visit, and the promised wonders of the new gas illuminations to admire. Everyone was astounded when David, also, declared that he would be attending – David, who never went to any such things! He laughed off their surprise, pleading the lure of those bookshops, but his real reason was an unease, a dread feeling of impending doom.

"At eighty-five I am much too old for any such silliness," declared Susannah. "But, David, must you go? It's so unlike you…"

But he insisted, and all she could do was pray, commending them all to God's care. Unable to say it aloud, she could only hope that he wasn't taking the notion of being the real father too seriously.

Isabella also had an uneasy feeling about it. She buried it in the great task of sorting appropriate clothing, not only for herself but particularly for Mary-Eliza, who was now seventeen and attending her first grown-up society ball. Properly presenting a very marriageable daughter was no small task. When there was finally time to just sit, on the train, Isabella proudly considered her record of having, despite a bleeding heart, raised such a fine family. This ball should be a culmination of all that achievement, but the nauseous lump inside her persisted.

Phillip, though typically impatient with the tiresome requirements of court appearances, was innocent of any premonitions. He too had much to be pleased about, having so successfully furthered his position as a leading and respected member of the Colony's gentry. Among the discussions on bloodlines, land deals, and political issues, including those pesky chartists with their shocking notions about every man, no matter how mean and uneducated, having a vote – they called it democracy – there would also be the fact that he had a very attractive daughter for whom a suitable husband had to be selected.

So the main players converged on Hobart, along with thousands of others, all wanting to take part in the many festivities. Around seven thousand school children were given a medal and a bag containing an orange, an apple, and a small cake, as they filed individually through a marquee on the domain. The smell within the tent, some ladies of the volunteer corps later remarked, was enough to make you faint. Every club in town had dinners for its members; endless rehearsals of the national anthem took place, performances, orations and presentations were attended, and booths selling refreshments were set up everywhere. On the night, however, it was noted that there was very little drunkenness. The brilliant blaze of the new gas light illuminations was dazzling to all, but particularly to those accustomed to the ancient darkness of the country.

The grand ball at Government House held more excitement. Nine hundred had been invited. The vice-regal band played the Queen's Jubilee March while everyone stood. Then His Excellency and Lady Hamilton led out the first quadrille, and the rest of the evening was a gay sight with the predominantly white and cream satin gowns interspersed with the scarlet uniforms of the military. It was a dream night for all except the hard-pressed staff and those responsible for the smooth functioning of it all.

David saw nothing to concern him throughout the evening, and – exhausted by the effort of exchanging polite conversation with people he did not know – was glad when it ended. Gavin was clearly having great fun, dancing lustily and scoring several attractive young ladies to escort. His father Phillip introduced him to numerous worthies, and young Mary-Eliza was quite the belle of the ball. They all agreed it had been a very satisfactory evening.

Late that night the wind sprang up. It howled down the streets, rattling windows, setting signs a-creaking, and clanging loose roofing iron. David, who had chosen to stay at the more modest All Nations Hotel, was woken by the unaccustomed racket. As he lay uneasily, a more familiar sound came to him. On the back of the wind he distinctly heard the crying. Go home, go home, it seemed to be urging. What are you doing here? It was so insistent he decided to leave on the first train north that he could get a ticket for.

At the station, he found that the only remaining ticket for the next several days was on a train scheduled to leave inside 30 minutes. But that would not do – had he not promised to take Gavin to Walch's bookshop this very morning?

As he backed away, he bumped into the man standing behind him. Astonished, he recognised Marner Larkin, the mysterious labourer who had worked with him years ago to rebuild the fence and old hut in the foothill of the Tiers.

"Are you going on this train also?"

"No, no, I have a commitment….but how good to see you…" David stammered, shaken. *Marner?* Of all the most unlikely people, what was *he* doing here?

"Come," said the latter, looking hard at him, "here is a ticket. *For you.*"

He thrust it at him, but David declined again, determined not to let Gavin down. As he walked away something tugged sharply in his chest. He knew he was doing a great wrong by turning away, but did so anyway.

✳✳✳

Phillip was not a reader of books. Corinthia's well-stocked library, established by his father, added a desirable touch of gentility, but his own interests were limited to the newspapers and occasionally the London Illustrated News. That morning, as he strolled from Hadley's up Murray St on his way to the Tasmanian Gentleman's Club, though he had noticed Walch's Bookshop near the corner, he would not have had any reason for stopping. But some unholy urge made him cross the street and enter the shop.

David and Gavin were entirely absorbed, pouring over some new book, and did not see him. Their heads so close together, sharing such intimacy, struck Phillip like a knife. Here was his eldest son, giving his Fairfield uncle that easy friendship that he had failed to form with his own father. Phillip's first impulse was to march between them, but something detached clicked in his brain. Watching them more closely, things he had observed but never quite taken on board over the years began to surface. How different the boy really was. How much he looked like David. How his mother was always there to smooth over these awkward moments. Dozens of small incidents, inconsequential in themselves, but adding up to something. What, exactly, he could not fully name just yet. But there was an unease in him, something – what was it now? – from the early days of their marriage. Something that wasn't quite the way it should have been?

Phillip quietly left the shop. Instead of entering the Club, he continued past, walking up Macquarie Street, through South Hobart and into the foothills of the mountain. Around him, the trees creaked and hissed in the still persistent wind. Sitting on a log, he began to consider his wife in a new and thoughtful depth.

On that same morning, Isabella had declared a period of rest, but young Mary-Eliza was ready to go shopping and fretted till she got her way. The two ladies set out from Hadley's Hotel, unaware that something fundamental had shifted. Both complained about the pesky wind, still strong, that upset their bonnets and tugged at their skirts in a most unseemly fashion.

David made some book purchases and took his leave of Gavin. Back at the All Nations Hotel, he chanced upon another Midlander who was also anxious to get home and bewailing the impossibility of places on the train. The two men decided to hire a wagon between them, and after much effort succeeded. Wasting no time, they set forth that very afternoon, David as unaware as Isabella but with a strong urge to get away. The knowledge that it was now too late, that the damage had been done, already sat in his bones but he had yet to acknowledge it.

***

Only two weeks later, mourners gathered at Kirklands Church for Susannah's funeral. While they had all been away at the ball, she had taken to her bed, and after a week's quiet retreat, had handed her soul to God. Though distressed, Isabella was grateful that her grandmother had been spared the scandal that would now surely rock the local community. The way Philip started looking at her when she and Eliza-Mary returned from their shopping spree, had knocked all complacency from her.

However, he had said nothing, and accompanied her to the funeral in the most natural manner. Many of the extended family was there, for they had all respected Susannah, and some had loved her dearly. David, looking bereft and shaken, kept well back. Gavin seemed a little bemused but it was difficult to say what the cause was.

The church service and burial complete, the gathered company prepared to go back to Fairbourne. While waiting for the carriages to line up, Isabella retreated back into the little church to sit.

"He knows, doesn't he?" said David, who had also sought to hide in its recesses but came out when he recognised her.

"Oh David, David," she sobbed as he put his arms around her.

"I'll take you away, dear love," he murmured. "We can disappear, make a new life together somewhere far away, Queensland perhaps. I have enough put by to do that..." hungrily drinking in her still sweet and fresh womanliness. She turned slowly, wonderingly, and for a long time really looked at him.

This was not the man she had for so long been in love with. Twenty years ago, David had still been in his prime, and that is how she had pictured him from then on. Now, he was a frail, ageing man in his mid-fifties. He had none of Philip's solidity or direction, but was rather a weak dreamer who largely let life happen to him. Suddenly, the romance was gone. Stabbed to the heart – for now it was too late – Isabella understood for the first time properly the true value of her husband An enormous regret rose up in her. She also saw her full guilt, and knew she had to expiate it. Running away was not an option. So she left him, desolate, alone in the church, and went to face whatever Philip chose to hand out to her.

The latter had thought long and hard about it. While he didn't know the exact details, and didn't care to ask, he had the sense to stand back from his initial fury at being duped, and counseled himself against any impulsive action. The servants bore the brunt, as he charged around the estate, ordering massive cleanups, a whole new program of ditch-digging, and a complete overhaul of the farm machinery. In the evenings he went for long walks, thoughtfully making his decisions, and by the time of the funeral, he had calmed enough to attend. He even offered a supportive arm to his wife as they stood at the graveside, for he had decided that the family's honour and good name were more important than personal feelings.

"No, my dear, I am not going to disgrace you publicly as I certainly could," Philip told her later that day, after they had returned to Corinthia. Exhausted by the emotional strain of the day, Isabella had sat at the dinner table with her head bowed, unable to keep back the tears. Somehow, he sensed how it was with her, that she also had deep regrets, and, not being a deliberately unkind sort, was moved to release her from her agony.

"You may continue as Mrs. Philip Cowley, attending to the raising of our children and managing the house as you have been doing. But I do not want to see *your* son again. I have made arrangements for him to receive a letter from my solicitor, requesting him to leave Tasmania immediately, to not come back, and to make no further contact with you. I am writing him out of my will, completely disinheriting him, and he will no longer exist as far as I am concerned. And you, my dear, will make no attempt to communicate with him. This I absolutely require of you. Nor will you ever see your David again; no visits to Fairbourne will be allowed for as long as he is there, and if by some mischance you come upon him in public, you will have no private conversation with him. Albert will be raised as my official heir, as is most appropriate for he shows every aptitude in that direction."

And so it was done.

Gavin, stunned and bewildered after being ordered so abruptly to leave Corinthia, and denied permission to see his mother – rode over to see his Uncle David. It was the moment when David could have proudly claimed his fatherhood of Gavin, and put hope and structure into the darkness the boy was now plunged into – but found not the courage. It was lost in a whirl of uncontrolled grief and confusion. For his mother's sake, Gavin agreed to go without fuss. David gave him all the money he had, to help him along, and the solicitor's letter had held a generous bank draft also. With this small comfort, Gavin simply vanished. Officially, he had left to gain wider farming experience with relatives in Western Victoria, and in time he was forgotten by most.

David lived on for another six years before the sadness overcame him completely and he was laid to rest beside his mother in Kirkland's small cemetery, under the shadow of the towering Western Tiers.

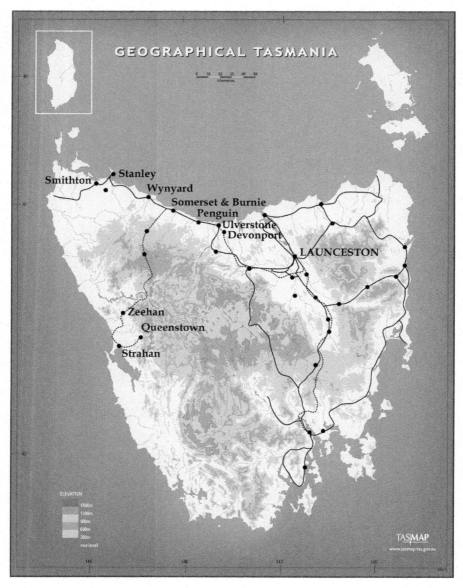

Map 6 – *Tasmania circa 1905*

By 1905, a large part of the North West Coast had been cleared of forest and turned into farmland. Roads remained a nightmare, turning to deep mud in winter, and rivers remained barriers except where bridges had been built. There were frequently washed away by floods. Most trade was done by coastal shipping, until the arrival of the railway around 1900. Until the 1920's, the spur lines into the hinterlands were the farmers' principal means of getting their produce to market, and enabled the creation of many small rural communities.

THE EX-CONVICT TURNERS
1835 – 1914

Man is born free, but everywhere he is in chains.

Jean-Jacques Rousseau

16. GEORGE

The woman moaned and tried to shift away from the pain. Already weak with malnutrition, she lay on the lumpy sacking mattress stuffed with decomposing straw without hope and put up no fight, just waiting for it to be over and another dead child to slide from her. Her first-born, Howard, had come lustily enough, but then they still had some dignity and enough to eat. Their second child had found not enough nourishment to come to a live birth, as by then the potato market had collapsed and there was nothing to eat except rotting potatoes. It would be just as well for this third one to be the same, for they were even worse off now.

The bark hut stood deep in the dark forest, hastily built by George in a hidden corner at the back of Drew's 500-acre timber concession in which he now worked, perforce, as a splitter again. His little son, barely five, sat outside the door, frightened by the strange noises his mother was making, and desolate, knowing his father would not be back till much later. Vaguely he felt he should help, but could think of nothing but doing more of his usual jobs, gathering kindling and bringing up water from the creek. So he kept on till his legs gave out. He was getting hungry, though he was used to that. His mother had gone quiet; after a while he thought it was too quiet and peeked in. A foul, fetid smell assailed him.

The woman lay asleep and by her feet was something horrible, covered in blood. He backed away, and continued sitting, scratching at the ground with a stick, a lonely little figure. The darkness hovered around him, sliding silently through the huge trees and pooling in the gullies.

His father George, on his way back to the hut, was full of bitter thoughts and hatred for Thomas Drew. Having been cheated by the latter so as to leave them without anything at all, he and some other men in a similar position were now being ripped off as well, paid only in basic goods and a pittance insufficient to keep a mouse alive, for the palings they laboriously split in the forest. Drew, the bastard, was an ex-convict like himself, for all his fine airs, and he should've been fair in his dealings, at least with his own kind.

Thomas Drew had stolen two horses in England and been trans-ported for life, arriving in Van Diemens Land in 1832. How he managed to be a carrier in Launceston with his own horse and dray within only a few years is not clear. He prospered even then and had a keen eye for business, and the very fine timber stands of the NorthWest Coast promised riches. He bought a small schooner, and by 1840 he was not only collecting the palings, shingles, posts and more from the rivers, but he engaged his own splitters, hired more boats, and began to make real profits, particularly in supplying the new town of Adelaide with housing materials. By a fortuitous good chance, he was in the right place to overpower two bushrangers and deliver them to the prison in Laun-ceston. For this he was rewarded with the lease to a 640-acre block of crown land on the banks of the Don River, and by 1842 – the year in which he also received a full pardon – he had purchased it. Not only was the land alongside the river where a safe anchorage could be developed, but it was also on some of that fine, rich, chocolate brown soil that the NorthWest would soon become famous for. But first, the enormous, dark forest had to be removed from it.

It was at this point that Drew, already a sharp dealer, began to overstep the line. He had no scruples about exploiting his former convict peers. If they didn't have the gumption to make something of themselves, like he had done, well then they deserved all they had coming to them. So he let his fine land to poor tenant farmers, usually in 21-acre lots on condition that they cleared it for him, and tempted them in with low rental rates. He didn't bother explaining to them the fine detail of the lease terms, which were cleverly worded to enable him to evict tenants off their piece under certain conditions. And he made sure that each one finally found themselves precisely in those conditions – unable to pay the annual rent. It was so simple: he bought the timber they cleared at a very low price, so they had very little to spare after buying the basic essentials and the necessary seed potatoes to sow. He also insisted that a high proportion of the land was properly grubbed out, thus largely disallowing his tenants the earlier opportunity of sowing produce around the ring-barked trees, which was the method most other farmers were adopting around them. So, after years of slaving away, the tenants found that they could not adequately supplement their incomes, or even grow enough of their own food, and inevitably sooner or later they defaulted on the rent.

George Turner had been one of those hopeful tenants. Excited at the chance to finally farm a bit for himself, he had signed, with difficulty after 15 years of not having held a pen in his hand, his name to a lease with Drew in 1842.

His time as assigned convict with the VDL Company had finally come to an end seven years earlier, and he was able to apply to Magistrate Horne for his ticket-of-leave. With two more years on probation before he could apply for his full freedom, he was meanwhile free to take paid work wherever he wanted. His goal was Launceston – work could surely be found there, and perhaps someone from Pontefract found, who might know something about his family. It was thirteen years since he had his last despairing court-room glimpse of his mother.

George had left Circular Head in the company of John King, a kindly overseer contracted to the VDL but so appalled by the conditions there that he left, with his family, after only three years. He invited George to join him on the way, even paying for his passage on the *Fanny*.

But George couldn't handle the noise and bustle of the town. The years in isolation had affected him, and his strange eyes drew unwelcome attention from all he met. Adrift without a structure that directed his days and actions, he was terrified of getting into another bad situation – which was all that life had dealt him so far. When the extra shillings

King had given him ran out, and he had still not fallen on his feet, he retreated from the fray by taking a job as a wattle bark stripper at Port Sorell. An immediate start, four shillings a day, and the *Rebecca* would take him there when she left on the next tide. George, grateful to have something settled without having hassles over it, left the town without accomplishing either of his original intentions, to find work away from the isolation of the hinterland and to seek news of his family. In his hurry, he also forgot that ticket-of-leavers were required to advise the local magistrate of their movements if they wished to leave the area they were registered to be in.

So once more George found himself on a boat going west, although this time it was not far along the coast, and not as a convict – he was going to work for a wage of real money. He joined the group of men working along the Rubicon and Green's Creek, living in simple bark huts and working steadily for weeks until, somehow, a keg of rum would find its way into their midst and for a few days they had a wild break. The men were all single, and mostly decent enough, but in their drunken bouts unnatural things would happen, and George, with no hope of a woman, did it too. What else was there? Later he was deeply disgusted with himself, but at the time it was all a man wanted.

Gradually there was less and less wattle bark to be found within transportable distances, so their employer Charles Friend decided to move on to bigger things. There was fine timber standing around the Mersey and Forth Rivers, and splitters were needed there.

Until 1838 the area west of Port Sorell was seen as an inaccessible and largely useless wilderness covered by an enormous gloomy forest. The only known areas were the mouths of the rivers, the Mersey, Don, Forth, and Leven, investigated by captains seeking safe shelter. But the 1830's brought about a broader interest in those parts – the recent development of the Port Phillip area which needed supplies of all kinds, the growth of Adelaide calling out for timber, and the fact that virtually all imme-diately useable land elsewhere in Van Diemens Land had meanwhile been granted away, leaving none for new immigrants or for the native born children of those already settled. Ex-convicts, also, were looking for somewhere to live and they, too, had children.

One of the first to live there and work the land himself was James Fenton, son of a well-connected Irish Protestant family, who applied for, and then bought, 1000 acres in the Forth River area in 1839. As he began to harvest the timber, he discovered the rich soil beneath the rainforest. He also pioneered the method of ring-barking the trees that subsequently made it possible to clear the entire NorthWest and turn it into farmland of the finest quality. A rush for the land followed, led as usual by speculators who were mostly absentee owners, and either did nothing with their blocks or else let their large acreages in smaller parcels to applicants on particular terms.

But none of them had terms quite as harsh as Thomas Drew, to whom George now applied for the piece of land that would get him started, he believed, on the road to respectable self-sufficiency. Hard work would not be a problem – he was used to that. He was already an experienced splitter, a handy carpenter, and strong in all manner of general labour.

Overjoyed at having secured a lease, he looked at his piece, some little way up the Don Valley with what would now be described as million-dollar views, and began to build a slab hut. But not just any hut – this was to be a home, for George had finally got his eye on a girl who might just be willing to marry him. And now that he was on his way to being respectable, he found the confidence to seriously think about asking.

Whilst working as a splitter on the Mersey two years before, George had encountered there an Irish family. Martin Meagher, an ex-convict, was unable to find work once the probation system began, and did what many of his compatriots resorted to: retreating to the fringe of the great forest, he built a small hut out of casual sight of the authorities and cultivated some potatoes in hastily scratched-up soil. Over time, a large group of such poor families developed into a separate class, reviled and considered the lowest of the shiftless low. Any drunken brawls, thefts or other mischief was immediately laid at their door, often with good reason, and agents and bailiffs were forever trying to move them on. Brewing up the sly grog was one of the ways such families got by.

But George had noticed fifteen-year-old Rose, thin as a rake and no beauty, who had the same wheat-coloured hair and blue eyes as his mother. Shy and awkward with her, he persisted in spite of himself, glad that she didn't seem to mind his odd eyes, and somehow it began to be understood that Rose and George were going to be a couple. He vowed that he would provide a decent home for her, and when the lease with Drew appeared to offer exactly that opportunity, he asked her to marry him. He had saved up the license fee, and though he had not the means to take them to Launceston in search of a minister, he promised that he would ask the first one to visit these parts to solemnize the union. Thus Rose and George moved onto the 20 acres on the hill behind the Don Heads, into the hut he had built and fitted out with a box bed, a table and a fireplace.

"There's room for the cot there," he said shyly but proudly, and in due course the same was filled with his son Howard.

These were George's few best years – the time from 1840 when he first met Rose to after the birth of his first-born. He set to work with a will, felling the best trees to turn into palings that Drew collected regularly. He fenced a bit for a vegetable garden, which Rose tended, and one day he even brought back a small clutch of chickens. He was just forty, still vigorous, he had a wife and a son and the prospect of becoming respectable. For a short while he was almost happy.

It wasn't long before it all went wrong.

The 1840's were bad time for the increasing number of small farmers in the area. A severe economic depression had hit the whole island, collapsing the price paid for potatoes along with almost everything else. Only those with spare resources and a broad base of operations could hang in there with reasonable comfort. Louisa Meredith, wife of the newly-appointed local police magistrate, wrote that never in her life had she seen such poverty and starvation as in the forests of the NorthWest, noting the many desperate families who had nowhere else to go, trying to hang on till things got better. At first, George and Rose with little Howard were still managing, and late in 1843 he had an unexpected visit from John King, the kindly overseer who had helped him depart from the VDL Company in 1835.

Two years earlier, King had bought 640 acres of crown land at Table Cape, good land on the River Inglis, near where the town of Wynyard would eventually stand. He was the first settler in the area, living in isolation with his wife and their six children, setting about the gruelling task of clearing and fencing. Want of supplies had brought him to Launceston, and on his return journey on horseback, after making enquiries, he stopped at the Don Heads to see George Turner.

"I've often wondered how you went. You kind of disappeared from Launceston – wasn't till recently I heard you were out here," he greeted him, and was proudly introduced to Rose and little Howard, and taken on a tour of the work done so far on the 20-acre lease. "I'm glad you've got something solid now, married and a father, too!"

King gave them his own news, and also mentioned that the VDL Company had been letting leases, small and large, around the area of Emu Bay. Not only that, but they were even guaranteeing the price of potatoes grown by their tenants. George looked a little anxious – had he missed out again? – but consoled himself that he did have a lease, after all, and that he had no wish to be landlorded by that awful VDL Company. Besides, Emu Bay was a lot further away to the west, a wild and lonely place that he remembered uncomfortably from his convict days, and he had no wish to go back there.

"Well, not really knowing where you were at, I thought you might have liked to know," King said. "You seem well set here now. But you know where I can be found, if you have any need."

George's need would soon be very great, but by the time he tried to follow up on that offer, he found that King was dead, drowned in the Cam River in early 1845 as he was returning from another trip to Launceston. Yet another of the few men George had risked liking was lost to him. That same year, Drew evicted him mercilessly, and the Turner family became homeless, skulking illegally in the little bark hut at the back of the timber concession, barely alive on the few shillings and supplies that George's work managed to earn him. His hatred of mankind grew along with his inner certainty that he had no chance in this world where only some were powerful and all the rest like himself were mere pawns to fate's whims. Had he not tried, worked so hard to be decent? On his way back to their desolate little hut, he bitterly contemplated that, despite his efforts, all had been taken away again.

Finding his little boy mute with misery and the dead bundle at his wife's feet, he raged inwardly while he did what he could to make them comfortable. That night, he walked miles back through the bush to the nearest homestead and stole a chicken. Ticket-of-leavers were not meant to have guns, but not being able to shoot his own game meant starvation for his family. Now that he had stepped back over the line into criminality again, George started planning how he might steal a gun, too. The chicken became the stew that revived his wife, and the next day George showed up for work as normal, afraid that an absence might lead to him being connected with the missing bird.

His position was altogether precarious. Having failed to report his place of residence from the time he had left Launceston, as was required of ticket of leavers, he had not applied for his full pardon either when it became due, fearing it might be refused. By the time a minister was known to be in the area, for the same reason he did not ask for his marriage to be solemnized, nor did he report the birth of his son. He managed to dodge the muster of 1841. Unsure of the possible consequences, George was constantly full of fear. All he knew was that the world had it in for him, and he needed to move on yet again. But a gun was essential, and close by was James Fenton's homestead...

A few nights later, he roused his wife Rosie, told her to gather Howard and their few rags. Their cooking pot he used, for want of a satchel, as a container. In it went what was left of the flour, a twist of tea, some salt, and a few potatoes and turnips.

"We're going west," he said, "to Emu Bay. I've heard there's work there."

Too dazed to protest, she followed him through the dark bush, he carrying the whimpering child and she the pot and their blanket. He had something else with him, but it was not until daylight, after he had pushed them hard to cover several miles, that she recognized it for a gun.

"George – did you *steal* it?"

"Yes. I've had enough of bloody starvation. Once we're well away, I'll be able to hunt and we'll have a decent feed."

"Oh George...."

Their change in status came hard to her. Going from respectable poor to real criminal was a big step down. But what could she say? Being proper had failed them. She stumbled on, consoling little Howard, whom George was mostly carrying. He wasn't heavy, poor mite, there wasn't enough meat on him to make him so.

By late morning George felt it safe to stop. They had not been following the official track to Emu Bay, as the risk of detection along there was too high. One might get away with stealing a chicken, but not a gun. Although James Fenton, from whose house he had taken it, was a decent sort, he was still supposed to report such a theft to the local police constable.

"Fenton – it's odd," thought George, "it was almost as though he'd cooperated with the theft?"

George had planned it carefully, watching the house until he was sure it was empty, and sighting a window likely to be vulnerable, had made a successful entry, quickly finding a choice of guns and ammunition as well. He took the only kind he was familiar with – one that looked like the ones Herbert Fairfield had issued to his shepherds – and much hoped that he was choosing the right shot and powder for it. Grabbing as much of the latter as he could and climbing hurriedly out again, he had caught sight of Fenton walking back towards the house together with another man, and felt he'd been seen. But Fenton had turned back, deliberately it seemed, to his companion…he could've raised a hullabaloo instead… why didn't he…?

George couldn't wait to find out. He had got his family away as quickly as he could that night, and however hungry they might be, he couldn't risk the sound of a shot that might be heard by someone. But now he settled Rosie and Howard in their miserable blanket and sought a small clearing near a stream, where he hunkered down to wait. An hour earlier he had tested the gun with a single precious shot, and to his relief found it worked well enough. All that remained was to hit something effectively, a wallaby by preference. Surely he could manage that.

He did, and they lit a small fire. The stolen gun filled their bellies for the first of many times. They were deep in the forest, more than six miles back from the coastal track, and after two days of feasting and resting, they made their way cautiously and slowly along, gradually finding themselves in an unexpected network of faint pathways and, eventually, humble huts and other people who were also living precariously out of sight of any authorities. They were all the same, desperately poor, either ex or runaway convicts, usually Irish. Some had stories like George and Rosie's, others had something more sinister to hide; all were united in their hatred of those who had means. But they shared unstintingly the shelter of their simple bark huts, a place to sleep, information and tips on how to manage. Rosie's obvious Irishness opened the doors to them. A few of their hosts were better established, with potatoes and turnips growing in small areas cleared between the trees, but most were not as permanent as that, just trying to survive on theft, sly-grog brewing, and amazing ingenuity that made something out of nothing.

Bit by bit as they moved further west they learned of what was happening, who was living where, and who could be trusted. If he hadn't had a family, George would have happily fitted in and stayed, but the sight of Rosie, so like his mother, trying to keep herself and Howard warm in their pitiful rags, kept him moving. And she was expecting again…he had to provide for her, and soon.

It was true that he'd heard of possible work in Emu Bay – John King had mentioned how some of the first to lease land there were doing quite well. Gibson, the VDL Company's new manager who had replaced Edward Curr, started the tenancy scheme there at a low two shillings an acre. But to prevent 'undesirables', Gibson accepted only tenants with capital, at least £400. This meant occupiers had enough resources to clear, fence and prepare the land efficiently, and it also meant that such people often had work to offer. It was there that George was headed. As they went along, they heard of one farmer in particular – Cornelius Morris, who was also from Ireland and who was said to be a good man.

Good men. Every time he had been helped by someone, it had been by a *good man*. What made a good man? George was not given to much deep contemplation, but he had noted one thing – they usually had an active church connection. Not that George himself had any time for the regular church, as it was part of the hated authorities, but Rosie said that this man Morris was a good Catholic and therefore must be alright. The experience with Drew had made George unwilling to trust anyone, but since he had to find work somewhere, then this man might be the one to approach.

And so it proved. Cornelius and Mary Morris had emigrated from Ireland, initially to New Zealand, but in 1846 they arrived at Emu Bay, and leased 160 acres on the coast and into the hills up behind, alongside the Cooee Creek. Here they established themselves successfully, eventually purchasing their land, becoming respected pioneers of the district.

Mary Morris was a trained teacher. Even she, together with some of the older of their seven children, worked on clearing the land. They built a cottage beside the Cooee Creek, and by 1849 they were employing several men to help. When George and Rosie knocked on their door, Mary took one look at the young woman, obviously pregnant, and immediately took them in. George began to work for Cornelius who appreciated his obvious skills with timber, and with a regular wage coming in, a cosy little hut, and surrounded by friendly folk, he began to hope again. There was even a school for young Howard, as Mary taught the neighbouring children part-time, usually in the evenings. Presently Rose gave birth to a living child, whom they called Henry. By 1850 she was expecting another, and life was almost good again.

But fate never smiled upon George for long.

His expectation that everything good would be snatched away from him before he had time to enjoy it, came painfully true once more at the end of that year, first when Cornelius Morris drowned in the Inglis River on returning from a visit to Gibson at Stanley, and secondly when Rose died, unable to deliver the breech baby. Mary Morris was giving birth to her eighth at the very same time, and was therefore unable to help, being both in childbed and prostrated by the sudden loss of her husband. The Morris child lived, but Rose, swollen with her unborn, was buried in Emu Bay's first proper cemetery, now vanished, along the Romaine Creek in what is now Brooklyn. This was up the hill from the original company store in Emu Bay, where, nineteen years earlier, George had dug two graves for the blacks, one of them being Tom Kickerterpoller.

The darkness came pouring out of the trees, flowing over the sand and pursuing George who was running, howling, along the beach at Cooee...the same beach where he had seen the black woman axed to death, and Goldie dragging her child and the other woman into captivity. Their screams filled his ears just as they had then when he had stood by and done nothing to help them. In the blackness was Henry Hellyer, too, whose name he had failed to defend properly, just to save his own skin. The specters of John King and Cornelius Morris rose from their watery graves and joined the macabre dance. By the next tree stood his mother, stricken in the court by the magistrate's decision to send him to Van Diemens Land. The darkness grew, and swirled about him, now filled with Rosie's terrible screams as well, flowed into his mind and filled it completely.

The small community then had another to bury – George, who had come back from the beach, taken a rope from the barn and had hung himself among the trees further up the slope. They put him in the little cemetery beside Rosie, even though he had taken his own life, as the ground was not yet properly consecrated and the case too sad to do anything else. Mary Morris, still too unwell to attend, had the care of young Howard, nearly eight, and his toddler brother Henry. There was nowhere for them to go, so Mary simply added them to her own brood of eight, where they grew into sturdy young men.

17. HOWARD

Forty-two years later, in 1893, as Howard Turner was turning fifty, he sat looking out the window in his cottage at Deep Creek near Wynyard. The special chair his brother Henry had built for him after the accident, held him upright. Outside lay his own thirty acres. Half was wholly cleared, cattle grazing placidly on it. He had purchased it outright in 1881, after leasing it from Moore & Quiggin Sawmillers for a number of years. Nearby lay Henry's fifty acres. The two of them had found work with the Wynyard timber mill in the early 1860's. Soon they earned enough to start putting some money by, and presently both got married. Now they had growing families, a weatherproof home each, a measure of security and an awareness of the opportunities unfolding around them as the area developed steadily and the population numbers grew.

Howard, confined by his long convalescence to the special chair, had time to consider how they had reached such a measure of stability. After the tree fell on him and smashed most of the bones in his pelvis, he had been angry and despairing, but in time a measure of good sense reestablished itself in his mind. His wife's steadiness, Henry's ongoing assistance, and the unstinting help from his fellow-believers among the Christian Bible Gathering, all helped. Now he also paid silent tribute to the woman who had not only given him and Henry a home when they were orphaned, but had taken their upbringing as seriously as that of her own eight children.

Mary Morris, still reeling from the sudden death of her own husband, included the two boys into her own family partly out of pity and Christian charity, but also because it was the simplest way of dealing with the problem. Mary was a most practical lady, and now, with her oldest boy having to take full responsibility for the farm still being clawed from the forest, and increasingly cultivated and stocked, she did not have the time to hunt up a magistrate in Launceston, who might have been able to make some decisions regarding Howard and Henry. She was already feeding eight – two more would make little difference. Besides, she had gathered during the barely two years that she had known their parents – poor ones! what a horrible way to die! – that there were no relatives at all for George and that Rosie's were not a reliable sort, even if they could be found. She also sensed that George would rather not be brought to the attention of any authorities. Not that he had done anything bad, of that she was sure. It was just an unfortunate combination of circumstances, underlined by ignorance and a lack of education.

Education was Mary's forte, and she was running a lively little school. The classes were held mostly in the evenings as many children, including Howard, had to work during the day. She was a firm and kindly teacher, expecting good work from her scholars but not without humour and a keen musical appreciation. At the end of the week, there would be a lesson in country dancing, accompanied on an upright piano or the viol played by one of her children. The piano was Mary's pride and joy, as there were not many such to be found along the coast at the time. It had been Cornelius' last gift to her; he had arranged to have it shipped over from Melbourne in one of the small cutters that called regularly at Emu Bay for timber and potatoes. Getting it safely off the ship and up to the house at Cooee had been a major operation.

Howard and Henry had both repaid their kindly adopted mother not only with hard work on her farm, but by becoming literate, thoughtful and largely sober young men. Despite the early tragedies of their life, the two boys had better opportunities than either of their parents had ever had.

The Widow Morris, as she was widely known, became an important figure in Burnie. By 1860, she was the official teacher employed by the Board of Education at £30 a year. Mary was retired only after many years of service, when an officious new inspector decided that her Irish and Catholic primers would no longer do. She continued to teach privately, especially the poorer settlers and their children, back in her cottage in Cooee, from which she had walked all these years, in rain or shine, all the way to the town school. It was well-known, her white house with unusual-shaped windows full of diamond panes and pit-sawn timber floors, not only for her classes, but also practical help. Mary was skilled at herbal simples and all manner of medical treatments, and she never withheld her services from anyone who couldn't afford to pay. Her children and all the neighbourhood loved and respected her, including the Turner boys.

"Thank you, Mrs. Morris," thought Howard, shifting in his chair to ease the stiffness of his joints. "You gave us so much."

It had been a steady progression for them from the farm at Cooee, both finding work quite readily in a variety of labouring, farming and timber tasks. More and more people came to the area, each needing help to get established. From the Mersey River in the east to Circular Head in the west, a string of towns developed along the coast. The country behind each was penetrated and cleared, road trusts opened up the vital access to the backblocks, without which no farmer could sell his produce, and bridges were constructed over the rivers with their treacherous sandbars. Thus Forth, Ulverstone, Penguin, Burnie, and Wynyard, with many a smaller village in between, forever changed the "impenetrable and totally uninhabitable wasteland", as the coast had been described in 1823, into a fine and fertile farmland, famous for potatoes, and presently, dairying.

But first the land had to be cleared, and there was big money in it. William Moore and Robert Quiggin were brothers-in-law who had studied engineering and mill design before emigrating to Australia. They quickly selected 4000 acres south of the Inglis River, and over the next twenty years became the biggest timber trade business in Tasmania. Moore & Quiggin also developed a trade in financial affairs and investment, so it was not hard for the Turner boys, who by then had proved their worth, to get their leases at an affordable rent, and which enabled them to own the land quite quickly. It was the penultimate achievement, and on the way to it they also found the time to get married.

It all came about through of the Christian Bible Gathering.

In the 18th and 19th centuries, in the USA and in England, there were a series of great Christian revivals, the best known no doubt being that led by John Wesley of the Methodist Church. The massive 'Outpouring of the Spirit', as the movement was often described, had a dramatic effect on the lives of thousands of people everywhere, particularly the working man.

Those who were drunk, wretched or hopeless suddenly discovered a new way to live, felt infilled by the spirit, and many began to live sober, industrious and orderly lives. It was a most remarkable social transformation.

For convicts, who often came from very non-religious backgrounds, attendance at services had been enforced, thus uniting religion with hated authority in the minds of many. As they became free and joined the labouring classes in forming a large part of the new communities in the forests, beyond the unrelenting hard work there was no culture or inner life, and very little education, amongst them. The Christian message, when preached powerfully as it was by fiery missionaries in the 1870's, came as rain in the desert to many, providing a greater sense of community, purpose and inner satisfaction. The sense of loss, dislocation and alienation in a strange land was replaced with meaning and belonging. Many were drawn to the simplicity of the gathering chapels, the absence of lengthy ritual, the inclusion of every man as a potential preacher with no attention to social rank, and the strong structure of clear beliefs.

Howard and Henry also began to attend the newly-formed Christian Bible Gathering, initially held in local homes and presently in a small chapel. It was a long walk to attend, but the two young men did it willingly, responding with deep conviction to the word of God, and to take their places as part of the respectable believers. And not least because there were some daughters among the families attending.

In time Howard at just thirty married Anne, and Henry wed Evelyn a few months later. Both girls came from country labouring families who had arrived in the 1860's from England, with the help of the St Andrew's immigration society. Soon children were born. Some died young of illness and accident, including Howard's first, but others grew strongly. His third child, Silas, was thirteen when he saw the timber fall on his father.

The general practice of ring-barking the larger eucalypt trees and leaving them upright to die slowly over some years while cultivating the ground around them, was useful but brought its own dangers. Storms like the great gale in May 1893 could bring down the crowns of these giants, and sometimes the whole tree itself. But occasionally, on still days, a huge branch that had been previously weakened could snap and fall suddenly without warning. Hurtling down from a great height in less time than it took to look up, the shattering pieces flew like missiles in all directions. Howard was harvesting potatoes, and would have been pulped outright had not the horse with the cart taken the full force. As it killed the animal, the settling branch gave a final twist, swiping Howard off his feet by hitting him in the pelvis with an outer tip before scattering the last of its deadly load around the fallen man.

Young Silas, further down the row with his own sack to fill, was physically untouched. He came running up, terrified as to what he might find, but there was nothing he could do. The timber was far too heavy to move. He flew like the wind to get help, and was met partway by Anne who had heard the crash. He didn't need words for her to know. It had happened too often in the area. "Run for Henry!" she cried, and she too could do nothing at the scene except call out Howard's name and pray.

It took several big men to free Howard, and then they brought him back to the cottage, laid flat on a door, still mercifully unconscious. There was no hospital to take him to. A man skilled in bone-setting was found, who straightened out and splinted the injured man. Neighbours and friends, especially from their own Bible Gathering, prayed over him. It seemed a miracle that his back was not broken after all, and that he did, very slowly and painfully, recover. As he got better, Henry built him a special chair of a comfortable height and with a supporting back, which they padded. The bones knit together sufficiently to allow him to walk again, clumsily and never without pain, but it was more than could have been hoped for.

"Truly, God was with you," they all agreed.

And they all turned out to help, bringing the rest of the crop in, sowing grasses and later finding some extra stock to put on it, for Howard would clearly never farm again. Some of the church members quietly took Anne aside and enquired about the family's finances; others simply pressed a few coins into her hand. Silas at thirteen was still in school but pitched in too, and Anne learnt to be a nurse as well as managing the family, garden, the daily round of milking their six cows and selling the milk to the new butter factory established by Mr Fenton. That milk was their saviour, providing a monthly summer income of around £12.

Besides Silas, they had Gwen at 15, old enough to work alongside Anne, and both Margaret, 11, and Nellie at 7 could help. Little Daniel was but a toddler, a joyous curly-headed ray of sunshine. And glad of them all they were, for begetting children was another thing Howard would never do again. Anne spent long weeks changing his dressings daily and keeping him clean, and it was no doubt due to her diligence that no infection set in.

Once he was able to sit up, Howard would stare out of the window for hours.

"I'm no use to anyone anymore…

Some days he would sit in bitter, depressed silence, and Anne would have her work cut out to coax a smile from him.

But little Daniel always managed it. Anne would leave him slumbering in his cot near where Howard was sitting while she and Gwen went out to milk, and presently the little one would wake, chirping like a happy bird, and come clambering up onto his father's lap. Drawing in the baby smell, such sweetness mixed with the acridity of a soaked nappy, Howard remembered the good things he did have. A loving and loyal wife who didn't shirk her work, helpful children, a farm he owned outright even if it wasn't fully cleared, a brother nearby, many real friends who had helped generously and some still did, turning up to cut and stack firewood, help with a harvest, do some essential fencing or other maintenance. Presently Margaret and Nellie would be heard in the kitchen, stirring up the fire and getting the breakfast together. Holding Daniel and waiting to be relieved of the ever-growing damp patch on his lap, Howard learned to count his blessings.

"I'm lucky after all. It could have been a lot worse…"

And he equally gratefully thought of the new Cooperative Butter Factory, which had been started by CBM Fenton only the year before. "CBM", as everyone called him, was the son of James Fenton, the first settler of the Forth area and the man from whom Howard's father George had stolen a gun, though Howard did not know that. Being well-read and travelled, CBM knew of the recent developments in refrigeration and saw the possibilities of a butter factory. His hunch proved right – the factory paid a 10% dividend after only six months of operation and had fully paid for itself inside eleven years. Surplus profits were returned to the farmers in the form of extra payments on their milk supply. The Factory took all their milk and relieved the farmers of the onerous and time-consuming chore of making and selling their own butter. More and more cows began to be milked in the district, and in a very few years, the Factory's annual report noted with satisfaction that "many farmers were at last able to call their farms their own".

That, however, was still in the future. In 1893, during the Factory's first year of operation, Howard was simply grateful that its existence meant the family had a small but regular income. And in the long months of enforced sitting, he began to read. Not that there were normally any books, apart from the bible, to be found in a typical farmer's household like Howard's. But now Mary Morris' schooling came back to him, and he let it be known that he would gladly receive any papers or journals that might be spare and available. And with that, his horizons began to widen.

"Look," he said to Anne, "this John Harrison of Geelong that's just died, he reckoned refrigeration could be used in butchering, too."

Not long after, a friend called by after he had been to Launceston, and chanced to mention Bender & Co's fine butcher shop, where he had bought some excellent sausages and some good meat that was as fresh as a daisy despite the summer heat.

"He had a special cool room where he kept it," reported the visitor. "He went in there to get my order, and came out with sawdust on his boots, but the meat was really fresh and sweet."

Butchering was a laborious and time-consuming process, usually done by agreement with several farmers gathering together to dispatch and process a number of pigs and sheep, plus the occasional steer, in one long session. The carcasses had to be dunked in boiling water, stripped and cleaned, cut and preserved, all inside a few hours – the joints hung to be smoked, other pieces salted, some ground to make sausages inside the intestines which first had to be cleaned – it was very hard work done under great pressure, and even then the meat sometimes would go putrid before it could be fully used. How gladly the farmers would give it up, and buy it instead, if only there were a butcher in Wynyard to do it for them – and to safely preserve the meat, too, with this new refrigeration!

For that was the perfect answer. With the right help, there was surely a chance for a Turner's Butchery in Wynyard. He would start small, and build up slowly as he learnt the trade. There would be many a good sausage recipe to be found among the wives of the area, too.

Howard scanned the agricultural journals, sending away for catalogues on steam generators, ice-making and refrigeration equipment, and on one of his first tentative trips out – lifted up onto the cart with much cushioning to protect him from the jolting – he went to see the Butter Factory's De La Vergne refrigeration plant. Stumbling and still unsteady on two sticks, but at least walking, he was shown around by F Calloway, the manager. All the locals had been touched by Howard's accident, and – unlikely though it seemed that a simple cocky farmer should start a butcher's shop – they were all anxious to help. And they respected the drive that had him reaching into new areas in a bid not to be defeated.

Soon there was a large group of willing workers who volunteered their time, as they were able, to put together the building that would eventually house the shop in front, and the family behind and above. The money, too, was found, in part by a loan underwritten by several respected business men of the area. It took three years to bring it all together, but in 1896 Turner's Hygienic Butchery opened in the main street of Wynyard.

It was a success from the start. Howard employed the son of a neighbour, big hefty Aaron, as his chief butcher, and together by experience they learned the trade. Soon he went from paying two younger lads to engaging several more, as demand rose for deliveries to be made, and the volume increased. He also hired out cool room space to families, acquired an ice-making machine, and expanded his range to include brawns, germans, and various corned, spiced and potted meats. Ten years down the track, he was also selling eggs, butter, lard, dripping, honey, and mutton birds. He became a well-known figure, seated in a special wheelchair he had had manufactured for him, and keeping a sharp eye on his shop and butchery. Though Anne had to care for his personal cleanliness till the day he died in 1908, she also got an easier life with the move into town, and the steadily growing bank balance. When the great bushfires of 1906 devastated the backblocks and killed much livestock, including some of theirs, she was grateful to be safely in town.

She could afford to enjoy its amenities, too, for the business continued to thrive and the family had a measure of comfort undreamed-of not long before. There were shops, including Mr Farmer's Up-To-Date-Store with its fancy selections, which only got better still when the River Don Trading Co took it over in 1903. A grateful wife, she remained her husband's devoted servant to his last day. Howard was becoming agonisingly stiff, his poorly-knitted joints causing him much pain, until finally he was a curled-up cripple unable to leave his bed. Kinch the Chemist's supply of laudanum had to be increased steadily; perhaps it was a too-large dose of the opiate that brought about the blessed release.

His brother Henry had meanwhile taken over much of the running of the business, effectively overseeing the shop, the deliveries, the butchering, and trying to keep big Aaron in line.

The latter's activity was becoming an issue, for Aaron was the leader of a bunch of wild young men who patronized the local hotels to excess and consequently caused much trouble in town. At that time, Wynyard had considerable notoriety as a watering hole, with three hotels – The Royal, the Commercial, and the Mt. Lyell. To fight the nefarious drinking, the Temperance Society opened a coffee palace, and issued certificates of abstinence to over 80 members. They were so effective that one hotel manager left town to open up in Waratah instead. And they saw it as a sign from God that the Commercial burnt down in 1900. Alas, their own palace met the same fate 14 years later. But the drinking wasn't going to stop; the men kept coming and the carousing continued. As long as Aaron did his butchering work efficiently – and mostly he did; in fact, he was virtually indispensable – that might not have mattered, except that he had included Silas into his unruly crowd of ne'er-do-wells. Perhaps Silas had chosen to join them, his young blood itching to get away from the pious restrictions of the family's religion, but Anne and Henry preferred to think he had been seduced into sinning by that Aaron.

18. SILAS

Meanwhile, up among the back blocks, something was moving. The darkness that had come into the land with the death of Tom Kickerterpoller took on new forms. As the vast forest was steadily destroyed, this strange presence slithered among the huge white ghost trees, twisting up into their limbs left bare as the sap ceased rising and giving life. Great flocks of screeching white cockatoos descended, their raucous derision at man's foolish doings punctuated by loud cracking as they hunted for bugs under the dead bark of the tortured trees. Sometimes this Thing would flow down a lonely valley, curl around a settler's hut, and open its jaws through the gaps, sending the inhabitant out in screaming fear. Some went mad, some turned their guns upon themselves, and some disappeared in the dark of the remaining forest. Nothing much was ever found of them, the devils cleaning them up quickly enough, filling the bush with their snarling and growling as they fought over the feast. Every time it happened, the Thing would leave a pool of itself in that place. Those men who were doing well were mostly too comfortable to see it, this ancient reptilian curse that had been released into Eden, but those on the margins, who had no fat on their bones to cushion them, knew it well. And sometimes the Thing would slip into an unguarded heart.

Silas was twenty-eight when his father died. Well grown and strong, he had regular features, dark blonde hair, and a pleasant smile. He would have passed anywhere without remark except that he had inherited his grandfather George's different coloured eyes. One brown, one blue – anyone seeing him for the first time took a mental step back.

"He's of the devil" it was whispered.

Kinder people recalled the old myths and said that he could see heaven as well as the earth. Whatever their view, Silas was condemned to be different, unable to mask it, and few treated him without at least some wariness. He'd had a bad time of it in school, and was glad to leave early from there after his father's accident. At fourteen, he was already carrying the heavy farming load of a grown man. He would come home dead beat, full of a kind of hatred, having little to say to anyone and avoiding his father's sickbed as much as possible.

"He's working hard," everyone commented approvingly but Anne knew that not all was right with her son.

He was sixteen when the butcher's shop opened down in the town, and when the family moved there too, he gladly stayed behind on the now lonely block up the Deep Creek, guarding the precious cattle. He couldn't bear to see his father struck down, reduced to an impotent cripple; it made him feel sick. Even later, as Howard demonstrated his tough persistence by creating the shop and managing well despite his disability, his son could not stand to see that strong body smashed, its physical power gone. For Silas, a man's glory lay in his rippling muscles and he couldn't forgive his father for no longer having them. Good book-keeping, taking orders, and kowtowing to customers were no substitute. He hated the very smell of illness.

His family's religious observances left him cold, too. He'd objected to attending the services and Sunday School already at the age of ten, and his parents gave up pressuring him when Anne, knowing his social horror, was able to look past her expectations and said to let him be.

"He's doing his bit in other ways," she added, and fielded her community's hints of 'falling away' with a cool stare. Silas was different; not that she could fully explain it, but the mother's heart wanted to protect him. So he worked hard in his lonely physical world; so very, very physical. It brought him some relief, though soon it wasn't going to be enough as his body matured and a man's urges came upon him.

It was as well that he had privacy then, up there on the lonely block. His sexuality was powerful, filling him up, and he gave it free rein. Being alone, he pleasured himself whenever the feeling came. It simply was, like eating or sleeping, and he didn't give it a moral dimension until gradually some other young men starting turning up. How they found him was a mystery, some secret code that filled the air, or maybe the Thing that slithered among the remaining trees had passed the message on. They were mostly all young, and they brought tobacco and powerful bodies urgent in their young manhood. Silas was barely comfortable with his sisters and saw only Anne as a faint source of comfort, though being his mother, she didn't really count as 'female'. But men, now, that was another thing, uncomplicated, no mystery and no words required, as everyone understood. They would meet in the evenings, after the work was done, and be impatient if seasonal harvests or emergencies got in the way. There were many of those – houses burnt down regularly, fences were breached and livestock escaped, wagons broke down or got bogged, accidents happened. The community always turned out to help.

One accident in which Silas couldn't help was the crushing of his little brother. Seven year old Daniel was playing outside in the main street with a group of other children, having escaped from Nellie, who was momentarily distracted by the intricacies of a dress pattern that was proving difficult to cut out. The children were playing hide-and-seek among the carts and wagons parked along the street, accustomed to darting in and out past horses tied to fences, and thinking no more of the clopping of hooves than the singing of birds. In a shrieking chase, Daniel rushed out from his hiding place, straight under the wheels of the passing passenger coach. The men's curses, horses flailing to a halt, the sudden horrible silence before the screams began – Nellie would never forget it. Perhaps that was why she could never bear to pay attention to pretty dresses again.

They brought the poor broken body inside, and someone was sent to fetch Silas, who had loved his little brother – the only one in the family he had had a warm relationship with. He took one look, and went out, having no words for his shocked parents or the hysterical Nellie. Gwen and Margaret, his two married sisters, were also there; though saddened, they had learnt about life the hard way and took it more calmly. He left it to them to do what was needed, and went to hammer together a little coffin, his anger expressed with every blow. He stood mute at the funeral, and afterwards it was Aaron, the one who did the butchering in the shop, who took him along to the hotel and bought him a drink.

He'd known Aaron for some years; seen him at his work behind the shop among the blood and the carcasses, wielding his axe and knives and turning the dead animal messes into steaks and chops and joints ready for roasting. Later, Silas regularly brought down the cattle he'd raised and delivered them to their fate in Aaron's meaty hands. Till then, they'd had little in common, Aaron being married and several years older, but now they sat side by side at the bar. Another drink turned up, and much later, when at closing time Silas could barely stagger, Aaron bedded him down in the shed at the back of his own house.

From then on, Silas would go drinking regularly with Aaron and his rough crowd. Word soon got back to the Turners, where there was outrage and reproaches. He endured them silently and then withdrew back to the mercifully silent block on the Deep Creek. His silence made him impregnable, quite apart from the fact that there he was nurturing a vital part of the family's economy. As long as he did that, he could remain acceptable. It only remained to make him respectable also, and that meant married. For years Anne had vainly plotted, and invited suitable girls, but Silas, when he could with difficulty be persuaded to eat an occasional meal with the family in town, would simply slide away afterwards, apparently unaffected by the charms of the girl on offer.

Inevitably rumours started up. After she had become a widow, one worthy church elder came to see her. Did she realize that Silas was 'different', he said, using the word in its ugliest connotation and barely concealing his gleeful fascination. It was a disgrace to the church and they couldn't keep the son, even of one of their important families, within their flock if the matter wasn't rectified. This was pure hypocrisy, as Silas had not darkened the church door for many years, but it had its intended effect on Anne. Silas must marry, and must do so very soon.

She sensed his discomfort with women generally, so looked as close to home as possible – what about his cousin Lavinia? One of the younger children of Henry – her dead husband's brother – they had grown up together. The girl was a silently compliant young woman with no views of her own, doing what was expected of her and unquestioningly reflecting the prevailing opinions around her.

"Lavinia will do well," thought Anne. "She's passably competent, neither frilly, opinionated nor pretty enough to put Silas off, and already familiar to him. He's probably not seen her in years, but that can be remedied."

Having ascertained that the girl had no potential relationship with anyone else, Anne worked to bring the matter about. She enlisted her brother-in-law, his wife, her own daughters, and those of the church community whom she thought might bring influence to bear in the right places. Somehow, the word went out that Lavinia and Silas were to be married, and in due course Silas himself heard of it.

Of course, he had known of the expectation. It was normal, after all. And he was aware of the not so pleasant comments that had been made about him lately. The only way to counter those was to marry, and if it had to be done – Silas viewed the idea with more than reluctance, almost horror – then Lavinia would do well enough. Gradually, he allowed himself to be drawn into the scheme, knowing it inevitable, glad that other people were doing it all for him and all he had to do was turn up when requested and be polite to the girl. Detached though he was, he sensed that his mother had a grip on things, and would only arrange that which would be, in the circumstances, acceptable. He agreed to everything that was proposed, and in time realized that a wedding date had been set for May 1914. When the war call-up came only a short time later, it was a blessed release to him, but meanwhile he had done his duty. Lavinia had had the good sense to just lie there, and now she was expecting and her life focus would soon be filled with a little one, not her silent husband. Not that he was unkind in any way. He just wasn't 'there', and he frequently escaped to the block. Anne had suggested that they make their official home here with the family in Wynyard town – the house was large enough, after all, with only herself and Nellie inhabiting the space now. Having his sanctuary in the hills invaded by an unwanted wife was unthinkable.

"The girl needs company," Anne declared. "She'll feel much more at home here."

And Wynyard was acquiring some of the exciting sophistications and entertainments that were so rapidly changing the daily life of its inhabitants in the era before WW1. Touring theatre performances, including comic opera, arrived regularly. A bioscope was demonstrated at the annual fair, closely followed by the wonder of moving pictures. Motor traffic began to increase to such an extent that an Act of Parliament was required to give the police control of it. Mining and other magnates would drive proudly through parts that had never seen a real motor car before. By 1911 Wynyard's horse-drawn passenger service to Burnie – the one that had crushed little Daniel – was replaced by Mr. George Nicholls' bus with hard benches down the sides of the truck body. It was an appalling bone-rattler, but reduced the travelling time greatly, and was quite the 'in' thing to be seen travelling on. A garage and mechanic's shop opened up. Larger commercial operations installed the new telephone. In 1912 people heard of the amazing possibilities of wireless communication, although the radio in the average home was as yet un-dreamed of. Larger towns were getting electricity supplies; Turner's Hygienic Butchery hooked up to the grid not long after the war, and thus dispensed with the timber-greedy steam generator out the back. It had served them well, but was not regretted. They, too, installed a telephone and began to take orders that way. It was so very convenient.

None of these exciting inventions touched Silas' life up on the Deep Creek. He found some peace in the silence there. The dogs and cattle didn't care about his odd eyes or his 'difference'. He loved to watch the birds and refused to keep clear the scrub around the cottage despite the fire danger, so the small native birds would find a haven in them. They became quite tame, often hopping onto his fingers as he laid his hand on the verandah rail. He knew their seasons intimately, as he did those of other animals that gradually collected, refugees from the devastated forests, into the ever-spreading green oasis around him. As some larger trees grew up again, the mopoke owls came also, filling the night air with their soft calls. He watched the swamp hawks in their skillful hunting, heard the devils at night, and merely cursed the swift and deadly quoll when it had decimated his chickens yet again. He had no notion of the horror with which his grandfather George had viewed the forests and the life therein, but the moving Thing remembered. It left Silas mostly alone, though, as he genuinely sought, and found, peace in the living nature around him. That was the grace that saved his daily life.

The Thing raised its head and sniffed the air. The news of the war had come drifting up the valleys, and it sensed rich pickings here. Men would readily enough put aside any moral compunctions about 'thou shalt not kill' for the sake of adventure and a paid job in the army. Joyfully the Thing slithered its way among them, unseen but real, making sure as many as possible signed up.

The other young men no longer came, now that he was married. He missed their uncomplicated company, and when the call for enlistment came, he joined immediately. By October 1914 he was part of the 12th Battalion, having been sent for training at Pontville, and was landed in Alexandria in Egypt on the 9th of December.

Later, a much-delayed letter reached Silas in the trenches in France. He had a son. They were calling him Daniel, in memory of his little brother.

THE DUTCH DIJKSTRA FAMILY: 1877 – 1952

"I have suffered much".
from 'Max Havelaar' by Edward Douwes Dekker, 1860

19. NO HOME FOR YOU HERE

It could have been in a painting by Vermeer: old Minna sitting so close to the window facing the canal and straining to read a letter in the setting light. Her nephew Hendrik had sent it from Java, the great Dutch colony so far away, to which he had emigrated four years ago, in 1873.

He was, it seemed, doing well out there in the humid jungle shrilling with unfamiliar sounds and dripping with warm rain. *Warm* rain! Minna marvelled, unable to imagine such a thing here in Amsterdam, where it was frequent and always cold, lashing at ships' masts and stinging your face as you battled along the narrow streets. For the benefit of his aunt, of whom he was very fond, Hendrik described further the stunning flowers, butterflies and birds, the locals' colourful garb, and their teeming markets, filled with exotic produce. He spoke of the spicy food, which he was learning to like.

"For all that, I do miss your wonderful cooking," he added.

He did not mention the other side of the colonial life. That the indigenous locals were angry and resentful after more than 250 years of colonial rule, which included many bloody wars fought by the specially-created Netherlands East Indies Army, all aimed at 'pacifying' the region and securing this important source of Dutch wealth. The latter had established extensive plantations for tea, sugar, coffee, rubber and quinine, and the locals particularly resented the Cultivation System, which effectively forced them to labour on the estates run by the Dutch. Acts of sabotage were common; a sugar crop might go up in flames just before harvest time. For many an adventure-seeking Dutch boy becoming a soldier in the exotic Indonesian Islands seemed attractive; but many died there. Others settled permanently, joining the Dutch colonial families who were firmly established as the ruling class and operators of the administrative system.

Hendrik, through his job in an Amsterdam trading house with links to the East Indies trade, had been offered work on a tea plantation. It sounded fun, and he settled in quickly, though he was ambivalent about what he saw. As a very young man he had read a book that had shocked many Dutch at home, *Max Havelaar*, detailing the abuses of the colonial system and the suffering of the Indonesians. The estate he was on seemed to him particularly harshly run; as soon as he was able, he changed his work to a sugar plantation which was managed by a family with a more kindly concern for their staff. Along with good conditions, they provided an annual harvest festival, involving both the Dutch and Indonesian communities. It was at one of those that Hendrik met and later married the daughter of a colonial family. Soon they had several children. The doings of this Indonesian branch of the Dijkstra family were recorded in letters sent regularly back to Amsterdam, and old, old Aunt Minna heard of it all and dreamed of faraway isles where space was unlimited and the rain warm, until she died in 1903, aged 84. She was spared details of the savage local rebellion against the Dutch in 1888, equally brutally put down by the Dutch army, but the dramatic effects of the Krakatoa eruption in 1884 was described in detail.

In the manner of colonial custom, Hendrik's boys Edgar and Albrecht were sent to Amsterdam to get a university and mercantile education, thus meeting their European Dijkstra cousins. Albrecht liked it enough to stay, but Edgar returned to Java where he felt at home, and in turn started his own family there. His son Berndt was born in 1924 on the same sugar plantation that Hendrik had settled into, and Edgar, by now the manager, had the leisure and resources to pursue the arts and raise his children with a love for literature. Classical music played on their piano frequently filling the airy rooms of an evening. Young Berndt and his siblings grew up in a warm-hearted setting, and to them the Indonesian staff were part of the family.

Some of the colonial abuses had been rectified during the so-called Liberal Era, with substantial Dutch investment in infrastructure, railways, ports, gas and electricity, and funding for schools, both for the ethnic Dutch and the Indonesians. With the resultant air of self-satisfaction, and with the Dutch army always ready to keep firm control of the situation – as they frequently did; in 1906 they massacred one thousand Balinese at point blank range, in order to take over the last remaining independent part of the island – the future looked good.

It was not to last. After 350 years, the Dutch East Indies Empire crumbled, partly through the world-wide rise of nationalism in colonised countries, but specifically driven out by another invading force: the Japanese, who arrived in 1942 as part of their WWII Asian expansion program. In 1941, Berndt, his two brothers and his father all were called up for duty in the local Dutch forces, but soon had to surrender, their outnumbered troops placed in immediate internment. The Japanese also rounded up all Dutch and many other European ethnics, mainly women and children, and interned them also, often in pitiable conditions where many died. The men fared even worse; Berndt himself barely survived three appalling years at the Pakan Baru camp working on the Sumatran railroad; his brothers and father died there.

In December 1945, after the defeat of Japan, Berndt was shipped to Singapore by the Allied Forces who were helping survivors. Through the Red Cross he was eventually reunited there with his mother and two remaining sisters. Little Betty had died in the camp, but later he was more shocked still to hear that Jan, just turned 20 in 1944, had been forced by the Japanese into a military brothel and used as a 'comfort woman'.

"I would rather have died, along with Bet," Jan sobbed, as they sat together, thin and ravaged, covered in ulcers and tropical boils, but alive. "And then, after the Japs went, the Indonesians themselves started attacking us in the camps – we had nowhere else to go – oh Berndt, it w-w-w-was so awful…."

In January 1946, the shattered remnants of the Dijkstra family left Singapore on the *Johan van Oldenbarneveld*. By the time they arrived in Rotterdam, wearing winter clothes donated by the Red Cross, the reality had sunk fully in. They had nothing left in their homeland, Java, where their house had been destroyed along with the entire Dutch administration – never to rise again, though some further savage military attempts were made by the Netherlands government to regain their former colony. But by 1950, Indonesian nationalism had firmly risen. The Dijkstras and thousands like them had little choice but to return to their European families as homeless refugees, crowding into their relatives' tiny houses and, once the initial excitement had settled, to ask themselves: what next?

They missed Java, its indolent warmth, easy life, the space and abundant nature there, so very different from the dour grey crowds hastening through the narrow city streets where Berndt felt horribly confined and alienated. The place was often bitterly cold and the rain equally so. Every dog that had survived the war had apparently chosen Berndt's very street to drop his stinking business in. The place was dirty and uninviting, and though he understood that the war had left its scars, he also noted that there were few parks or open spaces, that the canals stank horribly and were crowded with rotten, rat and flea-infested boats, and the air heavy with soot and dirt. Nor had he any wish to further stretch his cousin's hospitality, though that was difficult, with simply no spare housing available.

Finally the massive Marshall Plan came to his rescue. Repair of the thousands of destroyed bridges and dikes, re-opening Shiphol airport, and starting up the phenomenal expansion of Rotterdam as the future Europort, provided ready work. Berndt moved into single men's accommodation on the port reconstruction site. His now-frail mother remained in his cousin's care, and poor, shattered Jan along with his younger sister Lotta found work in the city, both still sharing a tiny bedroom in the attic.

Glad no longer to be a burden and to have secured an income, Berndt could not warm to his new setting. Like other Dijkstras before him, his mind was set on a far away land. Late in 1952 he met Anna, and one day, after he had shared his restlessness and desperate need to get away, she started talking about another island far away. Somewhere in town she had noticed a poster advertising it. They wanted migrants. It was green and beautiful and there was plenty of room. It was named after one of their own great seafarers, Abel Tasman.

PART THREE

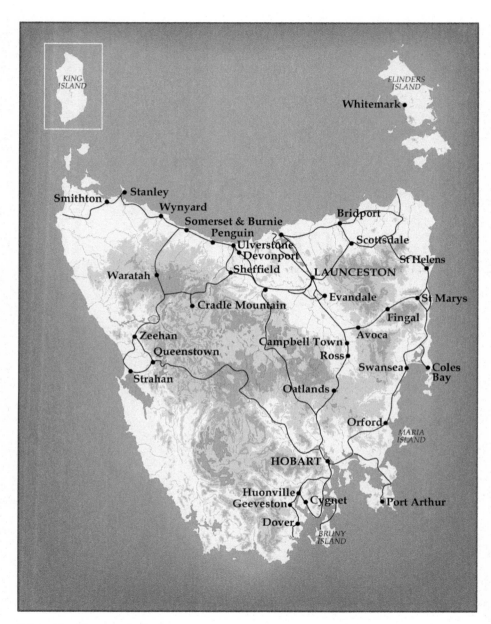

Map 7 – *Tasmania today*

THE ABORIGINES: from 1938

VICTOR & JAMES MAYNE

We are all in the gutter, but some of us are looking at the stars.
Oscar Wilde

20. VICTOR

1938, Flinders Island

Harry's father had told them the story of Matilda, laughing and pretty with her wild red hair. Every boy on the Islands was in love with her, had fought to be the one to lead her out on the dance floor, or spent a whole week's wages on buying a new shirt so she might be impressed. One had teasingly chased her out into the night, from the dance that evening back in 1897, threatening to put a live lizard down her neck. They had skylarked together along the beach till they sat on the rocks for a breather. Next minute she was dead, the head with the flaming hair falling forward as the boy lunged to catch her. Her heart had simply stopped.

It was a sobered end to the barn dance, one of many held regularly on the islands. The Harleys and the Hammonds, the two families on East Kangaroo Island, held smaller dances in their well-furnished houses, where there were pianos and hand-made lace curtains. But the big dances, which were also attended by families from neighbouring islands, were held in the woolshed. It was from there that Matilda's last laughter rang out amid the waltz she was dancing with Boyes, whose own son Harry now stood, forty-one years later, at Matilda's second grave.

"She really had red hair," muttered the young man. "I could see it through the broken coffin..."

He shivered. Erosion had washed away the shallow covering of the original grave, necessitating a reburial in the deeper soil of Flinders, and he had just laboriously brought the clumsy box over on his boat from East Kangaroo.

Now he and many others, including his friends Victor Mayne and Ted Maynard, stood silently for the solemn occasion. They all attended barn dances regularly, fun occasions that were not usually touched by the shadow of death come suddenly and too soon. Yet only a year later those same young men were off to the war, along with about twenty other Island boys. They went with the 9th Division of the A.I.F. to the Middle East, where Ted would die, but Harry and Vic made it back.

In 1943, Vic found himself stationed at Wangaratta, for some further military training, and it was in those few weeks of comparative calm there that he had a chance to digest the enormous changes that had thrust themselves upon him with almost the same speed as that unholy hail of bullets and bombs loosened by WWII. One of those changes came to him by meeting other Aborigines – the men from the all-Aboriginal platoon at Camp No 9.

Vic was born on Cape Barren Island in 1920, a fourth generation Islander and an eighth-caste Tasmanian Aboriginal. Not that they called themselves that – they were the Straitsmen, or more commonly the Islanders, descendants of the original inhabitants, the white sealers and their black wives, and now masters of the wild and dangerous seas around them, builders of fine boats, and fiercely independent. Since 1830 his family, along with about ten other original ones, had fought for recognition and a corner of their own. Lucy Beeton had led the charge until she died in 1886, achieving the official reserve on Cape Barren Island for them, and schooling for their children. After that, their external fate was largely in the hands of do-gooders and churchmen, some of whom meant well but all of whom believed that the Straitsmen needed to be told what it was that they needed. Gradually, all the other islands including big Flinders were invaded by white men who wanted the land for grazing, or a share of the mutton bird harvest. They had money, alcohol and business ambitions, and among them were some who had no time for the 'lazy black crows' who didn't want to work regular-like.

There was some gradual melding of the two groups through inter-marriages, but many Straitsmen retreated to Cape Barren where they could live their own way among themselves. Their young men worked away on the other islands in shearing, on the small trading boats, as stockmen or fence and road building. Some families established themselves on Flinders, the men labouring on farms owned by whites; the women making do in simple huts, sometimes even tents. Their humble circumstances never stopped them having fun, though, and local dances were never missed; wonderful dance dresses were sewn even though their homes had no electricity.

On their Cape Barren Reserve, however, life was free, simple and mostly good. A few families ran sheep or cattle, and nearly all had vegetable gardens. There was only the one store on the whole island.

"I'm not paying their fancy prices," Vic's mother declared. "Andrew's going over to Flinders shortly..."

She and other families would buy their flour, tea and other basic staples at Lady Barron, where the cost was lower. They lived very self-suf-ficiently, on rabbits and wallaby, home baked bread and mutton birds, salted, fried, put into pies, or casseroled. Fishing and craying provided excellently for the table, and tomorrow took care of itself.

The year's highlight was the birdin' season in March. Families spent several weeks together on Badger or Chappell or Babel Islands, depending on where their sheds were. Despite the unrelenting hard and dirty work, this annual get-together was full of fun and gossip, looking over the girls and dancing the night away. Here they could set aside the resentments of not being allowed to purchase drinks inside the regular pub, and of being seen as the least desirable among the population. It was a hard life that challenged a man, and not until the war took Vic away from the Bass Strait Islands, did he realise how different the rest of the world was.

The showers at the soldier's camps were a marvel to him. So was the telephone at the station, constantly informing the officers of all that was going on. Clean sheets on their bunk beds. Daily newspapers. Cities with trams and cars and girls in doorways. The bazaars in Cairo, and the power of his uniform which proclaimed that he had a wage and could be ripped off for it. Even the basic army food, arriving daily in the canteen with no effort on his part, except when he was on kitchen duty roster, and of which he could eat as much as he wanted, was a miracle. Vic soon realised that not only was he a darkie, but an ignorant country bumpkin as well, even by the simple standards of the rough lot of soldiers he was among, and it might have gone poorly with him if it had not been for Mike Johnson.

Mike was one like himself, but from Eden on the south eastern coast of Victoria. In the 1820's, white men started whaling there, also, and soon found that the local Aborigines made excellent boatmen. It became a tradition, and the Johnson family carved itself a niche in that industry, supplying strong men to build and man the boats. Some of their sons found employment elsewhere, as Mike had done by knocking around the wharves in Melbourne. Vic met Mike when they both signed up in 1939 and found themselves travelling to the Middle East together. Mike's experience helped Vic avoid many a green-horn mistake, and in the barracks the two together got less picked on than one on his own would have been.

"You don't know about the Australian Aborigines League?" Mike was astonished, and explained how it had been formed by William Cooper, an Aborigine himself. Cooper led many petitions to Cabinet for parliamentary representation, enfranchisement, and land rights for his peoples. He petitioned for justice, for black returned soldiers to be granted farms the same way as white soldiers were, and his League recorded the many rejections and continuing injustices, the forcible removal even of the few lands left to the Aboriginal missions and the residents then having nowhere to go except into shanties around the larger towns. There, their children were considered 'neglected' and taken. The government of the day, led by Joseph Lyons, did not consider the matter important enough to do anything about it. Together with the Aborigines Progressive Association, Cooper arranged the first Day of Black Mourning on Australia Day 1938.

"Why, he even led a delegation to the German Consulate to deliver a petition which condemned the 'cruel persecution of the Jewish people in Germany by the Nazis'…"

This is the only known private protest, delivered while the rest of world's civilized nations sat by and watched silently.

Vic Mayne was stunned to learn all this – the existence of wide-spread protests by Aborigines, the horrifying list of on-going abuses, and the shining figure of William Cooper, who like Vic himself was 'just' another part-Aborigine. He heard that Cooper had educated himself, attending adult education classes and reading widely, and the value of education was not lost on Vic. Gradually he realised that his little corner of the world – the lovely but wild Bass Strait Islands – was possibly the most isolated and ignorant place anywhere.

"No one has a radio there, let alone a telephone, there are no daily papers, no library, and what is taught in school, is mostly about as useless as learning to knit when you need to be an engineer. When I get back home" – and he longed for it; none of the city amusements and wonders could replace the wide horizons of the seas, and his head ached with the continual noise – "any family that I might have will get that wonderful thing, an education, no matter what it takes. No one is going to call *my* children ignorant!"

From then on, he made a point of reading, slowly and painfully at first, being barely more than basically literate himself, but in time he learned. He had the time, and made use of the local library at Wanga-ratta. In the evenings he read on his bunk, straining in the inadequate light. Eventually he and Mike served in the Pacific, on New Guinea, and it was another three years before he finally made it back home.

Vic had no physical damage but the war left him baffled. What on earth had it all been for? It made no sense. He was sure, too, that no God would sanction the killing he had seen. Back in his routine of casual work around Flinders, he was grateful for the comforting familiarity of his home ground, but kept up his reading and thinking about what he had learned. The exoticness of the East and the northern jungles made great yarns, though the torn bodies and men screaming in agony as they died he kept silent about. And Bessie, with her big brown eyes and strong hands, who made him feel more light-hearted than he had been for a long time, began to take up much of his free time.

She was part of his childhood, from a neighbouring family of his own kind. They had gone to school and church together. Even when her family left Cape Barren and moved to Pine Scrub on Flinders, they met regularly at the mutton birding, Christmas, sporting days and dances. The memory of her smiling face had followed Vic to the war, and kept him from the girls in the doorways. There was something clean and simple about Bessie that was balm to his lacerated soul.

They decided to marry in May 1948. With a wife and family in the offing, Victor Mayne, returned soldier with six years' service on the front lines behind him, put in an application for a farm on the brand-new Soldier Settlement Scheme that was just being started on Flinders Island.

It was a big operation. The Agricultural Bank put the money up; bull-dozers came to clear the land, to cut drains and level roads. Fences and houses were built, cattle for the intending farmers imported. Suddenly, there was work for agricultural advisors, vets, builders, mechanics, and labourers. All but the latter were flown in, the Whitemark Pub constantly booked out until the Department put up more houses. The only generator in town, its roaring a familiar backdrop to all, was not very reliable and inclined to fail at critical moments, especially early on Saturday evenings when all those dresses were being pressed for the night's barn dance.

The ordinary labour was supplied by locals as well as new arrivals from the war camps of Europe, all housed in rough, single men's accom-modation at Summer Camp, in the middle of the area being drained for the new farms. Here men who had only a few words of English, but could sing wonderfully in Italian or play a harmonica to Polish dance tunes, relaxed together after the day's work. Shell-shocked men, stunned by the great canopy of brilliant stars and the vast silence of this island they had landed in after weeks at sea, rested their lacerated souls. They were good workers, these silent men who had seen too much, willingly doing their two years' indenture in return for a ticket to a land that had no war.

Also among the workers were some of the applicants for the new farms. They came to help build the houses that they would soon live in, drain the land and sow the clover that their cattle would soon graze, and erect the fences that would hold their stock from straying. There was an excited buzz as the new three-bedroom homes came into being, all much the same design but with fresh kitchens and new appliances such as electric stoves, for the Scheme also brought the poles and wires that would eventually be hooked up to a proper electric supply. Flinders was finally joining the rest of the world!

Vic was among these men also, though he had not yet had word on the progress of his application. Meanwhile, it was paid work, which he needed as Bessie presented him with daughter Rachel in 1949 and son William in 1951, and James a year later. They lived at Vinegar Hill in Lady Barron, where he rented a small cottage for them, thumbing a lift back to his family on Friday evening. The money was welcome, and he had no qualms about leaving Bessie to cope. She was strong and able, glowing with married happiness and young motherhood, and many of their relatives lived in the same street and would give her any help she might need, including her own parents, Una and Bill.

She was a fine one, his Bessie grown up on Cape Barren to be competent and independent, her olive skin smooth and her black curls an enchanting tangle always escaping from a colourful band. Strict about cleanliness, proper talk and no cursing, Bessie would have gone to church on Sundays, till she realised that the war had made Vic unable to believe. Loyally, she accepted that without fuss. Sundays became precious family days doing the chores together, taking the children to the beach for some fishing and paddling, or playing games inside in poorer weather. Bessie made their simple home a happy place; there was plenty of warm generous love, food and laughter for all. One Friday he had come home to find her washing baby James in a tin tub before the kitchen stove, and the other two tumbling about just outside, and his heart glowed with happiness. Soon he would present her with a proper house, one of those bright new ones he was helping to build, and they would have their own cattle and the children would attend proper school at Whitemark.

Presently a Dutchie, Berndt Dijkstra, joined the working team. Initially, Vic kept well back from him, as he had heard stories during the war of arrogant Dutch officers letting their men die through sheer uncaring, even cowardly, incompetence. In time he realised that this Dijkstra had himself spent two years as a prisoner of the Japanese in Indonesia, and now had a pregnant young wife boarding with a family in Ulverstone while he worked off his time. Vic could identify with Berndt, and as the latter had reasonable English, the two formed something of a friendship.

One still evening at Summer Camp, their conversation got around to ghostly things, several of the men contributing accounts of strange sightings, of ships seen gliding through the mist even though officially they were sunk, of men's voices heard where there was nobody, and unnamed monsters moving in the jungles.

"We got one of those right here," said Vic.

"Ach, go on with ye," laughed the men. "Tell us another one."

"Nah, it's true," insisted Vic, "'tis an old story but there's something to it. And it wasn't far from here, either, at Jack's Lagoon over by the Patriarchs." For the benefit of the imports, he pointed to the east. "Them hills over there."

"Well, one day nearly a hundred years ago, some hunters were sittin' round their dyin' camp fire there, when this thing with glowin' eyes came out of the scrub makin' weird noises, and walked right through them and *through the embers of their fire also* until it burnt its feet and started a terrible screechin', runnin' off. T'was truly awful to hear, the men said."

"Oh yeah, and just what was it supposed to be?" his companions asked, to humour him.

"A monkey, they said. Left behind by the doctor of the Lady Nelson ship that foundered nearby, in the 1830's. The ship had been to Cape Town for supplies, and badly needed a doctor. The only one qualified and willin' to join it was this mad German who insisted on bringin' his pet monkey. The captain didn't want it on board, but really had no choice. The story goes that, when the survivors were finally rescued after the shipwreck, the monkey had escaped and couldn't be found. That's why the two islands just out there are also known as The Capisheens."

Berndt looked thoughtful. The keeping of capuchin monkeys *was* popular some time ago; he himself remembered children's story books showing roaming music men often accompanied by such a monkey trained to rattle bells or pass a hat around, miserable in the cold Netherlands air as the fancy little red jackets they were made to wear did nothing much to keep them warm. It was perfectly possible, and he shivered a little, feeling sorry for the lost and disoriented animal.

"A bit like me," he thought, "homeless and without a base, or even a master."

He thought longingly of his wife Anne, now heavily pregnant, and hoped that he might be able to hitch a lift on a cargo flight out soon for a weekend.

"You lucky Vic," he mused, "you'll have a farm here soon to bring your family to, and I've still got a year and a half to work off before we can even hope for something proper of our own."

It made him determined to investigate future possibilities, and to improve his English.

Vic also was thinking of his future farm, but a small element of doubt was creeping into his mind. As a returned soldier he was as qualified as others who had already been allocated one, some of whom knew nothing at all about farming and had been sent to learn at Rob Archer's 'Landfall' farm in the Tamar Valley. He, Vic, was a true local, had handled cattle all his life on the islands, and really knew the weather here, unlike some of the other ex-soldiers, several from NSW and one even from Queensland. Why had he not heard yet? Uneasily he remembered the many cases listed by the Aborigines League, in which coloured returned soldiers had been denied re-settlement farms. But that was after WWI, and things had surely changed since then. Many more Aborigines had fought in this second war, as bravely as anyone, and nobody could deny their war records.

But they could, and did, deny him a farm. Vic had eventually and reluctantly written a painstakingly careful and polite letter to the Board, to remind them of his application, and after three weeks had received a reply that all the new farms were now allocated and he was not among the recipients. They were sorry but the list of applicants had been unprecedentedly long, and the successful ones naturally had to be those best qualified for the job. On behalf of the Agricultural Board, yours truly....

Vic knew this to be a lie. The rejection was solely because he was an Islander, a darkie, and not deemed fit company for those fine others who happened to have an all-white pedigree, which was more important than whether they had the right skills or not. He also knew that there was nothing he could do about it. The bitterness cut deeply into his heart, and he couldn't bear the thought of disappointing his Bessie.

21. JAMES

It was Bessie who made light of it. Instead of bemoaning the loss of the farm, she saw the best in the situation.

"We could move to Launceston. There'd be work there for you, and better pay, too. And the children could go to better schools, maybe even go to the higher grades, and get proper training. Wouldn't that be good, Vic?"

"You'd be willing to move there?"

"Sure. Why not?"

He admired her quiet resilience, and was once again deeply appreciative of this fine woman who had thrown her lot in with him. He would find a way of doing her proud somehow.

Bessie's family was, among the Islanders on Cape Barren, one of several who had kept their pride. They had moved to the Reserve there when it was granted in 1881, built their snug home and fenced a productive vegetable garden around it. Their sons always managed to find work on the various islands. But Cape Barren was home, and their women were house proud, deftly making do with simple furnishings that were always scrubbed clean, going to church regularly and insisting that their children attended school. Visitors from the outside were always astonished by the excellence of their English, their deep courtesy and unfailing hospitality. The more common image of the Islanders on Cape Barren was quite the opposite: lazy, uncooperative, living in squalor, drunken and unreliable. Of course there were such families also, and human nature being what it is, it happily focused on the no-hopers and forbore to look closely enough to see those others who walked tall and took the Christian commands of decent living seriously. But a humane government lawyer, A W Burbury, commissioned in 1929 to write a report on the situation of the Islanders, had noted: "In manner and courtesy they set an example which would put to shame many white folk".

Due to his recommendations, in the 1930's the Islanders began to receive a regular unemployment allowance, and assistance was given to repair roads and homes, erect fences and keep cattle. Burbury even recommended that the entire island of Cape Barren be given to the half-castes, deeming the Reserve, comprising a mere two thousand hectares, to be insufficient for effective economic activity. This however was ignored, and from the 1940's on the government and the Flinders Island Council pursued a deliberate policy of persuading the Cape Barreners to move off the Island. Many families did, mostly in pursuit of work, but a core of them, nurturing a deep hatred of the whites, refused. They feared, not without reason, that even a temporary absence might see their land forcibly taken. The Reserve had been granted them in recognition that Tasmania itself had been wrenched from their forbears – something acknowledged by Burbury – and they were not prepared to yield a single square foot of it, despising those of their numbers who had given in and left. They also loved their free way of life, not restricted by time and the tight confines of the urban life.

Vic and Bessie soon discovered that those downsides were real enough. Moving to the humble suburb of Invermay in Launceston in 1953, they found themselves among the poorest of the poor; families who were used to plenty of outdoor space were now crammed into small mean rented houses with tiny backyards, outdoor toilets and few facilities. The elevated noise levels, the continual coming and going to precise time tables, rent days to be remembered…

"A man's thoughts are no longer his own," Vic felt.

He had no choice but to get used to it, and could only be grateful that he had found work on the railway, bringing a regular weekly wage to his Bessie. And she managed wonderfully, quickly making friends among neighbours and locating other Island families nearby. Soon she had a network going and the mothers would sit together gossiping over their mending while watching the children playing in the street. Their Rachel attended the local school, conveniently located on the next corner, and young William, quickly becoming streetwise, would start the following year. Toddler James would soon have company, too, as Bessie was expecting again, and in 1954 Erica was born. Bessie's parents meanwhile decided that they also would leave Flinders Island, and Bessie was glad to have them nearby, both for family ties and help with the little ones. Her father Bill died soon after the move, and with Una suddenly a widow, Bessie's brother Ted left the Islands also and moved in with his mother for a while.

They formed a close community, those transplanted Islanders, needing mutual support against the racial taunts that regularly came their way and the harassing by the police. Yet there was also warmth and fun, with singalongs and musical evenings, and their homes were always open and hospitable and no ex-Straitsman ever needed to be lonely or hungry in Invermay. In the face of hardship, they held together and rejoiced over each hard-won success, a job landed here, an upper grade achieved there, and their children grew into the fabric of the city. Though Launceston's glory days as a wealthy mining town were long past, in the 1960's there were still factories, jobs and a reasonable education, so with persistence anyone who tried could become respectable and accepted.

Vic and Bessie had just begun to settle, when they had an unexpected visitor. The firm knock on the door revealed Vic's wartime comrade, Mike Johnston, with whom he had been to the Middle East, as well as New Guinea.

"Found you at last," roared Mike as he banged Vic on the back heartily. "Hell, I've been all over the Islands, looking for you!"

"But Mike, I didn't know…great to see you…this is my wife Bessie."

Mike swept his cap off, and greeted her.

"And four in the family as well, eh? It's more than I've got – I never did manage to settle down after that war."

Bessie set another plate and directed Rachel to find a spare chair, and soon they were talking animatedly over her good stew. Vic was thrilled to see his old friend.

"But what brings you over here?"

"I was at a loose end. I had a job with Sheilton & Co, metalworking, but then they built a new factory a long way out and I didn't really want to be travelling that far every day. Kinda got sick of the work, anyway, but I had a bit put by so I thought I'd take a break and come over to see this Island you'd been blathering on about. Only to find, after much mucking about, that you weren't there after all! Then someone told me the *Shearwater* would be coming over to Lonnie and I hopped on. Nice guy, that Captain Jackson – had some fine yarns, too. He told me where to find you, so here I am."

The children listened with fascination to the adult conversation about the beauty and freedom of the Islands of which only Rachel had some slight memory, intrigued by the exotic strangeness of the man who lived and worked in Melbourne, the fabled city across the water. Vic seldom visited the local pub, but sensed that Mike would not come out with the real reason for his visit in front of the family, so after the meal the two men went down the road for a pint, not before the visitor had been offered a bed for the night.

"No, thank you kindly, Bessie, but I'll find a boarding house." They could not dissuade him.

It took several drinks before Mike admitted to it.

"I'm scared, Vic. I can't stop thinking about it – the bullets and the explosions and the men blown to pieces. It gets me most nights, and I get the shakes. So I drink too much, trying to blot it out, but that's no good either – makes me unfit for work. My hands aren't real steady anymore, can't do the tooling work that's expected…thought maybe I could get work in the country that I can still do, like fencing, and that it would be quiet out there on your Flinders Island…"

Vic had had some nightmares about the war himself, and a tendency to black moods. He knew how much he owed his Bessie for pulling him out of it with her steadiness.

"No woman, Mike?" he asked.

"Nah. Couple of casual connections, you know, but I'm not fit to foist myself onto a nice girl. Besides, there's not many in Melbourne that would go with me – I'd have to go back to Eden to find my own kind and then there'd be no work there, leastways, not readily found. Anyways, I'm getting on a bit and I'm no catch with me waking up screaming most nights."

So that's why he wouldn't stay the night, thought Vic. Thoughtful of him. Sadly he observed his friend's ravaged face, the over-thin frame, the nervous tremor.

"Been to see a doc about it?"

"Yup. But he was no use – just told me I'd get over it. Don't think he really wanted to know. Bit like them New Guineans that they forced to work for the army; made them leave their villages but made no provision for 'em. The poor beggars were more than half starved, stumbling along with the packs and if one fell over, they just left him to die."

Partly to distract his friend, Vic told him about his dashed hopes for a farm in the Soldier Settlement Scheme on Flinders. Mike was sorry but not surprised. Vic went on:

"I don't think there'd be much casual work out there now, with the Scheme virtually completed. Maybe you should take your chances back home at Eden after all. Bit of family support and all that – you've got some there, I know, you've told me about them?"

"Yeah. Mum's alright. Dad's a rough sort but I've not seen any of them for many years. Maybe he's mellowed a bit by now. Got some brothers, too – last I heard, a couple of them were still working on the boats there. The Johnston's were always known there as good crewmen, and could find work readily enough because of it. But I never had that feel for the sea – prefer a solid ground beneath me."

Not that Mike was looking particularly well-grounded at the moment, thought Vic. He wished he could help his lost friend, but all he could think of was to urge him to return to his home ground and seek some solidarity there, and some rest for his shattered nerves. Mike stayed around for a couple of weeks, eating Bessie's hearty meals and sharing many a yarn with Vic while he considered his options. In the end, he took a berth on a small steamer heading for Melbourne, and Vic wondered, as he saw him off, if he would ever hear from him again. He didn't, and sometimes speculated if Mike had still been on board when the ship docked across the water. Perhaps he had chosen to seek a different eden.

***

Over the years, the Mayne family prospered modestly. Rachel eventually trained as a teacher; William got an apprenticeship in the service section of a car yard, and a full mechanic's ticket at the Technical College. When he married, he took out a mortgage on his own home. The youngest, Erica, would later go to university – the first of the family to do so. Materially, they reached a level of comfort unimaginable to the Islanders of Cape Barren where Vic and Bessie had grown up, and Bessie certainly appreciated having a washing machine, and an electric stove in a bright, modern kitchen.

The third child, James, moved to his grandmother Una's house up the road to be a help to the widow. As a teenager he began to gather with the other Islander boys down by the river. Not welcome in regular dance halls and pubs, the remaining quay sides of Launceston in the 1950's became the natural place for them, where the few boats still plying from the Islands arrived with feathers, mutton birds, fish and, above all, relatives or news of them. Eventually, the city embarked on sanitizing the river front, in preparation for the high levees to control the flooding that the area was prone to, but even before then the police conducted regular raids in the area.

James had been there too. In that crowd, it was easy to drink even though he was underage. Once, also, his uncle had to turn up at the police station to bail him out, after he had been roughly yanked away for being 'vagrant, drunk, and a public nuisance'. But he hadn't been bothering anyone; just quietly minding his own misery along with the others who all were not wanted in the streets, shops and jobs that the white people had. It was his grandmother Una who turned him around. The old lady encouraged him to join the football team.

"Don't let them get you down, laddie," she said. "Show 'em how you can play, instead," and backed up her words with hot tea and hearty sandwiches when he returned.

Eventually he earned his team's respect and became one of their stars. It also channeled his rage away, for he had lost a couple of casual jobs by hitting out at taunts. Then his uncle found him that plumbing apprenticeship with a decent, fair-minded boss who gave him the chance he needed. That was what enabled him establish his own business, after he had married Ellie and started their family.

His father Vic died quite suddenly, of a heart attack, and his mother decided to stay on in Invermay. Erica still had some schooling to do, and with the older two at work and James now living with her mother, Bessie began to foster homeless children. It just started happening – word would go round of a little one unkempt and begging, and somehow it got directed to Bessie's welcoming warmth. In time, the welfare heard about it and sent her a few children officially, but no one was ever turned away from her door, whether a darkie or not. Youngsters arriving in the city heard that here a meal and a bed could be found, and a few otherwise hopeless lives were turned around in Bessie's kitchen. Even those who continued on their own ways were permanently marked with the experience of a rare acceptance.

Gradually, Bessie got to be a respected elder of her community. After the national referendum in 1967, which removed discriminatory clauses from the constitution, things began to change. People no longer openly spoke of 'half-castes', or even of 'The Islanders'. The Tasmanian Aboriginal Centre was established; Michael Mansell – the first trained Aboriginal lawyer in Tasmania – took a petition to the Queen; an Aboriginal university course was developed; and a pride in being part-Aboriginal began to grow. Crafts like shell necklaces and basket weaving were rescued from oblivion. Truganini's bones were retrieved from the vaults of the museum in Hobart and scattered, after a ritual cremation, with solemn ceremony in the waters of Bruny Island, where she had been born more than one hundred and seventy years earlier. The museum's patronizing diorama of 'a vanished people' – their only Aboriginal display for many years – was dismantled and much later a new section telling the story of the displaced people with more sympathy, was opened. Stories were gathered and written down, genealogies pieced together, and the first definitive history published in 1981. Bessie was frequently consulted during these processes.

Mt. Cameron, Rocky Cave, and other important sites were given Aboriginal names, and officially protected, though there remains a redneck element in Tasmania who regularly and deliberately destroy such places, rip down signs, smash up caves, and drive four wheel cars and bikes over middens. Officially regretted, not much is actually done about it, but in 2004 the government handed Cape Barren Island over into Aboriginal management, and the community there began to re-group. Encouraged by his mother, James went to visit.

"You were only a little tacker when we left Flinders, but it's still your first home ground. You have relatives there, too..."

Flinders Island struck him as very beautiful, and he immediately responded to the freedom and open spaces there. Sparsely populated, the huge silence at night struck him as awesome, and fishing on wildly beautiful beaches fringed with turquoise water and terrific red rocks was a fantastic experience. What a great place to camp with children, he thought. He felt less comfortable on Cape Barren, despite being warmly welcomed by his Uncle Ted's widow, sensing that the locals felt he had taken on too many of the white man's ways.

"Well, what did they expect?" he expressed to Bessie on his return. "There is far more talk these days about being Aboriginal than there had ever been in our family when I was growing up. Back then, we had to work hard just to be ordinary like everyone else, to get a steady job, buy our own home, and find simple acceptance... To get that, you had to be like everyone else, and where you came from just wasn't something you ever talked about. It's not like now, when the fact that they can claim to being different is the biggest thing in their lives."

He didn't say it to his mother, but the fact that he had some indigenous blood meant no more to James than if it had been Irish or Asian or Creole. It was simply a fact from the past, and while interesting, it made no difference to who he was now.

THE FAIRFIELD DAUGHTERS, from 1953

The stranger that is within thy gates...
Book of Common Prayer

22. ANTHEA

Once again, Tasmania was in a frenzy over a Royal visit. This time, however, it was the actual reigning monarch, the recently-crowned young Queen Elizabeth II, who would be gracing the Island with her presence. The preparations for this momentous event had begun several years earlier, when Her Majesty was a mere princess, although she was already married and had two children. Her husband, Prince Phillip, was no stranger to the place, having been invited to the Northern Midlands property of Connorville in 1943, while in Melbourne on leave from naval duties. Among the welcome committee had been two nieces of Mrs O'Connor's, who suggested that the handsome (and then unmarried) young naval officer could do with some rest at their aunt's fine place in the lovely and peaceful countryside nestled under the grand Western Tiers and only a short drive south of Launceston.

Connorville lies an even shorter distance from Fairbourne, and a number of properties surrounding it were held, or had been, by descendants of the prolific Fairfield and Gatenby families. Some had intermarried with O'Connors, who claimed descent from the royal line of Ireland, with long-standing connections to the British monarchy. Besides, the local word had it, the last five miles of dirt road from Cressy to Connorville would, in honour of the Queen's visit, be finally macadamised.

Locals were stunned by the security precautions taken for the royal visit. Volunteers from the RSL clubs were drafted in, a man to every bridge and intersection along the entire length of the road, which was closed to all other traffic. The Queen, who had flown up that morning from Hobart to Wynyard, and travelled in a motorcade along the North West Coast waving to the massive crowds all the way, must have been grateful to find herself approaching Connorville for a few hours of completely private rest with only Mrs O'Connor, her son Roderic, and the inevitable retinue of staff around. It can be hoped that she did not have to use the specially-installed direct telephone line to Buckingham Palace, except perhaps to talk to her own children, left there in the care of a nanny. She had been away for many months travelling the entire Commonwealth, and the peace and privacy of Connorville must have been a true gift.

The locals, on the other hand, piled on as much excitement as they could. The big crowds that had gathered earlier to watch the Queen pass by, dispersed only slowly, many making their way into the local pubs. In the Cressy pub, a rumour was slipped to journalists about poor fire safety at the old property. It was entirely unfounded, but had newspaper editors scrambling to change their headlines for next day's editions until advised of the joke. Excited children, allowed out of school for the day, ran off to play as soon as they could, though many older ones were taken to attend a final practice session in Launceston for the massive display being prepared for the Queen's benefit the next day. Some wondered if all the decorations and effort had been worth it, given that Her Majesty only spent two hours touring the city before flying out again.

Anthea Reid, born a Fairfield, gladly travelled with her small daughter to the social given for the special occasion by her brother at Fairbourne. It was her home ground, that cosy old house dreaming among the trees where she had grown up with the freedom only rural children get. But her restless spirit had been endlessly frustrated by the petty restrictions of the boarding school residence in Launceston. At sixteen she was nearly expelled for being caught out in the town after curfew. Intelligent and capable of excellent work when she could be bothered, she was rapidly becoming something of a beauty who turned heads and found men much more interesting than writing essays. Her parents' intervention and promises of better behaviour didn't last long; during the summer holiday in 1948 she found herself a job in the furnishing section of the largest department store in town, and simply announced that she would from now on be self-sufficient.

It caused a great outcry at home. *Nice* girls stayed at home till they married! They certainly didn't take *common* sales girl jobs – but her parents knew her well enough not to argue too seriously. Perhaps they were really quite glad to have the willful girl off their hands. To scandalised busybodies they explained that she was unusually clever and needed an opportunity to prove herself.

Anthea found a tiny but affordable flat. It was rather poky and not in the best part of town, much to her parents' dismay who would have preferred her to stay respectably with relatives. Any housing was hard to get in the wake of the war, so she appreciated her luck. At the shop she turned out to be an excellent employee, showing great flair for good colour combinations and learning the basics of quality furnishings in record time. Despite her youth, she had exactly the right manner with the wealthier customers, and the store manager, who had engaged her more on the basis of her good looks and smart appearance, found her a valuable addition to the staff. As long as she kept the sales flowing, he was not concerned about occasional malicious whispers among the other employees, mostly older ladies, who considered her loose and shockingly forward.

"Look at how much leg she's showing – it's downright indecent!"

"You should have seen her fawning over that man!"

The unkind remarks hurt, and she kept largely to herself, spending her lunch half hour in the park or the library. She had recognised the look in the manager's eyes, and knew her position to be safe. In time, she did get a salary raise, but rather than spend it on a better flat, she bought, on hire purchase, a sewing machine and learnt to make herself a really good wardrobe, cleverly adapting old clothes into new styles. Despite the restrictions left over from the war, at work she always managed to look as though she had stepped out of Vogue, which did nothing to endear her to her colleagues.

It did do a great deal to attract male attention. The morality of the era disapproved of girls going to pubs, but every Saturday the dance halls were great places to meet men, and soon she had plenty offering to take her to the cinema, and out to tea. Men were intrigued by her – she clearly wasn't a 'common' type of girl and yet she lived alone? Her natural come-hither look drew them like bees to the honey pot. Anthea was careful of her reputation in the small town, but all her resolves broke down when she was introduced to Terence Reid.

The attraction was immediate. Terence, ten years her senior, roman-tically tall and with a worldly air, was the youngest son of a well-off local family. She fell in love with him too quickly to observe the dilettante's casual ways, too quickly to wonder why he wasn't already married, and much too quickly to ask herself all the right questions. She only knew that she was in the arms of her Rhett Butler, dancing dreamily to Tara's theme from *Gone With The Wind*, the 1947 MGM-release she had just seen. Her parents saw through him readily enough.

"…a good family but a no-good runt in the current litter…"

Not to be persuaded otherwise, Anthea soon sealed her fate by becoming pregnant. A wedding being inevitable now, both families made the best of it, and early in 1952, Eleanor Suzanne Reid was born. A quietly happy child, little Ellie was no trouble to her mother. Even her father, when he was home, was quite taken with her, and as an adult she remembered dimly a few moments of shared laughter when she was tickled by his moustache and he made funny faces for her.

Anthea was halfway through this brief marriage when she drove down to her brother's Queen's Visit Party. Joining the crowds along the road, she held up little Ellie so she too might catch a glimpse of the passing Queen, and then continued to Fairbourne. Glad to escape for a night from her increasingly unhappy union with Terence, she was grateful that he had chosen not to accompany her. She sensed her parent's disapproval and was beginning to realise that they might have been right, but was too proud to admit it publicly. After Ellie was asleep upstairs, she joined the guests and pretended to be happy. She bitterly regretted having had to give up her job in the department store, knowing how well she could have done there. Much better than the mess of a marriage she now had on her hands. Towards her daughter she felt ambivalent; half of her responded maternally to the little one, but the other half resented the imposition on her time and activities.

Terence did not have the staying power required to be a good husband or father. Well-meaning relatives had offered him a variety of positions in their businesses, none of which he held down competently, and it was not long before his good looks led him into an affair. He escaped the disaster by vanishing to the mainland, never to be sighted again by either wife or daughter, just after Ellie's fourth birthday. A few years later Anthea served him divorce papers through a solicitor; these were agreed to with no contest, and that was the end of that.

For a while, Anthea took refuge with her parents who had meanwhile moved to one of the smaller Fairfield farms nearby, leaving her brother to manage the original Fairbourne homestead and farm. But it was close by and his two children, Michael and Ruth, were cousins and childhood companions to little Ellie. Her grandparents adored her, and she was happy there.

And it was a very busy place – after the greyness of two world wars with a depression in between, the early 1950's brought a great agricultural boom to Tasmania, benefitting the Midlands graziers greatly. Wool for soldiers' uniforms in the Korean war in particular drove the demand, and thus the price, up. In other ways, also, it turned out to be a golden time – costs were still low, prices for other produce were stable, and mechanical innovations finally lowered the physical workload.

The new local Macquarie Soldier Settlement Scheme brought with it conveniences like electricity and telephones. Dairy farmers finally could install milking machines. Artificial insemination improved their stock and its yield; freezing techniques meant the establishment of vegetable processing factories. Potatoes were still in high demand in Sydney and elsewhere. Many farmers were now able to renovate old homes, install modern kitchens and bathrooms. Newly purchased family cars made shopping in the city easy. Shops were finally able to stock an exciting range of new goods – luxuries like silk stockings and makeup, as well as inexpensive ready-made clothes, fashion magazines and, in 1960, the biggest wonder of all – television, although Launceston viewers had to wait two further years before TNT9 began to broadcast. Those who could afford it had erected huge aerials to receive the Melbourne programs that had been available since 1956, and so the world moved in on sleepy Tasmania and changed it forever.

In the Northern Midlands they had their own, very worldly, excitement – Grand Prix Motor Racing. In Longford, a seven kilometre track had been developed on existing roads, involving some very sharp bends and two narrow bridges, and for fourteen glorious years, it became internationally known as a fast track to be taken seriously. World-famous champions like Stirling Moss, Graham Hill and Jack Brabham zipped around it at speeds up to 225kmh, joined by some locals like Bob Jane and John Youl. Massive crowds attended these events every March, until in 1968 new safety regulations made the cost prohibitive. Longford sank back into a quiet conservatism, which in the countryside generally held on a lot longer, keeping the rural homes in a dreamy state in which children thrived, even if some adults couldn't wait to escape it.

Thus it was for Anthea. Grateful though she was for the parental bolthole in her time of being a deserted wife, it took only a year of country-living before she could no longer contain her restlessness.

"Would you like to keep Ellie here while I go to Launceston to find work and establish a home for her and myself?" she asked her parents, who agreed readily, having become very fond of Ellie. So the small girl was granted another two years, as it turned out, of traditional family life which included frequent visits to nearby Fairbourne and playtimes with her cousins Michael and Ruth.

A bit wiser this time, Anthea arranged her new life in Launceston with care. Necessity initially obliged her to occupy a spare room in the house of a relative with two daughters. No positions were available in the department store where she had done well before, but the same manager provided her with a reference readily enough, along with a knowing wink. In 1957 the old social mores still dictated that an attractive woman who was single was automatically seen as 'one of those'. It was stultifying, insulting, and Anthea loathed it. She couldn't help her good looks, and it was hardly a shortcoming to have good fashion flair, surely. Nor was it her fault that she attracted men without even trying, but to be hated for this was hard to take. Yet rotting in the countryside was worse. The place that would really suit her was a genuine city like Melbourne, but there was Ellie and she would have to make the best of it in provincial Launceston.

So she tried to ignore the knowing looks, the unkind whispers, the demeaning judgements. She was a man's woman in all she said and did, and it was a long and bitter learning curve before she understood that the men around her were utterly incapable of respecting her. For that, she was simply too attractive, calling forth in them a sexual response that made them chase but dislike her. That they, the men, were responsible for their own reactions, was in that era not a common thought. In time, she would earn their grudging respect in her work, but that balm was still a long way off as she set out to rebuild her life.

She enrolled in a garment manufacture course at the Technical College, and with hard work was soon able to add 'dressmaker' to her qualifications. This got her a position in a dress shop that offered alterations and bridal wear. It was not a great salary, but the place was fashionable and willing to take her on the basis that she could leave at 3pm every day in exchange for doing some of the sewing work at home. For Saturdays – a busy day in the shop when she had to be present – she arranged that Ellie could spend the day with Mrs Rathlow, with whom she was currently living. It was a big house with a garden and a pet dog and cat; enough, surely, to keep a seven-year old happy?

Finding a place to live that could include Ellie proved harder to solve. Nothing within reach of a suitable school was in her financial capability. The availability of housing had not kept up with the exploding demand, driven by the post-war immigration. In the end she had to ask for help from her parents, and with them taking on half the rent, she was able to settle on a small but sunny flat with a little balcony, in a block of several.

Then she sent for Ellie.

23. ELLIE

It was a hard adjustment for them. Both tried, and both failed, though Ellie, with the natural adaptability of children, settled in more readily, especially after she was promised a kitten from the next farm litter. Feeling miserably confined in the small flat, she looked forward greatly to any holiday that took her back to Fairbourne.

Anthea found the loss of her personal freedom quickly outweighed the satisfaction of having done the right thing by her daughter. Initially, she made great efforts, helped by having the work from the dress shop to do at home. It gave them some common ground, for Ellie also loved to stitch, and would make pretty dresses for her dolls with her mother's help. For all that, they remained awkwardly polite strangers, constrained by their separate unhappinesses that they couldn't express to each other.

Once Ellie learned to read, she escaped into the wonderful worlds of fiction, cuddling her little cat, while Anthea quietly fretted, finding little to interest her in ordinary domesticity without a man, and relief only at her work. There, she shone, and for her lunch break she always carefully chose a place where she could be seen by the wider public, preferably male.

Eventually she started an affair with a married man. It required great discretion, and they settled on a regular evening once a week.

"Mother's gone back to the Tech, to complete her diploma, on Wednesday evenings," Ellie reported while back at the farm for a brief holiday. "Natalie, from two flats down, comes to sit with me."

At ten years old, she did not visualise what might really be happening. But her mother was suddenly much happier, and would assuage her occasionally guilty conscience by bringing some special treat home that day – a lovely end-piece of brocade from the shop, a few sweets, or the ingredients for Ellie's favourite meal. And on Sundays Anthea made more effort to take her daughter to interesting places. A rare treat was Sunday lunch at a hotel. Ellie noticed how her mother changed in that kind of setting, settling back as though she were suddenly in her proper sphere. Anthea always looked faultlessly elegant and at ease, as though she were a lady of means, and head waiters usually responded with the best service. Ellie enjoyed the fuss, but never felt entirely comfortable with it.

Her weekly evening with Natalie was a highlight. The girl brought along one of the new transistor radios from which flowed the latest rock n'roll music. Their flat had no television, telephone or record player, and though both she and Anthea listened to some regular radio programs, Natalie's pop music was a whole new dimension, fun, exciting, and different from her mother's world.

Despite that, Ellie was happiest back at the farm. Summer holidays were her great joy, and she spent much of them with her cousins Michael and Ruth at Fairbourne. Particular fun were the occasions when her uncle would take them all up to the hut in the foothills of Miller's bluff for a camp out. In the evening as they sat around their fire, he told stories, often about the old times, pointing to farms in the distance, dimly seen in the fading light from their eyrie, where bush rangers had attacked, hayricks been set on fire, desperate rides for a doctor done, and many other adventures had. These were among Ellie's happiest moments, along with times in Grandma's kitchen learning to cook, or in the garden, the cooing of doves a soft crooning background of peace.

As she turned fourteen, there were boys at school who began to notice her. She did not have her mother's arch beauty, but radiated an earthy attractiveness compounded by her unfashionably thick, much sighed-over, honey-blonde hair. Shy and unsure, not knowing how to handle such things, she shied away from the boys' awkward approaches. Much more confronting were the leers and suggestive remarks by an older tenant in the flats, who seemed to be lurking on the stairs every time she returned from school and on several occasions made attempts to touch her. Ellie feared and loathed this man. His threatening presence filled her days, making her afraid to come home to her cat and homework.

These things were not spoken about, so she said nothing, unconsciously carrying the dread that her sexual presence evoked. She did not know that the man had long noted her mother's single status and lusted over her, restrained only by the likely icy dismissal he would get from Anthea. But the daughter, now that was easy prey, and he was going to get that one. Ellie devised all manner of avoidance tactics, such as going to the library after school, or even meeting her mother as she was returning from work, but it was simply not practicable to do this all the time. Then she would run up the stairs, schoolbag swinging and key at the ready, petrified.

One day he got her, shoving her into a doorway, ready to rape quickly before anyone came. He had her mouth covered before she could scream, half-stunned as her head hit the frame, gagging on his stink. She was saved by the flat door opposite opening, and Mrs Talbot emerging with her shopping basket. Her startled exclamation enabled the distraught child to run up to her flat on the next level, slamming and locking the door.

Ellie knew that she would have to handle this on her own. She scrubbed his filth off her mouth, changed out of her school uniform and laid out her homework ready on the table. She made herself a cup of tea, the hot sweet drink calming her a bit, but the heavy, sick feeling in her stomach stayed. Ashamed as though it were her fault, and unable to express herself to Anthea, she made plans for running away. She couldn't face this any longer.

Meanwhile, however, Mrs Talbot had not been idle. Changing her mind about going shopping, she pulled up a chair by her open front door and sat there knitting, intending to have a word with that Mrs Reid. That woman might be of loose morals, and certainly not a proper mother, but compassion for the lonely, always polite, daughter overcame her prejudices. And she knew all about the man from downstairs. He'd slunk away instantly, but she had recognised him all the same. His poor wife! They said he was one of those who visited the brothel down at the gas works.

Anthea, flustered and shaken by her neighbour's outrage, said nothing to her daughter at the time, but took practical measures to protect her. Abruptly she announced, the following day, that Ellie was returning to her Fairfield grandparents, and would continue her schooling at the Campbell Town area school. As a reason she indicated that the flat lease was almost up, and rather than have Ellie upended by the uncertainty of a new move, returning to a stable setting that was also familiar would be a more satisfactory solution.

***

Back at Fairbourne, Ellie's grandfather had meanwhile taken on a new farm labourer called Pietro.

Pietro from Italy and Jurek from Poland had met on an immigrant ship in 1958, on their way to Australia, the land where there was no war and which was looking for labour. Both were single, having lost families in the WWII conflagration. Liking each other, they had stayed together as they worked off their obligatory years in return for their free ticket, and in the course of that had ended up on Tasmania's hydro-electric works, along with hundreds of others like themselves.

Jurek never forgot the wondering awe that his first sight of the wild western mountain ranges inspired in him. Raised in Krakow, he had visited his Polish country side on a few occasions but never went beyond ordinary farms in valleys cultivated for thousands of years into a quilt of fields and villages. The untamed vastness before him, as the truck disgorged the men working on the raising of the Clark Dam near Mt William, and later on other equally spectacular sites, simply stunned him. Like his fellow European, Olegas Truchanas from Lithuania who had also fled the war and had arrived in Tasmania in 1948, Jurek could not believe that the locals – some of whom worked alongside the immigrants on the hydro projects – could be so completely indifferent, even hostile, to this stunning beauty. His companion Pietro had seen the Appenine Mountains of northern Italy, and the Alps behind them, and was less astonished than Jurek, but he liked it all the same, and in their free time the two often went walking and camping in the bush. When their time with the hydro finished, they drifted into farming jobs, and at the time when Ellie returned to Fairbourne, both were working there – Pietro on the farm itself and Jurek on a neighbouring one.

Pietro's open admiration in Italian style for the blossoming Ellie added a new note to her life. Yet she never feared him like she had the man in the flats. His soft Italian whistle was spontaneous, genuine, and would never open the door for any disrespect, she knew instinctively, and smiled back at him cheerfully. Jurek, whom she saw a few times when he came to collect his friend at the end of the working week, had a more old-fashioned and shy courtesy, which Ellie liked even better. The two between them did much to restore her, just by their friendly but undemanding presence.

For Ellie, it was not only the answer to prayer, but a welcome one, for she loved the country life and Fairbourne in particular. A small part of her regretted leaving the city, her current school friends, and that pop music, but that was made up for by being with her cousins Michael and Ruth, with whom she got on well. Over the next two years, however, her feelings for Michael began to deepen.

***

It was an age of change. Suddenly, in the mid-sixties, echoes of the great revolution in Europe and North America began to resound even in the rural tracts of Tasmania. The Beatles arrived in Australia to scenes of near-hysteria by thousands of fans. The Seekers' and the BeeGees' songs were everywhere. Bob Dylan sang it: the times they were a'changing. And hemlines changed dramatically when Jean Shrimpton famously arrived at the Melbourne Cup in a skirt four fabulous inches above the knee. News of student protests overseas inspired the Brisbane campus to one of their own, which was promptly and brutally put down brutally by the local police. Anti-Vietnam demonstrations attracted evermore numbers, and Gough Whitlam, rising star of the Labour Party, promised to end both conscription and to bring the troops back home.

The change was irresistible. It tapped into something that had been stoppered up for too long, and the young people, who had nothing to lose except their parental approval, opened their souls to it. Even gentle Ellie began to hitch her skirt higher and higher, at least the moment she was outside the farm gate and before the school bus arrived, and if Pietro saw her – which somehow he frequently managed to do – his appreciation sent her on her way satisfied that this was *it*. None of these gay youngsters, nor their despairing parents, really knew what exactly it was, this unstoppable new thing wrapped up in the flood of mad music, self-expression, and sexual awareness.

Practically overnight, the boys went from respecting women – at least those whom they had classified as 'good' girls – to expecting them to be sexually available. If a girl refused, she was simply not in the running anymore. By doing this, the boys ceased to care whether a girl's first sexual encounter was an experience sufficiently good to make them think that sex might be pleasant or even just fun. And in most cases that initiation was anything but: rough, painful, embarrassing, fast and furtive; few girls were lucky enough to come away from it with a good feeling. It became a very difficult time for girls. If they 'did it' they were called sluts, and if they 'didn't', they were out of the running. Many felt used and cheapened. It was time of personal confusion, of no clear guidelines that seemed to lead to anything satisfactory, and while that new excitement made things seem fun, after the dancing and night-clubbing many girls were privately at a painful loss.

Ellie was also drawn into the whirlwind. Before she was sixteen, she had a boyfriend at the Campbell Town school who took her virginity but seemed to set no store by it. It was apparently a complete non-event. They had been going together for a few weeks, but once she said 'yes' to his constant demanding, he seemed to lose interest, and soon after she saw him smooching with another girl. She had three terrified weeks wondering if she was pregnant – mercifully not – but the complete alone-ness that his disinterest engendered, marked her painfully. Hurt and confused, she withdrew into herself, brooding a lot around the farm. But her non-virginal state sent its own signal, and one day cousin Michael noticed it.

They had been good mates since their earliest years. For Ellie, his safe familiarity now suddenly transforming into something more personal, was very comforting. Not particularly handsome, he was a likeable sort, relaxed, laid back, with laughing blue eyes, strong and confident, with a natural courtesy. He was, after all, the future laird of a fine Midlands sheep property. Ellie curled herself into his presence like a coming-home, and was glad that he was content to be restrained. Their shy and tender love blossomed in long walks on which they held hands, exchanged a few kisses, and spoke of themselves.

Ellie's joy was not shared by Michael's parents. She was a nice enough girl, but there were daughters among some of the other established pastoral families of the district, like the Camerons or the Archers, who would be much more suitable. Privately, they felt that Anthea, Ellie's mother, had let the side down on the family tradition with her poor marriage, and anyway, a first cousin was a bit too close. Mr Fairbourne decided to have a word with his son about his responsibilities and that he had better not raise the girl's hopes too much. It was a good thing that Michael would soon be going to the mainland to attend Agricultural College.

***

Pietro observed her heartbreak as Michael, conventional enough to bow to the inevitable, began to distance himself from Ellie. Two rejections within barely a year was a lot for the young girl to take. Well aware that it was not his place to make any personal remarks to her, *la figlia del padrone*, all he could do was lay on the appreciation that any attractive thing raised in his romantic Mediterranean mind, with a few soft whistles and gentle, non-threatening expressions of admiration. He hoped it might help to cheer her up a little, poor little one. Saddened to see her so downcast, he was almost glad that he would soon be gone. He and Jurek had been accepted for work – at better pay than farm labouring ever brought – on the upcoming water scheme nearby at Poatina.

The agricultural boom of the fifties continued into the next decade, bringing more changes. One of the biggest improvements had been the wiping out of the rabbit plague with myxomatosis. Ellie was frequently distressed at finding furry heaps in their death throes, or with their eyes picked out, but the farmers rejoiced. As the occupants of the Macquarie Soldier Scheme farms found their economic feet, their chances were further improved by the imaginative and practical notion of using the water from below the Poatina water power installation to irrigate the surrounding area. Around twenty kilometers of canals were built initially, to supply forty farms, the first water flowing in 1971 and enabling much more diversified agriculture – poppies, mustard, pyrethrum, vegetable crops and their seeds, and assorted grains. All thrived alongside the dairying, turning that part of the Tasmanian countryside into one of the most productive on the Island. Above it, high up in the Western Tiers, lay the lake whose waters brought the wealth to the region by a 5.6 km tunnel drilled through the rock to the power station.

Pietro and Jurek worked for a number of years on the Cressy Irrigation Scheme. Like many reffos, as the immigrants were often labelled, they had their share of unkind jibes and back-turning to contend with, but both remained quietly grateful for the haven they had found on this Island halfway round the world. They bitterly missed the cheerful family life of their home country, but the war had left them with nothing to go back to. They spent the rest of their working lives on various development schemes, living in single men's quarters, and eventually retired to Moonah, a suburb of Hobart with a large Italian population. Unassuming, likeable men, they helped build homes for new families, laid out gardens, and brought songs and cheer to those who were still feeling a bit lost.

While they remained in the Northern Midlands, they never quite lost touch with the Fairfields, where they had always been genuinely welcomed as part of the family. Pietro's cheerful whistling had been missed after he left. On some weekends he and Jurek dropped by to say hello, Pietro gently asking after Ellie and how she might be getting on in Launceston?

***

Ellie had fled away from Fairbourne and back to the city as soon as she finished grade ten at school in 1968. Old enough to get work, she found a room to rent and a job in the haberdashery section of a department store. Like her mother twenty years earlier, she did well there, and once settled, began attending the College of Advanced Education in the evenings.

Really enjoying the learning environment, she eventually completed her leaving certificate there.

Despite the torrid times that the late sixties ushered in, Ellie mostly remained in a self-chosen quiet backwater, content to direct her energies into work and study. Her mother Anthea had meanwhile married a second time, somewhat more successfully, and was living in her husband's home on Canning St. With his help, Anthea had opened her own dress shop, and was doing well with it. Ellie visited there regularly for a meal once a week, where they would have polite conversation but essentially remained strangers. In time, she made friends of her own age, going to the cinema with them and occasionally even to a nightclub, where she danced to the sexy beat of the Rolling Stones. Being attractive in the natural way of the young, she had admirers who took her out, but her previous experiences held her back.

It would have to be a special man to sweep her off her feet, and it took more than two years before James walked into the department store, needing buttons for his shirt.

THE EX-CONVICTS, from 1950

*Beyond the London-in-1840 atmosphere of Hobart and the
ordinary people living ordinary lives, there hovers in another
dimension: a kind of miasma from the putrescent remains of old
bad dreams, old lonelinesses and lunacies, old and calculated sins
against the Holy Ghost...*
Written by Hal Porter ca 1950-60

24. THE THING IN THE HILLS

Reginald Turner was a highly respected man, an elder in the Christian
Bible Gathering, serving on the local council several times and operating
the best butcher's shop in town. Naturally, he marched every Anzac Day
in the memory of his Grandfather Silas Turner, who had not returned
from the Great War, thus providing his family with that extra status
which his living presence would most certainly have sullied, given
those nasty rumours that had been circulating about him. The Turners,
privately grateful for his demise, now could bask in his courageous, quite
possibly even heroic, death in the trenches.

Fortunately for the family, the lamented Silas had managed to sire a
son just before rushing off to war. That boy, Daniel, was raised mainly by
his grandmother Anne, while his Uncle Henry ran the shop's accounts
and big Aaron, who had survived the war virtually unscathed, returned
to continue slicing up his carcasses and lovingly shaping them into
steaks, ribs, chops and sausages.

By a mercy Daniel had not inherited Silas' strange eyes. Altogether,
he turned into a perfectly normal young man, strong and neat-looking,

minimally interested in schoolwork but brilliant in the footy team. He married a very suitable girl in 1941, having been excused from going to WW2 on the basis of being a primary processor of agricultural produce. For once, the community had mercy and accepted this, thinking perhaps that all this war effort would need full stomachs to keep it going, or maybe they remembered his grandfather Howard's indomitable spirit after the tree had crushed him. In a tough and wordless community that saved its praise mainly for worship in church, Howard's fight to build the butcher's shop despite his broken body had been widely admired. And here was his only grandson, such a pleasant young man, taking on the same shop and honouring his grandfather's singular effort.

The shop made Daniel very aware of technological advances, which he embraced enthusiastically. Turner's Hygienic Butchery always had the latest in refrigeration and slicing machinery, an efficient delivery van, and offered the widest range of processed and smoked meats. Soon the family had a car for their own pleasure and convenience. They needed it, too; in 1944 Reginald was born, followed quickly by several other siblings. One day in the mid-fifties, Daniel went up to the old block on the Deep Creek Rd, which the family had kept, though none of them had lived there since Silas' time. It was the perfect place to build a nice large family home on.

It was an exciting time. Other farmers and traders were doing much the same; brand new houses suddenly dotted the countryside, their kitchens had convenient laminex surfaces and laundries by the back door with efficient washing machines.

Daniel had his neat garden properly fenced off, a new driveway graded, and every large tree in the vicinity felled. The brick house was wonderful, bright and new and easy to clean, but the children most liked playing in the old one, a haunted cave of rotting grey weatherboards, spiders and dust motes, left standing drunkenly over by the trees that filled the Deep Creek Valley. Daniel's children had enormous fun here; only young Reginald vaguely sensed the strange vibes that still surrounded the place.

His father Daniel had a model life, genuinely content with his shop, his wife, his children, and the material advances that his industry brought him so pleasantly. There was a modest holiday away on the Gold Coast, on which they experienced their first flight, but none of it altered Daniel's quiet satisfaction with life. The teachings of the church fulfilled him also; he took his turn preaching regularly and many remembered his quiet sincerity. He was of the last generation to be thus.

His children grew up in a completely different world.

It touched young Reginald most of all. Bitten by the restlessness in the air, he joined the boys who got together in cars and rode out of town, radios blaring, or gathered in out of the way corners, smoking and drinking. Girls started coming, too, and there were a few teenage pregnancies. If there was anything to disturb Daniel's contentedness, it was his son's wild behaviour.

"I've arranged for you to go to work on the Robert-Thompson farm, out on the Cape," he presented his son with a gently-worded ultimatum. "They'll pay you the regular farm labourer's starting wage, and you can live there, too. Do you good to learn something new."

Mainly to get away from home, Reg agreed. And the experience did steady him – the host family was travelled, educated and functioned with a dignified courtesy that he had not encountered before. He settled in well, the work hardening his muscles.

"There's a correspondence course in business basics that might interest you…"

"Your father has a ready-made, successful business. He wouldn't want to push you into it, but you could do a lot worse than that…"

"Aileen's a nice girl, decent and no slacker. We know her family well…"

And so Reg took on a formal apprenticeship in his father's shop, with a view to taking over the business in due course. Once qualified, he married Aileen, and when his two daughters were born, the family started attending church regularly. It looked as though all was back into its proper place.

But it wasn't. Somewhere along the way, the Thing that moved among the hills had managed to breathe on Reg, probably at Silas's old cottage, perhaps when the boys had held a drinking party there. Something kept drawing him back to the old place, where he had a secret stash of drink, cigarettes and dirty magazines, his imagination going to strange dark places. He and Aileen had bought a neat weatherboard home in Wynyard, but he found excuses to go up to the block, officially to visit his parents where he rarely stayed long, slipping over to the cottage before returning to his wife. Daniel sensed his son's divided being, but the good man could not begin to imagine what had captured Reg's heart. Outwardly, Reg had a pleasant enough manner, but inside him was a cold, empty space. His wife Aileen got to know it too. Her helpless and anxious servility only served to irritate him all the more.

So his home grew into a sad loveless place, every effort reserved for the keeping up of appearances. Aileen, deeply lonely, devoted herself to the two girls, church and local affairs, unfailingly supporting her husband as he eventually took over the shop and made his mark as a respectable local citizen. The home and block on the Deep Creek Road were sold and Reg's parents retired to a small unit in town. Reginald's siblings had all found work and marriages elsewhere, so he was the only one left to carry on the Turner name in Wynyard.

In his younger years, he had been a regular player in the Wynyard Football Team, and was part of the infamous 1967 Premiership. The North Hobart Team had been within a whisker of winning, when the local crowd prevented such an indignity from befalling their own team by invading the ground and removing the goal posts. The pubs benefitted for some time from the hearty celebrations.

"I'll have to give up coaching the boys on Saturday mornings. Paying Will for those extra hours doing the shop is simply too expensive – I'll have to do it myself."

He did not tell his wife that, in fact, business was no longer as lucrative as it had been. A Rolf Vos Supermarket had opened in town, with an extensive charcuterie, and many people liked the convenience that saved them going further up Goldie St to get their chops at Turner's. Besides, it was cheaper. By the time Reg quietly put the business on the market, the writing was on the wall, and he could find no buyer. But he kept up the appearance – a habit that had become second nature to him

– of a solid and secure retailer, and managed to keep surviving on the few remaining customers, a contract or two, and some speciality sausages and smallgoods that he was known for.

His position as elder in the church was his remaining satisfaction. The Christian Bible Gathering, being literal bible believers, quite enjoyed some hell and damnation and rigid rules that were not to be questioned. An intensely practical people, they had no time for intellectual ideas or philosophical speculation, and derided anything new. Underneath the mantle of proper behaviour however seethed fear and hatred, especially for anything sexual, and when AIDS became world news it gave Reg license to thunder forth exultantly and dramatically on the fate of Sodom and Gomorrah.

There were some genuine believers among the attending families, wonderful folk who sincerely tried to live the Christian life. They welcomed strangers, selflessly attended the sick and disadvantaged, and fostered damaged children. Most of the congregation however attended merely out of habit and for social respectability, without the inward conviction. Some may have had thoughts about their preacher's obviously unhappy wife and disenchanted daughters, but none could guess at the alien dark thing that was coiled in Reginald Turner's heart. It was the arrival of a family of innocents that would show up his true colours.

***

By the 1970's the transformation of the North West Coast of Tasmania was virtually complete. The green pastures and productive paddocks spread like a quilt over rolling hills, charmingly dotted by farmhouses with pretty gardens. All the ghostly dead trees were gone. White mist flowed magically along the valleys in the early morning. The chocolate brown soil was deep and rich, particularly fine for potatoes and other vegetables. Dairy cows could be seen streaming to the milking twice a day. Fat cattle grew fine steaks and on the slightly scrubbier land, sheep were kept. It was a pastoral landscape of great beauty, astonishing to visitors, and much treasured by locals. The whole was girt by a magnificent coast line, ranging from dramatic cliffs to superb beaches, and the wilderness had been pushed back far enough to be merely a pleasant line of distant blue mountains.

Few now remembered the dark forest that had covered virtually all of this land, the battles to clear it, the great poverty and tough bitterness of life for many who had worked there. It was never spoken of; for most, it had been simply too hard, and all they wanted now was to enjoy the prosperity that had finally come. Gradually it was realised that the rest of the world actually valued ancient forests, so it was not the thing to speak about how the magnificent myrtle and blackwood forests had been destroyed – felled, burnt, wasted – and how with them also went the birds, the robins, wrens, firetails, honey eaters, pipits, quails, wattle-birds and many others. They were mostly replaced by starlings, pigeons, sparrows, and the horrid screeching white cockatoo. Only occasionally was the royal wedgetail eagle seen, and still in danger of being shot. The tiger had been hunted to extinction, and the shy quolls retreated. The exquisite wildflowers were replaced by huge banks of blackberries and other imported weeds. The land lay bereft beneath its cultivated beauty; a sudden sense of it could fill the heart with a strange fear.

Just beyond the cultivated areas, in the dark treed fringes, a tough breed of outcasts clung to a filthy existence, in houses that were little more than humpies, surrounded by refuse and piles of rubbish. Most had never seen a doctor or an educational institution. By the 1980's the system was beginning to catch up with them, and the smelly and wild-looking children, shunned on the bus, were made to go to school. In time most of the youngsters saw the possibilities of a better life, and even some of their parents gave themselves up to be tended in aged care places. Some stayed, unable to make the change, gradually dying out, and another part of Tasmania's history was gratefully forgotten.

But the feeling remained.

Those who made it out of the isolation often joined other broken and wounded families in the housing commission suburbs, especially in Burnie. In rural areas men roamed with guns, pot shotting road signs and the china insulators off the early electricity poles. Some rough communities hung on in scrubby corners; there were unsolved murders and disappearances. To the thousands of tourists, it was a magnificent wilderness to be admired; to those who lived there, quite another spirit was abroad. Men shuddered when they heard the Thing growling out there. Open graves were found in lonely cemeteries. Young half-witted girls had inbred babies, their own fathers most often the sire. None of it was spoken about. The worst cases were shipped off to institutions, and a special school built for slow learners.

Much more readily remembered were the stories of the proper old communities, where outlying families found a focus around a tiny church, school, and a playing field. It was hard, really hard. There were generally no medical services. A man who cut his belly open with an axe was sewn up on the spot with hair from a bullock's tail. Incredibly, he survived, but many didn't. Some were crushed by logs, children died of diphtheria, women helped each other give birth. Dentistry was so deficient that the easiest thing was to have all teeth removed and replaced by dentures. This was often a saved-for and desired 21st birthday gift – it set you up for life, even though the process was brutal. It was still happening in the area in the 1980's. The black tiger snakes were huge, numerous, and deadly. There were massive storms with destructive winds, sleet and rain, floods and bushfires. The hardship and labour were unrelenting, and yet, there was such wonderful community life, too.

Everyone helped out when needed, and everyone was known. There were church services, celebrations and school concerts, cricket, footy, cattle sales and occasional picnic excursions. Proper grading of the terrible mud roads, and the coming of the railway, opened up the districts and produce could finally be sent to the towns reliably and quickly. Community halls were built and weekly dances held. Gradually, stores and post offices opened, even the odd telephone line, and later still, electricity arrived. For a while, through the 1930's to the 1950's, things slowly but steadily got better and that time was fondly remembered.

By the 1960's it began to fall apart. Machinery, at first so wonderfully desirable and labour-lightening, began to reduce the paying work on farms. Children left to work in the cities, and rarely came back. Everyone acquired a car and the small communities lost out to the supermarkets. Even the weekly dances died out. One could go to the cinema in Burnie, instead, or sit at home in the illusionary world of television.

Wynyard hung on as a small town of no great significance. The hospital was closed. The passenger train services ceased. The small airport hopefully built a longer runway to accommodate the larger jets, but they never came. It did manage to retain the butter factory, which produced milk and cheese as well, and eventually was taken over by a multi-national company. Nearly all the old sawmills disappeared. The rural recession of the 1980's hit hard. Gradually, the community sank back into a glowering, inward looking and defensive attitude, deeply conservative, hanging on to the old certainties and tightly closed against the new. Under the respectable surface seethed some deep resentments, the feeling of having missed out again, of being the underdog, the one cheated by the 'big ones who had money', and – most terribly destructive of all – a savage homophobia. It had its roots in the early history of the island, and was fuelled by strict and judgemental church teachings. Tasmania had had an unusually high incidence of imprisonment for consenting homosexual practice, and the legislation that made same-sex practices legal in 1997 made little difference to the deep-lying local antagonism. Men were aware of it, feared it, but many were fascinated too. It was never spoken of, or admitted in any way, but the hatred it raised flowed palpably in the air.

None of that was visible on the surface. The land lay in its great beauty, looking paradisiacal to newcomers. Large prosperous farms spread over the hills, many with substantial homes. The beaches were superb, the rocky coastline considered one of the finest in the world, the air the cleanest. It was a wonderfully fertile and lovely-looking place, and it should have been blessed.

It was into this place that a family of newcomers arrived, from England and with no knowledge of any Tasmanian history, or the ways of the place. They bought a farm further up on the Deep Creek Road, milked a small herd, and suffered all the loneliness and disorientation that strangers experience anywhere. That it would take time to settle in was only to be expected.

But they were stunned to find themselves derided as 'imports' and have it made clear that they were unwanted. Unpleasant jokes were played on them, and their innocence exploited in rural dealings. Having come from warmly friendly Cornwall, with modern ideas such as organic farming, recycling, and caring for the environment, it was shocking to find all that derided and dismissed. It was a comfortless time, and when the local church went on a recruitment drive for their Sunday School, the family gladly took up the invitation to bring their three children. They started attending regularly, a bit nonplussed by the fundamental teachings and the preaching of Reginald Turner, but stayed, hoping to find some acceptance in a kindly community.

25. THE THEFT OF LOVE

Denise Turner grew up a stranger from her father. Later, she began to hate him, his unloving coldness, rigid discipline, his distance from his wife, the hypocrisy of the family that presented a bright face to the outside world while the reality inside was horrid.

"I'm not coming to church with you anymore! I can't stand it!"

Watching them go off with her younger sister Beth, and ignoring the latter's spiteful remarks, she settled into her bedroom with a romance and the music blasting. How could the church have any respect for her father? Couldn't they see what a sham he was? She despised them all.

Beth remained compliant; perhaps, being the younger, she had made a better experience of family life. In due course she began to work at the Burnie hospital, after training as a nurse in Launceston. It was without doubt she who started the rumour, by breaching patient confidentiality, that would eventually destroy the new family in the Christian Bible Gathering congregation.

Denise, on the other hand, was finding real life by hanging around with the boys, smoking, making herself as attractive as she could, desperately seeking love and acceptance. Indifferent to schooling she barely made it to year ten, then drifted around a few casual jobs in the supermarket and the cafes, coming home at any kind of outrageous hour just to clean up and occasionally eat something. Turner didn't speak to her at all anymore, and her mother fluttered around despairingly, pleading for her love, making her favourite foods, but chilled by the girl's indifference. Soon there was an attractive young man who lived in Somerset, a tiny town a few miles back along the coast. The place had a hairdresser, and they happened to want someone, so she took it on. It was a wage, the lowest legally allowed, but offset when she found a cheap room for rent nearby. So she left home, and remained mostly estranged.

That is, until some time later, in the blaze of her affair with James Mayne, she brought him home once – so proud was she of this fancy man who was paying attention to her – though their liaison was already doomed, falling apart in the maelstrom of his own divorce. Just before he left, she got pregnant with Tyson, and presently her mother, in defiance of her husband, came to find her in Launceston after she'd had the baby and was struggling, alone, and broke. In defense of her daughter and grandchild, the mouse of a wife turned out to be resourceful and courageous after all.

She brought them home, taught Denise the basics of mothering and nappies, made sure both ate well and kept them clean and warm. Her husband made no bones about the shame of an illegitimate baby in his house, and only 'what the neighbours might think' stopped him from throwing them bodily out. Not once did he inquire about their well-being, and refused to increase the household budget to allow for extra food and baby things.

His hatred got blacker. He pounced on the news, whispered to him by his other daughter Beth, that the husband of the new family had been in the Burnie hospital and that there might just be the likelihood that the man was *different*.

"What do you mean, 'different'?"

"Well, homosexual…the doctors put something on his record that suggested it."

It was enough. Now he had a real target. He'd disliked the newcomers from the start, silly foreigners who knew nothing about the place, with all their fancy notions on organic farming and environmental care. Turner had been quite taken aback to discover that even among his own conservative congregation, there was some support for these ideas, and the ladies in particular had put together a booklet on it, on such things as not using bleach blocks in toilet cisterns. So he really resented the influence that the much-too-good-looking wife of these intruders was having. Why, she was even teaching *vegetarian* and wholefood cooking to the ladies group!

But the man…. Something dark stirred in Turner, something deep and nasty and primeval. Something that drew him irresistibly, to spy on the man, to watch out for the smallest slip, to tear him to pieces with scorn or sarcasm. He hated him because the newcomer triggered a powerful sexual urge that was unmentionable.

But up in the hills, the Thing was watching. Pleased with its work, it crawled closer. Here really was something…

***

In 1940, a group of four women and a man were walking on the isolated highland plateau behind Cradle Mountain, admiring the magnificent scenery before them – the craggy blue mountain peaks, the vast wilderness between, lovely dreaming lakes, the reddish brown glow of the ferns on the moors. It is an area so outstanding that it is now a National Park, visited by thousands of international tourists every year.

Into their idyll, however, came the strangest, most disturbing experience. In the words of one of the people present:

"Experienced here the weirdest phenomenon. Moving over a flat expanse of rock Mrs Mackenzie heard a rustling in a low shrub and stooped to pick up a stone. Immediately a fairly high-pitched buzzing sound was heard and a swift moving force, invisible but powerful, zigzagged across the rock between Miss Tyson, Mrs Richardson, and Mrs. Mackenzie.

Mr Mackenzie had passed the spot a few seconds before, but hearing the extraordinary noise turned back to see the three women all staring in the utmost bewilderment at this flat bare rock. I heard a continuous and rising sound as though undergrowth was on fire and burning furiously in a high wind – a shrill, angry, fierce crackling sound.

We rejoined the others and could see nothing. Miss Tyson averred that there must be a blowhole, but we looked and could see nothing. There was no wind or water.

The commotion continued for at least a minute and, this dying down, we heard rustling in the nearest shrubs – snakelike, but much too big and powerful. Stones were thrown into the bush but nothing emerged and yet strange sounds were heard in the bushes. They were something between a human and an animal sound, a kind of grunt which we couldn't identify.

Mr Mackenzie followed the sounds from bush to bush but they moved away too quickly for him to keep up. Further eastward, when he was looking to see what could be there, the sounds became fainter and ceased, with everyone astounded, bewildered and most uneasy. The force was felt up to knee height. The day was calm, no wind before or after at any time during the day."

***

Sometime in the late 1980's, the Christian Bible Gathering arranged for an overnight expedition into the mountains of the South West. Intended as a youth group activity, numerous adults chose to come also, it being a particularly spectacular and not readily visited part. They included the wife of the new family with her older son, and a reluctant Turner, replacing a youth group leader who had fallen ill. Special permission was obtained from the National Park ranger to enter the area on a little used and rough gravel track, built by the Hydro Electric Commission a decade earlier, when they were still planning to flood the Franklin River. It ended at an area levelled as a helipad, and once the tents were pitched, the group walked on a bit further to the edge of the famous Franklin Gorge, peering down into its vast depth from the very top. It was superb. The panorama included the Frenchman's Cap and the West Coast Ranges, impossibly beautiful but coldly remote. The young wife was overawed, but shivered inside.

"This landscape wouldn't care if I died in it," she thought. "It's completely indifferent to us."

Back at the camp, fires were lit, billies boiled, stews heated, and the evening passed in singsong and story-telling. As the day faded away, the enormous silence got to everyone. The stars were utterly brilliant and under their canopy, they all turned in, oddly silent.

Turner, lying alone in a borrowed tent, had put on a good show as the hearty youth leader, but was now feeling very uncomfortable. A very adequate sleeping bag and plenty of clothing – enough to stave off the cold night and likely frost in the morning – did not stop the shivering that arose deep inside him. It had been sitting within since they had driven into this wilderness. Now it intensified. A rhythmic pain began to pulse through his left hip – had he wrenched it somewhere along the walk to the gorge? he had no such recollection – that got ever sharper and more frequent. Presently he was in a cold sweat, twisting in silent agony every time it hit him. Something gripped him, sliding through him every time the pain hit, vengefully forcing him to go through it. It held him down firmly, but there was nothing there. Despite the unyielding grip, the air above him was empty. It was the most terrible experience he'd ever had in his life. No point calling out to anyone – nobody would be able to help with this un-nameable thing that had no reason. They'd think him mad. Perhaps he was? Had something burst in his brain?

But no – it was too horribly real, this other-something. Overwhelmed, he lay panting till it finally eased away after what seemed an eternity. It left his hip in excruciating pain, and he could barely walk in the morning, when he finally emerged, white and shaken. Well, that at least could be explained. He'd slipped along the way yesterday… must have wrenched the hip somehow… an unfortunate movement, you know… not so young anymore… it sounded plausible. As for that other thing, the one that had held him down and inflicted this upon him, of that he couldn't possibly speak. His own mind was stunned. What *had* it been? How was such a thing possible?

The other campers were exclaiming at the rivers of white mist flowing fast down the deep valleys, and fading away as the sun rose. It was magically beautiful.

The rest of the day passed as planned, after driving back to the Parks gate, with a walk along the old railway track down to Pillinger, a now-deserted mining township on the shore of Macquarie Harbour. Turner, pleading his injured hip, remained seated in one of the cars, grateful to be left alone, and endured the genuine agony of being thoroughly shaken up on the return trip to Wynyard. The next day his wife took him to the hospital in Burnie for x-rays. To his astonishment, nothing was found. Just a bad sprain, then? ventured the doctor. Confused, Turner went home with a painkiller prescription and advice to take it easy. And, indeed, over the next couple of weeks the pain eased and eventually went away. As things returned to normal, he tried to understand it, provide some explanations, but was unable to get his mind around it. The sheer insult of having been taken over by something that he had no control over – quite apart from the really terrible pain it had inflicted – had shaken him up. It was quite monstrous, but he had no answers.

Instead, he put his angry energy into spreading insinuations about the newcomer's homosexuality, without ever checking the veracity of it. An abomination to the church! The fear – and fascination – of male-to-male sex sat so deep in the community that men who were otherwise perfectly decent, began to get caught up in it. The husband noticed sly looks, fielded some suggestive remarks, sensed that he was being watched. Neither he nor his wife understood the local mindset, and had no idea what was going on, except that something unpleasant was in the air. Unable to equate love with lust, emotionally stunted local men mostly gave their wives a poor time of it, but these women recognised the young wife's unconscious sensuality that bespoke of *her* lively sex life with her own husband, and they loathed her for it. Any discerning observer would have noted this, and wondered about the truth of the rumour, but discernment was not a local strength. They preferred to feed on the spicy scandalous gossip, and it blinded them to the harm they were doing.

Turner began to stalk the husband. He stirred up many of his acquaintances. The unstoppable hatred, of the kind that can only breed in an uneducated redneck community, grew. There were occasions when a gun was trained on the man as he worked in his paddocks. That he was never actually shot was probably more a matter of luck, maybe a movement just at the critical moment. The undercurrent swirled about the family, and it began to get to them.

One day in church after his sermon, Turner approached the couple and handed them a booklet that he thought 'they should read'. It was entitled "The Abomination of Homosexuality" and was thinly disguised as a warning to all, particularly as AIDS was then making big news. But what it really contained was the most gloating, graphical description of what happens in New York male sex clubs, every sordid detail lovingly described. It was pure verbal pornography of the most blatant kind. The couple read it in wonderment, and handed it back to Turner with no comment. Still so innocent that they didn't understand, they had no reason to see it as addressing them directly. Later, as realization dawned, they felt they should have stood up before the congregation and waved it around:

"See what filth your so-called respectable elder is reading! He loves pornography! Is that the kind of man you want preaching to you, and taking care of your children?"

One morning after service – it had been Turner's turn to preach, and he'd done so fulsomely – among the congregation gathered by the door, he caught the handsome wife looking straight at him, and he saw that she knew him for what he really was. Something reared up in him, made him want to strike her, no, strangle her, and he was unable to stop a look of pure hatred that transformed his face into that of a wolf. Horror and disgust made the wife step back, turn away. It was true that she had been thinking of saying something, leaving him and his blind or complacent congregation with a final coup de grace. But no, let it be. They could sort it out themselves. It was no longer her business, and never again did she come here, shepherding her children away to a safer, cleaner place.

They started attending a kindlier church in Burnie, trying to shake the bad taste, but the harm was done. The marriage was breaking up – there were of course other reasons for this also – but those might have been overcome if it had not been for the poison that Reginald Turner had so actively spread. Their children too were damaged, never forgetting the narrow minded hypocrisy of their early church experience, and therefore unable to bring any reality to faith.

Presently the wife left, escaping the horror of the North West, and the abandoned husband hung on for two more years, finishing the house he had started to build. Only the sheerest determination enabled him to complete the house and sell it. Then he, too, left the place, wandering for many lost years on the mainland, never able to recover. The Thing in the hills would have been pleased with its work.

***

Denise put up with the situation out of necessity. Coping with a baby's needs was not something she was cut out for, so she accepted her mother's help, if not exactly gratefully. Restless, she started what casual part-time work she could get, but quickly realized that for independent living, she would have to do things better. Her affair with James and then the baby, had got in the way of completing her TAFE qualifications, but she did have some experience in hairdressing. Soon she was back in the same salon in Somerset, this time with a better wage. It was a good arrangement, her mother only too keen to have a grandson to love and care for every day. Denise started an affair or two, but they remained casual. A single mother with another man's child might be good for bedding, but was not to be considered for a serious relationship.

Things settled to a routine, and in time Tyson started school. Turner himself had begun to like the little boy, once he'd passed babyhood, and made clumsy attempts to befriend him. The child stared back, his eyes opaque, quickly learning to extract treats from his grandfather, but never once did he respond with any warmth. Turner, jealous of the real affection between Tyson and his grandmother, made Aileen's life as difficult as he could. Forced to ignominiously close the shop, he was around a great deal, much to her dismay. His hip – the one that had been mysteriously attacked – began to cause him problems, first a twinge here and there, some difficulty in moving freely, and then some real pain. It started to seize up, causing a clumsy limp and adding to his foul moods. Not that he'd ever been one to control his temper for the sake of his family, but now he became impossible to live with.

"I gotta get outa here!"

He found reasons for driving to Burnie, where he drank at the pubs, not really hiding it anymore. Late one Thursday morning, after such a trip, all his frustrations came together and the mask finally dropped. Returning through Cooee, just before the Cam River Bridge at Somerset, he pulled over onto the newly-remediated area between the shoreline and the road.

For many years, this had been the site of an abattoir, Hawkridge Meats. Locals had got used to the gruesome sight of terrified cattle being herded up a ramp while only a few meters from them, a conveyor belt spewed out the fresh entrails and other waste from the newly butchered carcasses. Often, trucks would be parked nearby, laden with stinking bones, before carting them off for grinding. The place reeked of death, yet it was situated on a most beautiful shoreline. That in itself did not strike locals as incongruous. There were garbage dumps in places where tourists would soon gasp over the million-dollar views, such as the one at Trial Harbour – but the blood and gore, and the bellowing of the cattle, were somewhat confronting. All were pleased when the place closed up, and in time the council began to clear the debris and make some attempts to return the area to something close to natural.

Turner was in no hurry to return home and, needing to clear his head, decided to take a look at the recent improvements while getting some sea air. Clambering stiffly from his car, he painfully slowly limped along the shoreline. Little did he know that he was walking on the same beach where his great-great-grandfather George had stood by and watched overseer Goldie shoot one Aboriginal woman and violently catch the other, along with her child. Nor did he know that it was near here that the same George had decided to kill himself, unable to stand the cruel dispensations of fate any longer. Reginald Turner didn't care about the past, but it was not to be denied. It had been waiting, and now it rose up and made a madman of him.

Some couples were strolling along the same area. He had paid scant attention to them, until suddenly a familiar laugh caught his ears. Only a few meters further along, was his own daughter Denise, the brazen hussy who had brought shame on his family with her illegitimate child, and she was dandling with a man, too. Wasn't she supposed to be at work? (It was actually her lunch hour.) The fellow was kissing her, and in the brief side view of his face Turner saw him to be foreign-looking as well. A wog? She's messing with them as well? Something grew up in him, a blind black rage, and he grabbed a chunky piece of driftwood by his feet and hurled it with surprising strength at the couple. Then he was running towards them, shouting obscenities, pouring out all his hatred of sex with no more containment.

The two, totally taken by surprise, fell apart. The wood had painfully caught Gino on the shoulder, and in the confusion he stood back as Turner, now foaming at the mouth, grabbed Denise's blonde hair and began to hit her, grunting. He made a terrifying spectacle, the mask finally gone and a lifetime of contained and controlled filth welling up. It was a face of pure evil, and Gino, revolted, nearly fled. But the girl was screaming and being attacked, he couldn't just leave her. Fortunately, he was experienced in some martial arts, so he hit the man – devil? – efficiently enough to fell him, and grabbing Denise, he dragged her away.

"What the heck was that? Are you alright?"

She was sobbing hysterically, and began to run as the fallen man howled more obscenities after her. They reached the car, panting.

"Take me away, take me *away!*" she cried, and it wasn't until they were parked in the main street of the small township, not far from her hairdresser, that she managed to pull herself together.

For she had recognised her father, the horrible face revealing the man she had always known to be there. And that he was going to kill her, if he could.

"Who *was* he? Why did he attack you? Are you alright? Shall I take you to the police?"

Gino was understandably confused.

"No, no...." she pulled a big breath. "Thanks for rescuing me. I'll be fine, I just need a moment."

"Who was he?"

"Don't know. Just some old crazy drunk, I suppose. You didn't really hurt him, did you?"

"No. He'll live, more's the pity."

She looked in the car mirror, observing a big bruise swelling up on her cheekbone and a split lip that had smeared blood on her face and collar.

"Dear God, I can't go to work like that..."

"Here," he handed her a handkerchief, and she did what she could to clean herself up.

"Would you drive me home, Gino?"

They stopped by the hairdresser, where, amid their cries of alarm, she did more than make her excuses for the afternoon. She handed in her notice, determined that she would leave, now this instant and forever, not only her home but Wynyard and the North West Coast altogether. She spent the afternoon packing, fluttered around by her distressed mother, collected Tyson from school, and caught the last Redline Coach of the day to Launceston.

Turner, back on the beach, found himself surrounded by a small crowd of wary people, half concerned, unsure about what they should do. Was he a dangerous raving lunatic? Or a victim? By chance nobody had actually seen him attack the couple, though some had observed the young man swipe him and then run away with the girl. Concerned questions, offers to get the police – he waved them all away.

"Just *go*," he snarled, and they backed off thankfully.

Left sitting alone in the sand, he felt his bruises. But that was nothing compared to the relief of having let go. Forty years of active hypocrisy had spilled out and it was like lancing a tightly-swollen boil. All the stinking pus was out, and he was finally the real man. Sorry he hadn't hurt the girl more effectively, failed even to kill her, he roared his rage at the empty sea. Triumphantly, he pronounced curses on his sexless wife, the butcher's shop that had kept him a slave all his life, and the whole of the stupid Wynyard society, all of whom had believed him to be such a good man, the fools.

"*Good, ha!*" he spat the word out. "No more – fuck 'em all..."

For more than two hours, he sat there, shouting and cursing. The police, alerted by one of the walkers, watched from a distance. As he was apparently doing nobody any harm, all they could do was keep an eye on things. His identity had been quickly established via his car number plate, and the older cop had some thoughtful moments, seeing the pathetic wreck of the man on the beach. He knew Reginald Turner well enough – you wouldn't think such a man would end up like this.

Eventually the cold wind off the sea, and his own age and frailty, caught up with Turner. He crawled back into himself and tried to get up. He managed it after some attempts and stumbled back to the car, frozen to the bone and barely upright with the agony in his hip. With some fumbling he got the motor running, the heater thawing him somewhat.

He'd go and have a proper warming drink at the pub before going home. Waiting to turn west onto the Wynyard road, he had to give way to the big Redline Coach on its way to Launceston.

Turner's fall from grace was noted in town. He was seen in the pubs, generally drunk before turning home, and many felt sorry for his wife. The hip seized up more, crippling him seriously, and a replacement was scheduled. In the long wait for the surgery, he remained defiant, having nothing to lose anymore. Finally the hospital called, and on the operating table, the surgeon sawed off the diseased hip. Normally, he would just hand over the removed part to his assistant, there not being time for anything else with blood going everywhere. But this time he hesitated briefly, puzzled by the odd appearance of the old bone. He'd seen many, of course, but this one was different. He couldn't stop then, and passed it over. Later that day, writing up his notes, it occurred to him that the bone had looked *gnawed*. Yes, that was it – like teeth marks, that's what the difference was.

"You're tired, matey," he told himself, "don't be silly. It's just an unusual calcification pattern."

He forbore to make any note about it in the patient's folder, and left to go home. But the image of the odd bone stayed with him for a long time.

THE DUTCH, from 1953

I had most need of blessing, and 'Amen' stuck in my throat.
Macbeth, by William Shakespeare

26. BERNDT AND ALAN

Berndt and Anna Dijkstra had arrived in Sydney on board the migrant ship *Volendam* in 1953. Sponsored by the Dutch government, they made jokes about having been 'sold by their country and bought by Australia'. The first few weeks after their arrival were horrible. Along with hundreds of other immigrants, they were sent by train in 'not much more than cattle wagons' to the Bathurst Migrant Camp in NSW. The country was bare, dusty, hot in the day and freezing at night; accommodation in long, tightly-packed Nissen huts did nothing to mitigate the climate. Anna was feeling terrible anyway, being pregnant with her first, and the disappointment to both was bitter.

"It's nothing like the films they showed," she whispered to Berndt behind the curtain that was all that shielded their bed from the neighbouring families. "The land was green and fruitful, not this barren waste…and oh, I can't stand the horrible food!"

Mutton stew, often fly-blown, was the most regular thing served up in the communal dining area. She tried to stifle her sobs against his shoulder. It was much harder for her, as she had left a family and beloved home background. He, on the other hand, having irrevocably lost all in Java, and hardened to deprivation in the Japanese camps, was simply grateful to be on his way to a new life. This camp did however have unpleasant military associations for him, so he was as anxious as Anna to be out of it.

"I'll go to Tasmania and get work there, and then you can come too, as soon as I've found some place for you to live."

He patted her swelling tummy.

"We need you settled before it comes, eh? I've heard there are lots of folk from our parts there, and that it's a nicer climate, too. That's where all those green fields are. They're looking for men to work on the hydro schemes, so I'm sure to find something. You'll see, it won't be long before I'll be sending for you!"

"Oh Berndt, I hate it here so. Can't I come now too?"

But that's what the men did as soon as their families were safely settled into the camps – off to find work and a place to live – so she set to with the other wives to make the best of it. At least there were no bombs falling here, no Gestapo, and the food, though awful, was actually plentiful.

Berndt had saved diligently before they left Amsterdam, and decided to fly to Launceston in Tasmania, expensive but desirable as it saved time. Yes, this was much better, he thought, as the hills of the Apple Isle became apparent. Inquiries at the airport soon directed him onto a bus to the Northwest Coast, and in the small town of Ulverstone he quickly found a bed with a Dutch family.

"It's not only much better – why, it's downright beautiful!"

He took in the stunning coastline, the vividly blue sea, the clean air, the sheer and utter peace of it – no Japanese, no guns, no war-torn cities and shattered people – just a sleepy town with mostly friendly faces and magnificent blue hills behind the fertile coastal fringe.

"This is the place, we've got to live here!"

His hosts agreed. There were some problems, of course; the culture was different, the language hard to learn, a few of the locals weren't quite so pleasant, but after four years they had begun to find their feet very satisfactorily. And yes, there was plenty of work – what could he do? Well, no, no tea plantations here but if he was into farming, how about the government's clearance scheme on Flinders Island? They were currently looking for men, it would be an immediate income until he found something better.

"My wife is expecting," he explained. Would there be housing and suitable facilities out there? Well, no, it wasn't exactly what you'd call a developed place – that was precisely what the scheme was supposed to be bringing about.

"There are a good many families like us living here by now," went on his host. "We could find somewhere for Anna to board and keep an eye on her while you're away working. And there's a hospital here in Ulverstone, so you needn't worry."

And so it was arranged. The Agricultural Bank that was overseeing the Flinders Island Scheme took him on immediately. The single men's housing at The Summer Camp came at no cost, with only a minimal contribution to make for food, saving a lot of his salary. Regular cargo flights – weather permitting of course – would provide a free lift to see his wife now and then. A Dutch family had a busy mother who'd be glad of Anna's help and company, and yes, there was a small room she could have at no cost in return. Heart-warmed by the help so readily offered, Berndt wrote the good news to Anna, enclosing a ticket to Launceston. It all happened so quickly there wasn't time to think, and before he knew it, he was on Flinders Island.

In many ways, it was a shock. His initial flight included an unwelcome and foul-mouthed group of prisoners, sent up from Risdon Prison in Hobart to do some enforced labouring on the Scheme. The local cop deftly prevented their being landed, and had them flown out again with the aircraft's return.

"Don't want this kind of scum here, do we?"

During the scrimmage, Berndt – holding the paper from the Agricultural Bank introducing him as a paid worker – was left to stand, unnoticed, until finally a harassed-looking man asked him his business.

"You'll be needing a lift to the Camp, then," he said, and advised that Palmer's truck would be going that way later in the day. "Might as well introduce yourself at the local Ag Bank, meanwhile."

The Camp, when he finally got there over 14 kms of unsealed track, was horrifyingly similar to the internment ones he'd suffered in, and if it hadn't been for the sheer difficulty of actually doing so, he would have left the place immediately.

Gradually, though, he settled to it. The work of was physically demanding, but he was used to that. Several other immigrants, from various European countries and in a similar state of shock, made him feel less alone with their ready camaraderie and friendly sing-a-longs round the camp fire in the evenings. With nothing to spend his money on, they would soon have enough to get started with a small house – that thought made up for it all.

The Camp sat in a featureless area of waste scrub, generally known as The Flats, but in the distance reared the fine Mt Strzelecki and on flying in, he had caught sight of white beaches. He soon joined others on Sundays, hitching a lift with the truck and spending the day fishing in the most magnificent setting, readily rivalling his beloved Java, with the clean, wide and uncrowded expanses of sand and brilliant red-tinged rock framed by a turquoise sea. Gradually, the simple life and the great silence of the land spread a gentle balm on his war-torn soul.

He was interested in the idea of providing returned soldiers with free farm land – not only that, but preparing it for them as well as building them a house. It seemed entirely extraordinary. In time, he learned that there were problems with the Scheme – sometimes the wrong land had been cleared, or insufficient for commercial survival allocated, and some returned soldiers didn't know enough about farming to make a successful go of it.

"I applied for a farm too, but they didn't see me fit enough, even though I'm truly local and I've as good a war record as any," he was told by Vic Mayne, one of his co-labourers, "just because I'm part coloured".

"I thought all men counted the same in Australia?"

Berndt had not been aware of the existence of coloured natives – Vic was the only one he'd met. None of the films promoting Australia had shown anything but laughing, white, and very European faces. When Vic left and moved to Launceston, Berndt decided that he would do the same as soon as he could. Anna had meanwhile given birth to Roseanne, and no doubt there would be others. He now regretted having so hastily accepted the first job offered, but his desperate need to get them settled and some income coming in had made it seem the right way to go.

He made inquiries every time he had time off in Ulverstone. There was a large Dutch community south of Hobart, in a small town called Kingston, and he wrote to the Pastor of the Reformed Church there. An encouraging reply – yes, more families were welcome and help could be offered – got his hopes up and saw him through his remaining time of obligatory work. In 1955, with Anna expecting their second child, they moved into a little house in 'Little Groningen', as the community in Kingston was nicknamed, and from there he made a successful application to the Agricultural Department as an advisor and field worker. Alan was born next, and by the time his little sister Sabina arrived, Berndt had taken out a mortgage on 5 acres of fine land near the town.

"I'll build us a fine, comfortable house, here. Better than being in a crowded, dirty city, eh?"

With Berndt in a secure job, having adapted quickly from growing tea to potatoes, and Anna finding much comfort at the local Dutch church and community, they settled in quite quickly. On the basis of her letters home, her brother also emigrated to Tasmania, though he choose to farm at Elliott on the North West Coast, where he grew vegetables on contract for a processing factory in the rich brown soil. Visits to Uncle Tadd's lively farm were always much looked forward to, especially by the three young children. Outwardly, it was a successful story of assimilation and adaption, but the past is not so easily shed.

***

"If he lives, you need to face the possibility of permanent brain damage," pronounced the doctor over the comatose body of Alan. Berndt and Anna had rushed to the Royal Hobart Hospital, where their seven year old son lay after being hit by a car. His class had been on an outing, when the young boy, dreaming along by himself at the rear, impulsively ran across the road to catch up, without looking out for any traffic.

"He's always dreaming, that boy – it's time he pulled his socks up," his father was often heard to say, especially when a small chore had not been completed. Or, more sharply:

"Will you get on with it?"

Berndt, though unable to put his war experience into words, knew how easily a man's place in the world is lost, and he did not want that to be his son's lot.

"Hard work is the only way; see how we survived to give you all this."

And now his only boy was a barely-alive body. It was a bitter blow.

Eventually they brought little Alan home. He had awakened after seven days in coma, and the hospital released him to the flustered Anna with many injunctions to be careful with him. She took this literally, bowing her head under God's will, and many a time there would be a whispered comment to visitors about how delicate Alan was. His older sister was charged with keeping a special eye on him; any rough and tumble games were cut short or prohibited.

"No games or sports at school!"

The physical injuries healed promptly, and despite no actual evidence of any damage in the head, he was fluttered around by his mother and older sister for a long time. Inevitably, Alan grew up a solitary child, out of touch with ordinary life and unable to handle it, always conscious of his special status. The doctor's words, thoughtlessly spoken where the child could hear them, made him doubt his right to live. His father, quickly impatient yet uneasily guilty over his half shame at having a difficult son, retreated for the most part, leaving Alan's management to Anna. Only in one thing he insisted – that the boy complete his education, and do a science degree at university. On the strength of that, Alan secured a position in the Health Department, where he remained for the rest of his working life. Though he had no real interest in the work, he stayed, safely cradled in a system which provided a good salary, generous benefits, and no likelihood of losing his job. That is, until, in the wake of his affair with Denise, he thought he'd try being a hero.

Alan's sisters, Roseanne and Sabina, were both refreshingly normal, and did well. As their brother sank evermore into himself, they lost interest in him also and went their own way. His last ally disappeared when his mother died, still quite young, of cancer. Alan, physically tall and with a romantic sadness permanently hanging around his good looks, readily attracted female attention, but he had nothing to give in return for the love offered. The idea that he had to make an effort to be worthy of love had never crossed his mind. Presently he married and had a daughter;

his wife left him in despair after a few lonely years, and – once their daughter got nearer puberty – had denied him visiting rights as well. He had not had contact with either for years, though he faithfully paid the child maintenance until the girl reached eighteen. His own father had approved of that, at least. Alan did visit Berndt occasionally, but they remained strangers until the old man died. The funeral brought Alan together with his family for the first time in years; he was astonished at what he hadn't known about his father that the eulogy now revealed to him.

Berndt and Anna had made it to a safe haven in Tasmania. Materially they recovered all and more, becoming respected members of the local community and having a solid and comfortable house in a growing suburb. As they got older, they sold the surrounding land for development at a good price, keeping only enough space for a generously-sized garden. Katrijn Dijkstra, dimly sensing the future as she dreamed of distant lands by her window in Amsterdam in 1828, would have approved of the latter. But she would have been much saddened by the loss of contentment that had befallen the Dijkstra family. Katrijn's religion had been severe but a living thing, capable of giving comfort and direction. The cold rigidity that entered the church as it tried to defend itself against its stance in the war and the changing world, would have had Katrijn weeping. The arrogance of Dutch colonialism in Indonesia, followed by the terrible deprivations under the Japanese, would have given her simple soul nightmares. Tasman's fabled island held so much promise, but what use was that when man came to it with his heart already full of the shadows of war?

PART
FOUR

THE TASMANIANS

JAMES MAYNE, ELLIE FAIRFIELD, DENISE TURNER, ALAN DIJKSTRA – AND TY

> *"Don't let the old break you; let the love make you."*
> Bertrand Russell

27. THE BEGINNING

I'll take him with me to the Western Tiers, thought James Mayne as he sat watching his son. To the old hut at the back of Michael's place, high up there where you can look out over the whole country.

The boy, unaware of his father's plans for him – unaware, indeed, that his father was even there – struggled to maintain his 12 year old cool in the face of adult doings. They were sitting in the Family Court in Hobart, where his mother Denise was waiting to hear the magistrate's decision on how to manage her son's misdoings.

James studied Denise, also. She had not changed much in thirteen years. More stylish in her clothing, perhaps, and her formerly wild hair tamed into a fashionable straight cut. She still had that sharp edge – how could he ever have found her attractive? That he had strayed from his 20-yr marriage with the steady Ellie was perhaps not too surprising. Denise's petite angularity was a new experience after his wife's comfortable and generous curves. But it was still only a regrettable lapse into a bit of temporary lust, best forgotten, which was now not possible, for before him was the consequence that now had to be faced: one lost boy.

It had seemed like the merest chance that James should find out about the matter just in time for this case, but he did not believe in coincidence any more – he had a role to play in the unfolding drama. Observing the child's confusion, James was overwhelmed with sorrow, remembering his own years of youthful dislocation, that desperate time of hanging out with other wild youngsters, often drunk, on the riverbank in Launceston, forever chased by the police as half-caste scum from the Islands. But for the loving support of his family, it might well have gone for him as it was threatening to for this boy, now in trouble and up before the court. He had only the vacuous flappings of an incompetent mother and a bitter, judgmental grandfather in Reginald Turner.

"I'm being somewhat unfair to Denise; she's probably doing the best she can, given her sad family setting…" He acknowledged that, for all her limitations, there was not a shred of meanness in her.

But the child needed a real father to hold him steady and teach him the man stuff. Somehow, he would get hold of him. Once the fuss had settled, he would take him out into the bush, or even to the Islands. There would be plenty to do out there, messing with boats, hunting, tasting the wind. Meanwhile, there was that small hut high up; they could hide out there together. All he had to do was plan it correctly, and soon. He was not leaving his son with the dysfunctional Denise, or to go to Ashley Youth Detention Centre. It's ok, Johnno Boy, I'm coming.

The court session ended in the boy being bailed to his mother's care with limited freedom until a psychiatric report could be completed. More idiotic nonsense, thought James, the boy needs love and stability, not psychological probings, as he walked out into Davey St and turned east. Crossing Murray St, he found himself looking straight at a tall man coming the other way. Something passed between them, a recognition, perhaps, that sent a strangeness rising up in him. What are you to me? He would see him again, he knew.

He reached his ute in the Wellington Car Park, impatient with having to descend round endless curves and levels. Bonnie, his half-cross kelpie, was back home, in Launceston, being fed by his neighbour. He had missed her, all the way driving down through the Midlands to Hobart on his last-minute decision to attend the case. Not sure how long it might all take, or if he might have to stay overnight, it seemed wiser to leave her behind. Bonnie had been his chief companion for the last eight years, her happy delight at his presence filling his days with warmth. He looked forward to getting back.

***

Alan Dijkstra reached the government offices on Murray St after an unsatisfactory lunch. In fact, most things were not going right for him lately, and just to prove the point, here was another one of those reports on water quality. It was a difficult situation, one he couldn't quite get a grip on, and that upset him. For him, as the temporary acting head of the research section in the Department of Health & Human Services, to be factually out of his depth was embarrassing, intolerable. Damn that doctor out there in St. Helens with her bleatings about toxic water – how had she managed to get such a high profile program like the ABC TV's "Australian Story" to run not only one but two half-hour sessions on her insane claims about trees emitting poison into the water supply? It was entirely absurd, but many people seemed to be taken in by it. Enough to have the state government requesting extra information.

He had already provided the reports on water testing and other facts that clearly refuted Dr. Bleaney's assertions. But the media loved their dramas, and gave far more space to that doctor than his own carefully collated reports. In fact, rarely if ever did the substance of any of his public health related work come before the public. Alan did not expect it to; it was usually handed to his superior for further processing: the latter summarized the information and occasionally passed it on to the media.

Acting in place of his boss – who had been inconsiderate enough to go sick at this very moment – Alan now had to set out the relevant points and suggest reasonable guidelines with which the government would formulate their stance on in the matter. And they wanted it right now.

Alan wasn't more than very averagely ambitious. He had worked through university on the expectations of his uncompromising father, and his just scraped-in degree had made his long tenure as a Tasmanian public servant possible. Materially, he was well taken care of, and could expect to retire in a few years in comfort on a very good superannuation. He owned his solid house, which he had refurbished himself. In his spare time he made some astute investments that had survived the recent downturns rather better than most. He had enjoyed doing that, finding it absorbing to research the markets and do well in them. And it was very nice to feel, for once, superior while listening to others' woes about having lost everything.

It was a small satisfaction in an otherwise not very satisfactory life. In his blacker moments – and he had a great many of those lately – his permanent sense of failure, of not amounting to anything much, drove him to excessive drink or into a haze of marihuana. A reliable worker, unremarkable but solid, he had never taken an unnecessary day off in his entire life, and always met the required work deadlines. For all that, promotions passed him by. Occasionally he registered a comment about his not having the right attitude. How could you have the right attitude when all your colleagues were in league against you? Alan didn't feel included. He believed that they conspired their work intrigues without him, and occasionally directly against him.

Being made acting head was only by default. In the normal course of events, he would have remained two levels down, and retired quietly and uneventfully from there. But the official head suddenly went down with a terminal disease, and the logical successor, no sooner installed, managed to hurt himself badly in a motorcycle accident.

"Serve him right," thought Alan. "Fancy being that immature to still be showing off on such an ostentatious machine. Who is he trying to impress?"

His unacknowledged envy resulted in poor workplace relations between himself and the now injured man. The department, sent in a spin by the sudden departure of two key men, and as always short-staffed, had turned to Alan until the position could be filled. Unable to overlook the way he had got there – by default only, not because someone had recognized his abilities – he spent more time stewing on the injustice of it, rather than grasping the moment and proving them all wrong. The memory of his father sternly telling him to get a grip on himself still cut deep, but didn't help. He rushed away promptly at five – not that going home improved things, for his house was also empty of all meaning. But there he could hide from others' prying eyes and ease himself into the wine.

Alan spent the afternoon grappling with the required report, assembling the relevant studies, ordering them neatly, and writing a summary of the contents. But the premier now wanted some impossibly decisive conclusions, some logical and irrefutable argument to bolster the government position. This is how it is, and this is why. It wasn't only his inability to do exactly that, but also something in the matter of these supposedly toxic trees that just didn't add up in Alan's mind. Why would an established doctor risk her reputation, her work and her income if she did not truly believe she was onto something genuine? Had she not spent many thousands of her own money having those tests done? For all his lack of confidence, Alan was a fair man, and this made him genuinely uneasy. He heartily wished that they had found a proper head of department by now, one who could turn this complexity into a simple spin sentence or two, and thus relieve him of the responsibility.

He finally submitted his effort, knowing it to be unsatisfactory, and left the office feeling more depressed than usual. Crossing back over Murray St on his way to his car, he was reminded briefly of the guy who had given him such a searching look at lunchtime. What the hell was that about? Alan felt that a challenge had been extended to him in that moment, something that mattered uncomfortably. It made him uneasy and driving home he turned up the music extra loud to drown out the silly refrain that kept forming in his head. Dr. Bleaney's bleatings... Bleaney's bleatings....

***

Denise Turner left the court sometime after James had disappeared down the street. She had not been aware of his quiet figure in the public gallery. Though glad that Tyrone had been spared instant locking-up, she had little control over him, really, and knew that she would be unable to meet the requirements the court had imposed. Keep Tyrone at home all the time? Allow him out – apart from school – only when accompanied by herself? Not only would they both drive each other insane, but the boy would not put up with it – even locked in his room, he would break out somehow, sooner or later. But perhaps the fear of being taken into youth detention would be enough to buy some cooperation from him, to see that psychiatrist, at least, and keep out of more real trouble. Perhaps. If she could keep that Mitch away from him.

"Get in!" she snapped impatiently when they reached the car. The music blared up immediately, and as she focused on the road, Tyrone snatched her mobile out of her bag and was dialing his mate. By now in the moving traffic, he easily dodged her attempts to take it back.

"You good for nothing bugger, you know you're not allowed to do that."

Listening helplessly to the half incomprehensible mutterings, she was overcome with exhaustion. The prospect of having to put up with this disaster of a kid any longer overwhelmed her.

"So he's still here, is he?" Caleb greeted her at the Glenorchy unit. She eyed him with sudden, furious dislike.

"Yeah, and it's *your* kid that got him into all this trouble in the first place. He's the one that should be up in court, not Ty."

She turned on the boy.

"Go to your room, just get out of the way. I'll call you when tea's ready."

Tyrone went quietly enough, his protest expressed in the shattering volume of noise from his radio. It was only later that she realized that he still had her mobile.

Denise slammed around the kitchen, looking for stuff to make a meal with. She was hungry. Caleb sat back with a beer, watching her, wanting to know the outcome.

"How long will we be stuck with him for? When's that fancy shrink going to do the report?"

Something burst in Denise. The upset of having her boy charged with theft on top of a long saga of disciplinary problems at school, the police coming and then the social workers, trying to make sense of what the legal aid lawyer said, and finally the court session which really had resolved nothing – it was all too much. And now here was the man who had been no use to her in all of it, whose own son had led her Ty astray in the first place. Screaming at him to get out, *just get out*, she flung the open bottle of ketchup in her hand at him. He leapt up and grabbed hold of her. You bitch. Something dark rose in his eyes, but after a moment he backed off contemptuously and left. It was more frightening than if he had actually hit her.

Shaking, Denise sagged onto the lounge, staring at the ketchup mess. The bottle had ejected a long streak of sauce across the room, on the wall and glugging into the carpet. She started to sob. How had it gotten to this? After a while, she got herself a very large glass of wine from the cask, lit a cigarette, and just sat there numbly.

"You ok, Mum? Shall I make some tea?"

Tyrone was making some efforts to dab at the spilt ketchup. She had not heard him come into the room. The wine had had its effect and she had calmed, although she could feel it making her unsteady. Too much, on an empty stomach. He turned on the telly, and she just sat, letting him clean up the mess and make some noodles for them both. He brought her a steaming plate, and sat beside her. They spooned it up, watching the afternoon soapie without really seeing it, but soothed by the familiar noise.

"You're a good kid, really, Ty."

And he was. He could be really sweet, like now, though it was increasingly rare.

When she so precipitously fled the North West Coast for Hobart with Ty, she had been glad to find this unit to rent in Glenorchy. That the man two villas along also had a son, whose care he shared with his ex, seemed an additional bonus. Ty and Mitch spent much time together, but when she and the father, Caleb, began an affair, the boys started to wander further away. Denise paid little attention, glad that Ty had a friend to keep him busy and off her hands. She desperately wanted it to work, this new life she was making for them. She had found a position in a hairdresser's in Moonah, and her evenings were taken up with Caleb.

The change in her son came only slowly to her attention. Even when she found herself confronting him too often for sloppy behaviour, rude language and general non-cooperation, she thought nothing more of it than 'he's in those years'. She had berated him for the bad school reports, and then for playing truant. Not that she much liked the somewhat older Mitch, but they were just boys, weren't they, playing around?

Then the police arrived. Ty had been caught house breaking. An alert neighbour had called, and the boy was caught as he came over the fence with the laptop in his hands. Mitch, bigger and faster, had got clean away. She had not seen him since. Neither, apparently, had Caleb.

The following weeks were a nightmare for Denise. She felt belittled by the social workers suggesting she wasn't an adequate mother, and overwhelmed by the lawyer. Eventually she realized that the case was being taken seriously, that Ty could actually be placed into detention. Angry and defensive, she was also confused.

"Why did you do it, Ty?" brought nothing but a useless, scowling shrug. Then she also lost her job as the hair salon cut back on staff. She and Caleb, who mostly wasn't working at all, began to have fights as they saw too much of each other, their angry passion at night solving nothing. He was nice at times, taking her with him to the pub. The language there was coarse and the alcohol too much, but she went along with it; it was better than being alone. Now she was back on the dole, with a kid in trouble, her man stomped out the door, and the whole dream was falling over.

It was not what she had come to Hobart for.

She got herself another glass of wine, and put her arm around Ty. For once he allowed her touch. He'd been frightened too. Somehow she sensed it through the wine swirls.

"You're a good kid, Ty", she said again. "We'll get it sorted out, this mess, you'll see. I promise."

***

Ellie Fairfield sat back with a sigh of satisfaction, coffee in hand, the previous weekend's paper before her, and no immediate pressure to do anything. The late February sun was pleasantly dappled by the grapevine growing under the clear verandah roof, where ripening bunches of fruit promised sweetness to come. Beyond lay her garden, a riot of flowers and vegetables surrounded by trees where the birds were welcome. Ellie's cat, Susie, had been carefully chosen from the RSPCA for her advancing years which made it unlikely that she would chase the feathered inhabitants, and who was currently purring in a sunny patch on the mat beside her.

On this Monday afternoon, the week's prospect lay before her pleasantly. Ellie worked part-time with a charitable organization, assisting unemployed people to set up their own small businesses. She taught the basic management program in Launceston two half days a week, and shared the mentoring work with two other employees. Between them, they regularly visited clients who were trying to get an astonishing variety of business ideas under way. It was work Ellie loved, being a natural teacher and taking a real interest in how her students developed. Not all made any money from it, of course, but to Ellie this was not the point – it was the encouragement and personal growth that the program could offer. In this, she was at odds with her employer, who was obliged to strictly observe the dollars of this government-funded program. Clients were only a payable proposition if they succeeded sufficiently to leave unemployment assistance.

It was not her employer's fault, Ellie realized. But what had happened to the value of human beings? She really enjoyed the two days a week on the road, especially when they took her into places she would not otherwise visit. Ellie loved the Tasmanian country side, particularly the rural fringe where the grand Western Tiers reared up with a promise of wilderness. Her cousin Michael's land lay like that, running back from the plains of the Macquarie River to the foothills between O'Connor's Peak and Millers Bluff. The original land grant, given to William Fairfield in 1824, had comprised 640 acres. Over time, the family had acquired additional pieces, some running right up to the precipices. It was very suitable for sheep, and over the years more of the trees had been cleared. But some had survived, particularly in the deep crevices where the creeks flowed down and the mountain birds sang.

Ellie had spent many summer holidays there with Michael and his sister Ruth, running wild in those hills and camping out in what was left of the old shepherd's hut at the top of a steep incline. The view from there was fantastic, covering the entire Midlands area to the heights of Ben Lomond in the east. On a clear day, you could see the dinky-toy-sized cars moving along the highway far across the valley. When she and Michael both had their own families, they gathered there regularly. The men made the old hut a bit more weatherproof, brought in a woodstove and some basic furniture. Water was fetched from the creek until Michael and James installed a pipe to the hut, from whence it trickled back to the creek in a small stream, to the children's endless delight.

Those days were some of our best times, thought Ellie, with the two families together. Michael's wife Isabelle came along occasionally, and the four adults would sit together watching the last golden sun fade from the slopes of Ben Lomond and letting the silence settle deeper around them. Then the kids would erupt from somewhere, hungry as jackals, and a cheery supper round the stove would follow, with yarns told and card games played.

Ellie sighed again, a fleeting touch of sadness at the memory. A pity she and James had not made it through. Though Ellie had re-built her own life after the divorce, and was very happy with it now, she did envy those couples who managed to stay together. She could see the deepening warmth between them, that understanding and acceptance of each other, and – sometimes it came as a surprise – the physical affection that often seemed more intense after thirty or more years. She hoped her children would all be lucky enough to experience it. Only her oldest, Ian, was married; he and Janine had two children, whom Ellie baby-sat regularly, as Janine also worked. They were well suited, a solid, steady, somewhat conventional couple making a nice home for their family.

Her daughter Tessa had left for Melbourne after completing grade 12. Floundering initially, she had steadied enough to go to university, completing her arts/economics degree and now had very well-paid work in an upmarket advertising firm. Tessa, handsome and going through a long list of boyfriends with snappy cars, showed no sign of settling down. Ellie acknowledged the heady independence and material success of Tessa's life, but wondered if the girl would eventually feel cheated if she didn't have a family of her own. Was it possible to feel fulfilled without one, Ellie wondered, but could not decide on the matter. She, after all, had had her share of one, so her being content on her own now was no guide to Tessa's situation.

And her youngest, Jeremy. Dear Jeremy. The dreamer, the one with impossible ideas. Barely scraping through school, not for lack of ability but because:

"It's boring, Mum. They don't teach anything real."

He was drifting from one job to another, trying to make some kind of sense of what might suit him. Ellie wondered what was keeping him here, in quiet old Launceston with such limited prospects? Living in a share house with an assortment of youngsters who seemed to change every week, he came to her occasionally for a decent meal.

Ellie was glad that James had kept in touch with their children despite the divorce, seeing them regularly, at first awkwardly in a rented flat for some stumbling and embarrassed weekend outings, but later things settled more easily after he bought himself a neat small house in Kings Meadows. And he had caused her no material difficulty, paying child maintenance regularly, and leaving her the house, where she continued to provide a home. His sudden affair with that student had come as a complete shock to her, particularly as James always seemed a steady man, his solid presence filling the house and their life. Ellie made a point of not accusing James of anything before the children, allowing them to forge their relationship in the new circumstances as best they might. Tessa had once spat out her disgust over her father's actions, as she was leaving for Melbourne, and had taken Ellie by surprise with her venom. The two boys had never spoken of it to her, ever.

Still, she had done the best she could, and now was free to live life as she wished. She also had an on-going and complicated involvement with Keith, a journalist with the *Launceston Examiner*, which caused her both joy and deep grief. In recent years she had wandered rather casually into the community of the local Anglican Church, appreciating those who acknowledged God, though she had little liking for formal religion.

Her salary was enough to keep her in simple comfort; the house was hers with no debt. And right now she could enjoy a pleasant, sunny and unhurried afternoon.

Ellie opened the previous day's Sunday paper. Amid the usual articles of break-ins, court cases, and other human debris, was a large spread on the St. Helens doctor who claimed that the extensive tree plantations above the town were the source of a mysterious toxicity in the local water. It was an extraordinary statement, strongly denied by the State government, whose tests had declared the water perfectly safe. But the massive oyster deaths in the bay continued, and Dr Bleaney, well-established and liked by many, pointed to the unusually large number of cancer patients in the area. Sufficiently concerned to personally pay for independent water tests, she had concluded on their evidence that the selective breeding of the Eucalyptus nitens was causing them to shed an unknown but dangerous substance which was contaminating the whole catchment.

Ellie had missed both ABC "Australian Story" programs on the same subject, not being much of a one for TV watching, but she had heard various and very heated conversations on the matter just recently. She found herself wondering about the plantations on her cousin's property. The Fairfields, along with many other farmers in the rural recession of the 1990's, had leased land to the timber companies who paid well to get their trees planted in good soil. Ellie had not visited Fairbourne much in recent times, but recalled seeing those trees once when they were just three feet high. They were, she supposed, quite large by now. Were they the same kind as those mentioned in the article? Was their beloved romping ground being poisoned by some creeping, dangerous growth?

Ellie decided that she would ring Michael that evening.

28. THE DOING, 2010

The boy was playing around the shack with the dog. James watched with interest, observing the child's conflicting emotions. He had no fear that Tyrone would actually try and run away – not only because of the sheer daunting difficulty of it, but because, really, Ty was rather enjoying all this. It was natural for him to feel at moments that he should remain loyal to his mother Denise – after all, had he not been kidnapped from her? And who was this strange man anyway, suddenly turning up out of the blue? All the same, camping out in the bush with someone who could catch dinner and cook it on an open fire as well, was very exciting. And the man was actually rather a nice guy. Even better, he had a gorgeous, happy and playful dog.

Arriving late the previous evening, in the dark, had been a bit scary for him, already emotionally overwhelmed. He had dropped off as soon as James had indicated the bunk. The man had then settled down with a sigh on the opposite bed, still stunned that it had happened so readily after all.

Tyrone had no idea of the amount of thought and planning that had brought him up here, high on the side of the Great Western Tiers with a brilliant view out over the Midlands, doing some real bush living instead of being in dull old school in Glenorchy. James had agonized at length over the matter. It was not in his nature to go against the law, nor had he any wish to inflict worry upon Denise. Yet he was urgently aware of the boy's age, just at that vital time before full puberty when firm guidance could make a significant difference to the boy's future. In the absence of anyone else, James had to do it, right now, before the kid was permanently messed up.

Simply contacting Denise and offering to take the boy off her hands, was the only proper way to do this, he knew, but felt unequal to the task.

She might well react badly to his sudden presence – after all, she had not seen fit to tell him about this child – and he remembered how she could explode into a sudden wild spitfire of temper. Also, she was under an obligation to keep the child secure and to turn up for stupid appointments with psychologists. That decided him.

"Do it now, answer questions later! After all, you're not going to hurt the boy."

But how? In the end, he wrote a letter to Denise, explaining his concern and intentions.

"I don't want Tyrone to be swallowed by the system. He's not a bad boy, just needs a man's guidance, especially now, to help him get things together. It came as a surprise to find that I had this son – why did you not tell me? – but I want to help him. Please allow him to have some time with me, and then I will bring him back to you."

Joan found him Denise's address. They'd had a relationship some years ago, and had remained steady friends after the passion faded. She worked in the social services in Launceston and was aware of Denise Turner's case. He had told her why his marriage had broken up, mentioning Denise as the cause. Now Joan wondered who Ty's father was, commenting on the sadly common situation of so many fatherless boys in trouble. It did not take James long to work out that the dates fitted perfectly, and one look at Ty's face had been enough to confirm the matter. He's probably got my stubbornness, too, he thought. Still, that can be good – it helps to get things done.

Telling Joan what was on his mind regarding the boy, he found in her an ally.

"I shouldn't do this, but..."

They had a nice dinner together, during which she told of other lost children and broken relationships. All of it only strengthened his resolve. He gathered that Denise had very recently moved from Glenorchy to a small flat in Lenah Valley, and enrolled at the Polytechnic in Advanced Hairdressing. Ty was still attending the Ogilvie High School in Glenorchy. To return home, he caught the Metro bus, and then there was a rather long walk up the hill to the flat, where he would be alone for a while until Denise got back from her course. That was the moment, James thought, if any. He would offer him a lift home, and just keep driving, having dropped the letter into Denise's post box just before. It was a risk and might not work out, but she had to know that her son was safe.

He checked the boy's route home out, watched him from a distance on the first day, and on the second he had his ute parked on the quiet stretch alongside the children's playground at the bottom of the hill. Bonnie was tied up on the open back. Just before the boy was due, he deliberately dropped his bag of tools, which he had filled with many small items, off the back of the flat tray, and was busy picking them up as Ty came round the corner.

"Would you like to give me hand with this, sonny?"

James had an open face and friendly smile, and was accompanied by a black and white dog with a happy bark. And what boy would resist handling tools? As they gathered, he innocently asked where the lad lived, and when the job was done, he offered him a lift home. It was absurdly simple…

The next few minutes were critical – the only moment he would have to persuade Ty. He had decided to pull over as soon as they were just too far from home for an immediate sprint. Now he was praying: God give me the right words, let him understand that I mean well…

The boy had protested as soon as the car continued past his home – everyone knew of stranger danger and he'd seen far too many kidnappings in movies. But even in his fright something came across to him, enough to make him hesitate when the car stopped in the reassuringly normal setting of the car park beside the Brent St Takeaway shop; just long enough to hear "Listen, Tyrone…" and to see a kindly face looking at him with genuine interest. With his hand on the door handle, the seat belt already undone, he stopped.

"You can go if you want to, Ty. I won't stop you. In fact, I'll drive you back home if that's what you want. But will you first listen for a moment?"

"Who are you? What do you want with me?"

"I saw you at the court. My name is James Mayne. I have a plumbing business in Launceston. I won't hurt you. I know your mother, and like I said, I'll take you back to her right now, if you really want. I know the trouble you've been in, and that you might still end up in Ashley. So I thought you might like to consider another, perhaps more interesting, possibility?"

The boy's astonishment fought with his need to protest, to be suspicious. But the man made no move to restrain him, and he didn't seem particularly threatening.

"What...?"

This was the crunch moment. James knew that if he didn't get the right words now, he would lose the boy. But he had to be straight with him, nothing less would do. He took a deep breath, and surrendered the outcome.

"It's like this. I kind of owe your mum a debt, from a long time ago, and when I heard about you and all that, I thought I might be able to help. I've got a shack up in the hills, right in the bush, where it's kind of nice, bit wild and lots of animals... we could do some hunting and maybe see some eagles..." he pulled himself up. "It's a man's life, up there. I thought it might do you good, better than being assessed by some psychologist who doesn't know anything much about real life. You could stay with me for a while, till all the upset settles down. Then maybe you might feel a bit better about everything, and perhaps we could even talk some sense into all those busybodies from the social services."

Ty was so astonished his mouth almost fell open. This man was a stranger, yet he knew exactly what was going on.

"But, but... why this? Couldn't you just talk to Mum, if you know her?"

James smiled. "I could, but I don't know that she'd be allowed to let you go. The court said something about her being responsible for you and making sure that you turn up for all these appointments. It was part of the deal that kept you out of Ashley, wasn't it?"

Ty nodded. Denise had made it very clear to him that if he did not come straight home, every day, without deviation, he would be taken to the youth detention center. Her trusting him, and him continuing at regular school, was all part of her attempts to 'sort out the mess', as she had promised. They had moved to this flat, away from Caleb and Mitch in Glenorchy; she had enrolled to get proper qualifications so she could get a reliable job, and if he would get his grades, maybe the situation could be salvaged. Her desire to make good for both of them had been so genuine and desperate that he had promised, and meant it, and so far he had kept his word.

"So, if we asked your Mum, she'd have to say 'no', wouldn't she? But, if you just disappeared without her having anything to do with it, then it wouldn't be her fault, would it? I left her a letter that she'll find when she gets home. In it, I told her what I had in mind, and where you would be. But, like I said, Ty, I'll take you straight back to her now, if you'd rather."

It had been enough. The boy still had thoughts, unformed questions, needed to work things out, but he had heard enough to be intrigued. James just sat quietly, keeping his thoughts in the moment, waiting for the boy to set the next note. The child's confusion and hesitation were natural, but he wasn't silly. Would he have enough pluck to run with this? James surprised himself when he realized that he was very much hoping so.

Ty was struggling with it all. Why should he trust this man? Who was he, anyway? Was he telling the truth? Yet he was offering something with a ring of adventure, a breaking out, a real man thing to do. Ty had long fretted under the restraints of living in a small space with not much to do. He turned his doubting, questioning face to the man, who smiled back gently and had big capable hands lying openly and easily at rest on his thighs. This man was at peace... it was not something Ty had come across before, and it was attractive.

Still, he had to assert himself. "What about Mum? I can't just disappear."

"Well, we could ring her if you like, along the way, when she gets home. That would reassure her."

"But she might get into trouble, too, if I'm not there?"

James liked the boy's concern for his mother.

"Hmmm... like I said, if you've been kind of taken away without her being consulted, then it's not her fault, is it."

This was a tricky one. He knew that, if Denise reported that the boy was with his real father and in no further trouble, there would probably be some breathing space. But he wasn't ready to tell the boy who he was in relation to himself. He wanted Ty to come without that pressure, to make a decision that was not further confused by more personal and emotionally fraught revelations.

"What about school? I have to sign in every day. They'll ring the services if I don't turn up."

"There are only three days to the end of term. We could probably persuade your Mum to ring in and say you're sick..."

"Hmmmm..."

The whole thing was getting sticky. James wavered, suddenly beset by doubts and wondering what he, a grown and responsible man, was doing. This was nothing other than plain kidnapping, and he was putting the boy unfairly through a lot of upset and doubt and tempting him to do something possibly dubious. What had he been thinking of? Why he had not gone the conventional way after all, and found the courage to confront Denise? There had been a good reason, but now it seemed less valid. He was about to say that he would drive Ty back home now. As he reached to turn the key, he caught the boy's look, and saw a real gleam of hope and excitement behind the doubts.

"Ok," said James, putting firm authority in his voice. "You decide: what shall we do?"

The rest of the day was a blur. With Ty's "Okay..." a sense of adventure returned. They were two guys, up to something big. They were going to defy authority, best it with their cleverness, and prove them all wrong. First, they got out and bought some food. James already had plenty of dry provisions in the back, but they munched burgers and drank coke with satisfaction as the car hit the Midlands Highway. In the tray at the back, Bonnie caught their excitement and barked happily as they bowled along. Strange, how quietly she had sat during that conversation, as though she sensed the gravity of it. James bought her a treat and Ty gave it to her.

"Nice dog. What's she called?"

They rang Denise from near Oatlands, using James' mobile. He gave it to Ty, to say what he liked, and after the boy's confused babbling explanations of which the mother could make little sense, he took over and spoke to her. She had meanwhile found the letter, was over the first surprise, and she was very, very angry. How dare he! Taking her boy like that! She was calling the police right now! He let her say it out, not attempting to defend himself, then quietly but firmly pointed out that Ty was happy to come, that he had given him the choice, and that he wanted to give the boy a chance to grow up a little in the company of his – he nearly gave himself away then, just managing to turn away enough so that Ty, who was patting Bonnie, couldn't hear the word – father.

"This isn't about you or me, Denise. It's about Ty and giving him a chance. He'll come to no harm, and I'll bring him back when he's had a bit of time to sort himself out. He's had enough of the police, Denise, and enough of the social service do-gooders. Let him be a man for a while, learn something real, and give him some space. I'm not hiding him, you've got my number, and my address is in the phonebook. Denise... I know it's a bit sudden, and you haven't seen anything of me for many years, but he's just at that age. Trust me in this?"

In the end she did. Perhaps the relief of not having the problem for a while played a part. Maybe the memory of the man himself, whom she knew to be fundamentally decent, worked through her fury. Instinctively, she could recognize that this mad, absurd situation could possibly have something good in it. As the white ute sped up the Highway towards Ross, she had just enough sense not to ring the police and make a big drama. She deflected her anger into several glasses of wine instead. Part of sorting out the mess had been a promise to herself not to drink so much. But Ty wasn't here to see this. It fought off the sudden feeling of aloneness, the emptiness of the small flat, the wrenching in her gut at the turn of events, the disappointment of her efforts to make good suddenly turned upside down; the whole incomprehensible mixture of emotions. And through it all, the sound of Ty's voice so excited, off on an adventure that she, his mother, couldn't provide and was excluded from. She felt defeated. The wine brought the tears, then drowned it all away.

At Ross they turned off the Highway onto the gravel of the Ashby's Road. The radio blaring, the dog barking, the ute raising a cloud of dust, it was just great. They'd be at the shack in a bit over an hour, and tomorrow they'd shoot a rabbit and cook it for dinner.

***

Putting off the unavoidable trip to work for another five minutes, Alan lit a cigarette and sat on his back deck with his cat, Ranger, on his lap. It was a big, black creature, getting on in years, and almost as grumpy as its owner. Once, when the world was younger, they had played together – Ranger a kitten from the cat's home and Alan a man with still some hope. But the man was comforted by its faithful presence, and the way it awaited Alan's return in the late afternoons, sitting in the driveway till the car pulled in.

In the office, there was a flurry of activity. The two administrative assistants – slinky, modern young women, unpleasantly self assured in their smart suits and forever smirking together about him, too, he was sure – had papers ready to dump on him; more impossible demands for explanations that he could not make. Something wasn't right and he could not ignore it quite so easily anymore. The strange behaviour of the doctor on the East Coast, for a start. Then the fudging of that health report. He was missing some essential link, and it gnawed at him. He escaped it all at lunchtime, heading for the nearby St. David's Park, where one could still smoke after the new draconian law that disallowed it even at the outside café tables.

A sudden gust of wind scattered the papers a woman on a bench further along had been looking through. He watched idly as she tried to gather them back up. *Her* business, he thought, not being generally attracted to thin angular women, but she was clearly losing the battle. He went to help, at a glance noting that they were official documents, and handed them to her as she straightened up. A slim, small thing she was, about forty he guessed, with a sharp face that was not unpleasant but currently distraught.

She took the papers, trying to stuff them into an inadequate bag.

"Oh, thanks…"

He nodded and would have turned away. What arrested his normal reflex to withdraw? Certainly not her messy struggle. Perhaps the look from those blue eyes, in which there was some uncertainty – not of him, he knew – or maybe it was the luscious blonde streaked hair. Who knows?

"Can I help?"

He surprised himself.

So they sat together on the bench, he holding her bag while she sorted the papers, helping her to control them in the wind, until they were finally stowed in some kind of order.

"Thanks," she said again. "This bloody wind…"

"It's a nuisance," he agreed. "It blows the leaves all over my lawn and into the driveway."

What a daft remark! She must think him some tame domesticated male fussing about inconsequential things. He made sure she could see his ringless left hand, and added:

"I do it for the exercise, of course, gathering the leaves every few days. I live in Lenah Valley; lots of trees there."

"I live there too!" she said, with a too-eager smile. He noted that her teeth were white and even.

There was a moment's pause. He prepared to move on, but this time it was she who reached out.

"Do you come here often? To this park, I mean?"

"I work just around the corner – it's handy here for lunch. I do research in the Health Department."

That sounded better than gathering bloody leaves, at least.

"Oh…"

A public servant, was he? That was impressive. Her mother always thought it was the ultimate career path. Not like a common hairdresser, especially a jobless one trying to get some real qualifications. And he was rather good-looking, too. She blundered on, anxious not to have him leave without some kind of contact being established. The Polytechnic was on the other side of the city – no way could she get away with suggesting that her lunch, also, was a regular event here in St. David's. Nor did she want to mention being encumbered with a son, especially not one who was in trouble with the court that was located just across the road, and from whence she had just come.

"I like to walk, here among the trees… it's peaceful."

Well, that was true enough. And why not develop a daily walk, for health's sake? It was the fashionable thing, after all.

"And I do it for my fitness – I work in Campbell St so it's a good bit of exercise, walking across the town. I don't usually stop and drop papers everywhere – that was just today."

He knew she was fudging something, and had noted the papers that held the official heading of the family court, but he didn't really care.

"What do you do, work wise?"

I'm a student in hairdressing wouldn't sound real good. She cast around for something that was close to the truth, for she had a certain bitter honesty.

"I teach at the Polytechnic, in the beauty department."

This wasn't entirely untrue – she had not long been enrolled when her previous practical experience became obvious, and her teacher had used her assistance with the real beginners in demonstrating some of the basics. It was a lie she could probably get away with.

Alan delayed only because going back to the office held no attraction for him, even less than the woman beside him. He fished in his pockets for the tobacco, and asked:

"Do you mind if I smoke?"

"Oh no, I do too! Would you like one of mine?"

She offered a pack of Horizons. They were cheap and nasty, but she owed him something for his help. Looking through the shrubbery at the traffic on Davey St, and the old building now housing the Royal Tennis Court, he said idly:

"I used to play badminton. Had to stop because of an injury."

This was not true. He had stopped because he found himself no longer fast enough to keep up with the younger ones. The game held no interest for him if he couldn't compete effectively, and was an insulting reminder of his increasing age. For a while he missed the sense of a vital, taut body but by now he had settled for a heavier frame. He still wasn't fat, by any means.

"I don't really have time for sports. That's why I walk through here most days. Have you been in the Tennis Court over there?"

"Yes. It's pretty good. A fast game, too."

He had been, but not as a player. The premises were sometimes let to functions, and he had attended one of those, reluctantly, in the course of work.

"How did you get hurt, playing?"

"I wrenched my shoulder. It's never been quite strong enough since."

"That must have been painful... is it still?"

He shook his head, and she cast about helplessly for something more to say. It was difficult, not wanting to go into the possibly tricky subject area of work, nor her personal situation, yet reluctant to let him go. But their cigarettes were coming to an end, and she pinned her hopes on the next day, hoping that she didn't sound too forward.

"Well, thanks again for the help. I'll be walking here again tomorrow – maybe I'll see you then?"

She stood before him, clutching her silly unpractical bag, and smiling brightly. Really, she wasn't too bad at all, and it was a while since he'd noticed an eager smile directed at him.

"Maybe. I might be here if they don't overload me in the office. The Premier wants a report, quite urgently, so I might not be free."

She looked suitably impressed.

"I'm Denise. Good luck with the report. I might see you around, some other time."

She walked off, swaying her hips and glad of the more formal clothing she had chosen that morning for the meeting at youth justice department, to sign that yes, her son was with his natural father and that she had – under pressure – agreed to this arrangement. The boy had been sick, so had missed the last week of school, and with his father belatedly showing an interest, it had seemed a good idea to let the boy go to him for the holidays. Yes, this was the name and the address. He would be back for the next term, and yes, she would bring him to the next child psychologist appointment. None of which she was sure of, but as long as it kept them off her back for the moment, she was willing to agree to it all.

That evening she decided to walk through the park again tomorrow at the same time. Being holidays, she had no classes to interfere with that plan. He – what was his name, she wondered, he hadn't said – was decidedly attractive. Or would it seem too pushy to be there the very next day? Maybe she should wait till Thursday? Yes, that would be better. One shouldn't be seen to be too keen. And, it would give her time to brighten up those streaks in her hair. She bustled about happily, thinking how she would impress him with her witty comments in conversations she fondly imagined might happen. It never crossed her mind to wonder what personal qualities and values he might have. He was a well-positioned man, not a loser like Caleb, that was enough. To do her justice, his likely salary was not a factor in her thinking, other than the possibilities of dining out in a fancy restaurant or two. A real public servant would have good taste in such matters. She was keen to get something happening before Ty came back and limited her movements.

Alan meanwhile returned to his prison. He hated himself for not having the guts to leave a job he disliked and felt unequal to. But it was too good a setting, the income high, the super building up, only four years to go and he could honorably retire with no financial penalty. If, on the other hand, he left now, he would miss out on a lot. Besides, what would he do? He feared that a life without a structure, however unsatisfactory, would get him down even more than this miserable existence. Sunk in his negative contemplation, he entirely missed the look of genuine concern that the two girls exchanged as he wandered through.

There were a hundred and one administrative details to attend to in his newly elevated position, but he was conscientious, and once settled to them, he worked through the pile methodically, doing a far better job than he realized. Getting back to the water report, he found a site on which that doctor in St. Helens had posted her views. She did not sound as nutty as had been suggested – her comments were thoroughly backed and referenced, and her point that water monitoring would never be accurate until pesticide activities were always reported and promptly tested, was reasonable enough. But then this astonishing bit: *"...an unknown chemical from the genetically improved E. nitens is responsible for the constant toxicity in the water of the George River"*. Was it really possible? If it was, it had enormous implications. But surely it was just nonsense?

He looked up the department's response. According to Dr Bleaney their final report was inadequate, used no further data collection, and simply assured the St. Helen's ratepayers that any toxicity in the water was within acceptable limits. That report was apparently backed by the Environment Protection Authority, the Ben Lomond Water, and the director of Public Health. This, too, was entirely correct.

Alan sat back and mused. He had submitted many reports on various aspects of public health, from recommended vaccination programs to veterinary practices. He also knew that a great deal of the information he had submitted never reached the public. Somehow, in the hands of those above him – his now absent departmental CEO, for instance – only certain aspects seemed to get any publicity. What Alan had always dismissed as poor reporting or inadequate media relationships, began to take on a different hue. How quickly, for instance, had the high number of child convulsions consequent to vaccinations turned into "a few", a "temporary batch difficulty", and "no reason to consider not vaccinating"? Was it possible that someone with vested interests in E. nitens plantations had leaned on the legislative member for the area to make that scathing attack on Dr. Bleaney and to suggest that the ABC should pay for the damage and the fright caused to the residents of St. Helens? Or could it be that CEOs of health departments were told by someone, possibly pharmaceutical companies, to keep public faith in vaccinations, irrespective of whether they were safe or not?

Could such large scale corruption really be going on deliberately? Surely not… It was simply insane to think like this. Enormous amounts of resources were being sunk into genetic research. Everybody was doing it – all the big companies around the world. Everyone expected that some dramatic cures for major diseases would result from it, although, Alan had to admit, he had yet to hear of any. But he was uncomfortable, thinking that the doctor in St. Helens had risked an awful lot for her beliefs. What if Bleaney was onto something after all, in those bleatings of hers?

But no, he wasn't about to subscribe to some lunatic conspiracy theory. After all, *he*, Alan Dijkstra, wasn't doing any dirty dealing. He was simply submitting his carefully collated reports, and it was none of his business what happened to them afterwards.

So he told himself, as he completed the current report and put it into the out tray with a sigh of relief. *He was just doing his job.* Later that evening, he heard the same phrase again. It was plaintively expressed by an actor playing a German Nazi in a concentration camp.

***

"But they're poisonous, Michael! They put out something that affects the water. Didn't you see the story on it?"

Michael smiled at his cousin Ellie, thinking that she was still a handsome woman at 58. He had always liked her steady, good com-monsense and felt that his two children were well cared for by her on their shared family holidays. Really, that James had been silly to leave her like he did. Was some minor straying really worth the loss of what had seemed a very wholesome marriage? True, James came from poor stock, thought Michael – Ellie could have chosen better. Maybe that was it – no staying power? It crossed Michael's mind that he had not heard anything about James in recent years. Not that he saw his cousin Ellie all that often these days. Her call a few days ago came as quite a surprise, and now here she was.

"Yes, I did see it. It seemed like a lot of rot to me. We use genetic modification all the time. Take the wheat – less wind-prone with shorter, stronger stalks, more yield with bigger heads – what's wrong with any of that?"

"I haven't thought about that. But surely there must be something to all this? That Dr Bleaney must have a reason for saying what she did about the water having something in it? They say she paid a lot of her own personal money to have the tests done – you wouldn't do that if you didn't believe in what you were on about. Anyway, you've got some of those trees, haven't you?"

"Yes, we do. We've got about forty acres of them, and they've been in for nearly ten years. They're on the back slopes – on the way to our shack. They look like perfectly normal trees to me. I'll let you know if they start doing any triffid-like things."

He was gently teasing her, waving away her comments about how could he know if he hadn't had the water tested.

"Come on, say hello to Gabrielle and I'm sure lunch is nearly ready. If you like, we can drive up through the trees this afternoon. Would that satisfy you?"

Ellie often felt like the poor unsophisticated cousin in Gabrielle's company. The latter came from one of the wealthier pastoral families of the district, the Camerons, and liked to remember her position in society. Several times a year, she would travel to Melbourne or Sydney for some expensive shopping. She had also extensively remodeled Fairbourne with exquisite taste. Ellie had to allow that Gabrielle had carefully studied the 1828 structure with its plain but solid Georgian style, even pouring over the simple sketches that William Fairfield had made, back in 1826, on the kitchen table of his first cottage. Nothing in the surviving family papers suggested that any real architect had ever been employed; William had clearly possessed a good eye and an ability to combine the practical requirements of his family with an attractive and gracious style. Gabrielle honored this by introducing the necessary comforts in discreet but effective ways, with wonderfully heated bathrooms, a modern kitchen, and a large conservatory, providing anything from a sun splashed playroom to a fine formal dining area when required. And it often was – Michael and Gabrielle entertained frequently. For their daughter Alison's 21st, they had held quite a ball on the grounds, supported by a large marquee and a small orchestra. Ellie, duly invited with her own children, had felt something of an outsider and was glad when it was over.

But Gabrielle was always faultlessly polite to Ellie, even if the two found little in common. It was Ellie who romped with the children at the shack on the hill, and Gabrielle, who mostly preferred the comfort of her own bed, would turn up only occasionally for the evening meal, bringing something delicious that had been cooked in a proper kitchen. Michael stood amusedly between the two, appreciating both for their own qualities, but mostly happy with his elegant wife. Lunch finished, he now looked across at her and announced the intended afternoon drive.

"Ellie wants to see the plantation trees. Those disputed E. nitens that Dr. Bleaney is making such a fuss about. She thinks we might all be well on the way to being poisoned by our water. Would you like to come?"

"It's entirely irresponsible of that woman in St. Helens to frighten the locals like that with her fanciful theories. She should be struck off. And, no thanks. You two go. I've got plenty to do here."

"So, how's life with you?" asked Michael as the Landcruiser turned onto the unmade track.

"Great, Michael. I'm really happy. I love my work – it's so interesting to visit all my small businesses and see how they're doing. I really feel I can help them, be an encourager for them. And I get to see so many places I would never otherwise visit. It's the best of jobs, especially as it's only part-time and I don't feel overly pressured. Almost as good as being in the country proper!"

"Ha, you should be here at shearing time if you want some real pressure. Getting 6000 jumpy merinos properly processed is no picnic. What about your personal life – got anyone to share it with?"

"No. Nor do I want anyone, Michael. I'm loving the peace of having the place to myself, and being able to do what I want, when I want it. I'm still good friends with Keith, but I'm perfectly happy to keep it that way – just friends. And it's nice being my age – men don't notice me anymore so I can be relaxed and be just who I am without worrying about measuring up. It's great."

"But you're still very attractive, Ellie. I'm sure Keith knows that too. He's probably breaking his heart over you, trying to get through your independence."

Ellie and Keith had had an involvement for a few years, which seemed to have gently come to nothing. He continued:

"Ever hear anything of James these days?"

"No, not in a while. There's really been no need. He sees Jeremy and Ian and his family fairly often. As far as I know, he's fine. Plumbing still seems to be in demand; from what I hear he's doing okay with the business. Why do you ask?"

"No reason. Just occurred to me that you hadn't mentioned him in a while."

Ellie shrugged. She bore James no grudges anymore, was even able to view the matter after all these years with some humour and sympathy, but there was no point in wasting time over it. She had been forced to heal the wound, and had done so determinedly, firmly putting aside both regrets and anger. Now she just wanted to be left in peace over it.

The track got rougher, and the car jolted a bit. Michael stared at some recent wheel marks, clearly visible in damp patches. He was puzzled.

"Odd, that…who's been through here lately?"

"Has anyone? Oh, I see… that's a bit unusual, isn't it?"

"Could be someone out hunting, I guess. Nothing to stop them, after all. Anyway, here are your trees. Do they look as though they're about to attack you?"

"Do stop teasing, Michael! What am I to think? That doctor sounded pretty certain about it. Stop the car, I want to look more closely. Yuck, they're not pretty, are they?"

It is a peculiarity of this Australian eucalypt that, as a young sapling, its leaves are round and silver grey, which gradually transform into the more familiar, darker and longer shapes in its tenth year or so. Some two to three meters high, with their squat lower half still clothed in the twirling silver discs, their upper section was a dark reddish green of slender branches, as though someone had joined two different trees together in the middle, for a joke. Like the platypus, mused Ellie. But no, these trees were not attractive. They stood in military rows, marching away over the hillside, with nothing much growing beneath them. No creatures, either – there would be nothing much for any animal to feed on, under this dull canopy.

"They've poisoned the ground against weeds, haven't they?"

"My dear Ellie, some weed control is necessary. It would be impossible to work between the rows. I do the same on my crops. It wouldn't be sensible not to."

"And don't they put that other stuff out, what's it called, 1080 or something, that kills the wallabies and the wombats and all?"

"Yes, they did – back when the trees were first in. You'd want to protect your investment, after all."

"Don't you *mind*, Michael? To have people come and put all this nasty stuff on your ground? And kill all the animals? What about the food chain? Wouldn't the birds take the poisoned flesh and die themselves?"

"It's not whether I mind, Ellie. There's good money in these trees.

They are growing fast and will be harvested in about twenty years. Just nicely in time, when I'm getting too old to do any heavy work myself. Besides, there's no actual evidence that agricultural sprays are bad for us. They're mighty useful, if you ask me. I'm sure glad when they keep my seed crops clean."

She made a despairing gesture. They had been over this subject many times before, Ellie implicitly believing that organic was the only safe way to be, and Michael, pragmatically laid-back, interested only in what was seen as the best practice and filled the bank account. Yet, she knew that he loved his land dearly, and was proudly familiar with every corner of it. He was a highly respected farmer in the district, and his merino stud famous even among the best.

"I agree it's a pity about the birds, Ellie. But it's only for the first two seasons. They do recover. I hope."

He glanced at the strange tire marks again. Ellie followed his look.

"You're worried about someone being up there?"

"Not really. I don't mind if anyone wants to take out a wallaby for their supper as long as they shut gates and don't shoot any wedge tails."

"See. You *do* care about the birds!"

He turned to her.

"Yes, Ellie, I do care about the birds. *And* the wallabies. *And* the wombats and whatever else is out here. But there's got to be space for everyone, you know – what would you eat if there weren't any farmers?"

It was impossible to remain angry for long with Michael. His friendly laid-back nature and relaxed refusal to get angry over anything, won the battle every time.

"Okay, okay! Let's not fight, for goodness sake. But I don't like these trees, Michael. They're…they're…well, *dead*. Look – can you see any birds among them?"

He couldn't. Nor could he remember ever noticing any creatures in the plantations. Not that he stopped among them often, generally just driving around the boundaries at intervals to check on fences and the like. The only animals he was aware of amongst them was a massive caterpillar infestation that the timber company people quickly came and sprayed. Still, did it matter? Plenty of beasties further up the hill, where the natural bush stood. Up the hill, on his land… he wondered who was up there now. There had only been one line of tracks, so whoever it was, they were still there. There was no other road out.

As they rattled back to Fairbourne, Ellie – having given up trying to change Michael's view, for the moment anyway – returned to the matter of the tire marks.

"Do you really not mind someone being up there shooting?"

"I don't much like it, Ellie, but there are plenty of wallabies. I can spare a few."

"*You* can spare a few! But they're not yours!"

"Well, they're on my land…"

"Is it really your land, Michael?"

He turned to her in surprise.

"What do you mean? Of course it's my land! There's been Fairfields working it for six generations!"

Ellie made a gesture of peace.

"I know, I know, but before that. Before William came here, it belonged to the Aborigines, didn't it? And he didn't exactly buy it off them, did he? Does that ever worry you, Michael?"

He laughed.

"My, you are turning into a radical, Cousin Ellie. You've been listening to all that lot from the Aboriginal Centre, have you? That Mansell and his bunch making all their land claims, crikey, what are they on about! None of them ever worked the land and made it productive, did they? Not one of them sweated over shearing any sheep either, before we came."

He softened. "Look, I don't mind if they want some recognition. Sure, some nasty things happened back then. Let them have their ancestral sites and do their smoke ceremonies or whatever they want. I've got nothing against that. But don't let any of them suggest that they know how to look after a bit of fertile land properly!"

"Oh Michael, I don't know that it's that simple…"

Ellie was struggling to express her thoughts that there was more to existence than farming for money. Recently much taken by some of the documentaries and films about Aboriginal life, she felt that a great injustice had been done but not acknowledged. Increasing evidence of complex lifestyles, most marvelously adapted to the land, had caught her imagination. The Wandjina paintings were remarkable too, as were the dark sinewy bodies that fitted so perfectly into the landscape. She had been fascinated by the film 'Ten Canoes', which retold an Aboriginal story of proper living with much humour. Ellie also believed in rules for life, and found the evidence of God's thoughts, as reflected in nature and life generally, an important structure. She could understand others who had such ideals.

Michael was looking at her. Close from early childhood, in his youth he had considered Ellie most attractive until his parents had steered him rather firmly in another direction. To this day she carried a relaxed sensuality, mostly quite unselfconsciously, but it suggested nice things in bed. He had quite envied James a few times. That silly fool James, he thought again. Fancy letting this nice woman go! Had he got around to regretting it? And was Ellie really happy without a man, as she claimed to be? She looked very inviting with her thick honey-blond hair plaited around her head in the old-fashioned Dutch style; very definitely not classy in the modern sense but one couldn't help wondering how it would look, loose down a naked back. He pulled himself up, sharply. Come on, Michael, what are you thinking? He focused on what she was saying.

"It's something we have to think about, surely? I mean, these things really happened, and we can't keep on pretending that they don't matter. We can't change them, but don't you think we could acknowledge them at least?"

"So, what difference would that make?"

Again, she struggled for words. This was all very new, and not something that had ever been talked about in her family.

"Well, some kind of recognition that they were human too?"

"You're a sweetheart, Ellie. I'm sure the TAC will be pleased to have you on their side. For now, I could do with some afternoon tea. Gabrielle makes fantastic muffins."

As they sat over tea in the conservatory, Ellie looked out on the glorious late autumn afternoon, and wondered about those dark figures, moving among the trees out there over their ancestral lands. How would they feel about an alien tree with unknown properties and no creatures living around it, slowly creeping over the landscape, possibly poisoning the water, too?

***

James was enjoying himself. Tyrone was coping better than expected, even when things seemed very scary, like on their second night up here in the bush. The crashing on the tin roof was bad enough, but the breathy harking of the possum was positively creepy. James took him outside and swung the torch up in time to see the creature rushing up the nearest tree. Ah, a brushy... Ty had never seen one alive.

He taught the boy to sit still in the evenings, watching the bush come alive as the light faded. See, there's a possum coming down that tree from its sleeping nook now. There are a couple of half-grown youngsters in its wake. That dark shape there is a bandicoot. He knows we're here, is weighing up if it is safe to come and nibble the grass in front of the hut like he's accustomed to doing. There are several wallabies over there. Not so easy to see are the quolls, but they too are there. And there are smaller possums, the sugar gliders, up there in the trees.

Ty had already encountered a snake, coiled in a sunny patch on a log, James arresting his instinctive backing away. They're just as scared of us as we are of them. Don't move suddenly, just be still and walk away gently when you have looked enough. See? He's really quite beautiful, those dark scales glittering in the sun. Yet they would be quite cool to touch. Smooth, too.

The fading of the day's bush activity holds enchantment. Listen to those last calls of the magpie...he's been caroling during the day, down there on the plains, but now it's just a few single calls. The kookaburras, too – although they don't really belong here. They were introduced in the 1930's. But we've got used to them, and their chuckles and gurgles are part of the day. They'll be among the first to wake you, with all their explosions of giggles. Every day has its humour to them, and where would we be without some fun? There are the jayjays and the currawongs – they look a bit alike but call so differently. But really special are the little birds, the ones you neither see nor hear readily, like the little white eyes. They come in quite big flocks, but you'll only notice them if you sit humbly still and listen. There are many small ones, pardalotes, finches, wrens, robins....

Tyrone began to see a whole new world. Why had he never thought about all these creatures before? James showed him webs of spiders, found huntsmen under bark, warned him of the deathly bite of the redback, yet without fear. You've just got to be sensible, lad, about where you put your hands. This is their world, so you go by their rules, and you won't come to no harm. Shrieking flocks of white cockatoos amused him, and once he stood spellbound as twenty or so black parrots descended on a partly-dead tree and began to hack noisily on the timber in search of grubs, squawking belligerently all the time.

He also watched the dog, who seemed to know that her place was not really in this bush. While she was unbothered by all the life around her, she stayed close to the man and boy. Not that she missed a thing. Only once did she get actively involved, one night when an appalling growling and snarling erupted. Bonnie madly capered about, barking in turn, and James let her. It's ok, sonny – they're only devils fighting over a carcass out there. Don't know why Bonnie always makes a fuss over that. Mind you, you're lucky to be hearing them at all. They used to be common everywhere, but just lately something's been killing them off, and there's not that many left just now. They'll come back in their own good time, if we give them the chance.

They were golden days up there in the late autumn sun, with crisp cold nights when they were glad of the fire and a warm blanket. With a hot stew inside them, James told stories of the bush and the men who lived in it, like the bushrangers of the 1820's. Sometimes he let his imagination wander further, and spoke softly of the dark men who had been kings of this island before white man came. Realizing how little he actually knew about them, his own kin, he still was able to weave stories of warriors who could throw their handmade spears with deadly accuracy, of battles between tribes, and of spring gatherings for the exchange of gossip and the finding of women. And he wasn't far from the truth, for humanity is the same the world over.

He was not yet ready to tell the boy that he himself had a connection to those dark men, nor that he was his father. In the three weeks vouchsafed to them, before school went back for the winter term, all the boy needed was some space, do man things and experience the strong reality of nature. Later, when it was all sorted out, he would take him out to the islands, to see the wild sea and white sands, and do some fishing.

Fishing, lad, there's some good fishing to be had here, too. Further up behind this mountain there are lots of lakes, including a great one. One day maybe we'll go there. There's trout and salmon – did you know they brought both those fish from England back in the 1860's? He told him the story of trials and misadventures, till finally they succeeded with a hay-packed ice box of fingerlings that had started on the many-months long journey in a wooden ship from Scotland as eggs. And he told him of the great exploration journeys, of men fascinated by this strange new land, of early encounters between black and white, and of strange plants and animals. The French now, they did a lot of looking with no mind to any conquering, and we have some good idea from their writings and drawings about what it might have been like here back then.

Tyrone took it all in, a whole new and unsuspected world opening up before him. Suddenly he had so much more to think about, and it was both fascinating and exciting. Nothing like that had ever been presented to him. Even the awesome physical view that lay spread out across the Midlands from their elevated position was utterly absorbing. He watched the flocks of sheep seeking the first sunny patch to warm up in. Yes, son, they do have a thick wooly coat on, but they like the feel of the morning sun, all the same. But in the summer when it gets really hot, they go the other way, and crowd under the trees – what's left of them – to get some shade. That's what made so many of the trees die out there, sonny. Their roots couldn't take the trampling or the concentrated droppings. And who knows, maybe the animals also brought something with them that wasn't known here before.

Ty particularly loved the wattle bird, with its white-tipped tail and loud call that varied from a raucous chuckle to a quick flow of melodious notes. The two watched it rushing among the branches, often upside down, as it foraged energetically. When they stood together to have a piss, the man cut through any schoolboy sniggers by adding a simple adult gravity to the process.

The man watched the boy change, and started to give him jobs to do, gathering firewood, lighting it in the stove box, skinning rabbits – they went to the lower slopes most days to shoot one – and sharpening the knife. James refused to shoot any native fauna, saying that the rabbits were imported and a nuisance, and so could be shot with impunity, but one would only take a native animal if one really needed one. Then it would be okay, provided it was clean and quick. He initiated more physical effort into the day, taking the boy for longer walks through the bush, scrambling up steep hillsides and through gullies. Once they found a small waterfall and amid much laughter, both had stripped for an icy-cold shower.

The whole thing was an enchanted moment. Soon enough, the world would crowd in on them with its demands. The days slipped by ever faster towards that inevitable time. But for the moment, as he saw the boy turn towards manhood, James was glad that he had done it. Whatever the coming complications, this was worth it.

**

Denise was equally conscious of time running away. She was operating at a high level of excitement, at the beginning of a promising love affair that might lead to all kinds of things, and soon Tyrone would be back to bring a more mundane and domestic restriction into her sudden life as a high flyer. She paused momentarily to wonder what his return would be like, bringing James in his wake, for meet they would have to. Any deeper thoughts about James she cast aside in her fantasizing about Alan.

Yes, Alan. She had done it. It took some courage, deliberately approaching him in the park two days after they had met, but once past that it was easy to get a drink-after-work happening, then a dinner out, and soon he took her to his bed. She put much effort into the process, buying pretty clothes, polishing her physical being in every way she knew, pretending sexual fervour, anything to please him, to 'land' him, and to be in a relationship with this desirable man. Painfully in love, her need to be accepted made her insecure and desperately anxious for his calls, which were not frequent enough. She was doing most of the driving, as much as she dared do, for she was in awe of him and didn't notice his emotional absence. In her subconscious stood the specter of her cold and unloving father; as long as her need to win the approval of that parent was still there, she was destined to fall in love with unavailable men.

Alan simply let it happen. He did not find Denise particularly attractive, but it was nice to have some sex and a warm body in bed. He paid her enough attention to facilitate that, not difficult given her obvious enthusiasm. His emotions were as disengaged from her as they were from most things. His mind, left clear of any attachment, observed her accurately enough – a simple woman without much education nor any seriously inquiring mind, engaged on the surface with the dramas on the TV, fashions and celebrities. She was actually quite boring, but it made the whole thing easy and undemanding. A fancy meal out now and then was enough, and he watched with mild amusement her attempts to appear informed on what was gourmet food, which he really didn't care about at all. As he got to know her better he conceded that she had certain qualities, being willing to work for her qualifications and to fight for her boy. When Tyrone had turned up in her world it was to his dismay; children held no interest for him, especially other men's, and only made sexual relationships more complicated. He nearly backed off then, leaving it to her to sort out her domestic dramas.

His self-absorption kept him in his shell. The only thing that had recently threatened to breach the wall – the sudden wondering about the value of his work in the wake of that damned doctor and her fancy ideas – became less urgent as the department finally obliged him by appointing a new head. After a hand-over period, he was gratefully able to go back into his quieter and undemanding corner, collating facts and presenting them to someone else to deal with. He would have stayed there, too, if it had not been for, of all things, that doctor again.

***

"Women, well now, they're like our other half, Ty."

James smiled at the boy's look of astonishment.

"Yes, we don't always like that idea, do we, Ty, because it puts responsibilities on us that we don't always want. But that's how it is, and we can't change it without missing out."

He had deliberately begun to talk about the big themes in life, anxious to get Ty thinking in some healthy directions before his time of immediate influence was over. There were only two days left before they had to return, and who knows what might happen then? There were moments when he was tempted just to deliver the child and vanish back to Launceston, avoiding the complications of Denise, the Social Services, and all the rest. But he knew he couldn't do that; having interfered in the boy's life he now had to take on full responsibility, or at least as much as would be allowed him. James had spent much time alone, with only Bonnie for company, in recent years. A quietly thoughtful man by nature, he had mused at length over mankind and the meaning of life, concluding that relationships are the most important thing of all. To treat others decently, respectfully, to try and further their possible best... the abrupt arrival of a needy boy into his life seemed to James a gift, a chance to live out what he had learned. Besides, he liked this kid and ached to see him grow beyond the shallow place in which he had been trapped.

But getting Ty to readily accept a return to the humdrum existence of school, a small flat in town, and an always-on-the-edge mother, was not easy. So he started talking about relationships, women, sex, and a man's responsibilities, while he still had the boy's ear for his simple, thoughtful statements about Important Things. Nobody, he knew, had ever suggested anything like this to him.

"You can't just use girls for sex, Ty. They've got feelings too, and expectations, and it affects them much more than you might think. If she seems keen and eager, that might be because she wants your love, not so much the sex, and you had better not have the sex unless you're willing to give her the love, too."

Love, he said, wasn't about romantic feelings or even about sex. It was about deciding if she had good attitudes, was kind and generous and constant, had values you could respect over the years, and then sticking with such a girl, if you were lucky enough to find one who thought the same about you. That kind of thing mostly didn't just happen. It took some thinking and looking, and keeping a respectful distance, for the moment you went to bed together, you sure lost all ability to see her for what she really was. It was a nuisance, that, but that was the way of it, and if Ty wanted a happy marriage he would need to remember it.

James would also have liked to promise some future adventures together, to help Ty better handle the coming school term, but felt unable to do so without knowing what reception they might get from Denise. So he made up for it by talking, challenging Ty to start thinking for himself, and in much physical activity. Their three weeks had transformed the boy, and James mused happily over it as they sat together on the last Thursday evening. They had only one more day. What last adventure would they get up to? But it turned out quite differently, for on Friday morning the Landcruiser came grinding up the steep road all the way to the shack, bearing an astonished Michael.

"It's *you*, James! I knew someone was hanging out up here, but it never crossed my mind… But, good to see you, anyway. And who's this?"

The two men shook hands, and James introduced Ty as 'my young friend'.

"The son of someone I know; he needed a holiday and I remembered this great place. I knew you wouldn't mind, Michael. We've had a lot of fun here, haven't we, Ty? And how's the farm going?"

They discussed rural matters for a while, and Michael's family. The latter was wondering if he should mention the curious coincidence that he had been, only a few days earlier, in the foothills below with Ellie herself. He was interested to know what James's mind was on the subject of his ex-wife. In the end, due to the presence of the strange boy, he merely asked if James had seen anything of her lately.

"No, I haven't."

James looked into the distance.

"I know through the children that she's well. Sounds happy, too, and I'm glad to know that."

Then he met Michael's eyes squarely.

"I didn't exactly contribute to her happiness back then, did I? I reckon it's about time I went to see her, to try and put it right, somehow, if she'll let me. I owe her that much, at least."

As he drove back down the hill, Michael decided that he had done James an injustice. It took courage to admit one's folly, even more to try and make amends. What did he actually know about James's family? Not much; his own had always considered the Maynes a bit beneath them, not from 'good stock' – Michael smiled at the farmer's way of expressing it – but what kind of stock was it? Something pinged in his mind, something Ellie had said only days earlier, what was it now? Ah, the Aboriginal question... Michael sat up with a jerk. That was it – James was from an Islander family. "One of those half castes," as his mother had said once, privately. It was never mentioned again, and Michael himself had never thought about it in all those years when they had met regularly through the holidays and at a few family functions. James was just James, Ellie's husband and he hadn't seemed a bad one or different from anyone else.

Now that he thought about it, he could see the faintly olive skin, the deeply brown eyes, and the curly mop, now a rather distinguished grey, and neatly trimmed. Before, he would have put it down to some Gaelic, Irish probably, influence. Maybe a touch of the gypsy? But an Islander, now, that was a lot closer to home.

***

Denise was singing to herself as she tidied the flat. She was so happy these days. In a mere three weeks, her life had become joyous. It made her glow with pleasure, hardly noticing daily irritations that before would have driven her to distraction. That day, Ty was returning and she was determined that he should see how good everything was now. Had she not promised him that she would sort out the mess?

She was curious, too, about seeing James again after all this time. In her happy mood, she could not find it in her to be angry, and was glad – judging by her son's voice on the mobile that morning – that things had gone well. Denise had enough insight to realise that having James around could make managing Ty much easier, so she had a conciliatory smile when the two arrived, and a nice tea ready.

Yes, of course James could come and take Ty out for occasional weekends; that would be absolutely fine, and so good for the boy. No, there had been no real problems with the Social Services. As long as there was no further trouble – and there wouldn't be, would there, Ty? – and the psychologist's report was satisfactory, all would be good. And yes, she was getting on at the Polytechnic, even doing some teaching there, and soon would have her full qualifications and a steady job in a fine salon.

James, prepared for a great drama, now observed her with interest. Had she really matured that much? Somehow, it didn't ring quite true, nor fit the picture he had of her. That glossy appearance, the smart clothes, the trilling laughter? But he was glad of her cooperation, and arranged to collect Ty for the weekend in a fortnight. The boy had become very miserable as they packed up the ute for the trip back to Hobart that morning. Now he was finding his mother all smiling and happy, against all expectations, and went cheerfully out to say goodbye to Bonnie in the ute.

"I've not told him yet, about being his father, I mean…I'm just a friend of yours, from long ago. Best leave it that way for the time being – he's got enough to think about as it is."

Both relieved and disappointed at the same time, she had agreed. Never having said much to Ty about his father, just that he was the result of an affair 'that didn't go nowhere', she had imagined the drama of a grand revelation, the provision finally of a real father. But it was also complicated and delaying the inevitable explanations was a relief, too.

"Catch ya soon, Sonny."

Then he was driving slowly up the Midlands Highway, back to Launceston. As he cleared the Epping Forrest, the magnificent Great Western Tiers rose on his left. There were often massive cloud formations above these precipitous slopes, and that late afternoon the lowering sun behind them was gilding their edges with brilliant gold and white. Vivid purple patches streaked with orange, impossible to paint, added to the drama above the dark blue mountain range. Behind it all the sky serenely spread its canopy, ranging from an irradiant white to the deepest cerulean blue over the eastern hills.

It's truly beautiful, this place, he thought. We are so lucky to be here. I wonder how much of it Denise notices – it seemed like everything we did and said was new to Ty, like he'd never been out anywhere much at all...not much of a family setting he's had, poor lad, either. It will be great to take Ty to meet my mother Bessie. And later, out to the Islands – he'll have the greatest of fun out there. I guess one thing that is Aboriginal in me is my closeness to the sea and the creatures, although anyone willing to listen to the land can have that. But I do love a good mutton bird stew...

James laughed to himself. The short-tailed shearwater, commonly known as mutton bird, was definitely an acquired taste, its powerful aroma not welcome in most ordinary kitchens. Yet there was nothing like it, nor was there anything nicer than sitting with family and mates around the fire, and his big, comfortable mother yarning gently about the things they all used to get up to. He missed his grandmother Una. She had passed on just when things took a turn for the better, and he was sorry that she had not seen his eventual success.

Except for his marriage. Now that was not, in the end, a success. It's funny, he thought, we kinda never worried about things back then, the way it happens now – we just got on with it. There was no unkindness about it, we were mostly gentle with each other and the kids, and we worked hard, just doing whatever it took to make a decent home with no fuss. We ate together, took the kids camping and out to play. Ellie would read to them in the evenings, and we had lots of silly family games. Sex, too, was not something we made a big thing out of; it was just part of life and had its exciting moments but mostly it was just pleasant and comforting, and that was enough. It had a simple and uncomplicated goodness about it, and it should have stayed that way, but something changed in the 1980's.

He remembered meeting Ellie. The thick honey blonde hair, the curvaceous figure so inviting, the wholesome earthiness of her. By then he had a steady job as a young plumber, and could look her straight in the eye. Some buttons had come off his shirt, so he thought it was time he learnt to fix them himself rather than bothering his mum. He's gone into the haberdashery department where she happened to be working, and when she laughed and showed him how to put the thread through the tiny needle hole and then even how to sew the button on – it must have been a quiet moment in the shop – he was captivated. A few days later he went back, wearing the same shirt all sewn up properly. Would she have coffee with him? She said yes, and nine months later she said yes again in the small church. Her mother, a rather refined widow, was there and only a few other members of her wider family, none of whom he really remembered except Michael, who had come up from the country to see who his favorite cousin was marrying. James's own mob was there in full, and it was a simple wedding with no pretentions followed by afternoon tea in the garden of a modest hotel. Bessie and Ellie had got on well from the start, and saw each other regularly, but there was not the same easy warmth from Ellie's family. Though no one was unfriendly, they mostly kept their distance, and it was only Michael who came closer and willingly shared the shack on the mountainside.

Those were good days, thought James. What a pity I stuffed things up. For it was me, no doubt. Things might have gotten a bit dull and routine, maybe, but there wasn't anything wrong with any of it... she was always steady and kindly, her cooking was great and the kids happy. So I got a big head and thought myself such a fine fella with that teaching job at the TAFE, and having a bit on the side just kinda fitted. I never thought at the time what it might do to Ellie, how she'd feel about it, or at any rate I never let that thought get in the way. I was going to have that pert little Denise over in hairdressing with her wild hair and sexy walk.

Really, I must go and see Ellie. I owe her that apology. I never actually said it to her. I'll have to tell her about Ty, too... that might not be so easy, but it won't be a real conversation if I'm not completely honest. Ow...

***

Ellie had returned home, entirely despairing of trying to convert cousin Michael to any different views. Really, she thought, these lovely laid-back people whom we like so much for their unshakeable steadiness do have the downside of being so very sure of themselves. That's quite enviable, really, but what if they hold views that might just need changing? Then she laughed as she accepted that Michael's business was his, not hers, and after all, he was very successful with what he did.

Did those trees really have some bad effect on the land and the water itself? Surely that could affect everyone, not just the corner where a private farmer was making a bit of extra money? But how was she to know? She was not a scientist, and had no access to specialist knowledge. There were two opposing views, each one claiming to be correct. Who was one to believe? That doctor Bleaney, or the State Government? Ellie sighed. This kind of in-fighting was fudging most major issues of the day – the conservation of forests, building a pulp mill or not, vaccinating children or not, multi-nationals misleading everyone – nobody really knew, but many sensed that there was something deeply rotten going on. Those strange trees were just another symptom of it.

Trying to clean up the world was just too difficult. All she could do was live her own life as decently as possible.

"And, oh, I *do* love my peaceful life the way it is now. It is such a privilege to be here, in this pleasant little corner and with such a nice garden. I'm grateful, every day."

Ellie had learnt to be grateful, as a tool for managing life. It had taken her a long time to understand that actively being grateful, even for things that seemed very undesirable, actually made them better and often revealed unexpected silver linings. There were times when she struggled hard to keep that stance, especially when Keith Jordan kept coming back.

A journalist with the local paper, he had come into her life four years after her marriage to James broke up. It was the first time someone was attractive enough to break the ice around her heart, and she grew very close to him; his being as familiar as her own. It simply was so – perhaps they had met before in a previous life? In bed, too, they were comfortable and sometimes really passionate. Ellie was surprised at her own body's response. Sex with James had usually been pleasant enough, as he was vital yet thoughtful. With Keith, this extraordinary familiarity brought her a satisfaction she had not known before.

They never lived together. Keith did not want that. She soon realized that he was not willing to be committed, and suspected that he had at times other involvements. She was also very conscious of their age difference – she was several years older than him, and he had ideas of a younger woman for any permanent partner. In the absence of such a one, she was a very acceptable person, a cross between a comforting mother figure and a real sexual pleasure. He liked her more than he admitted, but ultimately he was simply using her, and she was allowing it. Over time her heart grew sad with it, and eventually she had to put a stop to it.

So one day she firmly said no, there would be no more sex, not unless he could learn to really want *her*. No sexual relationship could be acceptable to her unless it was within a committed situation. But we can stay friends, yes? She would often console him over the failure of his latest affair, and silently pray that God might quiet her heart.

He did. It was one of the ways she came to know God. One summer evening, after Keith had left and she was particularly desolate, the nature in her garden reached out to her. From the trees, from the wind soughing gently through them, from the brilliance of the late silver sky, from the very earth, came a living consolation to her. She saw the unspeakable beauty of creation with new eyes, was penetrated by its deep stillness, and she knew that all would be well. That evening, an ancient peace came into her like liquid silver. Her fate was in the hands of a Master after all; her task was to seek no selfish motive in any of her actions, and the rest would be taken care of. So she could genuinely wish for Keith that he might find a real loving relationship. It no longer mattered whether it was with her or anyone else, as long as he could find some happiness.

For herself, she found great compensation. The inner stillness spread through her entire being and all her thoughts. Her power to help others increased, her ability to discern the real truth in human motives sharpened. It made her very good at her job, able to support, encourage and counsel the clients, often long-term unemployed whose potential was obscured by years of defeat. Ellie returned daily to her little garden and found deep joy in the flowers, the flight of the birds, the silvering of a leaf in the wind. She was utterly content to know that she had work that helped others, and then could take her rest, sitting on her verandah in the evening sun, her cat beside her.

"You," she said, "you would not dream of catching a bird, when your dinner bowl is filled regularly and you have no need for extra, would you now? You are, after all, a cat of great honour, yes?" and Susie purringly agreed with her, but nevertheless reserved the right, at all times, to at least keep an eye on those forbidden birds.

Ellie was not entirely above human emotions, though, and had to draw on God's promise of peace very much when Keith kept coming back, at times – usually when he was between girlfriends – physically reaching out for her. Then desire filled her womb. She remembered the feel of his familiar body and ached for him, only barely finding the strength to turn him away. In time, the wild longings of her heart were stilled, and she even found it possible to be grateful. She had been able to give this man a maturity, as well as a sexual confidence, and she was glad and wished him well with it. When he left, she could slip back, in due course inwardly calmed again, into the solitary peace of her little house.

Meanwhile, coming up the Midlands Highway towards Launceston, was James, a new resolve in his heart, and he was on his way to see Ellie.

29. THE THINKING, 2012

Denise Turner did not know what to do. It was a great offer, just what she needed after a disappointing series of short hairdressing jobs, none of which seemed to appreciate just how good she was.

"You could start almost immediately," said Sue, a student colleague from TAFE who had found work in Launceston after they both completed their courses. Her boss was looking for more staff, Sue was explaining on the phone.

"But I'd have to give up my flat here. And move Ty to a new school, when he's just settled down here at New Town. Yes, I know his dad's in Lonny too, but he seems to drive down readily enough."

"This is a good place to work in, Denise. Mr Tabor's pretty ok, pays a decent wage. It's all above board, super and all – he lets us go to further training one afternoon a week, too. I'm doing beauty therapy now – it's great fun. All those fabulous products, Denise, you should see them. They give us some of the promotionals to use for ourselves."

It was tempting. She needed a full-time reliable job and this sounded better than anything she'd found so far in Hobart. Moving up there wasn't really that difficult – rentals were cheaper in Launceston anyway – and Ty would surely now be ok in another school. Since James had been turning up regularly to see the boy, Ty had settled down, and was applying himself fairly steadily to his studies, playing soccer and other sports, and was no trouble to her. On James' urging, she had moved him from Glenorchy to the Newtown High School, which had a better atmosphere. If she lived in Launceston, James might take the boy out even more often. There were a lot of pluses in the offer.

But what really held Denise back from accepting it was the fact that Alan was here in Hobart. Leaving him was unthinkable, and she would do nothing to risk that relationship.

"Thanks, Sue, I'll think about it."

"Don't take too long over it. It'll be in the paper this weekend."

***

Meanwhile, Alan had finally fallen in love, every bit as intensely as Denise, but not with her. His eye had lit upon a lady with an elegant and ethereal look about her, as remote as the ice maiden, and Alan's unconscious immediately recognised her as totally familiar. She was as unavailable as his mother's genuine affection had been for him. This was the woman he had to conquer, to finally take the sting out of his lonely childhood.

So he set himself to be his most charming and obliging, and for a while he was successful. Denise didn't see anything much of him during that time; he had all sorts of excuses about being importantly busy, but he never quite fobbed her off either. The Ice Maiden wasn't all that readily obliging, and keeping a bit of consolation going was quite convenient. Denise sensed his perfidy but was too desperate, too afraid to make trouble or risk his displeasure. Every time he did call her, she thought that this was it, she was winning out after all, and if she kept showing him how devoted and sexy she was, in the end she'd surely finally get him. It was in this scenario that she turned down the job in Launceston. Had she known how completely unimportant she was to Alan, she would have grabbed it and run.

The Ice Maiden was not intentionally unkind; she too had had her heart frozen at an early age, her father having disappeared. For a while she enjoyed Alan's attentions and shared some of her life with him, and he, being anxious to impress, listened carefully. Her major interest was living naturally, eating healthily, being as free from chemicals as possible, and she felt Dr Bleaney's claims were probably correct. That large companies – the big pharmaceuticals foremost among them – should have deliberate programs to obfuscate or falsify any inconvenient evidence, was her normal expectation. She showed Alan an impressive folder with cases of personal and environmental damage caused by such practices, and gradually what had been a few vague thoughts in his mind, turned into serious possibilities. He began to read, and look up websites, so he could maintain his conversation with her. Though his primary motive was to impress the Ice Maiden, he was the one being shaped into a new way of thinking. His was an orderly mind, satisfied by neat facts well presented – and she had plenty of them. It was a growing discomfort to him that most of them contained views that were at complete odds with the daily work he was doing.

They talked about the municipal water supply. She had the list of chemicals being put into it, along with a picture of the yellow drums marked with the skull & crossbones symbol for poison, in the shed at the Bryn Estyn treatment plant.

"It's chlorine, supplied by Orica, a multinational company in mining, explosives, chemicals and water infrastructure. This company has permanently contaminated the Botany Aquifer in Sydney; it's responsible for arsenic, ammonia, cyanide and mercury leaks, many of them here in Australia. The Environmental Protection Agency has expressed ongoing concern about such issues with Orica, especially at mining sites. And here we are, drinking their stuff without any choice in the matter! They also add in aluminium – for crying out loud, it's been connected with possibly causing Alzheimer's! – and lime. As for routinely putting fluoride in the water, who knows if that couldn't be the reason why everybody suddenly needs joint replacements – well, has your fancy department done any genuine investigations into the possible negative health effects of any of that?"

It hadn't. They were far too under-staffed and under-resourced to conduct such things.

"We rely on reports from elsewhere, particularly the CSIRO, such as their Drinking Water Guidelines. They've done the necessary checking up – why should we do them again?"

"And what if one or two members of that body, or any other regulating agency, were in the pay of someone like Orica? Indeed, looking at the lack of political will to actually do something real about the environment, plus the fact that political lobbying is allowed in this mock-democracy of ours, is it not equally reasonable to think that the Federal government has completely caved in to the demands of the big multinationals, and no longer looks out for the common man, even setting his health at risk?"

"That seems so unlikely. Putting chlorine and fluoride in the water is exactly intended to promote people's health. In fact, the government assumes that it could be sued if it didn't do it. And the very last thing they'd want is a large-scale outbreak of E. coli – it's nasty and can kill, or disable your kidneys. Even ministers are human and wouldn't want to risk inflicting such pain on people!"

"Wouldn't they? How many of them would forego huge payouts and privileges for a vague philosophical position? Isn't realising that precisely why a few courageous people like Dr Bleaney are willing to take personal risks to reveal the truth of what's really going on? She's onto something even bigger than just putting questionable chemicals in – not that it's a matter of "just" – which involves even larger companies like Monsanto. They won't want anybody questioning their practices!"

There it was again – that doctor and her toxic water. His unease grew, particularly about the way his employer had expected that matter to be handled. But he made a conciliatory gesture and changed the subject.

The Ice Maiden, intelligent and well-informed, took definite positions and adjusted her lifestyle accordingly. Her home was attractive, airy and light, the food wholesome and delicious as well. She kept no car, using only public transport or her bicycle. Her bathroom was astonishingly free of potions, bottles, and sprays. His own lax disinterest in the big issues did not show up well and one day she would get around to suggesting that he, too, by his very job with its comfortable income, was living a betrayal. To have his integrity questioned by the woman whose goodwill mattered to him, was painful, but he was running out of excuses.

"Giant timber company collapses!" Tasmanian headlines had screamed recently. "Market for wood pulp shrinks!"

Cheaper sources of pulp from overseas and buyers' concerns about eco-sourcing, were further cited. In the wake of that, a corruption scandal convicted one of the bosses of having used insider knowledge to offload his substantial share of the portfolio just before the crash came. The involved case dragged on and on, particularly bitterly for the many farmers who were now left with acres of plantation trees they could neither sell nor harvest, and for which they were no longer getting any payments. Their contracts even forbade them to touch the trees in any way, and with the undergrowth thus uncontrolled, concern about the potential fire danger also grew. Ellie's cousin Michael was one of the many thus affected.

Alan began to see himself as a possible hero in the Ice Maiden's eyes if he, too, took a firm stand. For years he had despised himself for putting up with a situation he disliked intensely, but he was afraid. Unlikely at his age to find similar employment anywhere, he knew that the loss of status and structure in his life would be devastating. He doubted if he could handle it. Surely one resigned only if one had something better to go to!

Yet the issue wouldn't let him be. No amount of alcohol drowned it out for long. The smoking didn't help either – another thing the Ice Maiden despised. Maybe he could make a whole new start? He had to admit that, really, he could easily afford to forego the extra super – his investments had continued to do well, and he did, after all, own his house, which was in a good area, in good order and worth a good bit. There was plenty in the bank. If he was free, he could buy a four wheel drive, cross The Outback, sleep under the stars. The thought of never again being at the mercy of a superior boss or the supercilious girls at the office was delightful. He finally persuaded himself that freedom had a great sound to it.

"I've handed in my resignation," he told the Ice Maiden.

"You did *what?*"

"I can't stand it any more. It's just not right. Someone's got to take a stand. I'm finishing in eight weeks."

She didn't fall into his arms, but studied him carefully.

***

"It has been an unexpectedly pleasant and satisfying evening," Ellie thought as she drove slowly home through a dark Launceston, at nearly 1.30am, which was unusually late for her. Returning from birthday dinner at her son's place, she had listened with interest to the ambitions of these younger people, pleased by their thoughtful gravity and concern for their children's best chances. Steady work, buying their homes, and planning for holidays seemed to be their main objectives. None of the many guests mentioned the environment, which she found rather odd.

A solitary corner pub, still brightly lit and with a crowd milling around the door, caught her eye as she drove along. To her astonishment she found herself pulling over, almost as if another hand had taken the wheel of the car.

"I don't go into pubs," she thought, "especially not late at night!"

But here she was, parking and crossing the road. Music rolled out into the night, unexpectedly harmonious, and the smokers outside were clearly going back in for more. She had been in this pub only a few times, mainly for their generous counter meal, but its late-night crowd was not familiar to her and she felt foolishly conspicuous. Pushing her way through the din to the far end of the bar, she bought a house wine and, wedged awkwardly on a stool in the corner, turned to study the source of the music. It wasn't the kind you'd normally expect in this kind of place, and she really stared when she located the performer.

It was a woman playing the violin. Striking in a floating long dress of shimmering blues and greens, her hair was loose and quite long, flowing past her shoulders. Ellie saw it was silver but couldn't place her age at all – anywhere between forty-five and seventy-five? The hair seemed alive, lustrously flying out with the wild and sad sounds coming from the violin tucked under her chin, as this astonishing apparition – in this common corner pub! – held them all spellbound.

For that was exactly how it was. The crowd was hanging on the performance, stamping and clapping along to some wild gipsy dance, the pub roaring to a passionate crescendo. Then she softened the tone, playing lonesome melodies of lost love, the crowd humming along. Then the "The Pub with No Beer" and "I still call Australia Home" brought them to a sentimental warmth.

Ellie finished her wine, and unaccountably got another one, all the while thinking she should be going home and what was she doing here in the first place but unable to escape the compelling power of the scene she had drifted into so unexpectedly. She sat watching, envying the woman her freedom – what a marvelous thing to be able to do, casting such magic over this unlikely group of people! – and puzzling over why she, staid, non-adventurous and respectable Ellie, had distinctly felt a strange force guiding her into this place.

"This is absurd," she finally thought. "Go home before you get noticed."

She set the glass on the bar, gathered her bag and jacket and started to push her way determinedly towards the door. At that moment the playing turned into a melody that stopped her in her tracks. It was a piece she knew well and loved, a modern hymn that was often sung in her church from the Scripture-in-Song collection. A *religious* piece in a pub? But nobody seemed to notice, the crowd kept humming or swaying along as if mesmerised...Ellie looked sharply at the performer and found her looking directly back at her, smiling and playing with an emphasis that said unmistakably: *this tune is for you.*

Ellie finally got out, fumbling for her car keys. I shouldn't be driving after this much wine, she thought, but the police were elsewhere and she got home safely and unchallenged. As she drifted into sleep, the words of that song came to her. "Seek ye first the kingdom of God, and His righteousness..." The piece was one of her favourites, something to sing joyously whenever it was in the morning service. But to encounter it in a pub, of all places, and in such extraordinary, and somehow personal, circumstances, left her uneasy. There was a message here somewhere, and she didn't think that she really wanted to hear it.

And then that extraordinary performer, surely not the kind normally encountered in a common pub. Ellie decided that she would go back to the pub the next day and ask who their performer had been.

It was quite a few days before she actually did that. True, she was busy just then with the current batch of NEIS clients coming up for approval of their business submissions, but Ellie knew very well that she was also, in an obscure corner of her mind, avoiding the answer even though at the same time she was genuinely intrigued by the violin player. If she had been a singer instead, her voice would have been golden. Who *was* she?

The girl behind the pub counter had not been working that Saturday night but obligingly pulled out the gig bookings sheet.

"It was Katie Rayner," she announced. This was a well-known local country and western singer, a popular girl of about 25 who accompanied herself on a guitar.

"No," said Ellie, "that can't be right. This lady was much older and anyway, she played the violin…"

The girl gave her a pitying look but, after serving some other customers, went to ask the licensee. He was heaving barrels around the yard but would be in shortly, if the lady didn't mind waiting? Ellie sat, beginning to wonder if she had imagined it all. Maybe she was turning mad in her old age? But no, she knew what she had seen – and heard.

She recognised the large man when he came in; he had served her himself on the night. He also studied the booking sheet and pronounced on Katie Rayner, but then remembered that Katie at the last minute couldn't come and had sent this friend to stand in for her.

"I was a bit surprised when she came, being that old and having a violin. But she said to give her a chance and it was ok – the customers didn't mind her. In fact, they all stayed much later than usual, and she sure kept playing the right stuff to keep 'em here."

"But who is she?" asked Ellie.

He looked non-plussed.

"I don't know…she never said."

"But you must have paid her, surely?"

"No, in fact I didn't. She just kind of went…suddenly she wasn't there anymore, and everyone else went too, so I shut up shop."

"What time was that?" asked Ellie, though she knew the answer.

"Ah, about two in the morning. Funny that, I can't even remember her packing up. I should ask Katie about it." He looked genuinely puzzled. "Odd woman, she was – kinda unreal…"

That was exactly it. *Unreal.* An angel perhaps? Come to play her a special message? That song about doing the right thing, the melody of which kept playing insistently in her head. And what if the 'right thing' was to give James a fair hearing? Ellie knew it, had known it all along, from the moment he had turned up on her doorstep, and she fought that knowledge.

Why should she let him change her comfortable life that she had finally established? She didn't owe him a thing! He was the one who had left, wasn't he – he the one who broke faith with their marriage and played around elsewhere. She didn't have to put up with this! She liked her life exactly as it was, relished her undisturbed self-determination and the peacefulness of being alone. Round and round went her thoughts, crossly seeking a valid excuse and hopelessly knowing at the same time that there probably wasn't one.

She couldn't deny the demands of being righteous, as the stupid song insisted. James had a right to be heard, to be considered. He had been totally genuine, his eyes clean and humble as he asked to see her. And of course she knew him to be basically a good man with no real malice in him. Probably he had been seduced in a weak moment, like so many men were, and had possibly regretted it long and hard since. Too proud to let her know that, still decent enough to do the best he could in the wake of his damage, paying for her and the children's needs generously, and independent enough to forge a life for himself without bothering her. All these were, really, virtues that she could admire, when she thought about it, which she did reluctantly, knowing every thought was pulling her back in, into this relationship with her real husband.

Oh, *damn* him! He's not my husband! We were properly divorced. He's *not* my responsibility. Maybe not in the worldly law, came back that unrelenting voice inside her, but really he is, isn't he? You married him and bore his children, didn't you? You spent nearly 20 years together. You know each other in the very fibers of your being, you've shared everything from your dreams to your weak, naked moments and the vulnerability of having sex together. Doesn't all that bring a moral obligation?

Ellie parked under the carport that had riotous jasmine all over it. Though tempted to slam in angrily, she forced herself instead to go slowly, gathering her work papers from the seat, stopping to sniff the exotic scent, picking a few blooms for the table vase, checking the letterbox, and smiling as the cat came down the path to greet her. By the time she had reached her front door, she was ready to acknowledge how lucky she really was. Calmly, she worked through the comforting home routines, lighting the fire, packing away her purchases, deciding what dinner would be. Later, she would sit down quietly and consider the whole problem, fairly and thoroughly, and for now she would take some time out to gather herself. Having made her decision, she sat by the warmth radiating from the wood heater with the paper and a rare glass of good red wine.

That evening, back at the pub, the licensee also took a moment to consider the odd problem of the mystery gig player. What, exactly, had she been playing? Initially worried, he'd relaxed after hearing the first few notes – folksy, popular, lightweight, a mix of easy tunes that everybody knew and nobody would object to, even if it wasn't what the program had promised for the evening. And indeed, more and more people had come, the evening stretching out longer than usual; he had done good business that night.

Once at ease, he hadn't paid her much attention, busily attending the crowd's demands. Yet, now that he was thinking about it, she must have been rather good, even exceptional. He did recall that wild gipsy dance with all the crowd stomping along, shortly before, in fact, the strange lady had simply disappeared without asking for her money. She had played something soft and gentle as her last piece; he couldn't put a name to it but it had felt familiar. Then she simply went, as though she had floated away. Still puzzled, the landlord gave up on the problem, finished his closing up, and went home. The moon flooded the sky. For a moment the man fancied he could see that same ageless and wise face in it. Geez, he thought, you're getting soft in your old age. But it was a nice feeling, all the same.

***

Now Denise was really desperate. Alan hadn't called at all lately, and when she rang him, he sounded remote. She demanded a meeting and it was a disaster, his disinterest obvious. It took that humiliation for Denise's anger to finally rise. She shrieked her fury and disappointment, calling him every name she could think of, finally hurling an empty vase from his mantelpiece not quite at him, before storming out. He had just sat there, waiting for it to finish, glad she was the one to do it. She was nothing but a nuisance now. Pity about the vase, though. It had been his mother's.

Denise's fury went on for quite a while but was wonderfully cathartic. Once home, she kicked things and slammed doors. To think of all the demeaning things she'd allowed him to do to her, sexual stuff she had never felt ok about but allowed because it seemed to be the thing to do. She'd done it well, too, but the bastard never appreciated how lucky he was. Her swearing and banging reverberated round the flat – it was just as well that Ty was away with James – and then the realisation that she no longer had a fancy boyfriend sank in, bringing shame at her foolishness.

In the morning, she made some sensible decisions. Since all men were bastards, it was better to arrange life without them. She now regretted turning down that hairdressing job in Launceston, which she knew had been quickly filled. But getting away from the humiliating mess she was in now made the northern town seem a good idea all the same. Rents were cheaper there, and James would be real close to keep Ty in order – all the advantages that she had previously discounted rose up before her. She could bring good reasons for going. How she had wasted her time on that rotten bastard Alan was, after all, nobody's business, and need not be mentioned.

By the time James returned Ty to her after lunch that Sunday, she had cleared up and was in cool control. She even made an effort to provide tea and a nice slice. Oh, she was thinking of moving to Launceston – would James help her with his ute, one time when he was down anyway? She'd look for a flat meanwhile; a friend had mentioned a possible job there.... she was sick of Hobart, and anyway, wouldn't it be good for James if he didn't have such a long run to see Ty anymore?

James, not entirely convinced, sensed an unstated agenda, but it was not his business where she lived. Certainly he'd appreciate not having to drive so many hours to keep up his commitment to Ty. Seeing the boy settle and develop into a thoughtful and less angry young man, had become a great satisfaction to James. He was proud of himself for having made the effort, and turned around a wrongdoing on his part. Not that it was always easy. At times the boy was truculent and uncooperative, making James wish he'd never got involved. Denise often struck him as silly and shallow, and he had to work on himself to remember her background. The sheer amount of time and driving involved felt like a burden then. What have I taken on here, he wondered. Must've been completely insane…he was tempted to walk out on it all. But, no. Ty was still vulnerable, and despite his unpleasant moments he was growing steadier and more thoughtful. Somewhere along the line, the understanding that James was Ty's father had crept in – nobody had actually said anything but after some months all three of them simply knew it, and Ty now quite naturally called him 'Dad'. No. There could be no turning back if James was to live in peace with his conscience.

"Certainly I'll help you move, Denise. Ty can pitch in too. Let me know when you're ready and I'll bring the trailer, also."

***

This could be interesting, thought James as he drove back up the highway to Launceston, Bonnie sitting inside beside him. He leaned across to pat her. Good old dog, eh? Ty sure enjoys running around with you. Together we're seeing a bit of life at the moment, aren't we now?

They certainly were. There had been the visit to Ellie, the stumbling awkward first moments when she realised that he was there for a painful and personal apology that couldn't be ignored. She had accepted it gracefully enough, and sometime later, when he had invited her out to dinner, he had told her about his son Ty. This took some adjusting to; her shocked surprise was clear. She softened as he told her of his efforts to put things right, and how successful it had been with the boy.

"And what of the mother, that Denise?" she asked. "Are you seeing her again, also?"

"Not in any personal way, Ellie. I feel quite sorry for her – she seems to be battling to achieve something solid. That business with the police shook her up badly, too – she's pretty hapless in some ways but she's not a bad person. She could do with some kindness. But no, she's not for me – she was, like I said, a mistake on my part. Not just in looking outside of our marriage, but also because she's just not my sort. Ty should never have happened, but he did, so now I'm doing what I can. I only see Denise in connection with that."

"Poor girl…" Ellie looked thoughtfully into the distance.

"Ellie? I know our divorce was my fault entirely, and I've lived to regret it. Do you think…is there any chance…that we could consider being serious friends, at least?"

"James! But why, after all this time? Haven't we both rebuilt our lives in our own way?"

"Well, I actually really *like* you. You're a special person…"

Though she didn't reject him outright, she did not seem to be warming to the idea either.

"Will you think about it, at least?" he ventured. "I don't want to put you under any pressure, or upset you in any way. But perhaps you will allow me to see you occasionally, like this, and see how it feels after a while?"

It had become a routine. James deliberately let time go by before calling her again. Gradually, as she sensed his self-sufficiency and his genuine interest, she relaxed and started to enjoy his company. They were both curious to rediscover each other in this way. It was as if the years of marriage were something they had just drifted into, because it was the done thing. Now they found that the initial attraction had not lied – they did after all have a quiet closeness, a shared communality of thought.

"That's probably why we were always ok with each other, back then," Ellie reflected, "despite the differences in our backgrounds. We had the same basic ideas about the things that really matter, and we still do now."

Despite these insights and the pleasure of his company, she fought the idea. She liked her life as it was, and was very unsure about having another person in it all the time. Another body in the bed, also? She had no desire for sexual activity for its own sake, but had to admit that he wasn't unattractive. Occasionally she found herself thinking that a hug from him might be very nice. But when she realised that she was automatically paying attention to her appearance and clothing before they went out together, she deliberately stopped doing it.

"He must like me for how I am, just in the everyday appearance of me. I won't dress up – we don't need to pretend."

He didn't seem to notice any difference.

"Perhaps we could just be lovers, keeping our separate homes? That would solve the problem, wouldn't it?"

She knew it wouldn't. This was a serious thing they were engaged in, a searching for the real and uncompromising thing, that full acceptance of another human being. A cop out would be an insult to both of them. Though she fought the idea, she was gradually drawn closer, mostly because he kept the sexual entirely out of it, making no attempt to touch her beyond a friendly arm round the shoulders or holding her hand. He slowly courted her, far more successfully than either realised, by his gentle and consistent attention to the person she really was.

They already had the children in common. Gradually there were family get-togethers over Sunday lunch when they were all present. After an initial look of surprise, their sons Ian and Jeremy made no further comment, somehow settling naturally to the idea. Ellie noted it, half with regret and half smiling at how readily they had accepted it as perfectly natural. But she kept her surrender to herself for the time being, and James, who sensed it, quietly kept on waiting. He'd won through with Ty, and maybe he'd win through with Ellie, too.

James considered the new situation. Denise moving closer did not worry him at all. He had been planning to take Ty out to the Islands; now it would be simpler to arrange, as well as having him meet his own mother, Bessie. She was Ty's other grandmother, after all, and James smiled at the thought of how Ty would take to that warm and kind old dear. And how would Ellie feel about all that? Sooner or later, she would have to meet Ty, possibly even start considering him part of the family. James very much hoped it would come about that way. As he mused, he remembered a remark Denise had made, just as he was leaving.

"I might even start my own hairdressing business."

He had no way of judging her skills with scissors and dyes, but he did know that she had no business experience and probably not much commonsense either, when it came to keeping orderly accounts. She would need help – and Ellie's job was to teach people how to start and run small businesses...

Was he expecting too much? Or was this perhaps a way for Ellie and

Denise to meet in a natural manner and develop a working relationship? Should he suggest it to Ellie?

"What do you reckon, Bonnie?"

***

It was simply beyond belief. Alan – having made such a fine personal sacrifice – had completely failed to impress the Ice Maiden. After her first surprise, she coolly announced that she wished him the best of luck in his new life, and what an opportune time because their relationship was over, also. She had met someone she intended to marry.

It sent him into a spin. No job – could he retrieve his resignation? No Ice Maiden – but he really loved her, did he not, how could she discount such heart-agonising as he had over her? And not even little Denise for some comfort in bed – when he tried to ring, prepared with feeble excuses for 'making up' and all that, he found the number had been changed. He had a few weeks left at work, and then he would be really out on his own. The thought terrified him. His dead father's stern image rose before him.

"Have you done it again, Alan? Don't you think you owe us something better than that? I came here and slaved in a strange place for years so you and your sisters could have a better life – took any work I could get, built us a decent house, got you through university – and you show no gratitude at all. This will break your mother's heart."

Alan knew well enough that his father had been badly treated by the Japanese in Indonesia and that he had later come away from war-shattered Europe with his young wife Anna, who was then already pregnant with Roseanne on the ship and had a terrible passage as a consequence. But both had grimly set to, to start a new life from scratch, away from all that was familiar. Alan knew it all in theory, but couldn't really imagine it. His own young life had been sheltered and stable, tumbling with his sisters in a peaceful, green and abundant world, at least until the car accident that put him into a coma for seven days. To an outsider it looked idyllic, and, compared to what had gone before, it was. His mother's devoted care of her injured son brought universal admiration. But his father's dark silences, and his wife's nervous retreat into the rigid rituals of the Reformed Church, provided the small boy with no emotional closeness. He had been inclined, as an adult, to blame all his problems on his parents' insufficiency.

But in his current distress, Alan suddenly thought of his mother, and for the first time regretted that she was also dead, from cancer, when he was still only in his mid-twenties. How he had hated the long process of sickness with its unpleasant smells, visiting helpers hushing the household, and the oppressive, darkened room in which she lay. Her passing was a relief to him then, but now it was too late to ask her – anything.

Too bloody late! It's always too fucking late! I'm always missing out on the real things! He built up his fury. His cat Ranger kept well out of the way, mostly in the garden, though once or twice he came in and pushed his nose into Alan's hand, as if to console him. But his master had no time for him, and he stalked out again, his catly dignity deeply offended. Inside, Alan in a rage gathered up all the books and paperwork the Ice Maiden had given him – what use was all that bloody information now? See what it had landed him in – and dumped it in the trash. As he came back into the room, he found he'd dropped some pieces, and in stooping to gather them too, his hand paused over the photograph of a smiling, attractive woman.

It was part of a newspaper article on Dr. Bleaney – the woman from St. Helens who had caused such an uproar over her claims of water toxicity a couple of years ago. The Ice Maiden had often talked about it.

"It's as bad, maybe worse, than the 1080 that was freely sprayed all over the place here in the seventies when the US offloaded all their unused agent orange after the Vietnam War. Our government gamely bought it, even though it was known to be a destructive and persistent poison. We're *still* using it, for God's sake, so they're certainly not going to object to the trees, or investigate any possible nasties from them, are they?"

She had much admired Dr Bleaney's willingness to stand up to the political bullying and willful blindness.

Alan studied the picture more closely. That was really quite an attractive lady, smiling there in her blue top and pictured against the river she was trying to protect, nothing like the tough female he had imagined her. An open, friendly face; he felt that she had no double agenda. Clearly he recalled his astonishment that she had risked her professional position and her own money, all because of what she believed to be the real truth. He put the photograph back on his desk. Later on, after a soothing glass, he admitted to himself that he would like to be like that too – admired and respected for, for, well, *for being real.* Perhaps his decision to resign at work wasn't quite such a disaster after all. Yet the terror of having no structure to his days, and no respectable position anymore, could only be held in check with drink and smoke, and he spent his last few weeks at work in a haze. Everyone was glad to come to the end of it; the obligatory goodbye lunch was a muted affair that he couldn't escape fast enough.

***

As the cooling dusk drew its mantle over the foothills of Miller's Bluff in the Western Tiers, the straight rows of the untended plantation trees on Michael Fairfield's land brooded quietly over their secret. Beneath them, the now unrestrained growth of weeds tangled with the lower branches that should have been removed by now. Wallabies had found this new shelter so close to cultivated fields most convenient, and now began to stir. Breeding there undisturbed, along with rabbits and feral cats, they set out to nibble away at the oats, barley, poppies and other valuable crops. Ordinary fences proved no barrier, and the few shooters about made little difference to their numbers. They drank the water from the dams filled with the runoff from the treed slopes. As the summer progressed, the undergrowth grew ever drier. A carelessly-thrown cigarette butt could start a conflagration any time there. Or even an empty bottle, its broken shards magnifying the sun's heat onto some dry wisps. And with the strong wind eddies among those foothills, there would be no telling how it might go, up the mountain or out over the fields to the homesteads. Or maybe both.

30. THE MATURING, 2013

"This is incredibly beautiful," said Ellie, surveying Castle Rock and Marshall Beach running north. The colours were stunning – red lichen covering the yellow and grey rocks, the sea ranging from turquoise to the deepest blue, with patches of white and purple in between. To the south reared the Mt Strzelecki Peaks, now a National Park, and to the north, Mt Killiecrankie and Mt Tanner provided a natural focal point. The air was clear, the silence awesome, the possibilities infinite. She, James and Ty had just walked to the famous Rock, bringing a picnic lunch, after spending some time that morning at Wybalenna. The chapel there was the only building remaining of the village that had been built in the 1830's to accommodate the Aborigines rounded up in Tasmania by G A Robinson.

They had come to Flinders Island for a holiday. James and Tyrone had been before, and had much fun camping around the Island. This time, they were staying in cabins at a holiday park, Ellie in one and the two men in another.

"I won't impose on you, Ellie," James had said when he suggested the trip. "This is just a nice relaxed time to get to know each other – and it sure is a nice place to visit."

Not long before, Ellie had finally met Ty. She surveyed the grave young man, now fifteen, growing tall and strong, and any awkwardness was quickly banished by his open smile. The brown eyes, so like James' but topped with Denise's blond hair, held none of the surly disinterest common among teenage boys. James really did rescue this one, she thought, and stretched out her hands in welcome. There had been several family times since. One Sunday lunch was at their son Ian's and his wife Janine, their two little girls, and Jeremy. The latter and Ty got on well immediately, looking so absurdly alike that Ellie could hardly suppress her laughter. *Our* sons, she thought, which was an unusual phrase for her after so many years of being apart from their father, but now there's three of them, not just two...

She wished their daughter Tessa could have been there also, to complete the picture, but the girl – woman, now, Ellie reminded herself – was deeply into her advertising career in Melbourne and, while not unfriendly or particularly detached, saw little reason to spend time in a backwater like Launceston. Ellie understood it, hearing echoes of her own mother's restless and unhappy confinement in the morally judgmental small-town attitudes of the 1950's. That now elderly lady had become a widow in recent years. Her second husband had left her well provided for, and Ellie still visited regularly, always hoping for that closeness that had so far eluded them. She had a much warmer relationship with James' mother Bessie, with whom she had stayed in touch despite the divorce.

All the family complications blew away in the fresh air on Flinders. The weather was magnificent, and every day they drove their hire car to some beautiful place, most of which were remote and empty of all humanity.

But the brooding sadness at Wybalenna had touched Ellie deeply. She shivered at the thought of the Aboriginal graves, unmarked and empty, having been robbed and the skeletons sold to collectors. Later, some Straitsmen themselves had dug up the few that remained and reburied them in secret places, to protect them from further desecration. It was said that they planted a particular herb to mark the sites. She shook her head, too, at the idea that Aborigines would welcome the restoration of the chapel, done in the 1970's by the white community.

"It's a bit like expecting Jews to rejoice at the restoration of Auschwitz, isn't it?" she said to James, as they settled in the warm sand for their picnic.

"The land there has been given to the Aborigines, and they manage it now. One can understand that they don't want much to do with it, other than it be respected and left alone. It must be, to them, full of very sad ghosts."

"You speak of 'them' as though they were not a part of you, James?"

During their twenty years of marriage, his part-Aboriginal descent had never been mentioned between them – it simply wasn't in their consciousness, just as it had not been, at that time, for most Tasmanians. Other things in life had mattered much more. Ellie felt she herself was much more conscious of it than James. She was curious to know his view.

He hesitated. Both watched Ty, poking along the water's edge some distance away. Then he said:

"You know, it doesn't really make much difference to me. It just happens to be my background, just like you've got yours. Apart from your cousin Michael, you're not real close to the rather fancy Midland pastoralist's notion, are you, that you could claim if you had a mind to? It's a bit like that for me..." He cast around for the right words. "You know, I loved and respected my parents – they were a great example, as was Grandma Una. Being half-castes wasn't really the issue – not that they were, anyway; both were fourth generation and therefore watered down quite a bit. Anyways, they thought it right to discern a man by his actions only, not according to his racial colour."

James sat up a bit straighter, and stared out over the picture postcard scenery before them. The waves were curling majestically up on the golden beach, the water dazzling in its glitter, the sky an endless blue. In his mind's eye he saw his father, so anxious to provide well for them, so upright in his quiet dignity. In his mature years, James had begun to understand his father's occasional silences as a defensive retreat when overwhelmed by things, and mentally thanked him for choosing a non-violent response. Bessie's constant optimism would pull Victor back; she had really held the family together. Presently James continued:

"But they weren't ashamed to be known as Straitsmen, either – no one spoke about 'Aboriginality' back then – and they'd tell us stories of how their own parents and others before them had learnt to survive in this dangerous sea here. It's pretty enough right now, isn't it? But in it lies a fearsome power, not to be messed with casually." He turned to Ellie with a smile. "I wouldn't be game to take us out in a dinghy even today. You need real knowledge here, real experience, for that."

"So no fishing trips for us?" she smiled back at him. She had been sitting very still, listening intently to his words.

"Definitely not. But my father could've done it readily enough. And

350

they were proud, too, in a quiet way, of how they'd survived in real hard and lean times, and made do in clever and inventive ways, sharing and helping each other, and making their own fun, too." James drew his hand through the sand, enjoying its soft whisper. Then he balled his fist around some. "Something Mum once said makes me think the hardest thing for them to stomach was the general prejudice. All the officials ever saw was squalor and intransigence. Yet Mum was most insistent that we kept clean, and were decent in our language and behavior. She'd spend hours turning our shirt collars, to make them last, of course, but to make them look neat and tidy, too. I guess it was that, more than anything, that drove them, once they were in Launceston, to assimilate and try to be just like anyone else, in the outward, material sense, that is. No one dreamt, back then, about trying to be Aboriginal like now. It was quite the opposite – we worked hard to be like everyone else, so we could line up for the same jobs."

"Wow," smiled Ellie. "What a long speech!"

To herself she thought that the Maynes had been very successful at proving just that, at least in James. She puzzled, though, over the strong sense of resentment and anger that came across from the current Aboriginal community, particularly from the group she thought of as Mansell's mob.

"You seem to have a very different attitude to some of them. There's that spokeswoman – I've seen her on TV – she seems a bit hard faced and bitter, what's her name, Erica something?"

"That's my youngest sister…"

"*What!*"

"Yeah, she is. Changed a bit, hasn't she, from the couple of brief times you saw her way back then? She's done some growing up since… But you're right, we don't have a lot in common. Funny, that, she's the one that went to uni – Mum was so proud of that – but whatever she learnt there hasn't made her particularly happy. Mind you, she's just that bit younger and it put her into a different era to Rachel and Billy and me. All we wanted was to be accepted like everyone else, to have a job, a house, and just be allowed to get on with it, so I guess for me it is too late to be any other way." He spread his work-worn hands on his knees as he considered his sister. "Things changed real quick, all of a sudden, in the seventies, and if you weren't already formed by then, it sure got you, like it did Erica. She gets quite a kick out of being angry on behalf of the hard-done by Aborigines, and demanding land and rights and all...fills her life, I guess. I've not seen her in a long while."

"But you can't blame her, or the other Aborigines who are demanding all this recognition – after all, they were truly hard done by with some really awful things, quite apart from having their land taken from them."

"Sure, that's true enough. And why shouldn't they seek redress? They are, it seems, achieving quite a bit, thanks to Sis and her friends. Uni courses, learning about the old culture, well, it's all got its place, surely more so than learning about Brit kings and queens! And a better attitude to the land is really needed. This new language they're cobbling together, though, seems a bit odd to me, to try and make a new one out of the bits and pieces of several old ones – why would you want to learn that, unless it be to make you deliberately separate? I suppose it's fairly harmless, as long as they remain honest about it not being a historically true language. But getting to own and manage some significant places, especially Cape Barren Island, and being accepted despite having their own ways and stories – why, that is some progress."

"What you mentioned about making a new Tasmanian Aboriginal language makes you sound as though you don't agree with the idea of being different, or being culturally diverse, to use the PC word?"

"Well no, that's not quite what I meant. If an ethnic group has a cultural habit or art that contributes to mankind, there's nothing wrong with that at all. If I sound as though I'm against 'difference', that's only when people make themselves deliberately separate, because as a principle it's not a good thing. If families separate, that causes heartbreak and dysfunction. In a nation, we've got to be of a united mind on the basic things, otherwise it just won't work. But if within that, we can find room to enjoy diversity, why, that's great and it enriches life. After all, I like coffee and pizza as much as the next person."

That's fair enough, she thought. Then another thought struck her:

"What's in all this talk about being different just because you happen to have some Aboriginal blood in you? Why do some people like that seem to focus on that so much, and seem to completely ignore the other influences, such as Irish or English or even Maori? Can they really hear or see things in a different way from us?"

"It's got more to do with what you choose to focus on. If identifying Aboriginal gives you an identity and community, why not? I mean, some people do the same thing by joining churches or clubs. It's a good feeling when the people around you express much the same thoughts and ideas. Just as long as you can resist the urge to think yourself as better than any other group, of course."

"But do they really see in a different way? Do *you*?"

James laughed. "Do I strike you as different?"

"Well no, you're not rampantly and aggressively Aboriginal as some of them make out to be! But you're not entirely like ordinary everyday whites, either, are you?"

"Look, I don't really know. You're probably asking the wrong person..."

He stared into the distance for a while. Ellie watched his hands, broad and strong. Real workman's hands, she thought.

"I think there is something to it, though," James said. "It's more to do with where you come from – like, an English person presumably knows their land well and its ancient agricultural practices and probably has a deep closeness to some of its iconic images, like a small village huddled under the protecting spire of its church, set in a fertile valley – the sort of thing we see so much of in the English family sagas on TV. Yes? And if your blood roots are here in Tasmania, however much they might have been watered down, I think you probably do still have a special closeness to the place, a special attunement to the way the wind blows or how the natural creatures move. I'm not sure if you can also hear or see more than others, but it probably makes you feel that way. In some places I do get strange and dark feelings, and sometimes I do think I can hear something unearthly in the wind. Wybalenna sure is full of crying ghosts, given what happened there – but then, couldn't you find that in an English graveyard too – leastwise one that's had a particularly tragic history? Does that answer your question?"

Ellie liked the way James had thought things through. I could readily live with his values, she mused – you could rely on him to consider thoughtfully anything that arises.

"Do you think anyone – from any background, like say us Europeans – could have this same attunement if they are open to it?"

"In principle, yes, but I don't think it happens quite so readily. There has to be a familiarity that can only come with time. I guess there will come a time when the whites do know the place well enough, for it to have seeped into their bones as you might say, and then perhaps they will start to treat it right and begin to belong here in the true sense."

"Like the Aborigines already do?"

"Something like that…"

"So what grates about the Mansell mob isn't what they're asking for, which is probably perfectly reasonable, but rather the fact that they seem to cultivate an attitude of anger and resentment, just like your sister does?" she ventured.

He lent back in the warm sand, smiling at her.

"That's pretty much it, Ellie," he answered. "It's just not a nice way to be. Mind you, here in Tassie they've got a particularly tough audience to try and convert. European tourists who go on specialised Aboriginal Experience tours might be open to their message, but Tasmanians for most part are not. This story here is too raw, and too close…"

Ellie knew that to be true. Few locals really wanted to know. The Federal Labour governments had set the note nationally for reconciliation in the 1980's, but the conservative Liberals had since reversed that and were largely opposed to any such sentiment, focusing instead on the – mostly white – heroics celebrated on Anzac Day. And the local Tasmanian Labour government, though initially enthusiastic, had proved weak and incompetent; Aboriginal matters, as far as they could avoid them, were not on the agenda beyond a bit of lip service. Not, at any rate, since Premier Bacon had died. Now it was all go for big business at the expense of the common man. Just like the companies that promoted those strange trees.

"That reminds me, James, what do you think of those trees that Cousin Michael has growing below the shack?"

"Hmm, they're not much of an asset in the landscape, are they, nor, from what I'm gathering, in his pocket either, at the moment. I promised Ty a few more days up there sometime soon, before the summer break ends. Maybe around the beginning of February?"

Just then, Ty came wandering back with some find from the beach, and hungry, too, so they unpacked the picnic basket and the rest of the day was spent in laughter and a deep appreciation of the beauty they were in and their own comfortable company. Soon they would fly home, and Ellie knew that sometime quite soon she would say 'yes' to James. She had come around to realizing that she was exceptionally lucky, being offered a relationship by a good man who was also willing to see her as a real person. That was a rare privilege indeed. Would we have come to this same place, she wondered, if we had stayed together?

***

"Are you alright, Alan?" Roseanne's voice was concerned, making in Alan's opinion a good show of being interested in his wellbeing while probably only wanting something. He never heard from his sisters unless that was the case, didn't he? Not that they would have turned him down if he had shown an interest in them, and that he was free to do so anytime – indeed, that *he* should initiate it – simply wasn't a factor in his thinking. So contact remained limited to major family functions only, both girls having long written him off as 'a problem'. Alan knew this and resented it.

But this time he was only half right. The younger one, Sabina, had heard on the grapevine – Hobart is a small town – that he had resigned at work. Knowing this to be premature in terms of years, she had mentioned it to Roseanne, which resulted in the latter making the call. Concern for him was ingrained in her ever since she'd been put in charge of the fragile child recovering from the accident, and though she now knew that much of the fuss at the time was not justified, there always remained the possibility of something being actually wrong. Some undefined fragility had remained.

"You're not at work anymore?"

This was a raw, painful subject, a move he still regretted, so he made light of it, saying that he was sick of the work and wanted a change. He knew better than to give the lofty philosophical reasons he had tried to beguile the Ice Maiden with. Roseanne knew him too well to buy that. She was still puzzled – it didn't quite add up, yet she was reassured that he was, at least, there and apparently not ill.

"So what will you do now, Alan?"

"Don't know yet… I'm thinking of buying a four wheel drive and going around Australia…"

A fortnight later, Alan received another call, this time from his Uncle Tadd on the North West Coast, inviting him to come and stay. Surprised – he'd had no direct contact with his mother's brother for a very long time – but taken by the genuine warmth in Tadd's voice, he agreed to drive up and stay for a couple of days.

It wasn't really his thing, to stay with family. He disliked sleeping in guest bedrooms that tended to be uncomfortable and not really private, as well as having to share bathrooms. But he needed something to break him out of the severer-than-usual spiral of drink and dope he had fallen into recently. Getting out of the house would help.

Apart from some rather fun childhood holidays, he had only seen Taddeus Berema briefly at the funerals of his parents, and now he felt the omission. Alan also regretted that he had not been more friendly with Roseanne – she was his nearest relative, and once they had been close. She was the one who had held his hand and seen him safely to his class; she the one who had shielded him from school bullies. Maybe there was something to the family thing after all.

He was curious, too, about Uncle Tadd. A cheerful, friendly man, he had remained unmarried and presumably childless, nor had there ever been mention of any serious girlfriend. Alan knew that the farm's main business was the growing of assorted vegetables, and he remembered chickens, dogs and cats, and yes, there had been a horse too, that the girls got to ride, and he thought there might have been some sheep somewhere, too.

The farm lay fifteen minutes driving past Burnie, along Ocean Vista, elevated on the hills rising towards Elliott with a fine view of the sea. He arrived after the four-hour drive, a little self-consciously carrying a bottle of wine for his Uncle. Just call me Tadd, the latter said as he came out to welcome Alan. Here, you can have the studio, and he led the way across the yard, away from the main house, to what looked like a converted barn. To Alan's great appreciation, it turned out to be a self-contained and very well furnished apartment, almost luxurious, and certainly private, with a lovely outlook through big windows. Clearly, Uncle Tadd had set up some holiday accommodation; Alan wondered why it was empty at the height of the holiday season – almost February it was, right in the shimmering heat of summer – and later still he wondered if his Uncle had turned away business just so that he, Alan, might stay there? I think you'll find all you need here, his host continued. Settle in and come across when you're ready. Had a good drive up?

The main house held further surprises. Though nothing was aggressively ostentatious – in fact, everything showed remarkably good taste – the general statement was that life was for enjoying. There was a generously stocked drinks cabinet, easy chairs around what would be the cosy warmth of a big wood heater in winter, a large dining table and quality appliances in the open-plan kitchen. Floor-to-ceiling windows took in the brilliant view to Bass Strait, the sliding doors standing open to a partially-covered sandstone patio with attractive outdoor furniture.

Uncle Tadd himself was another surprise. For an elderly man – at least 75, Alan calculated – he was remarkably fit and light on his feet, his powerful frame a testimony to constant physical work done with energy and pleasure. This man could still nimbly climb up into his tractor cab, heave hay bales or wrestle with recalcitrant calves. Alan felt his defensiveness rising, thinking his own physique inadequate and, worse, even inconsequential. But again his host disarmed him, easily fixing drinks and leading the way out onto the patio, in a manner that showed no condescension, only genuine interest.

And thus it went. The two got on well. Alan, relaxing into a longer stay than the anticipated two days, phoned a friend in Hobart to call by daily and feed his cat. During the mornings, Uncle Tadd was busy about the farm, it being the middle of harvesting a large acreage of French beans. This was done by contractors who brought their big, lumbering machines into the paddocks in the morning, and sent the fragrant greens off to the factory in equally large trucks.

"Nothing romantic about it these days, is there?" laughed his host, as he climbed into his overalls. "Make yourself comfortable – or feel free to travel around, as you wish. I'll be needed out there till lunchtime, but help yourself meanwhile to anything in the kitchen. I've put a roast in the oven for this evening."

The slow-cooked meat was delicious and deftly served by this astonishing man, who was, Alan had to remind himself, actually part of his family. He was also taken aback to discover that his two sisters had not only brought their own children up here regularly for holidays, but continued to call by. Alan could see why, with such a royal welcome, but wondered how he'd been so completely unaware of it all. *Missing out again?* whispered his demons.

"I'm so glad to get to know you, Alan. I've often wondered how you've been getting on," Tadd said one evening when the mellowing effect of wine had relaxed his guest.

"Having such an accident at a young age has the plus that the body heals quickly and well, but it's also a very impressionable age. I did feel that my sister fussed over you too much. She only meant well but it must have been a very difficult thing to manage back then. She and your dad would have had a very big stake in being seen to be doing the right thing."

No one had ever broached this subject with Alan before, or with such understanding and an opening to speak of how it really was. Half embarrassed, he made consenting noises.

"It is now known," Uncle Tadd went on, "that the human brain, if suddenly jarred or severely hit, can result in the suspension of consciousness. It might have seemed that you came out of your long coma – seven days, wasn't it? – without any apparent harm, but this peculiar suspension can result in someone feeling as though they had lost their grip on reality. As though, you might say, they no longer quite knew their proper place in this world anymore."

This was so painfully accurate that Alan almost squirmed. Yet Uncle Tadd's kindly concern robbed the words of any sting.

"Yet you've done incredibly well to have held a senior job in the Health Department for so long, Alan. And now you've taken a bigger step still, resigning as you have. That really is courageous, I reckon, because as a little boy you once took an impulsive decision to run after your school mates and it resulted in a very hard bang. That's a painful lesson for a little one, and I can see it would make stepping out from the familiar very challenging. So I really admire you for that."

Tadd refilled their glasses and continued:

"I love my work here and this place, but even for me there have been moments when I wished I'd had the courage to walk out and start something new, especially in the earlier days when it was still really hard going. When I first came here – that's fifty-five years ago now – the locals called us imports (that's when they were being almost kindly; they had a few less flattering expressions for other times). We were not very welcome, especially in the farming sector. They paid us badly, played nasty tricks on us whenever they could, and were envious when I got on through sheer hard work. I bought this farm after only five years, when many still thought that I didn't have a right to any land of theirs, and it took another thirty very hard years before I could even start to afford what you see here now. I'm happy to say that attitudes have changed around here, for most part, and I've found many nice friends since, but I'm very much with you when it comes to the difficulties of making a new start in anything..."

Despite himself, Alan was drawn into the conversation. Unable to admit to the real, silly and superficial reason why he'd left his work, he spoke lightly of the possibility of buying some quality photographic equipment, a suitable vehicle, and travelling around trying to capture the beauty of nature. The idea had only just come to him, possibly inspired by a fine landscape photo in the guest apartment, but it was better than confessing that, really, he had no idea.

"Very suitable for a loner," he laughed.

Tadd looked at him: "You're wondering why I haven't done the usual thing and got married?"

Alan admitted it.

"It's quite simple, really. I just never found quite the person I really wanted to settle with. Oh yes, there have been a couple of longer rela-tionships that might have gone that way, but somehow by then I was quite content and didn't feel a huge urge to have someone around all the time. I guess I worked a bit too hard in my younger years, when it would have been easier to be beguiled by some nice girl…" Tadd smiled into the distance. "There were a few nice ones about, too, but I was kinda shy and felt I should have something solid behind me before I could venture to ask any of them, so somehow the opportunity passed me by. And yes, in some ways it's a regret to me. But since I've learnt to love my solitude, that quiet time in the evenings when I can read what other people have thought and experienced, and think quietly about it. I love the peace of that. And in the silence I can sense that there's a Greater Being out there somewhere that made all the beauty around us. Every time the tiny wrens hop around on the grass out here, or when the morning mist flows down this valley, I have that thought confirmed to me, so I know I'm not really alone."

He turned to offer his guest a bowl of roasted nuts.

"Funny old codger you must think me," he continued. "Not that I've much time for the priests and their cant. I find enough that's holy right here. Have you ever walked in the mighty forests on the West Coast?"

Taken aback, Alan had to admit that he had not ever really done so.

"Put it on your bucket list," smiled Uncle Tadd. "But I'm not just a solitary hermit. I do have several good friends – in fact, I've invited some to come and meet you over dinner in a couple of days." Alan felt a rush of fear curl into his stomach. His Uncle continued: "I've seen a lot of Sabina's and Roseanne's children, also; they've become my family in a very real way. And now I'm so pleased to be renewing my connection with you, too."

The next evening Alan found himself telling his Uncle about his own daughter, lost to him for years.

"Her mother put pressure on her to say she didn't want to see me, that it was too upsetting. I knew it was a put-up job at the time, but what can you do? The women have all the power in these things."

"There may come a day when your girl seeks you out for herself. You are after all in the phone book." The old man settled back for a little sermon:

"Meanwhile, the power to arrange your own life is here with you, every day, and it can be lived fully. You could do worse than taking beautiful pictures, learning to really look at what's there and trying to capture its essence. Really looking, now, that's an art most of us have to learn again – little kids have it but we somehow overlay that ability with stuff, mostly useless chatter, that's already in our heads and it blinds us… I missed a lot in my younger years. You could say it kept me on the straight and narrow, and I did achieve what I was aiming for, but it came at a price. It was a long time till I began to really see other things. Not just nature's beauty, either, but people and what motivates them, and to try and find their goodness in among all their shortcomings. Nowdays, except when it's harvest or the like, I take it slowly and have learnt to enjoy things just for what they are. Savouring, that's the word, savouring the richness of life, and that way life becomes very full and interesting. And it's all out there, right in front of us, we don't even have to go anywhere special to find it – all we have to do is take the time to look, and enjoy…"

That Uncle Tadd enjoyed things was evident all around him. But Alan knew that he wasn't talking about material stuff only. He suspected that the man saw him for what he really was, a shallow failure, yet he was disarmed in the gently accepting atmosphere his host wove about him. He went to bed, deeply thoughtful. He wanted what this man had, this inner contentment, and was reminded once more of that doctor in St Helens. She too, would have that same attitude, an inner freedom that allowed one to take risks without being upended if it should happen to go wrong. But what was this elusive thing? And how did one get it?

Alan stayed almost ten days, trying to fathom the answer. Once during that time, some of Uncle Tadd's friends over for dinner. Alan could see how carefully he prepared beautiful food for them, brought genuine interest to each, and how skillfully he, Alan, was included into the group. Referring to his intention to take up photography, Uncle Tadd added:

"You could probably take some very fine pictures, Alan, but I wonder how long it would really satisfy you? I think you may have another talent. Have you considered sculpting? Either in wood, stone, clay, or even casting in bronze? That has such a solid, permanent feel to it, challenging your eye in really positive ways, surely? There would be much to learn, of course, but you've got the time now. I can quite imagine you creating some pretty magnificent life-size sculptures…"

The others guests took up the theme, each one having something to say about a sculpture that had impressed them. Names that Alan had never heard of before were readily mentioned, and at one point his host brought out a large book on the subject.

It was both humbling to realise how much he'd missed out on by not seeking to know his Uncle before, and to see such a different way of life. Perhaps getting it together was not impossible after all – maybe something could be salvaged from the ruins of his own utter stupidity.

When he made his goodbyes, struggling to express himself adequately, Uncle Tadd merely smiled and reminded him that there was always a welcome for him here, anytime. He also handed him the book on famous sculptures to borrow till his next visit.

Alan drove away through the landscape shimmering under the intense February heat. Bush fire alerts had been broadcast. It was Thursday of the last week before school returned, and along the Coast families were crowding to the beaches. In the Northern Midlands, four youngsters from Campbell Town, one with a new provisional driver's license, decided to take a joy ride in the old farm ute, up the Poatina Road to the Great Lake. North of Fairbourne, just where the quiet country road comes close to the rising foothills of the Western Tiers and the eucalyptus nitens plantation, one of them threw an empty vodka bottle out of the car. It shattered on a small rock and the clear shards fell down into the tinder dry grass.

***

That same Thursday morning, James arrived slightly late to collect Tyrone for the promised few days up at the shack. By way of thank you to Michael for having let them use the place frequently, he planned to replace some of the rusty and loose roofing on the old building. It would teach Ty a few practical things, too, and he looked forward to working alongside the boy.

He had already obtained the roofing tin, and was up early to secure the cumbersome load on the back of the ute, along with tools and supplies. He topped it with a wheelbarrow and two sacks of cement, thinking to do a few other small jobs while he was at it. It was a big load, and he crammed some of the smaller items into the cab. James wondered if the ute would cope with it on the rough track. Ty might have to walk the last steep bit, he decided, but I think we'll be ok otherwise.

"Ok, Bonnie, hop in then. Why, what's the matter?"

His canine companion had aged in recent times, much of the bounce gone from her and her muzzle grey. Still happy to join in their adventures, today she just stood there, her tail drooping.

"Can't you jump into the cab anymore, old girl?"

James picked her up, noting how light she had become. She submitted quietly, for she adored him, and would follow him faithfully no matter what he asked of her. Even today, though every bone in her body indicated that something was wrong and they would be far more sensible to stay at home.

"Wow, it's a bit cramped in here," commented Ty, as he squeezed himself into the crowded cab of the ute, and hoisted Bonnie onto his lap. "Is she ok?"

"Just getting old, like me," smiled his father. "And finding the heat a bit much, probably. Still, there's usually a nice breeze around The Bluff, and the forecast is for cooler conditions generally from tomorrow, so it won't be too hard to handle the tin. I'm glad to be doing this job – Michael's been very generous and we can just fit it in neatly before you start in grade 10 and I have a big plumbing job on that new subdivision – a great way to finish off the holiday and be useful at the same time."

Was he justifying things a bit too much? Just before leaving his house, he had run back to the shed for some working gloves, and as he left, had felt a strange lurch in his heart. He had hesitated then, wondering if he should cancel the whole trip, but not wanting to disappoint Ty or let Michael down, pressed on anyway.

In the ute cab, Bonnie curled herself tightly onto the boy's lap, and whimpered quietly to herself.

***

Denise watched them drive away. She had made an extra effort and baked them some Anzac biscuits. Altogether, she was becoming more attentive to Ty's father, since the ignominious end of her fancy affair with Alan. How different James was, she reflected. He had helped her willingly with her move to Launceston, heaving heavy items with ease, even temporarily storing some of her larger items in his work shed. She noted his simple weatherboard house on its large block, much of which was taken up by his plumbing workshop. It was unpretentious but everything was neat and well kept. She began to look at James in a new light, observing his strong figure and the vibrant silver hair that was always closely trimmed, and contrasted attractively with his dark tan.

Presently she had secured a reasonably spacious flat, part of a larger converted home on the eastern slope along the Old Main Road. There were three other tenants in the building, and all could access the garden, which was a great help with a fast-growing teenager for whom no flat ever seemed big enough. Ty had enrolled in the local high school for the last term of grade 9, and Denise started the hunt for a job. Not much was around, so James had suggested that she might consider doing some NEIS training, eventually starting her own hair dressing business. This was a bit daunting, but better than being in the dole queue. She put it off for a while, enervated by the summer heat, but had just decided that she would make the application when Ty started grade 10, which would be next week.

For the moment, she would enjoy the few quiet days while the boy was away, and maybe try out a new hair colour that had caught her eye, and do some enjoyable op shopping for nice clothes. She wanted to look her best when James brought Ty back on Sunday. Returning with a satisfying armful of clothing, she noted through her east-facing kitchen window that a bushfire was burning in the hills on the other side of Ravenswood.

***

Alan spent that morning idling along the Coast, in no great hurry to get home to his empty house. In Devonport he stopped for a coffee, and flipped through the book his Uncle had loaned him. He was astonished at the sheer magnificence of some of the sculptures – figures raw with life hewn out of timber, splendid torsos cast in bronze, and ethereal beauty lovingly shaped in clay. Many were larger than life and impressed him with their powerful presence. It *would* be very engrossing to do something like that.

He continued on and at Longford, on an impulse, turned off the Midlands Highway onto the quiet country road that ran down through Cressy and along the foot of the Western Tiers. It would make a nice change from the noisy and busy main road, which it rejoined near Ross. There was no hurry, after all. Presently the road drew close to the mountain, and Alan suddenly realised that he was driving along a eucalyptus plantation. Was this the kind that Dr Bleaney claimed might be the source of the water pollution? When he saw a small track leading up into the foothills, looping along the edge of the plantation, he turned into it, intending only to go a short distance, but the track remained obstinately narrow, offering nowhere to turn. The land was rising steadily and promised a nice lookout. Since there was apparently nobody about to object, he kept going – it had to lead to somewhere, after all. The road got steeper and rougher, really only suitable for a proper four wheel drive. He had to go quite a bit further than he intended before he found a slight widening that just enabled him, with some difficulty, to back around. Relieved, he pulled over into the small space, stopped the engine, and stepped out into the intense heat.

He was just at the point where the plantation stopped. Immediately below him were the eucalypts, all exactly alike, with a warren of weeds cluttering the rows between them; on the other side of the track lay natural bush, also stretching away up the mountain above him. The only sound was the swishing of the wind, rising now to what would soon be a very hot and strong northerly. The plantation trees did not appear to have the strong eucalypt scent he would have expected. Were they really oozing some kind of poison into the groundwater? It seemed incredibly unlikely, yet that doctor had staked her reputation – and a lot of her money! – on it.

Despite the heat, he felt an inward shiver. There was something brooding and eerie about the place, magnified by the silence. He didn't like it at all, and would rather have simply driven away, whe his Uncle's words about looking came to him. Look *properly*. Ok, he thought, I've come this far, the car is safely turned, so I might as well take a closer look.

At this point the track had taken a turn that hid the promised view from him. He decided to walk a bit further up, there being enough shade still that would make it bearable. A strange urge was suddenly upon him, to follow this track and see where it might lead, as though some other force were beckoning him on. After ten minutes of increasingly hot effort, just as he was about to give up, he came out onto the clearing in front of the shack, where James and Tyrone were discussing the plan of action for the intended repairs. They had arrived only thirty minutes earlier. The ute, still fully laden, was parked in the shade. It was Bonnie who alerted them to the arrival of a stranger. Alan would have preferred to quietly melt back down the track, but the dog's barking had come too quickly, so he stepped forward to explain his presence.

It was a surreal moment. Ty immediately recognised the man who had been his mother's lover. Alan took a bit longer to place him, as the boy had grown a lot since he had last seen him, and anyway, he had not ever paid him much attention.

"Hi, I'm Alan. Forgive the intrusion – purely accidental. I was walking along the track and didn't realise that there was anyone here. I'll go immediately."

"No, wait," said James, intrigued for he felt he somehow knew this man and had also caught an odd look on Ty's face. "It's very hot and you look as though you could do with some water."

"Well, I wouldn't say no to that. Thank you…"

James led the way into to the hut veranda, fished up some bottled water and indicated the camp chairs. Ty still wore a perplexed look. The three sat in the shade, drinking the cool water. To make conversation, Alan indicated the ute.

"Looks like a pretty workman-like set up. Planning to do some repairs?"

They told him about the roof, talked building matters and found common ground. Alan explained his interest in the plantation trees that had brought him up the track in the first place, and appreciated the view and general setting. The other two shared previous adventures they had enjoyed there. Around them in the bush, the hovering spirits waited.

"Wind's rising," commented James. "Going to be seriously hot shortly. We won't be doing any heavy work today – just unload and get everything ready. But we'll have some lunch first. Join us, Alan, before you go?"

His first instinct was to say no, but again something seemed to stop him. Soon the chops were frying in the pan. They settled around the table inside; presently there was coffee. Time slid by in more talk, until the dog began barking again.

"Oh my God…!"

James could smell the smoke as soon as he stepped out. Below them, on the northern flank of the hill, the plantation was on fire, the gusting wind pushing it up towards them. The only means of getting away was down the one track in a heavily laden ute with room for barely two people.

"Alan! Quick! Take the boy and the ute. You've got a chance if you go right now!"

"But Dad," cried Tyrone. "What about you? I'm not going without you!"

"Go, *NOW!* Take Bonnie with you, she's too old to run."

Despite his shock at realising that he had been irresponsible and had ignored warnings, a powerful, calm authority suddenly filled James. He clearly saw what had to be done to save the situation. He hustled the two into the vehicle, not broking any argument. Just before letting the brake go, Alan looked at him. *I do know you. You're the one who looked at me on that crossing in Hobart.* He reached out.

"Here, take my keys. My car's not that far down the track – you could make it to there ok."

"Thanks. Take care of Ty."

And the ute shot down the hill. It was a terrifying ride for both. Alan, unused to a manual and clumsy ute, struggled to control it. Frightened for their lives, the smoke at times completely obscuring their path, they passed Alan's car – thank goodness I put it to the side – but there wasn't time to stop. The boy, still clutching the dog, kept wailing: "what about Dad?" and Alan kept grimly on, fighting to keep the bucking vehicle on the rutted track, pushing it as fast as possible. *Take care of Ty.* The flames were coming closer on their left, only metres away, the air impossibly hot and burning their lungs. Their eyes were streaming. *Take care of Ty.* For once in his life, he would do something properly. They were almost at the bottom. Through a momentary gap in the smoke, he saw that the track curved round to the left, and then the trees right next to them exploded. There was nothing but to drive right through the wall of flame. *Take care of Ty.* So he did, pressing the accelerator hard and bearing to the left, not knowing if it would take them to safety or to a screaming, burning death.

***

The bush fire at Miller's Bluff was on the news around mid-afternoon.

"Forty hectares of plantation, several paddocks of poppies, and a considerable area of bush are already burned. Six fire crews are attending, concentrating primarily on preventing the fire from spreading towards homesteads in the area. The fire further up the hills is in steep bushland, difficult to access, and is currently out of control. Other fires are also burning in the Derwent Valley, Ravenswood, and…."

Ellie's heart froze as she heard it. She had turned the radio on a short while earlier, to accompany a sewing task she was completing. Now she sat, rigid with shock. She hadn't heard aright, surely? Not, not near *Miller's Bluff?* But that was where Michael had his plantation, and that's where the shack is, and that's where James and Ty are! She leapt to her computer, bringing up the ABC local news page. Oh dear God, it's true….

Frantically, she dialled James' mobile. *Out of network range.* Ty had one too, but she didn't know the number. Next she tried her cousin Michael. This one was operating, but he wasn't answering. She left a message, saying that she had heard the news and was on her way and to call her as soon as he could. Then she ran for her car and hurled along the road south, ignoring all speed limits.

On the other side of town, Denise also heard the news. She remained unconcerned. Bush fires were common enough in early February – there was one quite close to town – and she was not aware of the exact location of the shack that James so often took Ty to, beyond it being somewhere on the Western Tiers. Not so far from the road to Poatina, she remembered Ty telling her once. She would no doubt see the details on the TV news at 6pm, she thought, and continued applying foils to her hair.

***

The blackened ute exploded out of the fire before the astonished gaze of the men on a fire truck that had arrived only minutes earlier. Destabilised by its load suddenly falling off as the ropes melted away, the ute careened across the burnt and smoking paddock, hit a depression in the ground and rolled over a couple of times before ploughing to a jarring halt.

SES crews ran to right it and assist the two occupants, calling urgently for an ambulance while paramedics among them tried to stabilise the injuries. Both Alan and Ty had burns to the face and hands, all their hair gone. The boy's left side had taken the main impact with several broken bones and massive contusions. The man had been wearing a seat belt and seemed outwardly less hurt but internal injuries were suspected. As for the dog, it was best to put the poor burnt brute down immediately. It was given a dose of pethidine and a local, who had stopped on the road, volunteered to take it to the vet in Longford.

The ambulance crew reported that the boy had regained partial consciousness on the way to the Launceston hospital, and was mumbling something about his dad.

"Your dad's ok, he's here with us, he'll be ok, we're nearly at the hospital."

But he kept on, repeating about leaving Dad behind, and nobody at the time understood.

***

The TV news at 6pm spoke of the miraculous escape of a father and his son in a white ute. The man was described as a hero, having courageously taken the only possible route to safety through the flames. He and the boy were in the ICU at the Launceston General Hospital, and though injured and nastily burnt, both were expected to do ok.

This time Denise sat up sharply. A man and a boy in white ute? She peered closely at the pictures. Yes, it could be.... *Ty! Ty was hurt, and so was James!* But the man said they would be ok... In no time she was on her way to the hospital. She, the mother of the boy and the love interest of the man – she liked to think of herself as that, anticipating what she had begun to hope for – would be needed, for the paperwork and to sit by their beds. She arrived at the ICU all in a flutter, at first meeting incomprehension until a nurse confirmed that they were not certain about the identity of the boy's mother. The police had traced the ute as belonging to James Mayne, a plumber from Launceston. As neither had any ID on them, it was naturally assumed that he was the driver, and the boy with him his son, and they were registered in the hospital as such. It had taken a while for the disconnect to become clear – Mr Mayne had three adult children, and was divorced from his wife, so who exactly was the boy?

Denise as the mother was quickly established, and she filled in the forms around his admission and permission for his treatment before she was allowed to see him. Yes, Mr Mayne was Ty's father. No, they were not married, but… she allowed it to be assumed that they were in a relationship. The police had meanwhile sent an officer to speak with Mr Mayne's elderly mother, who was now too frail to leave her aged care home. He reassured her that James would live, and be ok – it would take a while but his injuries didn't appear to be life threatening. And wasn't he just such a hero to save the boy at such risk? Old Bessie Mayne knew all about Ty, as James had long ago told her the whole story, and despite her upset she was glad, too, that the nice Ellie would get her husband back after all. The officer left, saying she could ring the hospital anytime for updates, and that she would immediately be advised of any change in her son's condition.

Ty was not recognisable. Entirely covered in tubes and gauze, his inert body was being pumped and regulated by machines. He's in an artificial coma, to keep him stable, they explained to Denise. No, there is nothing you can do. She asked to see James, and after some hesitation, was allowed to take a quick look from the doorway. He too was inert and completely covered, surrounded by more ticking machines, tubes, and nurses.

The staff suggested she might need a cup of tea and showed her to a small sitting area. Holding the hot drink, Denise found herself thinking that something was not right. She puzzled over it for a while and stepped outside several times for a thoughtful smoke, but couldn't decide what it was. When she returned and asked after them, James had been taken in for surgery, and Ty was unchanged, so she went back to the waiting area to sit out the night.

Ellie meanwhile had found Michael, along with the police and fire crews, on the road to Fairbourne. He had called her back to advise where he was – the police was interviewing him, as the owner of the burnt plantation, and while he was there he had confirmed that his friend James with his son Ty had been up at the shack, intending to fix the roof, and yes, that crashed ute belonged to James and the scattered load of roofing iron confirmed it. He also told her that James and Ty had been taken to the Launceston Hospital, about two hours ago. Both were burnt and injured, and no, he didn't know how badly.

Ellie nearly fainted when she heard this and saw the blackened vehicle.

"Oh God, Michael, at least they're alive. I'd better go straight back there. Is everything ok at Fairbourne? Have you lost a lot of crops as well as the plantation?"

"The house is fine – no fires anywhere near it. But a fair few poppies here have gone. They, however, were insured, unlike the trees..."

To cheer her up – she really did look stricken, he thought – he made a joke:

"Well, at least you won't have to worry anymore about whether the bloody things really were oozing poison."

She smiled feebly, and they looked up at the flanks of the mountain, where the fire was still burning in the bush. It was clear that the shack was well and truly gone, the fire front having swept up over it. He laid a hand on her shoulder.

"They were incredibly lucky to get out. It will take some time for that up there to burn itself out, though the weather is set to cool tonight with the wind change. That'll help. Are you ok? Would you like me to drive you back?"

"Thanks, Michael, but I'm fine. Well, no, I'm not, but I can cope. I'd best be going."

"Let me know where it's at, as soon as you can. I'm sure you'll find them doing fine."

It was after 8pm before she got back to the city and managed to park near the hospital. On the drive up, she had found herself praying. Dear God, let them be alright... She was surprised to discover within herself, despite the worry and upset, a core of deep calm. The nurses at the ICU were puzzled. Here was a second lady, also claiming an interest in the two fire victims brought in that afternoon. No, she was no relative of the boy's at all. *Oh, for God's sake, how are they?* I'm sorry, but we only hand out information to family. *Oh, please, I know them both well. And, well, I'm Mr Mayne's former wife.* It sounded so stupid, but how could she explain that they were about to get re-married? *Please? You could check with his mother, that I'm her daughter-in-law...*

"Look, Mrs Fairfield, the two are both having surgery at the moment, and I can give you no further details. But you can go to the waiting room; the boy's mother is also there, waiting for news."

Ellie smiled at Denise and sat down in the small room. They were the only two there; the Thursday evening emergencies crowded in the main reception had not percolated through to this inner area yet. So, this was Ty's mother? Yes, she could see the resemblance. Gathering her courage for a personal exchange, she was about to address her when a nurse appeared.

"Denise Turner? The doctor is able to see you about your son now. This way."

Denise scrambled up and disappeared. The same nurse returned in a moment, holding a clipboard.

"You are Eleanor Fairfield?"

"Yes, I'm a close family friend. Please, how is he?"

"Mr Mayne's mother has confirmed your identity. He's just come out of surgery. He's been stabilised and, apart from the burns to the face and hands, there appears to be nothing seriously bad – just massive bruising and scraping, and a fractured arm."

"How bad are the burns?"

"We've seen worse here – he was lucky. They both were, though the boy has suffered far more other injuries. It seems some skin grafting will be needed, but the doctors don't think it will be a big problem. It will take some time, though."

"Can I see him?"

"Just a quick look from the doorway. He's still in coma."

Ellie saw much the same as Denise had, a short while earlier: a human-like form shrouded in white gauze, hooked up to tubes and machines. There was nothing she could do – James was getting the best medical care possible, and until he regained consciousness, she was only in the way here. As she was led away, she caught a glimpse, in the next cubicle, of Denise, seated near Ty, staring helplessly at the same incomprehensible bundle that was her son.

Presently, Denise decided to go home also. She got some sleep, and, before returning to the hospital the next morning, took care with her appearance. James should see a lovely vision of loving care when he finally awoke. And Ty, Ty, her boy… they had told her that his burns were not so bad, looked awful but really were only superficial, though he had multiple fractures on legs and arms, collarbone and a couple of ribs, along with lots of bruises and cuts. But he was young, none of it was life-threatening, and he'd eventually be just fine again. So she arrived with hope and bounce, the devoted mother ready to shoulder everything required of her.

Mr Mayne was awake. Warned that he wasn't a pretty sight, she insisted on seeing him, and was shocked at the bare skull, mostly covered in gauze, the wrapped hands, and the body… This time she saw immediately what it was that had bothered her the night before. James had a naturally stocky body, powerful and muscled. But this long, lanky form under the white covers did not look like that. Denise, accustomed to touching hairdressing clients and assessing their body shapes to match their hair styles, was startled. Then, to her shock, she saw – from the less swollen and red side of the ravaged face – a *blue eye* looking blankly at her.

"But this is not James! It isn't! It's someone else! Where's *James?*

***

After the ute had gone, James looked at the approaching wall of flames. They'd left only just in time, he thought, but if the man has the guts to keep going, they might make it. Now the smoke was coming thick, every increasing wind gust bringing more, the crackling and roaring was getting really loud. No wonder people die in fires; they come so quickly. Just the last few minutes had cut off any possibility of running for it now.

The sudden authority that had enabled him to make the man go and take Ty and Bonnie, settled to a deep calm. James looked at the flames without fear. He knew he was about to die, and he knew that it was alright. Ty was young and had a life to live yet, and that man, Alan, he had something to complete, also. There had been an early recognition, all that time ago, of their future interaction, though neither could have known how it would be. How extraordinary that Alan had turned up when he did, so completely unlikely and yet, James had no doubt, brought by angels so he could save the boy, and move on to whatever was his next stage. He was glad they'd taken the dog, too, and he thanked her for the many years of companionship. His children were old enough to be independent, Ian solid and well established, and Tessa too, in her own fashion, though he was sorry that he had seen almost nothing of her for quite some years. Young Jeremy would find his way sooner or later, with Ellie there to provide some stability till he did.

But Ellie herself – his one regret that he would not, after all, get to be her partner in the mature and rich relationship that they had begun to build. She'd be sad, too – he'd seen her growing love. It could have been good, the two of them together, perhaps too good, and that was maybe why it wasn't going to be.

He was choking now, the dense smoke and heat filling the air and driving the oxygen away. Not much longer now. The flames burst over the edge of the clearing. On his knees, he raised his arms.

"I'm ready…"

And the spirits that had been waiting came around, lifting him up, taking his soul from the burning body and soaring with it high above, away into the clear air. There he came in among them, the many who had lived and suffered and seen the land change, too. They who saw eternal hope in the glory of God's creation at every sunrise. They who tried to help when they saw man still struggling down below. And they who sometimes filled the wind with their crying.

EPILOGUE

It took some time for the police, the hospital, and the fire service to get their facts together. The first to indicate that Alan Dijkstra was missing was his cat Ranger, who had become very hungry and was loudly informing the neighbours thereof. He was rescued by Roseanne, finally contacted by the police. A day after Denise alerted the astonished hospital staff, Alan's burnt out car was spotted from a helicopter at the top of the plantation area, and later the police were called to a body further up. Not until the car had been traced to a man from Hobart was serious credence was given to the now-hysterical Denise, and the equally concerned Ellie. The police even considered the possibility of foul play, particularly as it took some time to interview Tyrone Turner. The cause of the fire was never officially established.

When Alan was released from hospital, he went to stay with his Uncle Tadd to recover. Although he had escaped lightly, he was shaken by the whole experience and it took a while for his fractured arm to heal. Tadd was particularly concerned that the arm should return to full strength – we can't have any impediment to the emerging sculptor, can we now? – and he would patiently massage and exercise it. Alan remained haunted by the dead man's words: *take care of Ty* and he forced himself get in touch with Denise over the boy's progress. He wasn't sure if this taking care might require anything more of him, but intended to do something. When he finally felt more in control, he returned to Hobart, where his cat greeted him with unprecedented enthusiasm. "Absence makes the heart grow fonder, eh, Ranger? Or were you just missing the indoor comfort? Well, I've got news for you – we are moving. Don't know where yet, but I'm selling this house, we're going somewhere new and fresh, and it will have a studio. And one of my first models is going to be a young man called Ty..."

Some years later, the State Government would decide that a large timber sculpture depicting heroic deeds of Tasmanians would be appropriate for the 225th Anniversary of Settlement. They gave the commission to the renowned artist Alan Dijkstra.

Denise Turner's total confusion at finding that the man who had rescued her son was actually Alan added, amongst other things, a comical note into the emotional upending that she had to sort through. James' death was hard to stomach. She had told nobody of her personal plans for James, but at least could cling to the belief that it might have been possible. They had not been able to tell Ty about it for some time. In the hurry to leave the shack, and clutching the terrified dog, the boy had not thought about putting the seat belt on – Alan had done his automatically – and so he had sustained very substantial injuries. His burns, though, could have been worse. He would in time require a skin graft on the left side of his face and his arm, but beyond some minor scarring was expected to look his normal self again. His young body tackled the job of healing, leaving him with no long term trace beyond a limp that put a stop to any formal sports. At night he sobbed over the loss of his father, who – he now realised – had sacrificed his life so he, and Alan, could live. But how could you leave me, Dad? he often cried silently, missing James desperately. In time, Ty grew into a grave young man and, remembering his delight at the natural world that his father had opened up to him, he chose to study environmental science.

Denise squared her shoulders and tackled the next stage of her life with dedication. When James' will was read, she found that he had altered it only a year earlier, adding a trust fund for Ty's education and a lump sum of a few thousands for herself. This left her nonplussed, but with the means now being available, she found the courage to actually enroll in the NEIS program to learn some solid business basics. This time she stuck to her plan and saw it through, in due course opening a hair salon that she managed to run with modest success.

Ellie Fairfield also spent much time in tears over James' death. When finally the full story was known, she was not really surprised at his actions. Yes, that's exactly what he would do, she thought. But, oh James, in the process you left me a second time and this time it's final, she railed at him in her darker moments. One day, though, after another bout of tears, a presence came to her. *It will be alright*, said a voice though no one was to be seen. A silver peace flowed through her to every fingertip and she was filled with a great accepting calm. Ok, she whispered.

She was happy that Ty occasionally came to visit her, giving her news of both his and Denise's progress. You left them a fine legacy, James, she thought. One of her NEIS pupils had been Denise, who worked quite hard and got her business plan approved. As the government kept tightening the money available to the NEIS program, and eventually made it almost entirely on-line only, she continued to visit some of her clients in her own time, just to encourage them, and Denise was one of them.

In the foothills of Miller's Bluff, the remaining trees were bulldozed and the ash ploughed in. It was a good outcome for Michael Fairfield – he had sole use of the area again. He too was shocked and saddened by James' untimely and tragic death, and wondered if the latter had ever got around to speaking with Ellie, as he had intended. Given her obvious concern on the day of the fire, he reckoned that James not only had done so, but that Ellie probably now had more to grieve over than most suspected.

"But better that you did say it, James, before you died, for all her pain now. You had the courage to heal the past. Good on you…"

"Although the world is full of suffering, it is also full of the over-coming of it."

—Helen Keller

On countless hillsides all over Tasmania, millions of Eucalyptus nitens trees stand in soldier-like rows. Time has proved that these particular modified and genetically engineered trees are not living up to the claims made for them. After a few years of dramatic growth, they slow down equally dramatically. Their much touted frost resistance is not much better than that of the native blue gum (Eucalyptus globulus), and they suffer from wood rot and wind blow. Forestry Tasmania in a recent report admitted that they probably would have done better to plant the blue gum in the first place. Dr. Alison Bleaney and her colleagues are continuing their research into the water toxicity in areas where the E. nitens stand. Poisonous algal blooms in the waters around Tasmania now occur regularly, even in the cold winter season where none had been experienced before, making the local seafood potentially deadly, and warnings are frequently published not to eat any. Meanwhile, the trees stand silently, holding their secret close.*

*For further reading see: article in Intl. Journal of Environmental Studies, Vol 72, 2015 Issue 1: *Preliminary Investigations of toxicity in the Georges Bay Catchment, Tasmania, Australia* http://www.tandfonline.com/doi/abs/10.1080/00207233.2014.988550

Lightning Source UK Ltd.
Milton Keynes UK
UKOW04f1939050917

308660UK00001B/182/P